Curtailing Corruption

Development of this book was supported by the
International Center on Nonviolent Conflict

Curtailing Corruption

People Power for Accountability and Justice

Shaazka Beyerle

LYNNE
RIENNER
PUBLISHERS

BOULDER
LONDON

Published in the United States of America in 2014 by
Lynne Rienner Publishers, Inc.
1800 30th Street, Boulder, Colorado 80301
www.rienner.com

and in the United Kingdom by
Lynne Rienner Publishers, Inc.
3 Henrietta Street, Covent Garden, London WC2E 8LU

Library of Congress Cataloging-in-Publication Data
A Cataloging-in-Publication Data record for this book
is available from the Library of Congress.
ISBN: 978-1-62637-052-4 (hc : alk. paper)
ISBN: 978-1-62637-056-2 (pb : alk. paper)

British Cataloguing in Publication Data
A Cataloguing in Publication record for this book
is available from the British Library.

Printed and bound in the United States of America

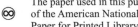 The paper used in this publication meets the requirements
of the American National Standard for Permanence of
Paper for Printed Library Materials Z39.48-1992.

5   4   3   2   1

Contents

Acknowledgments

Writing the acknowledgments for this book brings to a close a journey of inquiry and inspiration. First and foremost, I deeply thank the nonviolent activists and people power leaders whom I met as I did the research for the book. (They are all identified in their respective chapters.) You generously gave your time and shared your incomparable experiences, insights, and wisdom. I cherish your trust and goodwill, and marvel at your resilience, fearlessness, and unwavering efforts to gain freedom, justice, human dignity, and genuine democracy. Second, I would like to acknowledge the millions of people about whom I researched but will never meet. They are unknown heroes to us all. Yet, their successes, as you will come to read, are remarkable. They not only set a high standard of people power excellence, they also prove that we all have the capacity to collectively take nonviolent action for the common good.

My gratitude is extended to the founders of the International Center on Nonviolent Conflict (ICNC): Peter Ackerman, its founding chair, and Jack DuVall, its president, my intellectual mentors. They immediately understood how corruption is a form of oppression and grasped the practical and scholarly significance of finding and analyzing cases in which citizens, mobilized in nonviolent campaigns and movements, targeted corruption and impunity. Were it not for ICNC, this work could not have materialized. Over the years, ICNC provided an environment of intellectual inquiry and rigor. For their encouragement, productive discussions, advice, and help along the way, I thank my colleagues there, including Hardy Merriman, Althea Middleton-Detzner, Nicola Barrach, Maciej Bartkowski, Ashley Farnan, and Jake

Fitzpatrick, as well as former colleagues Maria Stephan, Daryn Cambridge, Suravi Bhandary, and Vanessa Ortiz. Appreciation also goes to Ciel Lagumen, Deena Patriarca, and Kay Robinson for their good cheer and encouragement.

There are two other organizations I would like to acknowledge. First is the Center for Transatlantic Relations (CTR) at the School of Advanced International Studies, Johns Hopkins University. CTR provided an academic home as I wrote the book; I benefitted from its activities, interactions with scholars and research fellows, and opportunities to discuss my work. To Dan Hamilton, CTR's director; Andras Simonyi, its managing director; and Kurt Volker, a CTR senior fellow, I extend my sincere appreciation for this experience and for your encouragement. A note of thanks also goes to Katrien Maes and Miriam Cunningham, and to the five CTR interns—Daniel Froehlich, Nathaniel J. Hojnacki, William D. Hudec, Ermal Vila, and Jozefien Willemen—who proofread my manuscript. The second organization is the indefatigable Nonviolence International. Mubarak Awad, its founder, and Michael Beer, its executive director, have been consistently supportive of the entire research project and book from the outset, offering constructive feedback, expertise, good ideas, and treasured friendship.

The people power field cuts across many disciplines, which contributes to its academic dynamism and relevance to the real world. A thank you to the following scholars for their insights about civil resistance: Cynthia Boaz, Erica Chenoweth, Tom Hastings, Brian Martin, Kurt Schock, Lee Smithey, and Stephen Zunes. Some among you were also my behind-the-scenes cheerleaders, and you made a world of difference. I extend a special note of gratitude to Brian Martin. You were my mentor for this book. You kept me on track, generously gave of your time, meticulously reviewed the manuscript, provided sound advice, offered continuous encouragement, and, in the process, became a friend.

I also would like to heartily thank several people for our discussions and your support, research leads, and contacts: Marinetta Cannito, Andrea Figari, Arwa Hassan, Geo-sung Kim, Giorgi Meladze, Nancy Pearson, Nils Taxell, Roberto Pérez-Rocha, Stefano Siviero, and Karen Volker.

This book, and the investigation on which it is based, would not have been possible without a grant from the United States Institute of Peace (USIP) and financial and material support from ICNC. I am deeply grateful for their backing. Thank you to my USIP grant officer, Steven Riskin, for your confidence in this endeavor and for our productive, cooperative interactions.

To my publisher, Lynne Rienner, her team, and the anonymous reviewers, thank you for your time, effort, and the constructive input that helped me to prepare the book manuscript for publication.

In closing, I thank my husband, Kanthan, who stood by me, honored this endeavor, and never had a doubt that I could turn a dream into this reality.

—*Shaazka Beyerle*

Introduction

Little did I know in August 2004 that a trip to Ankara, Turkey, would change the course of my professional life. The setting was the New Tactics in Human Rights Symposium, organized by the ever-innovative Center for Victims of Torture.[1] While speaking on a panel discussion, "Mass Actions for Public Participation," a fellow panelist riveted all of us in the room. He told us about a campaign in Turkey in 1997 that mobilized an estimated 30 million people—yes, 30 million—to fight endemic corruption and linkages between crime syndicates, arms traffickers, the state, the private sector, and the media. The campaign was the One Minute of Darkness for Constant Light, and the speaker was Ersin Salman, one of its founders.

I returned home inspired and intrigued. Here was an astounding case of people power that had gone unnoticed—in the international media, in the civil resistance realm, and in anticorruption circles. Regular people mobilized, truly en masse, not to oust a dictator or occupier but to expose, shake up, and begin to change a rotten system of graft, abuse, and impunity. How peculiar, it seemed at the time, that a campaign targeting malfeasance was highlighted at, of all places, a human rights conference. I wondered if the One Minute of Darkness for Constant Light was a rarity, or were more campaigns and movements targeting corruption going on in other parts of the world? My sense was that this case represented only the tip of the iceberg. Thus began a journey— yielding discoveries, knowledge, inspiration, and rich lessons about civil resistance and people power.

In the ensuing years, through the International Center on Nonviolent Conflict (ICNC), I began initial research and then immersion into

1

the anticorruption and accountability realms. By the end of 2009 I had embarked on an in-depth study. The project had four main objectives. The first was to identify, document, and analyze contemporary nonviolent campaigns and movements to fight graft and abuse, demand accountability, and win rights and justice. The cases took place over the past seventeen years or were ongoing. Corruption was the sole focus in some instances. In other cases, it was linked to overall public concerns (such as authoritarian rule, state capture, violence, impunity of authorities, dishonest politics) or to tangible grievances touching daily life (for example, the provision of basic services, endemic "petty" bribery, land expropriation, environmental destruction, and misuse of antipoverty and development resources). The multidimensional nature of most of these civic initiatives reflects the reality that corruption does not occur in a vacuum; it is both source and enabler of many forms of oppression.

The second objective was to ascertain common attributes and patterns, and distill general lessons learned. The third objective was to examine the international dimension and policy implications of homegrown, civic anticorruption campaigns and movements. The final objective was to offer recommendations for anticorruption advocates, donors, development institutions, and policymakers, based on actual case studies and the views of campaign leaders and civic actors.

Campaigns and movements targeting corruption often face decentralized targets rather than an identifiable dictator or external government, and can be found both in undemocratic and democratic systems. Graft and abuse are manifested in a systemic manner rather than a hodgepodge collection of illicit transactions. Consequently, this research brings to light new applications of civil resistance beyond the more commonly known cases against occupations, such as the Indian independence movement, and authoritarian regimes from Chile to Poland. It also expands our understanding about the dynamics of how people collectively wield nonviolent power for the common good.

Criteria and Methods

The focus of this research is on citizen agency: what civic actors and regular people—organized together and exerting their collective power—are doing to curb corruption as they define and experience it. Hence, the analytical framework is based on the skills, strategies, objectives, and demands of such initiatives, rather than on the phenomenon of corruption itself, which has been judiciously studied for more than two decades by scholars and practitioners from the anticorruption and development realms.

I selected cases that met the following criteria:

- They were "popular" initiatives. They were civilian-based, involved grassroots participation, and were led and implemented by individuals from the civic realm, rather than governments or external actors, such as donors, development institutions, and international nongovernmental organizations (INGOs).
- They were nonviolent. They did not threaten or use violence to further their aims.
- They involved some degree of organization and planning, which varied depending on the scope—objectives, geographical range, duration—of the civic initiative.
- Multiple nonviolent actions were employed. Thus, instances of one-off demonstrations or spontaneous protests were not considered. There are countless examples of such actions around the world virtually every day.
- Objectives and demands were articulated.
- The civic initiative was sustained over a period of time.[2]

I identified more than twenty-five cases (and the pace of new initiatives continues unabated).[3] Of them, twelve spanning the globe and touching upon various forms of corruption are featured, from Afghanistan, Bosnia-Herzegovina, Brazil, Egypt, India, Indonesia, Italy, Kenya, Mexico, (South) Korea, Turkey, and Uganda. Overall, the research found that graft and abuse can be curbed, particularly those forms that matter to everyday people. When citizens raise their collective voice and exert their collective power, they translate corruption from an abstract societal ill to tangible experiences of oppression and social and economic injustice. While the goals involve curbing negatives—graft, abuse, and impunity—underpinning their struggles is the desire to attain positives: information, accountability, participatory democracy, freedom, and last but not least, human dignity.

For this study I developed a set of research and interview questions, with input received from scholars and practitioners from the civic realm. Cases were documented through a review of scholarly literature; a review of databases, reports, and publications from international civil society and the anticorruption, democracy building, and development communities; articles and media reports; and phone interviews, written correspondence, and personal conversations with civic actors. These ac-

4

Case Studies

Context of Corruption	Type of Collective Action	Country	Organizers
Reconstruction and development projects	Civic initiative/ social accountability	Afghanistan	Integrity Watch Afghanistan— CSO
Overall endemic corruption	Campaign within broader social movement	Bosnia-Herzegovina	Dosta! [Enough!]— nonviolent youth movement
Political corruption	Ficha Limpa (Clean slate) —social movement	Brazil	MCCE (Movement Against Electoral Corruption) and Avaaz
Overall endemic corruption/impunity	shayfeen.com/Egyptians Against Corruption— social movement	Egypt	Egyptians Against Corruption— SMO
Overall endemic corruption/bribery	5th Pillar— social movement	India	5th Pillar—SMO
Efforts to neutralize the anticorruption commission	CICAK (Love Indonesia, Love Anti-Corruption Commission) campaign	Indonesia	Informal network of civic leaders, activists, and CSOs
Cosa Nostra mafia	Addiopizzo [Good-bye, protection money]—social movement	Italy	Addiopizzo—SMO
Parliament Constituency Development Funds	Civic initiative/ social accountability	Kenya	MUHURI (Muslims for Human Rights)— CSO-CBO
Overall endemic corruption	DHP (Dejemos de Hacernos Pendejos)— social movement	Mexico	Informal network of civic leaders and activists
Political corruption	CAGE (Citizens Alliance for the General Election) 2000 campaign	Korea	Coalition (1,104 NGOs, CSOs, citizen groups, YMCA/YWCA, religious organizations)
State-organized crime/paramilitary groups linkages	One Minute of Darkness for Constant Light campaign	Turkey	Informal network of civic leaders and activists
Police	Civic initiative/social accountability	Uganda	NAFODU (National Foundation for Democracy and Human Rights in Uganda) CSO-CBO

Notes: CBO = community-based organization; CSO = civil society organization; SMO = social movement organization.

tors came from bottom-up civic initiatives targeting corruption; local, in-country civil society organizations (CSOs) and social movement organizations (SMOs);[4] INGOs; and regional and country anticorruption and development practitioners. I also sought the counsel of scholars focused on democracy building, corruption, civil resistance, peacebuilding, and human rights.

The Plan of the Book

Chapter 1 explores the linkages among corruption, violence, and poverty, as well as the synergies between anticorruption and peacebuilding. Here I add civil resistance into the equation and summarize research on the efficacy and outcomes of nonviolent civic initiatives, highlighting people power movements against authoritarian regimes in which corruption was a source of public anger and one of the key grievances around which people mobilized. I also identify three related misconceptions about civil resistance and people power that are common in the anticorruption and development realms.

In Chapter 2 I scrutinize the traditional definitions of corruption from a people power perspective, presenting two alternative conceptualizations—one that is systemic and one that is people-centered—and discuss the ways in which civil resistance complements and reinforces legal and administrative approaches.

Afghanistan, Brazil, India, Indonesia, Italy, Korea, and Uganda are the focus of the seven in-depth case studies I present in Chapters 3 through 9. Chapter 10 features an additional five abbreviated cases—Bosnia-Herzegovina, Egypt, Kenya, Mexico, and Turkey—which complement the detailed examinations of the previous chapters.

In Chapter 11 I present a comparative analysis of the civic initiatives, focusing on common attributes, general lessons learned, and noteworthy patterns that expand our understanding of civil resistance, people power, and the practice of democracy. My focus in Chapter 12 is on the relevance of bottom-up civic initiatives to foreign policy; donor effectiveness; and overall anticorruption, development, democracy, and peacebuilding strategies.

As the international anticorruption and development communities have begun to acknowledge the impact of citizens on systems of corruption, two major policy issues have emerged. First is the question of what roles the international community can play in grassroots anticorruption initiatives. In this book I provide analysis and real examples that are relevant to key international concerns—for example, conflict and peacebuilding in Afghanistan and the Democratic Republic of Congo; consolidation of democracy in the Middle East; and political corruption, impunity, and economic decline in parts of the Global North. Second, an unsettling new trend is emerging to scale up—to systematize and extensively replicate citizen empowerment actions and tools—without strategic analysis and consideration of local contexts. Such attempts may not only lead to weak results or failure but can also divert grassroots efforts from more effective paths and potentially put civilians in harm's way.

* * *

For regular citizens, the experience of corruption can be a source of oppression and the denial of basic freedoms and rights. In spite of such bleak circumstances, or perhaps because of them, this research has shown that people can move from being victims and bystanders of malfeasance to becoming a force for transforming their societies. I have been inspired, informed, and humbled by the accomplishments, resourcefulness, strategies, and skills of these nonviolent campaigns and movements, and the modest yet great women and men—young and old, everyday heroes—behind them. I trust you will be as well.

Notes

1. Information about the New Tactics in Human Rights Symposium and the session titled "Mass Actions for Public Participation" can be found at http://www.newtactics.org/WorldSymposium and http://www.newtactics.org/WK416.

2. The term "civic initiative" refers to organized civic efforts that fit the above-stated criteria. It encompasses nonviolent, grassroots campaigns and social movements.

3. Research was also conducted on the Movement to Defend Khimki Forest in Russia. However, it was not included because of ongoing developments that could not be documented at the time of writing this book. As well, during this interval, new cases emerged that merited investigation, such as ongoing land-right campaigns in Cambodia and the 2011 Wukan village blockade in China. Unfortunately, initiating new research was not possible.

4. A social movement organization (SMO) is a nonstate entity that is part of a social movement. It can provide multiple functions to the movement, such as identity, leadership, strategizing, and planning, but the movement is not bounded by the SMO, nor are SMOs essential for social movements to flourish.

1

Corruption, People, and Power

People know they can make a difference when they come together in sufficient numbers and with a clear goal. Citizens, acting in coordination, can more effectively challenge governments, corporations, financial institutions, sports bodies or international organisations that neglect their duty towards them.

—Brasilia Declaration, Fifteenth International
Anti-Corruption Conference, November 2012

It afflicts dictatorships and democracies, the Global North and the Global South; it impedes development; it threatens peacebuilding. But not until late 2010–2011, when people around the world raised their voices, did the blight of corruption move to the forefront of the international stage. During the so-called Arab Spring, citizens valiantly defied entrenched dictators to say "enough" to malfeasance, and they have been risking—in many cases, sacrificing—their lives to demand freedom, democracy, and dignity. Taking inspiration from the Middle East, several months later the Indignados (Outraged) movement emerged in Spain, and Occupy Wall Street followed suit in the United States. The latter proclaimed, "We are the 99% that will no longer tolerate the greed and corruption of the 1%."[1]

These protestors are giving voice to the sentiments of many people in the Global North, as reflected in the 2010 Global Corruption Barometer conducted by Transparency International, the global civil society coalition against corruption. It found that views on corruption are most negative in North America and Europe; 67 percent and 73 percent of people, respectively, in those areas said that corruption increased over the previous three years.[2] Overall, the survey found that 70 percent of respondents claimed they would be willing to report an incident of corruption. In retrospect, these results presage the outburst of civil resistance that marked 2011. From India to the United States, citizens are making connections between corruption and unaccountability of state and corporate powerholders on the one hand, and excess, social and economic inequality, and the distortion of political and economic systems by special interests on the other hand.[3]

They understand a fundamental characteristic of corruption: it does not occur in a vacuum. To target corruption is to touch simultaneously the myriad injustices to which it is linked, from violence and poverty to impunity, abuse, authoritarianism, unaccountability, and environmental destruction. Thus, fighting malfeasance is not a superficial solution that avoids the underlying problem; it can be a direct attack on oppression, thereby impacting prospects for democracy, human rights, poverty alleviation, and postconflict transformation.

The Corruption-Poverty-Violence Nexus

The World Bank has identified corruption as one of the greatest obstacles to economic and social development, finding that graft undermines development by "distorting the rule of law and weakening the institutional foundation on which economic growth depends."[4] According to Transparency International, the global civil society coalition against corruption, a review of past and current efforts to reduce poverty suggests that corruption has been a constant obstacle for countries trying to bring about the political, economic, and social changes necessary for their development. The coalition concluded, "Across different country contexts, corruption has been a cause and consequence of poverty."[5]

A 2004 report of the UN Secretary-General's High-Level Panel on Threats, Challenges, and Change concluded that "corruption, illicit trade and money-laundering contribute to State weakness, impede economic growth, and undermine democracy. These activities thus create a permissive environment for civil conflict."[6] A risk analysis from the 2011 World Bank Development Report found that "countries where government effectiveness, rule of law, and control of corruption are weak have a 30–45 percent higher risk of civil war, and significantly higher risk of extreme criminal violence than other developing countries."[7] The report also found that in surveys conducted in six postconflict countries and territories, citizens named corruption, poverty, unemployment, and inequality as the main drivers of violent strife.[8] The official declaration of the Fourteenth International Anti-Corruption

Conference (IACC), held in November 2010, stated, "Corruption was identified as a facilitator and generator of civil conflict, as an inhibitor of peace-building, as correlated with terrorism, and as a facilitator of nuclear proliferation."[9] Finally, a European Commission checklist, on the root causes of conflict and early warning indicators, includes the corruption troika of bribery in bureaucracies, collusion between the private sector and civil servants, and organized crime.[10]

In addition to violent conflict, at an aggregate level, corruption has been found to be positively correlated with higher risks of political instability and human rights abuses.[11] Human Rights Watch cites a direct relationship between corruption and political violence, in which public officials use stolen public revenues to pay for political violence in support of their ambitions.[12] Corruption also creates an overall climate of impunity.[13] Human Rights Watch and the Center for Victims of Torture tie corruption to repression, as it hampers government accountability while benefitting officials and security forces that commit abuses for financial gain.[14] The Fourteenth IACC noted, "In trafficking, particularly of human beings, corruption is seen to play a facilitating role at every stage in the process, keeping the crime from becoming visible, buying impunity when a case is detected, expediting the physical movement of trafficked individuals, and ensuring that its victims stay beholden to the system that first victimised them."[15]

Corruption inhibits sustainable peace in multiple ways, some direct and others indirect. Corruption is often the venal legacy of violent strife and is embedded into the political, social, and economic fabric of the society. Cheyanne Scharbatke-Church and Kirby Reiling point out that war economies, by their nature, function through malfeasance; the parties in the conflict depend on fraud, bribery, and criminal groups to expedite the smooth functioning of the system.[16] Arms traffickers and transnational organized crime add to the deadly mix by readily providing weapons. The global illicit arms trade is estimated at $200 million to $300 million annually, and Africa is the largest market. As a result, the continent tragically suffers the most casualties from it.[17]

Moreover, corruption can draw out or perpetuate civil or regional conflicts because it functions as an enabler; violent groups themselves engage in illicit activities to acquire weapons and supplies. Nowhere is this process more wrenchingly evident than in the Democratic Republic of Congo (DRC), where approximately 3.5 million lives have been lost since the onset of war in 1998 and hundreds of thousands of girls and women have been systematically raped.[18] The military, rebel groups, and various foreign allies have plundered the country's diamonds, gold, timber, ivory, coltan, and cobalt, not only to finance their atrocities, but ultimately to enrich themselves, which has become an end unto itself.[19] Over the past decade, violent confrontations over the Casamance region have broken out among The Gambia, Guinea Bissau, and Senegal, and between Cameroon and Nigeria in the oil-rich Bakassi peninsula for an equal length of time. A US Agency for International Development (USAID) report concluded that corruption, more often than not, played a key role in fomenting and protracting these conflicts.[20]

Furthermore, when corruption is endemic—whereby a complex system of graft permeates the political system, economic spheres, and basic provision of services in a country—it can stimulate social unrest and foment violent conflict. For example, in the Niger Delta, insurgent groups are amassing weapons and recruiting young men from an impoverished, angry, and frustrated population that experiences little benefit from oil wealth while living amid horrendous environmental destruction from its extraction and processing.[21]

In the postconflict context, corruption can function as an inhibitor of sustainable peace, the latter needing human security and stability to take root and flourish.[22] First, graft can allow the entrenchment of the political status quo that operated during the conflict.[23] Second, it undermines the new government's legitimacy; rule of law; and capacity for reconstruction, economic development, and the provision of basic public services. For ordinary citizens, the horrors of war are replaced with grueling hardship, to which pervasive malfeasance adds another layer of tangible injustice, as is the case in Afghanistan. In a 2010 poll, 83 percent of Afghans said that corruption affects their daily lives.[24] As a result, the Taliban is recruiting new members from among the marginalized population oppressed by unrelenting graft and poverty. "People support armed groups to express their dissatisfaction with the government," contends an Afghan civil society actor.[25] At a 2012 US Senate committee meeting, General John Allen stated, "We know that corruption still robs Afghan citizens of their faith in the government, and that poor governance itself often advances insurgent messages.[26]

Corruption can also be an enabler of state capture in postconflict or fragile democracies, fueling yet more violence and claiming the lives of civilians as well as those who try to fight it.[27] Tragically escalating in Central America, narco-corruption refers to the interrelationship between transnational drug cartels and state security forces, as well as the infiltration of organized crime interests into politics, governance, and the actual functioning of institutions, leading to countries such as Mexico and Guatemala being called narco-states. During the six years of Mexican president Felipe Calderon's tenure, the drug war claimed an estimated 100,000 lives, while 25,000 adults and children went missing, according to leaked government documents.[28] The chief of the UN Office of Drugs and Crime has asserted, "Corruption, poverty, and poor criminal justice capacity make Guatemala extremely vulnerable to organized crime."[29] Not coincidentally, the country is experiencing the worst violence since the cessation of the thirty-six-year civil war in 1996. Approximately 5,000 people are murdered each year due to organized crime and gangs, now compounded by Mexican drug cartels' expanding south across the border.[30] By 2011, the World Bank reported that criminal violence was killing more Guatemalans than did the civil war during the 1980s.[31] Narco-corruption, of course, is not limited to the Americas. According to a confidential source, the drug trade in Afghanistan also serves as the main source of financing for the private armies of local warlords, which are connected to parts of the postconflict government. The Taliban is in on the game as well, exchanging drugs for weapons.[32] Anticorruption advocates point out that there cannot be genuine security and freedom for citizens when law enforcement is compromised by malfeasance.[33]

Peacebuilding and Anticorruption Synergies

Up until quite recently, the linkages between anticorruption and peacebuilding could be characterized as a "tale of two communities."[34] Traditionally, the former focused on technocratic and legislative policies and reforms, while the latter attempted to promote dialogue and reconcile competing groups and interests.[35] Yet they have much in common. First, they share overlapping challenges, including use of power, impunity, societal trust, and socially harmful notions, such as a zero-sum approach.[36] Second, the peacebuilding and anticorruption spheres both seek longer-term goals of social and economic justice; transparent, accountable governance; human rights; and equitable use of resources. Finally, they emphasize change at the sociopolitical level (for example, institutional practices, social norms) and at the individual level (for example, knowledge, skills, and attitudes).[37] Scharbatke-Church and Reiling aptly conclude, "As conflicts are riddled with corruption, peacebuilding work should be appropriately riddled with anticorruption efforts."[38]

Moving forward, the anticorruption realm needs to better comprehend postconflict dynamics when dealing with graft in such settings.[39] Indeed, there are promising developments on this front. One of the main themes of the Fourteenth International Anti-Corruption Conference in

2010 was "Restoring Trust for Peace and Security," which examined "the dynamic linkages between corruption, peace, and security."[40] As importantly, the peacebuilding community ought to fully address the corruption-violence relationship. Scharbatke-Church and Reiling assert that few peacebuilding agencies have developed capacities and programs that seek to impact "the vicious network of corruption and conflict."[41] Instead, peace agreements and international reconstruction actors have turned propagators of violence into postconflict winners. Organized crime bosses and warlords (sometimes one and the same) who used the conflict to reap profits are reconstituted as political and economic players. When they gain access to state resources, the opportunities for enrichment through corruption are vast.[42]

One needs only to look at Afghanistan, the Balkans, DRC, and Sierra Leone to witness such outcomes. In Afghanistan the post–Bonn agreement government gave warlords high-ranking government positions, which played a role in the endemic corruption and unaccountable, poor governance that has come to characterize the war-torn country.[43] Some notorious commanders maintain militias under the guise of private security companies, which provide protection, in some cases under conditions of extortion, for NATO troops and external aid organizations.[44] These commanders have moved into business (both licit and illicit) and won seats under flawed elections or have proxies in the Parliament.[45] Turning to the Balkans, mafia structures in Bosnia-Herzegovina and Kosovo endeavored to tie up their power by gaining control over local political and economic processes.[46] In Africa, former rebel leaders in the DRC were appointed vice presidents. They were allowed to place cronies in senior positions in state-run companies, from which millions of dollars were embezzled.[47] In Sierra Leone, Foday Sankoh, the deceased leader of the Revolutionary United Front (RUF), indicted on seventeen counts of crimes against humanity in 2003, had initially been pardoned and appointed vice president. He was left in control of the diamond mines under the 1999 Lomé Peace Accord, which ended the country's civil war. The agreement enabled the RUF to form a political party, gave it several cabinet seats in the transitional government, and granted all combatants total amnesty.[48]

Adding Civil Resistance to the Peacebuilding-Anticorruption Equation

One crucial element needs to be added to the peacebuilding-anticorruption equation: civil resistance and the power of regular people to bring forth change. Strategic nonviolent action scholar Stephen Zunes notes that when authoritarian or ineffectual governance is paired with endemic corruption, a vicious cycle can develop that leads to further delegitimization of authority and rule of law, which in turn reinforces authoritarian or ineffectual governance, impunity, poverty, and on and on.[49] The result is what nonviolent conflict educator Jack DuVall calls "fragmented tyrannies"—weak, fragile democracies or semiauthoritarian systems in which citizens live under conditions of violence, abuse, human insecurity, and fear perpetrated by multiple state and nonstate entities.[50] Zunes points out that civil resistance has the potential to activate an anticorruption cycle.[51] Nonviolent social movements and grassroots civic campaigns can challenge the corruption-poverty-violence nexus, in turn creating alternative loci of power, thereby empowering the civic realm to continue to wage strategic civic campaigns and movements that continue to challenge the corrupt, unequal status quo.[52]

Civil Resistance Defined

Civil resistance is a civilian-based process to fight oppression, impunity, and injustice through people power. It is also called "nonviolent resistance," "nonviolent struggle," "nonviolent conflict," and "nonviolent action." Civil resistance is nonviolent in that it does not employ the threat or use of violence, and popular in the sense that it involves the participation of regular people standing together against oppression. Maciej Bartkowski, a civil resistance scholar, summarizes it in this manner: "Whether overt or tacit, nonviolent forms of resistance are a popular expression of people's collective determination to withdraw their cooperation from the powers that be. People can refuse to follow a coerced or internalized system of lies and deception, and thereby, intentionally increase the cost of official control."[53]

While the terms "civil resistance" and "people power" are often used interchangeably, I draw a distinction. Civil resistance generates people power. Thus, it constitutes the means, process, or methodology through which people can wield collective power. What exactly is this form of power? It consists of significant numbers of individuals organized together around shared grievances and goals, exerting social, economic, political, and psychological pressure and engaging in nonviolent strategies and tactics, such as civil disobedience, noncooperation, strikes, boycotts, monitoring, petition drives, low-risk mass actions, and demonstrations. The pioneering nonviolent struggle theorist Gene Sharp documented over 198 types of tactics, and movements and campaigns, including those targeting corruption, are creating new ones continuously.[54]

The efficacy of civil resistance is not a matter of theory or conjecture. People power campaigns and movements have a rich history of curbing oppression and injustice and a proven track record of success over violent resistance. A landmark book by Erica Chenoweth and Maria Stephan documents that, in the last century, violent campaigns succeeded historically in only 26 percent of all cases, compared to 53 percent in the case of nonviolent, civilian-based campaigns, even facing extremely brutal regimes.[55] Thirty of the nonviolent campaigns studied occurred in countries that ranked as autocracies (between −7 and −10 on the Polity IV scale), and all experienced severe repression.[56] Nonetheless, twenty-one of them (70 percent) succeeded, an even higher success rate than average for nonviolent campaigns facing other types of regimes.[57] Finally, subsequent analysis overall found a high correlation between nonviolent campaigns and a democratic outcome five years later.[58]

Similarly, a quantitative analysis of transitions from authoritarianism to democracy over the past three decades found that civil resistance was a key factor in driving 75 percent of political transitions, and such transformations were far more likely to result in democratic reform and civil liberties than violent or elite-led, top-down changes. Of the thirty-five countries subsequently rated "Free" according to a Freedom House index, thirty-two had a significant bottom-up civil resistance component.[59] In contrast, the 2011 World Bank Development Report established that 90 percent of civil wars waged over the past decade took place in countries that had already suffered from civil war at some point during the previous thirty years.[60] In other words, nonviolent struggle not only has a greater chance of success than violent conflict; it lays the foundation for a more peaceful and fair aftermath. Thus, the historical record confirms what Gandhi understood decades ago: the form of struggle impacts the outcome. He wrote, "The means may be likened to a seed, the end to a tree; and there is just the same inviolable connection between the means and the end as there is between the seed and the tree."[61]

Corruption was a source of public anger and one of the key grievances around which people mobilized in many of the nonviolent movements targeting authoritarian regimes, including the People Power Revolution in the Philippines; the nonviolent resistance to Serbian dictator Slobodan Milosevic, catalyzed by the youth movement OTPOR; the Rose Revolution in Georgia; and the Orange Revolutions in Ukraine in

2004 and February 2014.[62] Well before the people power uprisings in Tunisia and Egypt, malfeasance was the target of citizen dissent in the region, part of a rich and relatively unknown history of civil resistance from the early 1900s onward.[63] In 1997, over the course of six weeks, the One Minute of Darkness for Constant Light campaign mobilized approximately 30 million Turkish citizens in synchronized low-risk mass actions to pressure the government to take specific measures to combat systemic corruption (see Chapter 10). In May 2006 a group of young men and women, communicating through text messages, launched the Orange Movement against political corruption in Kuwait. Their nonviolent tactics, including leafleting the Parliament, enlisted public support and participation, resulting in early parliamentary elections in which legislation to change electoral districts (to prevent corruption) became a major campaign issue and was later adopted.[64]

Founded by Egyptian women in 2005, shayfeen.com (a play on words meaning "we see you" in Arabic) increased public awareness about corruption, fostered citizen participation, monitored the government, broadcast election fraud in real time via the Internet, and proved their activities were valid under the United Nations Convention Against Corruption (UNCAC), to which Egypt was a signatory. The campaign spawned the Egyptians against Corruption movement (see Chapter 10). Endemic corruption was also one of the main injustices identified by the historic, youth-driven April 6, 2008, general strike (Facebook Revolution), which evolved into the April 6 movement that played a catalytic role in the Egyptian January 25 Revolution. We Are All Khaled Said, the second key youth group in the revolution, originally came into existence in 2010 following the torture and death of the twenty-eight-year-old, who had posted a video on the Internet of police officers dividing up confiscated drugs and money among themselves.[65]

Common Misconceptions About People Power in the Anticorruption Context

The capacity of everyday people to nonviolently bring forth political, social, and economic change controverts deeply ingrained notions about people and power—its sources, how it is wielded, and who holds it.[66] Three common, interrelated misconceptions about people power resistance regularly crop up in the anticorruption and development literature.

Myth #1: The need for a government or institutions willing to fight corruption. The underlying premise of this misconception is that citizens cannot make a difference unless powerholders also want to realize change. It is common to find pronouncements such as, "Thus, the predisposition of the state to citizen engagement in governance is a central determining factor for the success of social accountability."[67] If this were the case, then there would be little point for citizens to initiate efforts to tackle graft. In reality, people power has the capacity to create political will where it did not exist, apply pressure on recalcitrant institutions and governments to take action, and support those within the state or other institutions who are attempting to fight the corrupt system but have been blocked or threatened.

An unprecedented people power victory in Brazil illustrates this process (see Chapter 4). Following the failure of political reform bills, in 2008 a coalition of forty-four civic groups, including grassroots and church organizations, unions, and professional associations, formed the Movement Against Electoral Corruption (MCCE). It developed the Ficha Limpa (meaning "clean record" or "clean slate") legislation, which would render candidates ineligible to take office if they have been convicted of the following crimes by more than one judge: misuse of public funds, drug trafficking, rape, murder, or racism. The bill was introduced to Congress through the Popular Initiative clause in the Brazilian constitution, by a massive petition effort that gathered over 1.6 million handwritten signatures. Digital and real-world actions, coordinated by Avaaz, pushed the legislation through Congress in spite of fierce opposition as many sitting representatives would be impacted once the law came into effect.[68] It was approved in June 2010.[69]

Myth #2: A legislative framework, civil liberties, and access to information are necessary for success. Because of this myth, one encounters such deterministic statements as, "Formal democracy and the existence of basic civil and political rights is a critical precondition for virtually any kind of civil society activism that engages critically with the state."[70] If this were the case, citizens living in less than ideal situations would be doomed, while those living in more beneficent contexts should succeed. Fortunately, this misconception is refuted by the historical record and comparative research discussed earlier, as well as my investigation on corruption. In spite of difficult circumstances, or perhaps because of them, bottom-up campaigns targeting graft and abuse are most often found in places that are not paragons of accountability and rights, and many of the struggles seek to achieve the very things cited as prerequisites. For example, Integrity Watch Afghanistan is empowering villagers in community mobilization and democratic decisionmaking under conditions of ongoing violent conflict, negligible rule of law, human rights abuses, and limited access to information (see Chapter 8). The group trains local volunteers, chosen by peers, to monitor projects selected by the villages, in order to curb corruption and improve reconstruction and development (which can involve numerous players—from donors to foreign military, contractors, subcontractors, suppliers, national and subnational levels of the state, and nonstate entities). As a result, not only is graft reduced, people gain tangible results, such as schools, roads, and clinics. Moreover, relations with local state authorities often improve, and in some cases, the influence of warlords has been weakened as communities became more autonomous and confident to solve their own problems.[71]

Myth #3: Governments need to give people civic space to make their voices heard.[72] There are many varieties of this notion, which leads to claims such as, "Countries where technological advancement and rising voices of citizens are more tolerated have greater civic participation and a more vibrant civil society."[73] This misconception is based on the assumption that citizen engagement and action are dependent on governments to give them space, to allow them to express dissent, and ultimately, to refrain from repression. In the final analysis, this would mean that no matter what regular people do, they are ultimately dependent on the benevolence of the government, ruler, or authority. The reality could not be more different.

Comparative research on nonviolent versus violent struggles confirms that while the level of repression can shape nonviolent struggles, it is not a significant determinant of their outcome. The Chenoweth and Stephan study found that in the face of crackdowns, nonviolent campaigns are six times more likely to achieve full success than violent campaigns that also faced repression.[74] Nor do harsh attacks signify that people power has failed. In the corruption context, attacks can be a sign that the system is being undermined and vested interests are threatened. Successful nonviolent movements develop strategies to build resilience, such as the use of low-risk mass actions and dilemma actions, the latter putting the oppressor in a lose-lose situation and the civic initiative in a win-win situation.[75] The Dosta! nonviolent youth movement in Bosnia-Herzegovina was particularly adept at fusing humor with dilemma actions (see Chapter 10). Repression against such civic dissent can "backfire" by delegitimizing the oppressors, transforming public outrage into support for the movement or campaign, and shifting or weakening the loyalties of those within the corrupt system who do not approve of such harsh measures against peaceful citizens.[76]

States—and violent nonstate actors such as organized crime and paramilitaries—will still try to limit political and civic space. But through civil resistance, citizens have the capacity to claim space, expand it, and use it. Thus, civic space is neither finite nor dependent on the goodwill of governments to grant it. The 2011 people power movements in Tunisia and Egypt are examples of how—in societies where authoritarian regimes choked off virtually all space—people carved it open, mobilizing and wielding nonviolent power to the extent that two brutal dictators were forced to step down after decades of rule.

Beyond Structural Determinism

At the heart of all these misconceptions is an ingrained belief that civil resistance and people power achievements are structurally determined.[77] In other words, certain conditions are needed for success, and their absence is a harbinger for failure. The historical record, aforementioned research, this study, and a unique investigation conclusively prove otherwise. Utilizing Freedom House's database, begun in 1972—a regression analysis of sixty-four countries experiencing transitions to democracy—found that "neither the political nor environmental factors examined in the study had a statistically significant impact on the success or failure of civil resistance movements."[78] Civic movements were as likely to succeed in less-developed, economically poor countries as in developed, affluent ones. Nor was significant evidence found that ethnic or religious differences limited possibilities for a unified civic opposition to emerge.[79] The only exception concerned the centralization of power. It was found that among the small number of decentralized regimes, "The more political power was dispersed to local leaders or governors throughout the country, the less likely it was that a successful national civic movement would emerge."[80]

A meta–case study analysis emerging from the development and democracy realm echoes these results. This ten-year research program on citizenship, participation, and accountability concluded that citizen engagement "can make positive differences, even in the least democratic settings—a proposition that challenges the conventional wisdom of an institution- and state-oriented approach that relegates opportunities for citizens to engage in a variety of participatory strategies to a more 'mature' democratic phase."[81]

In conclusion, civil resistance and people power can succeed even in unfavorable conditions. Skills—in planning, tactical innovation, and communications, and in building unity, strategy, self-organization, and nonviolent discipline—play a critical role in overcoming obstacles. These capacities can change adverse conditions, thereby altering the political, social, and economic terrain on which the struggle takes place.

Notes

1. Occupy Wall Street website, http://occupywallst.org/ (accessed September 30, 2013).

2. "People See Corruption Getting Worse but Are Ready to Get Involved, Says Biggest Transparency International Global Public Opinion Survey," press release, Transparency International, December 9, 2010, www.transparency.org.

3. Thomas Friedman, "Two Peas in a Pod," *New York Times,* November 8, 2011, www.nytimes.com.

4. "Fraud and Corruption: Frequently Asked Questions," World Bank, http://web.worldbank.org (accessed September 30, 2013).

5. Civicus, "Poverty and Corruption" (Working Paper #02/2008, Transparency International), http://www.civicus.org.

6. *United Nations, A More Secure World: Our Shared Responsibility, Report of the Secretary-General's High-Level Panel on Threats, Challenges, and Change,* UN Doc a/59/565, December 1, 2004, 20–21, www.unrol.org.

7. *World Bank Development Report 2011: Conflict, Security, and Development* (Washington, DC: World Bank, 2011).

8. Emma Batha, "FACTBOX: World Bank Report Highlights Links Between Conflict and Poverty," Thompson Reuters Foundation, April 11, 2011, www.trust.org.

9. Fourteenth International Anti-Corruption Conference, "The Bangkok Declaration: Restoring Trust," November 13, 2010, http://14iacc.org.

10. "European Commission Check-List for Root Causes of Conflict," Conflict Prevention Section/External Relations, European Commission, http://www.ceipaz.org.

11. Philippe Le Billon, "Buying Peace or Fueling War: The Role of Corruption in Armed Conflicts," *Journal of International Development* 15 (2003): 413–426.

12. "Corruption, Godfatherism, and the Funding of Political Violence," Human Rights Watch, October 2007, http://hrw.org.

13. Daniel Kaufmann, "Human Rights, Governance, and Development: An Empirical Perspective," in *Human Rights and Development: Towards Mutual Reinforcement,* ed. Philip Alston and Mary Robinson, 352–402 (Oxford: Oxford University Press, 2005).

14. Arvind Ganesan, "Human Rights and Corruption: The Linkages," Human Rights Watch, July 30, 2007, http://hrw.org.

15. Fourteenth International Anti-Corruption Conference, "Bangkok Declaration."

16. Cheyanne Scharbatke-Church and Kirby Reiling, "Lilies That Fester: Seeds of Corruption and Peacebuilding," *New Routes Journal of Peace Research and Action* 14, no. 3–4 (2009): 4–9.

17. "Eradicating Arms Trafficking Will Further Peace in Central Africa, Say UN officials," United Nations News Centre, March 19, 2010, www.un.org.

18. The statistics cited have been sourced from Global Witness and UNICEF. See "Same Old Story: A Background Study on Natural Resources in the Democratic Republic of Congo," Global Witness, June 2004, 5, www.global witness.org; "UNICEF, V-Day Put Rape in Democratic Republic of the Congo Front and Center," UNICEF press release, April 12, 2008, www.unicef.org.

19. Global Witness, "Same Old Story."

20. "Conflict Prevention and Anti-Corruption Overview," USAID West Africa, September 2007, www.usaid.gov.

21. *Niger Delta Human Development Report* (Abuja: United Nations Development Programme, 2006), http://hdr.undp.org.

22. Martti Ahtisaari, "Violence Prevention: A Critical Dimension of Development Conference" (presentation, World Bank, Washington, DC, April 6, 2009).

23. Philippe Le Billon, "Thought Piece: What Is the Impact? Effects of Corruption in Post-Conflict" (paper for the Nexus: Corruption, Conflict, and Peacebuilding Colloquium, the Institute for Human Security, the Fletcher School, Tufts University, Boston, MA, April 12–13, 2007), http://fletcher.tufts.edu.

24. Craig Whitlock, "Pentagon Says Instability in Afghanistan Has 'Leveled Off,'" *Washington Post,* April 29, 2010, www.washingtonpost.com.

25. Confidential source.

26. Frank Vogl, "Afghan Corruption Imperils Future Success," *USA Today,* February 10, 2013, www.usatoday.com.

27. State capture occurs when vested interests influence and manipulate the policymaking, political, and bureaucratic processes for their own advantage.

28. William Booth, "Mexico's Crime Wave Has Left About 25,000 Missing, Government Documents Show," *Washington Post,* November 29, 2012, www.washingtonpost.com.

29. "UNODC Assists Guatemala to Tackle Organized Crime," United Nations Office of Drugs and Crime (UNODC), March 17, 2010, www.unodc.org.

30. Stephen S. Dudley, "How Mexico's Drug War Is Killing Guatemala," *Foreign Policy,* July 20, 2010, www.foreignpolicy.com; Mariana Sanchez, "Drug Gangs Fuel Political Violence," Al-Jazeera International video report, September 9, 2007, http://bravenewfilms.org.

31. *World Bank Development Report 2011.*

32. Jerome Starkey, "Drugs for Guns: How the Afghan Heroin Trade Is Fuelling the Taliban Insurgency," *The Independent,* April 29, 2008, www.independent.co.uk.

33. Fourteenth International Anti-Corruption Conference, "Bangkok Declaration."

34. Raymond June and Nathaniel Heller, "Corruption and Anti-Corruption in Peacebuilding: Toward a Unified Framework," *New Routes Journal of Peace Research and Action* 14, no. 3–4 (2009): 10–13.

35. Ibid.

36. Scharbatke-Church and Reiling, "Lilies That Fester."

37. Ibid.

38. Ibid., 3.

39. June and Heller, "Corruption and Anti-Corruption in Peacebuilding."

40. Fourteenth International Anti-Corruption Conference, "Bangkok Declaration."

41. Scharbatke-Church and Reiling, "Lilies That Fester," 5.

42. Phyllis Dininio, "Warlords and Corruption in Post-Conflict Governments," *New Routes Journal of Peace Research and Action* 14, no. 3–4 (2009): 27–29.

43. Ibid.

44. Antonio Giustozzi, "Afghanistan: Transition Without End," Crisis States Research Centre, London School of Economics and Political Science (Crisis States working papers series 2, no. 40, November 2008), http://eprints.lse.ac.uk/22938/.

45. Aryn Baker, "The Warlords of Afghanistan," *Time,* February 12, 2009, www.time.com; Tom Peter, "A Changing of the Guard for Afghanistan's Warlords," *Christian Science Monitor,* October 27, 2010, www.csmonitor.com.

46. Karen Ballentine and Heiko Nitzschke, "The Political Economy of Civil War and Conflict Transformation," Berghof Research Centre for Constructive Conflict Management, Berlin, April 2005, www.berghof-handbook.net.

47. "Congo's Elections: Making or Breaking the Peace," Africa Report, International Crisis Group, no. 108, April 27, 2006, www.crisisgroup.org.

48. Kendra Dupuy and Helga Malmin Binningsbo, "Buying Peace with Diamonds?" Centre for the Study of Civil War Policy Brief, International Peace Research Institute, July 2008, www.prio.no.

49. Stephen Zunes, panel presentation at the Thirteenth International Anti-Corruption Conference, Athens, October 31, 2008.

50. My colleague Jack DuVall coined the term "fragmented tyrannies." Personal communication with author, Washington, DC, July 2008.

51. Zunes, panel presentation at the Thirteenth International Anti-Corruption Conference.

52. The civic realm refers to the collective nonstate, bottom-up initiatives and relationships in a society, including nonviolent civic campaigns and movements; civil society organizations (CSOs); nongovernmental organizations (NGOs); community-based organizations (CBOs); civic coalitions and alliances; unions; professional organizations; grassroots networks, committees, and collectives; local citizen groups; activists, community organizers, and last but not least, citizens.

53. Maciej Bartkowski, ed., *Recovering Nonviolent History: Civil Resistance in Liberation Struggles* (Boulder, CO: Lynne Rienner Publishers, 2013), 5.

54. Gene Sharp, *Waging Nonviolent Struggle: 20th-Century Practice and 21st-Century Potential* (Boston: Porter Sargent, 2005).

55. Erica Chenoweth and Maria Stephan, *Why Civil Resistance Works: The Strategic Logic of Nonviolent Conflict* (New York: Columbia University Press, 2011).

56. The Polity IV scale is a conceptual scheme that examines "concomitant qualities of democratic and autocratic authority in governing institutions, rather than discreet and mutually exclusive forms of governance." It delineates a spectrum of governing authority from what are termed fully institutionalized autocracies through mixed, or incoherent, authority regimes to fully institutionalized democracies. The Polity Score is based on a 21-point scale ranging from −10 (hereditary monarchy) to +10 (consolidated democracy). For additional information, see www.systemicpeace.org.

57. Erica Chenoweth, "A Skeptic's Guide to Nonviolent Resistance," *Rational Insurgent,* March 9, 2011, http://rationalinsurgent.wordpress.com.

58. Ibid.

59. Adrian Karatnycky and Peter Ackerman, *How Freedom Is Won: From Civic Resistance to Durable Democracy* (New York: Freedom House, 2005).

60. *World Development Report 2011.*

61. M. K. Gandhi, *Hind Swaraj or Indian Home Rule* (n.p., 1938), chap. 16, http://www.mkgandhi.org.

62. For research on civil resistance and the history of nonviolent social movements, see the following: Peter Ackerman and Jack DuVall, *A Force More Powerful: A Century of Nonviolent Conflict* (New York: Palgrave, 2000); Adam Roberts and Timothy Garton Ash, *Civil Resistance and Power Politics: From Gandhi to the Present* (Oxford: Oxford University Press, 2009); Sharp, *Waging Nonviolent Struggle*; Maria Stephan, ed., *Civilian Jihad: Nonviolent Struggle, Democratization, and Governance in the Middle East* (New York: Palgrave Macmillan, 2009).

63. For additional information, see Mary King, *A Quiet Revolution: The First Palestinian Intifada and Nonviolent Resistance* (New York: Nation Books, 2007); Stephan, *Civilian Jihad.*

64. Hamad Albloshi and Faisal Alfahad, "The Orange Movement of Kuwait: Civic Pressure Transforms a Political System," in *Civilian Jihad: Nonviolent Struggle, Democratization, and Governance in the Middle East,* ed. Maria Stephan (New York: Palgrave Macmillan, 2009), 219–232.

65. Ernesto Londono, "Egyptian Man's Death Became Symbol of Callous State," *Washington Post,* February 8, 2011, www.washingtonpost.com.

66. For an in-depth examination of misconceptions about civil resistance and people power, see Kurt Schock, *Unarmed Insurrections: People Power Movements in Non-Democracies* (Minneapolis: University of Minnesota Press, 2005), 6–12.

67. *Reflections on Social Accountability: Catalyzing Democratic Governance to Accelerate Progress Towards the Millennium Development Goals,* United Nations Development Programme, 2013, 9, www.undp.org.

68. According to Congresso em Foco, a watchdog website, in 2010, 147 of the 513 members of the Chamber of Deputies of Congress (29 percent), and twenty-one out of eighty-one senators (26 percent), faced criminal charges in the Supreme Court or were under investigation.

69. UKAid, "Active Citizens, Accountable Governments: Civil Society Experiences from the Latin America Partnership Programme Arrangement," Department of Foreign and International Affairs, n.d., www.aidsalliance.org.

70. *Best Practices in the Participatory Approach to Delivery of Social Services* (Addis Ababa: Economic Commission for Africa, 2004), 8.

71. Lorenzo Delesgues, Integrity Watch Afghanistan cofounder, personal communication with author, April 2011.

72. Civic space is the arena for public expression and dissent.

73. David Sasaki, "The Role of Technology and Citizen Media in Promoting Transparency, Accountability, and Civic Participation," Technology for Transparency Network, May 27, 2010, 13, http://globalvoicesonline.org.

74. Maria Stephan and Erica Chenoweth, "Why Civil Resistance Works: The Strategic Logic of Nonviolent Conflict," *International Security* 33, no. 1 (Summer 2008): 7–44.

75. Dilemma actions put the oppressor in a situation whereby the actions it takes will result in some kind of negative outcome for it and some kind of positive outcome for the nonviolent campaign or movement. For information about dilemma actions, see Srdja Popovic, Slobodan Djinovic, Andre J. Milivojevic, Hardy Merriman, and Ivan Marovic, *A Guide to Effective Nonviolent Struggle* (Belgrade: Centre for Applied Nonviolent Action and Strategies, 2007), chap. 12.

76. Backfire occurs when an attack creates more support for or attention to whatever is attacked—in this context, civic initiatives targeting corruption and abuse. For information about backfire, see www.bmartin.cc/pubs/backfire.html.

77. Schock, *Unarmed Insurrections*.

78. Eleanor Marchant, *Enabling Environments for Civic Movements and the Dynamics of Democratic Transition,* Freedom House, 2008, www.freedomhouse.org.

79. Ibid., "Overview."

80. Ibid., "Principal Findings."

81. John Gaventa and Gregory Barrett, "So What Difference Does It Make? Mapping the Outcomes of Citizen Engagement" (Institute of Development Studies, Working Paper 2010, no. 347, October 2010, 54), www.ntd.co.uk.

2

Approaches to Curbing Corruption

The standard and most widely used definition of corruption is, "the abuse of entrusted power for private gain."[1] Another common definition is, "the abuse of public office for private gain."[2] These operational, succinct definitions depict the phenomenon at the micro level as a transaction between or among parties.[3] However, these conceptualizations have limitations. First, corruption is not only prevalent in governments, as suggested by the latter definition. It can occur in the economic realm and among nonstate sectors and groups in society. Second, abuse of entrusted power may not necessarily be for private gain but also to reap political gains or collective benefits for a third party, entity, group, or sector—for example, state security forces, political parties, businesses, financial services, and unions. Finally, this framework does not convey how corruption functions. It is not simply the aggregate of individual transactions between a corrupter (abuser of power) and the corruptee (victim or willing partner in the illicit interaction).

Corruption functions as a system of power abuse that involves multiple relationships—some obvious and many others hidden, hence the anticorruption community's emphasis on transparency. Within this system are long-standing interests that want to maintain the venal status quo. My preferred definition of corruption is as follows: a system of abuse of entrusted power for private, collective, or political gain—often involving a complex, intertwined set of relationships, some obvious, others hidden, with established vested interests, that can operate vertically within an institution or horizontally across political, economic, and social spheres in a society or transnationally.[4]

Corruption can also be defined from a human rights framework—

through the eyes and experiences of regular people. Once they are factored into the equation, graft can further be understood as a form of oppression and loss of freedom. Aruna Roy, one of the founders of both the Mazdoor Kisan Shakti Sangathan (Union for the Empowerment of Peasants and Laborers, MKSS) and the Right to Information movement in India, characterizes corruption as "the external manifestations of the denial of a right, an entitlement, a wage, a medicine."[5]

Limitations of Top-Down Anticorruption Approaches

Now into its third decade, the global anticorruption struggle has undoubtedly made progress, but real change appears to be modest.[6] Wide-scale national anticorruption programs, traditionally favored by donor countries and multilateral institutions, have had inconsistent results.[7] A literature review of approximately 150 studies identified through a bibliography of close to 800 sources found "few success stories when it comes to the impact of donor supported anti-corruption efforts."[8] Nor have public perceptions improved. Transparency International's 2010 Global Corruption Barometer found that 60 percent of those surveyed in eighty-six countries and territories said that corruption had increased over the past three years. Eighty percent stated that political parties are corrupt or extremely corrupt, and half asserted that their government's efforts to stop corruption were ineffective. Since 2006, payoffs to police are said to have doubled, while more respondents reported paying bribes to the judiciary and for registry and permit services than in 2005. Poorer interviewees were twice as likely to pay bribes for basic services as more well-off individuals.[9]

Traditional anticorruption approaches can be summarized by three main features. First, they have been top-down and elite-driven, with attention directed mainly toward administrative graft. Citizens and the potential of people power did not factor into the equation. Second, efforts focused considerably on developing norms, rules, and structures, resulting in legislation; institution building, such as anticorruption commissions; improvement of national and local government capacity; international agreements; and public finance management. In essence, these approaches were largely based on the experiences of industrialized Western democracies. Some governance experts argue even further that attempts to improve governance were based on a value judgment that "West is best" and what was needed was a correction of deficiencies in comparison to this ideal.[10]

Third, there has been a predominant focus on processes. According to Daniel Kaufmann, a development specialist, the fallacy exists that one "fights corruption by fighting corruption." This approach translated into ongoing anticorruption initiatives with more commissions or ethics agencies, and the drafting of new or improved laws, codes of conduct, decrees, integrity pacts, and so on, which, he asserts, appear to have had minimal impact.[11]

Viewed through the lens of people power, the limitations to elite-driven, technocratic strategies are manifold. Foremost, top-down measures have rested on the flawed assumption that once anticorruption structures are put in place, illicit practices will accordingly change. Institutions accused of corruption are often made responsible for enacting reforms. But those benefitting from graft are much less likely to stand against it than those suffering from it. Consequently, even when political will exists, it can be blocked—not because more political will is needed, but because too many players have a stake in the crooked status quo. Second, the grass roots was not included in the anticorruption equation—as sources of information and insights about malfeasance and top-down approaches to curb it; in terms of citizens' experiences of it; or as potential drivers of accountability, integrity, and change. Third, the systemic nature of corruption was often missed, and focus on corruption was limited in societal sectors beyond the state. Furthermore, one-size-fits-all types of frameworks aimed at replicating mature bureaucracies in the Global North were promulgated. Cumulatively, there was minimal impact on the daily lives of regular people.

A Paradigm Shift

To their credit, over the past decade, the international anticorruption and development communities began an earnest stock-taking, and a historic paradigm shift is under way in the anticorruption and accountability realms. These communities now recognize that graft cannot be fully challenged without the active involvement of citizens. The Fourteenth International Anti-Corruption Conference (IACC) in 2010, a bellwether of advances in these fields, launched a new interactive series of sessions on people's empowerment.[12] It brought together activists to feature innovative uses of ICTs (information and communication technologies) and profile grassroots civic initiatives.[13] The final declaration, presciently released one month before the onset of the Tunisian people power revolution, stated, "Empowered people create change. . . . This expanded element of our conference points the way for the future of the anti-corruption movement, one incorporating citizen mobilisation and empowerment, as well as the inclusion of youth."[14]

By 2012, the Fifteenth IACC's overall theme was Mobilising People: Connecting Agents of Change. Transparency International's Strategy 2015 plan includes people among the six priorities: "Increased empowerment of people and partners around the world to take action against corruption. The challenge is to engage with people more widely than ever before—for ultimately, only people can stop corruption."[15] In April 2011, signifying major inroads in the development realm, Robert Zoellick, then president of the World Bank, outlined a new "social contract for development" in which "an empowered public is the foundation for a stronger society, more effective government, and a more successful state."[16] Jim Kim, the Bank's subsequent president, reiterated this focus. While outlining the institution's anticorruption priorities, he said, "We need to empower citizens with information and tools to make their governments more effective and accountable."[17]

Top-Down and Bottom-Up: Two Sides of the Same Coin

Top-down and bottom-up approaches are not mutually exclusive. Both are needed. Moreover, there are multiple ways in which grassroots civic campaigns and movements, wielding people power, can complement and reinforce legal and administrative approaches, which are essential to build the anticorruption infrastructure needed for long-term transformation of systems of graft. Some examples follow.

Vertical Corruption

People power initiatives can curb vertical corruption functioning within an institution. The National Foundation for Democracy and Human Rights in Uganda (NAFODU), a grassroots civil society organization (CSO) in the southwest of the country, initiated a volunteer-driven, community-monitoring mobilization that targeted local police intimidation and extortion (see Chapter 9).

Horizontal Corruption

Grassroots campaigns and movements can impact horizontal corruption, which operates across institutions, groups, and sectors. Dosta! (Enough!), a youth movement in Bosnia-Herzegovina, challenged systemic corruption by zeroing in on a scandal involving the prime minister of one of the two political sections, as well as a former prime minister, a state company, government administrations, and later, the prime minister of Sarajevo Canton, the mayor of Sarajevo, and the police (see Chapter 10). After investigative journalists exposed how the prime minister, Nedžad Branković, acquired an exclusive apartment for approximately US$500, Dosta! launched a campaign through graffiti, Facebook mobilization, T-shirt mockery, billboard messages, and inundating police stations with phone calls. Branković's party subsequently forced him to resign.[18]

Systemic Approach

Organized, strategic civic movements and campaigns are particularly suited to a systemic approach to curbing deeply entrenched corruption and abuse by exerting pressure on other sectors and nonstate sources of graft in society. Launched in 2004, Addiopizzo (Good-bye, protection money), a youth-led nonviolent movement in Palermo, Italy, is disrupting the system of Mafia extortion (see Chapter 6). The movement does this by building an ever-growing group of businesses that refuse to pay *pizzo*; mobilizing citizens to resist through simple, everyday acts, such as patronizing *pizzo*-free businesses, and harnessing national and international support through Mafia-free tourism initiatives; seeking ethical public procurement practices; and cooperating with teachers, schools, and the education ministry to instill integrity and anti-Mafia values in the next generation.

Implementation

Although rules, regulations, and laws targeting corruption may exist on the books, they are not always implemented or compliance is low. Such is the problem that Transparency International's aforementioned Strategy 2015 also identifies institutions and laws among its strategic priorities. The strategy statement prioritizes "improved implementation of anti-corruption programmes in leading institutions, businesses and the international financial system."[19] The challenge is to ensure that commitments to stop corruption are translated into actions, enforcement, and results. Another priority is "more effective enforcement of laws and standards around the world and reduced impunity for corrupt acts."[20] The challenge is enforcing fair legal frameworks, ensuring no impunity for corruption.

Civil resistance can create pressure for such measures. For instance, the 5th Pillar movement in India strategically uses the country's Right to Information law (RTI) by encouraging citizens to file RTI inquiries (see Chapter 7). With the proper questions, it's possible to document misbehavior, thereby holding officials accountable. To magnify its impact, 5th Pillar links this action together with other nonviolent tactics, such as workshops in urban centers and villages, assistance in writing and submitting RTIs, "people's inspection and audits" of public works, leafleting, social processions, and backup for those wanting to approach the state government's Vigilance Department and the Central Bureau of Investigation's Anti-Corruption Division.[21]

Mobilized citizens can also play a role in implementing legal or administrative measures, particularly those won by nonviolent campaigns and movements. A review of the impact of donor funding on home-grown SMOs and social movements observed, "Ensuring that legislation is enforced may also require the capacity to monitor the activities of enforcement agencies. To enact this monitoring, social movements need more than a presence in official corridors and international arenas—the existence of a strong grass-roots network of activists on the ground is essential."[22]

Protection

Civic campaigns and movements can also support and protect honest individuals, within state institutions and other entities, who are attempting change. All too often, one or a small number of reformers cannot challenge or dismantle entrenched, multifaceted systems of graft and unaccountability. To defend the Indonesian Corruption Eradication Commission (KPK) and secure the release of two falsely imprisoned deputy commissioners, the 2009 CICAK (Love Indonesia, Love Anti-Corruption Commission) campaign mobilized citizens around the country (see Chapter 5). It utilized creative nonviolent tactics, including a 1.7 million member Facebook group, humorous stunts, anticorruption ringtones, and street actions.

The Dynamics of People Power in Curbing Corruption and Gaining Accountability

> History demonstrates that there is no reason to expect corrupt officials and political leaders to reform themselves.
> —*Pierre Landell Mills*

Some researchers of citizen engagement and accountability initiatives have commented on the absence of theories of change in their fields of study.[23] The dynamics of civil resistance and people power provide a conceptual framework to fill this gap. Grassroots campaigns and movements by their nature emerge from the civic realm and include the participation of regular people united around common grievances, objectives, and demands. Mobilized citizens engaging in nonviolent tactics make up a social force that can exert pressure on the state and on other sectors of society. This pressure comes from outside the institution or corrupt system, which usually cannot reform from within because those who are benefitting from graft and abuse circumvent technocratic measures and thwart political efforts at change.

Therein lies the strategic advantage of nonviolent resistance to curb corruption: it consists of extrainstitutional methods of action to push for change, when powerholders are corrupt or unaccountable and institutional channels are blocked or ineffective.[24] Mobilized citizens engaged in organized campaigns and movements generate people power through three dynamics. *Disruption* of the status quo or regular functioning of systems of corruption shakes up venal relationships and weakens enablers. The latter involves laws, practices, and professional services that can facilitate malfeasance. Hence, individually targeting or punishing every illicit interaction is not necessary—an impossibility anyway, given that most corrupt relationships are hidden and few power abusers willingly forsake their vested interests and gains. Civil resistance strategies of disruption break down the system and make business as usual more difficult and risky. MUHURI (Muslims for Human Rights) in Mombasa, Kenya, is empowering poor communities to fight poverty by curbing misuse of constituency development funds, approximately $1 million given annually to each member of Parliament (see Chapter 10). MUHURI conducts local education and training in a six-step social audit to monitor expenditures and public works, while using nonviolent tactics, such as street theatre and marches, to build support, mobilize citizens, and collect information.[25]

Engagement of people involves pulling them toward the campaign or movement—from the public as well as from various sectors, groups, institutions, and elites, including from within corrupt systems (e.g., political leaders, integrity champions, and honest bureaucrats). In the civil resistance realm, this dynamic is often described as shifting people's loyalties away from the oppressors toward the nonviolent civic initiative and producing "defections"—that is, individuals and groups within the corrupt system who refuse to go along with it. The engagement dynamic is based on the reality that not everyone is equally loyal, equally corruptible, and equally wedded to the corrupt system.

Engagement strategies strengthen citizen participation and campaign capacity, while weakening sources of support and control for unaccountable and corrupt powerholders, entities, and their enablers. The aforementioned NAFODU civic initiative in Uganda illustrates this process. By engaging local volunteers and citizens to report on police graft in low-risk ways, through radio call-ins and SMS texts, it shook up the illicit system and generated social pressure. At the same time, the initiative strategically sought to win elements of law enforcement toward the community, for example, by obtaining a memorandum of understanding with officials and conducting local integrity trainings. In an astounding shift of power relations, the police began to share their own grievances and asked for the help of NAFODU and citizens to give them a voice and make recommendations to the government.[26]

There is another dimension to engagement—joining forces with "institutional activists." Somewhat similar to the notion of integrity champions, these powerholder insiders within state (and conceivably nonstate) entities "proactively take up causes that overlap with those of grassroots challengers."[27] Their insider activism is often conducted independently of civil society. They can access institutional resources and influence policymaking and implementation.[28] Thus, in some anticorruption and accountability cases, they can constitute an essential ally and critical target of engagement tactics. The objective is not to shift the positions of such "institutional activists" or to encourage their defection from the system, that is, to step out or break away from it. Rather, nonviolent campaigns and movements could seek to join forces with them in order to magnify internal, top-down and external, bottom-up pressure.

Shifting power relations through the power of numbers is a third dynamic for generating people power. Large-scale public participation relative to the size of struggle arena—which can range from the community level all the way to the national and international levels—can create social pressure of a magnitude that becomes difficult to suppress or ignore. In other words, "When one person speaks of injustice, it remains a whisper. When two people speak out, it becomes talk. When many tell of injustice, they find a voice that will be heard."[29] Strategies activating the numbers dynamic can alter the loyalties of powerholders and strengthen honest changemakers within the corrupt system who are no longer alone, and thus, not easy targets to subdue. In 1996 Turkey was beleaguered by a nationwide crime syndicate that involved paramilitary entities, the mafia, drug traffickers, government officials, members of Parliament, parts of the judiciary and media, and businesses. In spite of semiauthoritarian rule and limited civic space to express dissent, the 1997 Citizens Initiative for Constant Light mobilized the public in the One Minute of Darkness for Constant Light campaign, through a low-risk mass action (see Chapter 10). They began with co-

ordinated switching off of lights, soon augmented by unanticipated out-
pourings on the street. At its peak, approximately 30 million people
took part in the campaign, which pressured the government to launch
judicial investigations resulting in verdicts, and exposed crime syndicate figures and relationships.

People Power Tactics

Nonviolent tactics constitute the methods of civil resistance that can
generate people power. Grassroots civic initiatives targeting corruption
have significantly expanded the civil resistance repertoire by creating
innovative tactics or engaging in conventional ones in novel ways (a
comprehensive list of the wide-ranging tactics employed in the twelve
cases appears in the Appendix). Such tactics include

- Noncooperation.
- Civil disobedience.
- Low-risk mass actions.
- Displays of symbols.
- Street theatre, visual dramatizations, stunts.
- Songs, poetry, cultural expressions.
- Humor, dilemma actions.
- Candidate "blacklists."
- Information gathering, right to information procedures.
- Monitoring of officials, institutions, budgets, spending, public
  services, development projects.[30]
- Social audits and "face the people" forums.
- Digital resistance through social networking technologies (e.g.,
  Facebook posts, blogging, SMS, e-petitions, tweets).[31]
- Education and training.
- Social and economic empowerment initiatives.
- Youth recreation.
- Creation of parallel institutions.
- Anticorruption pledges, citizen-sponsored integrity awards.
- Protests, petitions, vigils, marches, sit-ins.
- Strikes, boycotts, reverse boycotts.[32]
- Nonviolent blockades.
- Nonviolent accompaniment.

How do citizens curb corruption? How is people power manifested?
What are the results? The in-depth case studies presented in this book

progress from national campaigns and movements to more local struggles. Chapters 3 and 4 examine nationwide grassroots initiatives targeting political corruption in South Korea and Brazil, respectively. The abuse of power by political parties, elites, and legislators is common around the world. As documented in the 2011 Global Corruption Barometer cited earlier in this chapter, 80 percent of citizens surveyed perceive political parties to be corrupt. A 2012 Transparency International report on Europe stated, "Popular discontent with corruption has brought people out onto the streets in these and other European countries to protest against a combination of political corruption and perceived unfair austerity being meted out to ordinary citizens."[33] A 2013 poll of American voters found that 85 percent stated they had an unfavorable opinion of the U.S. Congress. When asked if they have a higher opinion of the legislative body or various unpleasant things, respondents indicated a more positive opinion of root canals, head lice, colonoscopies, and cockroaches (to name a few) than Congress.[34] In contrast, the South Korean and Brazilian cases offer inspiration and rich lessons of how to move from anger and disengagement from the political process to nonviolent empowerment and positive change.

Notes

1. "What We Do," Transparency International website, http://www.trans parency.org (accessed September 16, 2013).

2. Daniel Kaufmann, "Ten Myths About Governance and Corruption," *Finance and Development*, September 2005, 41, www.imf.org.

3. For a summary of traditional categories of corruption, see *United Nations Handbook: Practical Anti-Corruption Measures for Prosecutors and Investigators* (Vienna: United Nations Office of Drugs and Crime, 2004), 23–30, www.unodc.org.

4. This systemic definition was developed by the author, who wishes to credit, for inspiration, points made by Maria Gonzalez de Asis, World Bank, in an unpublished working paper.

5. Aruna Roy, "Survival and Right to Information" (Gulam Rasool Third Memorial Lecture, Forum for Freedom of Expression, Hyderabad, India, n.d.), 11, www.unipune.ac.in.

6. *Corruption and Human Rights: Making the Connection* (Geneva: International Council on Human Rights Policy and Transparency International, 2009).

7. Karen Hussmann and Hannes Hechler, "Anti-Corruption Policy Making in Practice: Implications for Implementing UNCAC," *U4 Brief*, January 2008, 1, www.cmi.no/publications.

8. *Anti-Corruption Approaches: A Literature Review* (Oslo: Norwegian Agency for Development and Cooperation, 2009), www.norad.no/en.

9. *Global Corruption Barometer* (Berlin: Transparency International, 2010), www.transparency.org.

10. Sue Unsworth, *An Upside-Down View of Governance* (Brighton: Institute of Development Studies, University of Sussex, April 2010).

11. Kaufmann, "Ten Myths About Governance and Corruption."

12. Disclosure: I had multiple roles at the Fourteenth and Fifteenth International Anti-Corruption Conferences (IACC).

13. "Changing the Rules of the Game," Fourteenth International Anti-Corruption Conference, http://14iacc.org.

14. "The Bangkok Declaration: Restoring Trust," Fourteenth International Anti-Corruption Conference, November 13, 2010, http://14iacc.org.

15. "Strategy 2015," Transparency International, 16, www.transparency.org.

16. Robert Zoellick, "The Middle East and North Africa: A New Social Contract for Development" (speech, the Peterson Institute for International Economics, Washington, DC, April 6, 2011), http://web.worldbank.org.

17. "Corruption Is 'Public Enemy Number One' in Developing Countries, Says World Bank Group President Kim," World Bank Group press release, December 19, 2013, www.worldbank.org.

18. Darko Brkan, Dosta! cofounder, April 2011, personal communication with author.

19. "Strategy 2015," 18.

20. Ibid., 20.

21. Shaazka Beyerle, "People Count: How Citizen Engagement and Action Challenge Corruption and Abuse" (paper presented at the International Peace Research Association Conference, Sydney, Australia, July 8, 2010).

22. Rita Jalali, "Financing Empowerment? How Foreign Aid to Southern NGOs and Social Movements Undermines Grass-Roots Mobilization," *Sociology Compass* 7, no. 1 (2013): 67.

23. Rosemary McGee and John Gaventa, with Gregg Barrett, Richard Calland, Ruth Carlitz, Anuradha Joshi, and Andres Mejia Acosta, "Review of Impact and Effectiveness of Transparency and Accountability Initiatives: Synthesis Report" (prepared for the Transparency and Accountability Initiative Workshop, Institute of Development Studies, Sussex, October 14–15, 2010), www.ids.ac.uk.

24. This conceptualization is based on the definition of social movements by Kurt Schock, "People Power and Alternative Politics," in *Politics in the Developing World*, 3rd ed., ed. Peter Burnell, Vicky Randall, and Lise Rakner (London: Oxford University Press, 2008), 202–219.

25. Social audits are a form of monitoring, consisting of multiple sequenced steps, such as information gathering, training citizens to interpret documents and budgets, monitoring expenditures and physically inspecting public works, community education and mobilization, public hearings with powerholders, and civic follow-up.

26. Joseline Korugyendo, former NAFODU head of programmes, March–April 2011, personal communication with author.

27. David Pettinicchio, "Institutional Activism: Reconsidering the Insider-Outsider Dichotomy," *Sociology Compass* 6, no. 6 (2012): 499.

28. Ibid.

29. This quote, without attribution, is from a video presentation that had been uploaded on the homepage of www.civicus.org in 2006. CIVICUS is an international civil society alliance.

30. Monitoring is a tactic used by civic actors—including regular citizens—in the anticorruption, accountability, human rights, development, governance, and environment realms. It can involve observing, recording, verifying, comparing, overseeing, checking, and inspecting. In the anticorruption context, the targets of such activities are people (for example, election candidates, parliamentarians, government leaders, public officials, civil servants, social service providers, and police); institutions (parliaments, public administrations, government agencies, judiciaries, state security forces, municipalities, corporations, universities, schools, and hospitals); policies (such as poverty reduction, education, and natural resource exploitation); budgets and expenditures, public programs, social services, public works, procurement practices, and procurement outcomes; and social and economic development projects conducted by governments or external actors. Monitoring can either be visible (for example, public audits or site inspections) or anonymous (for instance, mobile phone videos or SMS reports of public officials and police demanding bribes). Effective monitoring creates social pressure and disrupts corrupt practices within systems of graft and abuse.

31. Nonviolent tactics executed digitally—for example, e-petitions, online/SMS monitoring, SMS balloting, and mobile phone ringtones as displays of symbols.

32. Reverse boycotts occur when consumers support or patronize particular businesses or establishments.

33. Suzanne Mulcahy, *Money, Politics, Power: Corruption Risks in Europe* (Berlin: Transparency International, 2012), 9.

34. "Congress Less Popular Than Cockroaches, Traffic Jams," *Public Policy Polling*, January 8, 2013, www.publicpolicypolling.com.

3

Blacklisting Corrupt Candidates: Korea

If a man rises to high political office, his family will be financially set for three generations.
—*quoted in Glenn Manarin, "Striking Where It Hurts"*

Corrupt politicians, broken promises for change, backroom deals, cozy relationships with special interests, and abysmal choices on Election Day . . . these familiar complaints can be found in democracies and even in authoritarian systems where dictators often dabble with electoral façades. But what can regular people do beyond fuming, becoming apathetic, or voting for the least rotten apple in the barrel? In 2000, Korean civic leaders and citizens launched their own campaign to hinder venal, often entrenched politicians from running for office, and to improve the overall quality of candidates on the ballot for the Sixteenth National Assembly.[1]

Context

In 1970, four decades before Mohamed Bouazizi tragically died in Tunisia after setting himself on fire, Chon T'ae-il, a young textile worker in South Korea, took the same action and suffered the same fate.[2] In each instance, their self-immolation marked the onset of a civilian-based democracy movement. Korea's road to democracy was long and arduous. From 1948 the country endured successive dictatorships for decades. In 1987, led by student and labor groups, millions of people mobilized in what was called the June 10 Citizens' Democratic Revolt.[3] In the ensuing years, many veterans of this struggle went on to become leaders of civil society organizations focused on political and economic reforms to dismantle the old, corrupt system; strengthen democratic institutions; and consolidate representative rule. Foremost among these civic organizations were the People's Solidarity for Participatory Democracy (PSPD), Citizens' Coalition for Economic Justice (CCEJ), the Korean Federation for Environmental Movements (KFEM), and Green Korea United (GKU).

As in many other countries emerging out of authoritarian rule, corruption was proving difficult to dent. The country's financial crisis in 1997, followed by an onerous recession, exposed government incompetence and inefficiency and an overall lack of transparency in the political system.[4] "The crisis was the responsibility of the politicians who were pulling the strings of the economic system," according to political scientist Kim Young-rae.[5]

The public was becoming more and more disgusted. As they bore the consequences of the economic downturn, they were outraged by a series of scandals—graft across sectors; abuses of power and privileges; and bribery involving politicians, senior officials, banks, and *chaebols*, the latter referring to large business conglomerates with close ties to political figures and the state.[6] The ruling and opposition parties were both illicitly collecting funds. Legislators thwarted efforts to reform the Election Laws and crack down on political funding. They used—or, rather, abused—their immunity to undermine investigations. Law enforcement seemed to have little appetite to delve into political irregularities.[7] Korea's legislative branch became known as the "bullet-proof" and "brain dead" National Assembly.[8] Consequently, some civic leaders concluded that "corruption in Korea was so serious that it was the foremost obstacle hindering the progress of Korean society."[9] By the time the April 2000 National Assembly (parliamentary) elections were on the horizon, the public was distrustful of politicians, political parties, and the overall political system.[10]

Campaign: "Let's Change Old Politics with Citizens' Power"

Origins

Political reform and anticorruption have been central to civil society's efforts at consolidating Korea's democracy.[11] "The anti-corruption movement succeeds the democratic movements of the past decades," said Geo-sung Kim, a democracy movement veteran and chairperson of Transparency International Korea.[12]

PSPD, founded in 1994, launched a series of civic initiatives during that decade—from the Transparent Society Campaign in 1996, to pass a strong anticorruption law, to the Sunshine Project in 1998, which sought to modify the existing Freedom of Information Act, maximize its use, and expose budget mishandling.[13] By the early 1990s, civil society organizations began monitoring powerholders, initially for fair elections and "municipal congress watch" initiatives.[14] In 1999 a coalition of forty civil society organizations (CSOs), including the aforementioned PSPD, CCEJ, KFEM, and the Korean Women's Associations United (KWAU), took this tactic to a new level. On September 8, the Citizens' Solidarity for Monitoring the National Assembly Inspection of Government Offices was launched to record lawmakers' attendance, evaluate their performance, and scrutinize whether a list of 166 "reform tasks" were sufficiently addressed in committees.[15] When the monitors—civil society experts with relevant professional experience—were blocked from sessions, the coalition added street demonstrations and a phone/fax/email drive to its arsenal, which together generated media attention and public debate. On October 20 the campaign came to a close with the release of a report that ranked legislators on the basis of their performance. However, the initiative did not succeed to gain full access to the National Assembly's proceedings. This seeming failure had an unanticipated effect. According to Taeho Lee, a democracy movement veteran and deputy secretary general of PSPD, it catalyzed the civic realm.[16] After years of effort, civic organizations such as PSPD came to the conclusion that Korean political parties had not changed and politicians were not representing the population's interests.

The legislators' dismissive behavior became a public issue. Citizens were angered by their justifications, ranging from trivial excuses such as a lack of space in meeting rooms to arguments that civil society didn't have the expertise or even the right to monitor elected representatives. PSPD realized that there was a "need for more powerful action."[17] But what? Then, in October 1999, during a major television debate featuring National Assembly members and Lee, he declared that not only do citizens have the right to monitor lawmakers, they have the right to make them lose elections. After the program, a poll of viewers found that over 80 percent agreed with him. On that day, the seed for the Citizens Alliance for the General Elections (CAGE) 2000 was planted.

As 1999 drew to a close, fifteen civic organizations created a task force to explore the viability of a grassroots campaign to turn this new idea into reality—namely, a blacklist initiative. PSPD served as secretariat of the group. The idea of a blacklist originated from the aforementioned Transparent Society Campaign, which created a list of state pow-erholders—legislators, ministers, and deputy ministers—who were in-volved in massive corruption scandals that rocked the country.[18]

Strategic Analysis

From the outset, Lee reported, the task force strategically assessed the overall situation. The analysis was completed by December 18. Members assessed their potential strengths and weaknesses. They concluded that, in general, their strength was having the support of the general public, while their main weakness was that they did not have a nation-wide network and would quickly need to create one. They also identi-fied two principal obstacles. First, as the entire campaign to blacklist and defeat corrupt politicians would violate Article 87 of the Election Law, they needed to be prepared for the consequences and overcome qualms on the part of civic groups and citizens to become involved.[19] To address this challenge, they decided to systematically gauge the public's views and willingness to take action. Thus, in early January 2000, a sur-vey of a representative group of 500 people from around the country was conducted. Respondents were asked three key questions, which Lee paraphrased as follows:

1. Is it legitimate for civil society (CSOs and citizens) to evaluate, disqualify, and seek to defeat candidates for the National Assem-bly? (Result: 79.8 percent were in favor.)[20]
2. Although these activities are illegal under Article 87 of the Elec-tion Law, would you support a defeat campaign? (Result: 71.8 percent said they would support the effort, even if it is illegal.)[21]
3. Do you think this law should be changed? (Result: 65.1 percent said restrictions in the law should be changed because citizens have the right to conduct a blacklist.)[22]

As well, the survey garnered people's views about criteria for the blacklist. The task force concluded that people wanted the blacklist campaign, they wanted an amendment to the Election Law, and if that was not possible, they wanted civil disobedience and nonviolent direct action. The survey crystallized Lee's thinking that had been stirred dur-ing the TV debate. "Voters are the means to have rights," he reflected. Moreover, the survey gave civic leaders the ammunition needed to quickly convince CSOs, nongovernmental organizations (NGOs), and citizen groups to join the alliance. Finally, the survey enabled CAGE's planners to approach civic organizations, uncomfortable about breaking the Election Law, with reassurances that regular people supported mass civil disobedience.

The second obstacle was that powerholders would undoubtedly accuse civic leaders of political partisanship in order to undermine the campaign. To counter such attacks, they decided upon a policy of transparency. In practice, this involved publishing the blacklist criteria, basing assessments on publicly available information and releasing them on the CAGE website, involving citizens in the deliberations, and making no exceptions to the blacklist—regardless of the politician's seniority, power, or party affiliation.

Objectives, Strategy, Vision, and Plan of Action

With a little over three months until the elections, the task force quickly set to work on a campaign plan. They identified three objectives: (1) amend Article 87 of the Election Law, (2) improve the quality and integrity of candidates running in the April elections, and (3) remove "corrupt and incapable politicians" from the National Assembly.[23] The overall strategy consisted of a "de-nomination and de-election campaign by voters"—that is, discouraging corrupt politicians from being nominated and defeating those who still were selected as candidates.[24]

Ultimately, their vision was twofold. First, they sought to change the values of the political establishment, corrupt practices of political parties, and malfeasance of elected representatives. Second, they wanted to attain genuine participatory democracy in Korea, as enshrined in Article 1 of the Constitution, which states, "The Republic of Korea is a democratic republic. The sovereignty of the Republic of Korea resides in the people, and all state authority emanates from the people."[25] In other words, "We need to change the system and public consciousness," as Geo-sung Kim asserted.[26]

The task force devised a campaign plan centered on a defining method—blacklisting unfit candidates—around which a host of nonviolent tactics revolved.[27] The central elements were building a coalition, defining criteria for blacklisting, and breaking down the civic initiative into two phases: (1) Nakchon (Denominate)—including transparent assessment of potential party nominees, initial blacklist of unfit politicians likely to seek nomination, people power pressure on political parties to not nominate them, people power on parties to denominate—that is, withdraw those names from party lists who were nevertheless nominated; and (2) Naksun (Defeat)—releasing second blacklist of unfit candidates and mobilizing citizens to defeat these candidates in the April 14 parliamentary vote.

A Is for Alliance

Between December 1999 and early January 2000 the task force approached scores of national and local civic networks; NGOs; civil society groups; educational, professional, and religious organizations (Buddhist, Protestant, and Catholic); student and youth groups; cultural groups; community associations; and citizen groups.[28] It included such diverse groups as families of political prisoners to the entire YMCA/YWCA, and later on, a celebrity network and a cartoonists' association. "We proposed to them to join the campaign and presented the poll results and campaign plan," said Lee. Task force members pointed out the possibility of imprisonment and fines for breaking the Election Law and asked the heads of those organizations coming on board to sign an acknowledgment that they accepted these risks. In order to maintain a coherent focus and grow the alliance, it was decided to focus solely on corruption. "We needed to identify one issue everybody agreed on, and corruption is something that everyone is angry about," explained Lee. On January 12, 2000, amid fanfare at the Seoul Press Center, 470 organizations launched the Citizens Alliance for the General Election 2000 (CAGE).[29] The alliance presented a "Civil Manifesto for Political Reform" that declared, "Politics in Korea still remains in the time of the past century when the society and the people therein prepare their way into a new century as well as a new millennium. Political corruption in general is the worst obstacle hindering the progress of reform in Korean society that must no longer be tolerated."[30]

CAGE's very creation sent shock waves through the political establishment. The next day the headline of a major newspaper, *Dongo Ilbo*, was, "Political Parties Are Trembling: What If I Am on the List?"[31] Once the campaign got under way, the coalition grew to an astounding size—1,104 civic networks and groups.[32] "It became bigger than we expected," Lee stated.

B Is for Blacklist

Central to the campaign was the defining method of the blacklist, through which corrupt politicians would be identified as unfit to run for office while citizen mobilization and nonviolent actions would motivate voters to defeat them in the elections. Considerable effort was made to develop the criteria. Based on input from the January 2000 survey and discussions with citizens, the task force drafted a set of criteria that was reviewed and finalized by CAGE's Executive Committee, explained Lee. The criteria, as translated by PSPD into English, were

- Corrupt activities.
- Violation of the Election Law.
- Anti–human rights activities and destruction of democracy and constitutional order.
- Insincerity in lawmaking and activities against the (National) Assembly and electorate.
- Positions on reforming bills and policies.
- Suspect behaviors reflecting on the basic qualification for politicians.
- Failure of civic duties, such as military service and paying taxes.[33]

The first three criteria were considered the most important and decisive in determining the blacklists.[34] Politicians' track records were investigated for the following: convictions for taking bribes and violating Election Laws, serving in the authoritarian regime of Chun Doo-hwan as a member of the National Security Council's Legislative Committee, inciting "regional animosity" in order to acquire voter support from a particular area, recurrent switching of party affiliation, speculative real estate investments, going on costly overseas trips, or issuing statements "unbecoming to a lawmaker."[35]

Assessments were based on publicly available documentation, including National Assembly reports, mass media coverage and reports over the past ten years, judicial reports, reports from legislators, related books and pamphlets, and comparison of campaign pledges to actual activities while in office.[36]

In some cases, CAGE successfully pressured the government for the mandatory release of candidates' past criminal, tax, and military service records.[37] Anticipating opposition attacks from politicians named by the blacklist, campaign organizers built into the evaluation process three counteractive strategies: using public record information; sending politicians copies of negative documentation and giving them the opportunity to rebut; and reviewing legal matters, such as libel, via CAGE's expert Lawyers Advisory Team.[38] An intricate, participatory framework was created for the blacklisting process. PSPD's anticorruption team coordinated the assessments, which were conducted by a voluntary investigative group of civic experts, including lawyers and activists from such realms as anticorruption, environment, and women's rights. The results were given to several CAGE committees, teams, and organizational bodies.

Furthermore, CAGE deemed it essential to incorporate regular citizens into the blacklisting process, not only to remain true to the initiative's civic nature, but also to increase the blacklists' legitimacy and counter powerholder accusations of partisanship and inaccuracy. Task force members came up with an innovative solution: the 100 Voters Committee. The task force asked a polling company to help formulate the criteria for creating a nationally representative group of 100 Koreans (see table below). A matrix was created to outline the composition of the committee and guide the identification of potential participants. The next step was to randomly choose lay members from among the task force CSOs, who were regular citizens volunteering in the civic organizations rather than activists or staff. Out of this group, a cohort of individuals was identified according to the matrix criteria. The task force divided up the work to approach these people and invite them to join the Voters Committee. The committee "functioned as a jury," Lee reported.[39] Using the investigative team's results, the committee made recommendations for the blacklist to CAGE's Representative Board.

The 100 Voters Committee

Variable	Number in Committee
Gender	
Male	51
Female	49
Age	
20s	27
30s	28
40s	19
> 50	26
Region	
Seoul	25
Busan and Kyungnam	16
Daegu and Kyungbuk	11
Incheon and Kyungkido	25
Honam	11
Daejeon	2
Chungbuk	2
Chungnam	4
Gangwon	3
Jeju	1
Occupation	
Farmer	11
Self-employed	12
Factory worker	17
Office worker	14
University student	5
Houswife	33
None	8

Source: Eunyoung Kim, People's Solidarity for Participatory Democracy, powerpoint presentation, n.d. Obtained by the author from Kim's colleague Taeho Lee.

The final blacklists were determined through voting by CAGE's General Assembly.[40]

In the denominate phase, a total of 102 politicians were blacklisted. On January 24, with unprecedented live television coverage from the major channels, CAGE released the names of sixty-six legislators in the National Assembly who were deemed "unfit to be nominated by any party."[41] Many of them were bigwigs in both the ruling and opposition parties. CAGE's objective was to pressure the parties to refrain from nominating these individuals as candidates. The campaign released a second list of forty-six politicians on January 27, of whom forty-one were not presently serving in the National Assembly but were former legislators or senior cabinet members, as well as governors and mayors who were expected to seek nomination.[42] Out of this list, Lee recalled, ten individuals decided not to run, some because of their political situations and others because of the campaign—the latter constituting CAGE's first victory. The reaction of powerholders was what CAGE leaders expected—vitriol and charges of partisanship, conspiracies, and interference. Some political parties likened the campaign to "political terrorism."[43]

On April 3, ten days before the election, at a major press conference, CAGE released the final defeat blacklist, consisting of eighty-six candidates, including sixty-four from the original denominate blacklist. As the names were announced, CAGE members waved red cards, similar to those used by referees in soccer games, to signal the ejection of a player who committed a foul.[44] Moreover, the Seoul core identified twenty-two strategic districts in which concentrated efforts would be made to defeat particularly powerful and corrupt candidates. Campaign leaders were each assigned to be in charge of efforts in one of these precincts.[45]

C Is for Citizen Engagement

With the release of the first blacklist, CAGE launched a massive national signature drive that would continue until the elections. While the alliance did not come close to meeting its goal (10,000 voters from each of the country's 227 precincts), approximately 250,000 people pledged in writing that they would vote in the elections, but not for blacklisted candidates. It was a brilliant low-risk mass action tactic. It created a justification to interact with regular people and gather information about their views, educate them about the campaign, potentially win their support, encourage their involvement, and garner their commitment to reject corrupt candidates. In the run-up to voting day, local chapters intensified contact with citizens. Members—who chiefly were civically active citizens rather than paid staff—made personal calls to voters in their localities. Lee stated that they don't know how many calls were made in total, but in some districts, such as Incheon, local members called every single voter. The Seoul organizers also emailed local CAGE chapters with information about the blacklisted candidates in their districts, which some chapters forwarded directly on to voters.

D Is for (Civil) Disobedience

CAGE publicly declared a "principle of disobedience" against the aforementioned Article 87 of the Election Law. Civic leaders argued that people had the right to evaluate candidates. "Basically, the election is for voters as well as candidates, and freedom of expression of voters is guaranteed [under the law]," asserted Lee. CAGE pointed out that lawmakers also broke this law; the difference was that they were not punished for such violations, while the campaign did not hide what it was doing and was willing to suffer the consequences.

The basic principle, Lee stated, was that the national leadership would develop countrywide outreach initiatives and organize nonviolent actions in the capital designed to attract national media coverage, while local chapters would conduct their own activities. Shortly after the first blacklist of unfit candidates was released, the leadership core launched activities in Seoul that continued through the elections. From March 2 to March 6, organizers staged a Political Reform Plaza at Myongdong Cathedral, a symbol and site of citizen dissent since the 1970s.[46] Other tactics ranged from sit-ins at political party offices, demanding that unfit politicians not be nominated, to demonstrations, marches, a candlelight rally (March 5), hanging a huge banner on a building, street theatre, and humorous stunts such as fishing red soccer cards from a barrel of water.[47] Women's groups organized actions, including a broom demonstration, and also a rally on March 31. Youth held demonstrations and activities at schools and universities. Pickets were frequently used, and leaflets, red balloons, yellow and red soccer cards, buttons, and badges were handed out at many of the street actions. The latter two items featured the campaign's soccer card symbol or slogans, including "Out," "I Vote," and "Change/Change." CAGE secured the rights from a famous pop idol, Jeong-hyun Lee, to use her upbeat song, also titled "Change, Change!" Since street actions constituted acts of civil disobedience, activists created an adroit tactic to flummox the Election Law—one-person street rallies.[48]

In practice, as the timeline was so compressed in light of the April election date, the Seoul planners decided they had to step in to generate momentum on the ground and design tactics that energized local chapters, empowered their members, and engaged citizens. On January 30, CAGE orchestrated its first national mobilization—the Recovery Day of People's Rights. Rallies were held in Seoul and six major cities. As each name was read from the nominees' blacklist, people waved yellow soccer cards. Then on March 1, Korea's official day of independence from Japanese annexation in 1910, CAGE held a People's Sovereignty Day. Organizers released a citizens' Independence Charter and once more convened rallies in six major cities.[49] Again, yellow cards were distributed, and people waved them as the name of each blacklisted politician was called out. By mid-March, Lee recalled, the campaign conducted the first of two cross-country bus tours, stopping in nineteen cities to win support of citizens and collect their signatures for the blacklist pledge. Finally, core organizers developed an inventive tactic. To each of the twenty-two strategic districts, the campaign sent "a famous civil movement leader to act like a shadow candidate, someone who was a logical counterpart but a symbolic rival," explained Lee. For example, a candidate who was a corrupt prosecutor was shadowed by a respected human rights lawyer. In one district, it was a "macho male versus a diplomatic and petite female civic leader," he added.

In addition to these nationwide tactics organized by the Seoul core, some of the campaign's "departments" or special groups also initiated activities. Professors involved in CAGE held talks for students at universities, while teachers conducted special classes in elementary and secondary schools. The second week of March, the Korean Teachers and Educational Workers Union was reported to have convened Democracy Classes in all schools across the country, garnering national attention in the process.[50] The youth department organized the Red Festival, a massive event for young people modeled on the legendary 1969 Woodstock festival. Proclaiming, "Go, Play, Vote, and Change the World," it held various activities, the highlight being a concert with popular singers.[51] At the end of the performance, the audience waved a sea of red cards, chanting "Out" to the rhythm of the music. With an estimated 50,000 people, it was the largest on-the-ground mobilization of the campaign.[52]

By March, local chapters began initiating their own tactics, including candlelight rallies, local marches in cities, signature drives, and youth protests, for example, in the city of Incheon. In the southwest region, citizens organized a bicycle rally and farmers launched convoys. Rallies were held in the eastern provinces. In Daegu, a large city in southeastern Korea, a campaign event featured a children's protest along with a huge banner on which citizens left their palm prints.

Finally, the campaign also produced resource materials for voters on such key topics as political and judiciary reforms. The purpose was not only to arm voters with meaningful information but to drive the point home to the political establishment that the parties should include discussion about policy proposals during their election campaigns.[53]

Intimidation

As soon as the initial blacklist was released, the major political parties pursued legal action for defamation of character and violation of Article 87 in the Election Law.[54] On February 17, Park Won-soon, CAGE's Standing Committee chairman, along with a PSPD colleague, was summoned to the public prosecutor's office for breaking the Election Law. Lee recounted that a number of CAGE leaders were fined, arrested, and in some cases, both fined and arrested. Some civic organizations and activists faced "negative social pressure for standing up to blacklisted candidates," and some suffered "emotional difficulties," he added. However, overt violence was rare. On a couple of occasions, CAGE street actions and bus-tour activists were physically intimidated by campaign workers of blacklisted candidates,[55] but CAGE was prepared. Lee explained, "Tactically, we used our whole network and all our influence to blow up exposure about the events, in order to protect others, and then the candidates understood that violence will backfire." Their strategy proved to be correct. Not only was violence against the campaign muted, blacklisted candidates began to copy CAGE. "They tried to counter us with similar [nonviolent] tactics." When asked for examples, he cited mothers demonstrating in support of sons who were blacklisted candidates.

CAGE 2004

After the 2000 elections the alliance disbanded, having achieved its immediate objectives (see "Outcomes" below). CAGE's leaders thought that the nationwide mobilization was a singular phenomenon, a phase in Korea's overall political reform movement that would be difficult to repeat. However, new political scandals erupted before the 2004 National Assembly elections. Consequently, a group of civic leaders decided to conduct the blacklisting process once again. On February 4, CAGE 2004 was launched with 354 organizations on board. The difference, said Lee, was that this time around, the civic leaders did not plan for a grand coalition and massive citizen mobilization. Rather, the alliance launched a pioneering Click N Clean online initiative that focused on "Blacklisting, Money-Election Monitoring, Political Party Evaluation, and Voters campaign," according to a PSPD report.[56] It released two denominate blacklists (total of 109 individuals), and a final defeat blacklist consisting of two categories: 106 candidates who were deemed "unfit to run" and 100 legislators who voted for the impeachment of the president, Moo-hyun Roh.[57] The latter decision was not fully endorsed by alliance members, and the divisions over this issue weakened the group.[58]

Campaign Attributes

Leadership and Organization

CAGE had a highly developed leadership and organizational structure at the national and subnational levels, all the more extraordinary given the extremely short time frame available for planning, the pace at which the alliance coalesced, and the finite duration of the campaign. At the core was the Executive Committee. Comprising forty civic organizations (each represented by one person) with twelve cochairs at the helm, it constituted the leadership and made critical decisions throughout the campaign. At the next tier was the Representatives Committee, consisting of ten members from other civic organizations in the alliance. These two bodies worked in tandem, engaging in deliberations and planning. They presented plans to a wider body, the General Assembly (also called the Representative Board), consisting of 500 nationwide representatives of the coalition. In spite of the short time frame, a few meetings were held for the assembly. According to Lee, most decisions were made by consensus, with the exception of the first blacklist, which was put to a vote in the General Assembly.

At the subnational level, CAGE also had ten provincial/major urban units, and fifty-three county/local cities chapters. They operated autonomously, carrying out their own activities, communications, and citizen outreach and engagement. The central core provided the chapters with a campaign manual—a stage-by-stage, how-to guide for local activists. For the final ten-day push to defeat blacklisted candidates, CAGE's planners devised an additional organizational component. Each of the leaders of the civic organizations in the alliance was designated as a "marksman-in-charge," tasked with running the defeat campaign in an assigned election district.[59]

CAGE also had several functional departments or groups. Lee recalled groups for media monitoring; public relations, performances, events, posters, and symbols; online outreach; organized religion; and youth mobilization. Young people were considered a key group to activate, given that they represented 65 percent of the voting population.[60] An "expert professionals" group organized seminars, spoke on television programs, and generally provided expertise on relevant topics, such as elections and civil disobedience. There was also a lawyers group composed of legal professionals, including the former chair of the Korean Bar Association. It engaged in advocacy, provided assistance and counsel for arrested campaigners, and developed a legal manual for activists. During the one hundred days leading up to the elections, major civic organizations in the alliance assigned a total of forty members of their staff to work full-time on the campaign.

Image

CAGE cultivated two principal attributes that cumulatively had broad-based appeal among the population.

1. *Independence*—of corrupt politicians and of politics. "It builds on our notions of independence from Japan," explained Lee.
2. *Youthfulness*—in contrast to the entrenched, old-guard political establishment that clung to positions and privileges while hindering new young leaders from emerging.

Unity

For PSPD, the civil society organization that jump-started the campaign, unity was considered essential in order to achieve social change and was indeed founded upon this premise. By the end of 2001, in addition to fifty employees, it had 300 volunteer-experts and 14,578 citizen-members. Two of its leaders asserted, "Civic groups must not only attract and respond to the interests of the middle class but help mobilize laborers, farmers, and students to seek reform that will benefit them. In this way, civic movement and opposition mass movement can work together to create a more just society."[61] Hence, CAGE's planners considered unity a strategic necessity in order to confront the corrupt political establishment head-on and counter accusations of political partisanship. The massive alliance and the Internet were the pathways to engage regular people across multiple dimensions—geography, urban versus rural settings, age groups, gender, occupation, and socioeconomic status.

The coalition also energized individuals who then became active in the campaign. For instance, according to Hee-Yeon Cho, then chair of

PSPD's Policy Committee, strong support came from doctors, academics, teachers, clergy, lawyers, businesspeople, actors, and artists. They worked to involve their peers, in some cases individually and in other instances through respective professional organizations or unions. As well, a number took part in people power actions to defeat blacklisted candidates. For instance, some Catholic clergy formed a CAGE group and actively worked in Bucheon, targeting a candidate who was known for having committed human rights abuses during the dictatorship.[62]

Surveys confirmed that a large proportion of regular citizens supported CAGE. Gallup Korea carried out three polls, reportedly with almost the same questions regarding views of the civic initiative. When asked if the campaign was desirable or legitimate, 59 percent responded "yes" on January 12, 70 percent answered affirmatively on March 17, and 78 percent on April 14, the day after the elections.[63]

Funding
The campaign was funded through contributions from citizens, who largely responded through advertisements placed in newspapers and the CAGE website. PSPD stated that a total of KRW 350,191,652 (US$291,826) was collected from 5,667 donations, a fund-raising record for a civic initiative.[64] Leaders reported that citizens personally came to the headquarters to give money, while others made direct bank deposits or contributed via the Internet. The overall expenditures were KRW 328,851,681 (US$274,043), another milestone as donations surpassed final expenditures.[65]

Negotiation
At the outset, CAGE's leaders attempted dialogue and nonviolent persuasion with the political establishment. They reportedly had discussions with political party representatives and heads of the nominating committees in order to encourage them to "listen to civil society demands."[66] However, when the parties were unresponsive, the Seoul core was ready to launch its strategic plan of nonviolent action.

Nonviolent Discipline
CAGE leaders anticipated that their people might get harassed or attacked by political party supporters during the campaign, yet they vigorously rejected the use of violence under any circumstances. When asked why, Lee answered, "It was not necessary. We believed that violence is not helpful to our campaign because voting is a peaceful procedure, and even if we were hit, our opponents would use any violence to

say we are generating campaign violence." The campaign took a series of proactive steps to maintain nonviolent discipline, including drafting a Peace Charter that affirmed that CAGE would practice nonviolence, even though there was a strong likelihood that opponents would use violence. The national leadership as well as local CAGE chapters held multiple press conferences to announce it. CAGE also developed a nonviolence manual that was distributed to campaign participants. It included instructions on dealing with opponents. For example,

- In the case of physical fighting, sit down.
- In the case of people taking your campaign materials and petitions, let them do it.
- In the most serious cases, run away from the confrontation.

Digital Technology

The campaign sought to maximize the use of emerging communication technologies. For the first time, Lee stated, the Internet was rigorously factored into a civic initiative in Korea. It was used particularly to engage and mobilize young people. On M-tizen, a digital community, youth discussed the campaign, the elections, and political reform.[67] CAGE set up a website that literally became a big hit. The site was visited 856,090 times leading up to the April elections; the average number of daily hits was 10,569. Eight thousand emails were sent to the webmaster, and 45,674 messages were posted on the bulletin board.[68] The website featured the blacklists and documentation about the "unfit" nominees and candidates; for instance, on April 6, three days after the defeat blacklist was released, CAGE posted candidates' criminal records, generating 300,000 hits. The website also featured endorsements from popular music, television, and film personalities.[69] And in one of the earliest, if not the first, cases of digital resistance, 28,319 people posted their names in support of the campaign and signed up to receive e-information. CAGE capitalized on this unprecedented outcome by publicizing the results.

CAGE utilized SMS to communicate messages and developed a presence on Cyworld, an early social networking site created in Korea. Lee reported that mobile phone ringtones were also used, but they did not have a significant impact because "the technology was not so good then." Finally, media attacks by a few hostile newspapers backfired. They gave impetus to the fledgling alternative media and online citizen journalist initiatives, which began covering CAGE and digitally broadcasting key press conferences, thereby building momentum at critical points.

Communications

CAGE drew up a communications strategy and plan involving multiple divisions of the campaign. "It was very important," asserted Lee, "and not just part of the PR team, but also part of the main communications and planning staff." The plan included several components: key messages, targeted messaging, media relations, communication outlets, press conferences, and tie-ins with nonviolent actions. Core messages included "It's time for change!" "Withdraw Corrupted Politics," and "Banish Corruption." The yellow and red soccer cards—two culturally relevant symbols—encapsulated the entire campaign. The yellow card was used during the denominate phase and the red card during the final push to defeat blacklisted candidates.

Specialized messaging was developed for the four main targets of the campaign: citizens, the political establishment, media, and the National Election Commission. Citizens were urged to participate in the elections, to not vote for corrupt candidates, and to show "the power of voters—only the people power can change politics," Lee recalled. Political parties and lawmakers were urged, on the one hand, to not select corrupt, blacklisted nominees and to refrain from inflaming regional sentiments, and on the other hand, to make the candidate selection process more democratic and transparent.[70] The message to the National Election Commission was to make information available concerning candidates' criminal and tax records, and to exercise its power to stop the flow of illicit party funding rather than silencing citizens' voices.

Lee reported that campaign planners secured meetings with "main press staff to ask for coverage of the information on the blacklist." Central messages to the media were, "Do not manipulate the regional sentiment; help enrich political debates, broadcast the dark sides of candidates, and deliver full information about candidates to citizens," he added. Overall, the press was interested in CAGE and generally not hostile. Three major press conferences were held, two during the nominating process and one on April 3 to launch the defeat drive. In conjunction, they were bolstered by rallies, television appearances, expert meetings, local chapter publicity activities, posters, and graffiti.

Outcomes

Revision of election law. Prior to the 2000 elections, President Dae-jung Kim and the National Assembly amended the Election Law, thereby making CAGE legal.[71] Some provisions were changed, allowing press conferences, websites, and in-house newsletters, but printed materials and many forms of street actions were still forbidden.[72] As a result, while the campaign itself was no longer unlawful, it continued to engage in civil disobedience.

Denominating nominees. Ten individuals from the original blacklist of unfit politicians decided not to seek nomination. Of the remaining 102 blacklisted nominees, according to Lee, forty-eight failed to be selected as candidates by their political parties. Thus, in total, almost 52 percent of blacklisted politicians (58 out of 112) didn't get on the ballot.

Candidate pledges. Prior to the election, CAGE launched a drive to get candidates to promise to enact political reforms should they be elected. Between April 3 and 13, approximately 450 candidates signed the pledge.[73]

Candidate defeats. In the final elections, 69 percent of the blacklisted candidates (fifty-nine out of eighty-six) were defeated, including 68 percent (fifteen out of twenty-two) of the "most problematic" candidates in the strategic precincts.[74] There were some notable regional differences. In the Seoul area, nineteen out of twenty on the blacklist were defeated, and in Chungchong, fifteen out of eighteen lost. However, in Youngnam, only sixteen out of thirty-five candidates were defeated, reflecting the impact of strong regional loyalty linked to particular political parties.[75]

Improved caliber, new blood. The blacklists had an immediate impact on the overall nominations. Political parties generally screened nominees more carefully, and a large number of incumbents from the two major parties did not get selected.[76] Moreover, many new, younger faces, with no records of corruption, were elected.[77] On the whole, 80 percent of the new assembly consisted of first- and second-term legislators, including a sizeable number in their thirties and forties.[78]

Readjusted electoral districts. An attempt to gerrymander districts, based on bargaining by legislators of the major parties, was prevented.[79]

Disruption of the corrupt system; internalization of integrity. For Korean civil society, CAGE "dealt a serious blow to the structure of corruption and collusion among old parties and considerably weakened the influence of their corrupt bosses."[80] First, political parties started changing the ways in which candidates were nominated and selected to run. The process shifted from what sociologist Sun-Chul Kim summarized as "a top-down mechanism in which party bosses held sweeping power to the gradual adoption of primary elections where party grass roots gained a bigger voice."[81] As well, most political parties, even including those vehemently opposed to CAGE, incorporated nearly all of the blacklist criteria into their selection process. According to Lee, four years later, during the 2004 elections, each political party set up a committee to nominate candidates, utilized assessment criteria similar to those developed by CAGE, and even retained "relatively independent" experts to assess the qualifications of nominees. This was the most significant and lasting outcome of all, as the political establishment internalized values and standards of integrity and accountability set by civic leaders and supported by citizens.

Political reform. CAGE created an impetus for reforms in the political system, including election laws, funding of political parties, right to information about legislators' assets and legislative activities, and parliamentary transparency. It began almost immediately, as the incoming National Assembly formed a special committee on political reform and the amendment of political laws.[82]

CAGE 2004. In spite of the campaign's much smaller scale compared to 2000, it had a significant impact on the Seventeenth National Assembly elections. Among those judged unfit to run, 78 out of 106 (73.6 percent) lost. Of the one hundred legislators who voted to remove President Roh from office, fifty-one lost. In total, 63 percent of the combined lists were defeated. Scholars and Lee do not attribute the results solely to CAGE, given that the election became "a referendum on the impeachment of President Roh," according to sociologist Eui Hang Shin.[83] On the other hand, when one examines the outcomes for unfit-to-run candidates, the results are striking and suggest that citizens had been primed as a result of their success in 2000.

Transnational inspiration and exchange. News of CAGE's success spread quickly throughout Asia.[84] On April 18, five days after Korea's National Assembly elections, one of Japan's most influential newspapers, *Asahi Shimbun*, reported, "The South Koreans' resolve not to let incompetent and corrupt politicians get elected holds a lesson worth learning."[85] Soon after, a group of Japanese civic actors traveled to Korea to learn more about CAGE; in May, several members of CAGE visited Japan to share their experiences. Subsequently, in the run-up to the June 25, 2000, Lower House elections, seven key Japanese civic organizations and networks produced their own blacklists and together constituted the Movement to Expel Political Misfits.[86]

Case Analysis

Changing power relations, bottom-up democracy. "After the success of the campaign," Lee stated, "politicians became afraid of the voters' collective power. We could see changes in political parties and political processes for nominations. They were taking voters into consideration."

In essence, CAGE created conditions for bottom-up democracy. The campaign transformed citizens from passive voters, merely choosing from a fait-accompli set of politicians, to a dynamic force. They reclaimed their power to demand of political parties worthier representatives and defeat those candidates who had not acted in the interests of the people they were obligated to serve. In doing so, CAGE exacted accountability from both the political establishment and the individuals within that corrupt system.

People power dynamics. An excerpt from a publication by the Korea Democracy Foundation concluded, "The movement [CAGE] rode on a wave of citizens' anger at crooked politics and created a crisis in the political establishment."[87] It echoes the insights of Martin Luther King Jr., who said in 1963, "Nonviolent direct action seeks to create such a crisis and foster such a tension that a community which has constantly refused to negotiate is forced to confront the issue."[88] In Korea, after the civic alliance's efforts to negotiate with political parties were snubbed, voters collectively wielded power. They shook up a corrupt system to the extent that it could no longer smoothly function; it had operated as a political party–centered election system imbibed with undemocratic political practices that limited the participation of the civic realm in the election process.[89]

CAGE also demonstrates an adroit application of people power that combined mass civil disobedience—through the defining method of blacklisting and its associated nonviolent tactics—with a lawful, institutionalized mass action: targeted voting. The linking of technically illegal and legal actions had a synergistic effect. First, each on its own would not have been as disruptive. Second, casting a ballot was transformed into an act of defiance that was low-risk, highly participatory, and easy to carry out.

Ownership, collective identity, and legitimacy. CAGE's leadership meticulously cultivated a sense of ownership among citizens. The campaign employed multiple paths—from its very name, Citizens' Alliance; to the broad range of national and local civic organizations participating in it; to nonviolent tactics involving regular citizens, such as the voters' blacklist pledge, slogans and messaging, and reliance on thousands of volunteers. Citizen views, as well as local and regional input, were valued and systematically incorporated into strategy and planning, through representative polling and CAGE's organizational structure. Rather than dictate to the periphery, the leadership core encouraged—if not nurtured—local decisionmaking and initiatives. Finally, CAGE's fund-raising strategy was truly ingenious. By making a broad public appeal to citizens for financial support, each donation, however modest, became an act of resistance against the corrupt political establishment, bonding the donor's allegiance to the campaign and reinforcing his or her feeling of being a part of a larger struggle for reform, accountability, and democracy. All in all, these measures created a powerful quality of legitimacy that was difficult for corrupt politicians and political parties to damage, in spite of their concerted efforts.

Proactive approach and education. While it is impossible for any civic initiative to formulate every single step in advance and predict all outcomes, CAGE's strategists nonetheless proactively anticipated key challenges and took measures to address them. For example, it preempted violent skirmishes between parliamentary candidate supporters and CAGE citizen-members through the Peace Charter and a strict demand for nonviolent discipline. CAGE deflected hostile media and political party attacks through transparency, negotiation, and the legitimacy of citizen mobilization in the exercise of political rights. Education was also considered an essential step—hence the development of activist manuals on nonviolence, legal issues, and effective campaigning, as well as resource manuals for citizens on political reform that countered the political establishment's rhetoric and smears.

Positive framing. CAGE's leaders recognized that building the campaign around blacklisting corrupt candidates risked creating an overly negative character that could put off the public and dampen citizen action. As a result, the leaders sought to lighten the negativity through several approaches. They adapted popular symbols associated with positive activities, for instance, the soccer cards. They balanced serious tactics, such as candlelight vigils, with symbolic, humorous, fun, and upbeat actions, for example, the broom demonstration, satirical cartoons, and the Red Festival. The focus on unfit candidates was offset by support from pop stars and respected public figures. Messages and slogans largely emphasized empowerment and change, while the blacklisting process was framed in terms of positive outcomes.

Kingian nonviolence methodology. This civic initiative provides yet another affirmation that the nonviolent action methodology developed by practitioners of Kingian nonviolence is robust and effective.[90] Although CAGE's leaders had not been exposed to this particular set of practices, they intuitively adopted similar elements, including commitment to nonviolence, education (of campaign activists and the public), information gathering (about potential candidates), negotiation (with political parties and targeted politicians), and when that was not fruitful, citizen mobilization and direct action.

Learning from others. CAGE's core planners took inspiration from some well-known as well as unlikely sources. The overall strategy of a civil disobedience campaign that in its entirety broke an unjust law, and the adoption of sit-ins as a tactic were generally inspired by the US civil rights movement. The candlelight vigils were inspired by the East German nonviolent uprising against the communist regime in 1989. Dramatic images of this form of mass action captured the attention of many Koreans, who just two years earlier had won their own freedom from dictatorship. Lee recalled that they also learned from Bill Clinton's engagement of young people in the 1992 presidential campaign, which at the time was groundbreaking in American political circles. And finally, as evident from the name, the youth group took inspiration from the legendary Woodstock music festival.

Lessons Learned

Political Corruption and Bottom-Up Democracy
The CAGE 2000 campaign offers valuable lessons about political corruption and building bottom-up democracy. First, reform is not automatic after the transition from dictatorship to a democracy. Korean civic leaders described their emerging representative system as institutional politics "managed by strong cartels of politicians."[91] As a result, when voters end up having limited choices beyond obstructive politicians backed by corrupt parties, representative democracy alone cannot deliver accountability and justice, and can lose legitimacy in the eyes of the people.

Second, as in Indonesia (see Chapter 5), the leaders and activists of Korea's civic democracy movement became driving forces to transform the state and break down the intransigent remnants of the corrupt authoritarian system. Nonviolent struggle veterans form enduring relationships forged during the antidemocracy phase, based on common hardships, goals, and a vision for their country. Third, when the political establishment ignores the plight of citizens while engaging in self-enrichment, abusing authority, and protecting itself from justice, citizens have options beyond getting angry, abstaining from elections, or becoming radicalized. Through people power, they can pressure political parties to change, collectively block corrupt politicians from power by supporting honest counterparts, and set in motion a chain reaction that builds integrity. However, when facing an entrenched system of political graft and abuse, public consciousness of the problem on its own may not be enough to yield change. When this awareness is coupled with a nonviolent campaign or movement, social pressure can exact a toll on powerholders—in this case, losing an election.

Fourth, powerholder disrespect of citizens is frequently part of the core grievances that unite people and can be a potent mobilizer. In the case of Korea, PSPD asserted, "These corrupt political parties and politicians have had no respect for voters. Voters need to show their power to politicians by making use of their voters' rights, even if legal hurdles were [*sic*] put in front of voters."[92] Fifth, citizen mobilization and action can empower civic actors to frame the agenda for change in a corrupt system, instead of merely asking for reform and allowing powerholders to define the measures to be taken.

People Power

For civic leaders and concerned citizens, tackling political corruption might seem daunting, since it functions in a horizontal system that can involve dishonest politicians, multiple political parties, the executive branch, and the private sector, organized labor, or other nonstate interests. However, CAGE revealed a potent strategy:

- Tap widely held sentiments and grievances, in CAGE's case, public anger vis-à-vis unaccountable, venal legislators and discontent over the poor quality of candidates presented to voters.
- Link such legislators and candidates to a tangible issue with measurable outcomes.
- Zero in on a visible aspect of the corrupt system—for example, the opaque, undemocratic, crooked nomination process.
- Articulate clear demands—in this instance, withdrawal of unfit nominees and candidates from party lists and defeat of blacklisted candidates.
- Identify one or more mass actions—in this case, pledges and rejecting blacklisted candidates at the ballot box—that are low-risk and participatory in the given struggle context.

When confronting political corruption, CAGE 2000 demonstrated that political neutrality is particularly important in order to maintain the civic initiative's legitimacy and counter opponents' claims of partisanship and interference. Furthermore, as with other nonviolent campaigns and movements targeting corruption, legitimacy is vital. CAGE derived legitimacy through its civic, grassroots nature—in this case, the vast alliance and participation of regular citizens.

Like the community-monitoring initiatives in Afghanistan, surveys were a tool that yielded strategically useful information. On the one hand, they served as a mechanism to gather people's views, which was necessary for planning the campaign. On the other hand, they generated information that could be directed to the targets—in this instance, the political parties, nominees, and candidates.

As in many nonviolent struggles, most notably the US civil rights movement, civil disobedience can be strategically used to directly confront an unjust law—either as a tactic or, in the case of CAGE, by the entire campaign itself. When backed by public support and citizen mobilization, civil disobedience harnesses the power of numbers, thereby making the directive difficult to enforce and justify.

A strategic benefit of tactical diversity is that it can potentially engage a larger number of people. When a civic initiative relies heavily on one or a few tactics, it cannot fully involve a broad swath of people, and hence is less likely to maximize mobilization.

Social and cultural references can heighten the impact of a tactic, for example, through symbols, humor, and music. In CAGE's case, as Koreans are impassioned soccer fans, red and yellow referee cards became the predominant campaign symbols. In turn, waving the cards became a popular nonviolent action.

CAGE expanded the notion of the right to information. In addition to the right to "demand information held by government bodies," people also have the right to acquire relevant information about their elected representatives.[93] PSPD elaborates, "The citizens have a right to know what their representatives do in the National Assembly. The citizens have a right to know whether their lawmakers have been related to corruption."[94]

Organization and Unity

Both CAGE and CICAK in Indonesia addressed the need to balance core decisionmaking with internal campaign democracy, and centralization of planning with local autonomy. The choices are not mutually exclusive. An organizational structure can create multiple decisionmaking and planning options that incorporate elements of core leadership authority, consensus, majority voting, and core versus periphery action.

As with CICAK, one of the benefits of a broad coalition is that different groups can bring different talents and resources to the campaign or movement. For example, the involvement of the cartoonists' association in CAGE had a unique impact. Many members created satirical cartoons that were posted on the Internet. "They [cartoons] had a catalytic role in increasing the online campaign," said Lee. Lastly, endorsements and support from respected or popular public figures can be enhanced by dissemination through different channels, from ringtones to websites, concerts, and public statements.

Notes

1. Korea has a parliamentary system, with the unicameral National Assembly. The voting system is mixed: 246 members are elected by simple majority direct vote, and 54 are elected through proportional representation. In this book, Korea refers to the Republic of Korea, or South Korea.

2. Chon T'ae-il committed suicide on November 13, 1970, and Mohamed Bouazizi, on December 17, 2010.

3. In 1986 military strongman Chun Doo-hwan attempted to change the constitution to give himself a third term as president. After a public outcry he handpicked Roh Tae-woo as his heir apparent. Student and labor groups formed alliances with opposition parties to block this authoritarian succession. In early 1987 violent repression backfired when security forces killed a number of students. The middle class joined in mass demonstrations, and people power forced Chun to agree to an amendment allowing direct presidential elections. See Adrian Karatnycky and Peter Ackerman, *How Freedom Is Won: From Civic Resistance to Durable Democracy* (New York: Freedom House, 2005), 41; Gi-Wook Shinn and Paul Chang, eds., *South Korean Social Movements: From Democracy to Civil Society* (New York: Routledge, 2011).

4. Eui Hang Shin, "The Role of NGOs in Political Elections in Korea: The Case of the Citizens' Alliance for the 2000 General Election," *Asian Survey* 43, no. 4 (2003): 697–715.

5. Manarin, "Striking Where It Hurts," 38.

6. Ibid.

7. "Elections and Civil Society," Korea Democracy Foundation, April 16, 2012, www.kdemo.or.kr.

8. Ibid., 10.

9. People's Solidarity for Participatory Democracy (PSPD): "Using documentation to draw up a 'blacklist' of unacceptable political candidates and moving the public to vote against them"; see New Tactics in Human Rights, www.newtactics.org.

10. Shin, "Role of NGOs."

11. The phrase in the section title was the CAGE 2000 campaign slogan.

12. Manarin, "Striking Where It Hurts," 37.

13. *PSPD's Campaign for Transparent Society*, People's Solidarity for Participatory Democracy, Seoul, November 2001.

14. Hee-Yeon Cho, "A Study of the Blacklisting Campaign Against Corrupt Politicians in South Korea—Focused on the 'Naksun Movement' in April 2000" (paper presented at the Civil Society in Asia, Today and Tomorrow conference, Seoul, South Korea, December 5, 2003).

15. Samuel Kim, ed., *Korea's Democratization* (Cambridge: Cambridge University Press, 2003).

16. This chapter is based on interviews conducted in January 2010 plus sub-

sequent written communications with Taeho Lee, deputy secretary general of the People's Solidarity for Participatory Democracy (PSPD), who was directly involved in the campaign.

17. Eunyoung Kim, "CAGE 2000" (PowerPoint presentation provided to author, n.d.).

18. These included the Hanbo Steel scandal in 1997, involving former presidents Cheon and Roh in 1997, and construction project calamities, in which citizens lost their lives (*PSPD's Campaign for Transparent Society*).

19. Article 87 of the Election Law bans civic organizations from "election-related" campaign activities, which, according to Lee, include evaluating candidates and making recommendations to voters; Shin, "Role of NGOs," 703.

20. Kim, "CAGE 2000."

21. Ibid.

22. Ibid.

23. Ibid.

24. Ibid.

25. Ibid.

26. Manarin, "Striking Where It Hurts," 38.

27. The term "defining method" was developed by Kurt Schock.

28. According to Lee, the task force also approached unions, but at that time they supported a progressive political party and didn't join the nonpartisan task force or CAGE. The Citizens' Coalition for Economic Justice (CCEJ) also declined to join the civic initiative. It only wanted to disclose information about corrupt candidates and did not support a civil disobedience campaign, which it viewed as an interruption to the elections, said Lee.

29. The alliance included Korea's major civic and religious organizations. In addition to PSPD, KFEM, GKU, and KWAU, it involved the Citizens' Coalition for Democratic Media, the YMCA/YWCA, Citizens' Solidarity for Participation and Self-Governance, the National Association of Professors for Democratic Society, the National Council of Churches of Korea, Catholic Priests' Association for Justice, and the National Association for the Practice of Buddhism; "Elections and Civil Society."

30. Hee-Yeon Cho and Park Won-soon, "The Democratic Reform and Civic Movement in South Korea—Focused on PSPD," *Joint U.S.-Korea Academic Studies* 12 (2003): 1–17, 13, http://dnsm.skhu.ac.kr.

31. Sun-Chul Kim, "Power of Movement: Defiant Institutionalization of Social Movements in South Korea" (paper presented at the Politics and Protest Workshop, City University of New York [CUNY] Graduate Center, March 26, 2009, 2), www.jamesmjasper.org.

32. Lee confirmed that the correct number is 1,104, although various publications cite the coalition as reaching 1,053 and 1,101 members. After the elections, while preparing a white paper on the campaign, the CAGE secretariat conducted a final count of members that came to 1,104.

33. *PSPD's Campaign for Transparent Society*.

34. "Elections and Civil Society."

35. Shin, "Role of NGOs," 702.

36. *PSPD's Campaign for Transparent Society*, 2; Kim, "CAGE 2000," 3.

37. Manarin, "Striking Where It Hurts."

38. "Elections and Civil Society."

39. For additional information about citizens' juries, see Lyn Carson and Brian Martin, *Random Selection in Politics* (Westport, CT: Praeger, 1999).

40. Information about CAGE's Executive Committee, Representative Board, and General Assembly can be found on p. 49 of this chapter.

41. Shin, "Role of NGOs," 703.

42. Ibid.; Cho, "Study of the Blacklisting Campaign."

43. Shin, "Role of NGOs," 705.

44. Ibid.

45. Cho, "Study of the Blacklisting Campaign."

46. Ibid.

47. As soccer aficionados know, the yellow card stands for caution and signifies a warning to the player, while the red card indicates a foul and the expulsion of the player from the game.

48. "Elections and Civil Society."

49. March 1, 1919, is said to be the day that the twenty-eight-year Korean movement for independence began, when a group of cultural and religious leaders released a "Proclamation of Independence" and organized a mass demonstration; Bae-ho Hahn, "Korea," *Encyclopædia Britannica*, 2012, www.britannica.com.

50. Cho, "Study of the Blacklisting Campaign."

51. Ibid., 13.

52. Shin, "Role of NGOs."

53. Ibid.

54. Hyuk-Rae Kim, "Dilemmas in the Making of Civil Society in Korean Political Reform," *Journal of Contemporary Asia* 34, no. 1 (2004): 55–69.

55. Shin, "Role of NGOs."

56. "Blacklisting Campaign 2004," PSPD, January 19, 2004, www.people power21.org.

57. President Moo-hyun Roh was the leader of a tiny splinter party. In the midst of the run-up to the legislative elections, a political and democratic crisis erupted. On March 12, the National Assembly passed a motion to impeach him by a vote of 193–2, involving all the major parties. The grounds included violating the Election Law, accusations of illegal campaign fund-raising, and mishandling the economy. A large percentage of the public was opposed. It perceived the vote as a parliamentary coup against a democratically elected president by the entrenched political establishment and a concerted effort to thwart Roh's political agenda, which included rapprochement with North Korea. On May 14 the Constitutional Court overturned the impeachment, and he returned to power. For a detailed examination, see Eui Hang Shin, "Political Demography of South Korea: Cohort, Gender, Regionalism, and Citizens' Movement in Election Democracy" (paper presented at the Twenty-Fifth International Population Conference, Tours, France, July 18–23, 2005), http://iussp2005.princeton.edu.

58. "Elections and Civil Society."

59. Shin, "Role of NGOs."

60. Kim, "Dilemmas in the Making of Civil Society in Korean Political Reform."

61. Cho and Park, "Democratic Reform and Civic Movement in South Korea," 3.

62. The candidate was Sacheol Lee; Cho, "Study of the Blacklisting Campaign."

63. Sun-Chul Kim, "Power of Movement."

64. The South Korean currency is the won. Its currency code is KRW.

65. Kim, "CAGE 2000"; Cho and Park, "Democratic Reform and Civic Movement in South Korea."

66. Cho, "Study of the Blacklisting Campaign," 10.

67. Kim, "Dilemmas in the Making of Civil Society in Korean Political Reform."

68. Kim, "CAGE 2000."

69. Manarin, "Striking Where It Hurts."

70. Regional differences and biases have long-standing historical roots, dating back to the Three Kingdoms period (57 BC to AD 668). In the postdictatorship era, regional ties became influential determinants of voting behavior; David Kang, "Regional Politics and Democratic Consolidation in Korea," in *Korea's Democratization*, ed. Samuel Kim (Cambridge: Cambridge University Press, 2003), 161–180.

71. Manarin, "Striking Where It Hurts."

72. "Elections and Civil Society."

73. Shin, "Role of NGOs."

74. Ibid., 710.

75. Ibid.

76. Ibid.

77. Kim, "Dilemmas in the Making of Civil Society in Korean Political Reform."

78. Manarin, "Striking Where It Hurts."

79. Kim, "Dilemmas in the Making of Civil Society in Korean Political Reform."; Sun-Chul Kim, "Power of Movement."

80. "Elections and Civil Society," 12.

81. Sun-Chul Kim, "Power of Movement," 3.

82. "Elections and Civil Society."

83. Shin, "Political Demography of South Korea."

84. Cho, "Study of the Blacklisting Campaign."

85. David Johnson, "A Tale of Two Systems: Prosecuting Corruption in Japan and Italy," in *The State of Civil Society in Japan and Italy*, ed. Frank Schwartz and Susan Pharr (Cambridge: Cambridge University Press, 2003), 277.

86. Murakami Mutsuko, "A Gift from Korea: Japan's Election Process May Never Be the Same Again," Asiaweek, June 9, 2000, http://edition.cnn.com.

87. "Elections and Civil Society," 11.

88. Martin Luther King Jr., "Letter from a Birmingham Jail," April 16, 1963, http://mlk-kpp01.stanford.edu.

89. Shin, "Political Demography of South Korea."

90. The Kingian nonviolence methodology was developed during the US civil rights movement and is now encapsulated in a framework that is taught by Kingian practitioners around the world. It consists of a nonlinear, six-step strategy involving personal commitment, education, information gathering, negotiation, direct action, and reconciliation. The author participated in a Kingian Training of Trainers, led by Dr. Bernard Lafayette, at the University of Rhode Island, 2008.

91. Cho and Park, "Democratic Reform and Civic Movement in South Korea," 15.

92. *PSPD's Campaign for Transparent Society,* 1.

93. David Banisar, "The Right to Information and Privacy: Balancing Rights and Managing Conflicts" (working paper, World Bank, Washington, DC, 2011), 5.

94. "Blacklisting Campaign 2004," PSPD, www.peoplepower21.org.

4

Digital Resistance for Clean Politicians: Brazil

A military coup in 1964 inflicted over two decades of impunity and human rights abuses on the people of Brazil. In 1980, Catholic clergy informed by liberation theology began catalyzing civic dissent and a unified opposition to the regime.[1] Amid economic deterioration and repression, public calls to end the dictatorship grew, culminating in the broad-based 1983 Diretas Já (direct elections now) movement demanding direct presidential elections.[2] As millions of citizens took part in nonviolent mobilizations across the country, fissures grew within the junta.[3] Although the regime blocked a bill amending the constitution to allow direct elections of the president and vice president, Tancredo Neves, a civilian candidate, ran for the office of president. Defectors in the Electoral College sided with him and the political opposition, thereby ending military rule.[4] Neves died before taking office. His vice president, Jose Sarney, a defector from ARENA, the military's political party, was sworn in as president.[5] For many Brazilians, full democracy only came in 1989, when the citizens directly elected Fernando Collor de Mello. His victory was soon followed by infamy. Following mass demonstrations, in 1992 he was impeached for corruption, foreshadowing the political venality that eventually spurred the bottom-up Ficha Limpa (clean slate or clean record) social movement, the focus of this chapter.[6]

Context
Fast-forward two decades. Brazil is an emerging economic powerhouse, ranked the eighth-largest in the world.[7] But it is still beset with disparity

67

and corruption. Brazil is also rated the seventeenth-most unequal country in the world.[8] A 2010 study by the Federation of Industries of the State of São Paolo (FIESP) reported that corruption costs Brazil approximately US$39 billion (BRL 69 billion) a year, and per capita income would be 15.5 percent higher without this malfeasance.[9] Political corruption is endemic, and cynicism abounds—so much so that there is a common expression in Brazil, "Rouba, mas faz" (He steals, but he gets things done).[10] According to the watchdog website Congresso em Foco, in 2010, 29 percent of legislators in the Chamber of Deputies of Congress (147 out of 513) and 26 percent of senators (21 out of 81) either faced criminal charges in the Supreme Court or were under investigation. As well, many cases lapsed before they would be heard.[11] Some members—how many is not known—have been convicted in lower courts. The majority of wrongdoing involves stealing public money or violating campaign finance laws.[12] Poverty and graft interact in the political process, as politicians convicted of crimes continue getting elected through vote buying.[13] Finally, while a law on the books stipulated that those convicted would face impeachment and be prohibited from running again for three years, the few who were exposed in scandals avoided punishment by preemptively resigning, enabling them to stand again in the next elections.[14]

In 2010, twenty-five years after the generals were pushed away, the Ficha Limpa movement wielded people power once again—this time to root out graft, abuse, and unaccountability in the electoral system, and to restore legitimacy to Brazil's hard-won democracy.

The Beginning

Previous attempts to pass political reform bills failed in the Brazilian Congress. But in April 2008, forty-four civil society organizations (CSOs) joined together in a nonpartisan coalition called the Movement Against Electoral Corruption (MCCE). It included the National Conference of Bishops of Brazil (CNBB); grassroots organizations linked to the Catholic Church; unions, the Brazilian Bar Association (OAB), and other professional groups—for example, nursing, accounting, and biology organizations; and the Brazilian Justice and Peace Commission (CBJP). Their objective was simple yet sweeping: to prevent individuals with criminal backgrounds from running for elected office at all levels of government.[15] Marcus Faver, a judge who in the past had tried to hinder candidates with criminal records from seeking public office, proposed using a little-known legal instrument in the 1988 Constitution—

the Popular Initiative (Article 61, Paragraph 2), which allows citizens to submit bills to Congress.[16] Strict conditions for eligibility apply: the collection of handwritten, documented signatures from a minimum of 1 percent of the electorate from no fewer than five different states, in which the number of signatures from each state total at least 0.3 percent of the constituents.[17] Only then can the legislation be submitted to the Congress, where it is reviewed by relevant committees and must pass in both the Chamber of Deputies and Senate. Finally, should these hurdles be cleared, the law is presented to the president, who can either accept it or veto it. The MCCE's vision was twofold: to clean up Brazilian politics and to change cultural attitudes about corruption and vote buying, by directly involving the population in the solution.[18] The movement was launched with the slogan, "A vote has no price, it has consequences" (*Voto nao tem preco, tem consequencias*).[19]

The original legislation was drafted by a group of lawyers in Rio de Janeiro. Members of the Brazilian Bar Association certified its constitutionality. Candidates would be rendered ineligible to take office if they have been convicted of the following crimes by more than one judge: misuse of public funds, drug trafficking, rape, murder, or racism. Furthermore, the penalty for politicians accused of such wrongdoing was toughened; they would be barred from public office for eight years. Finally, the legislation was designed to prevent politicians from using constitutional loopholes such as preemptive resignation to avoid prosecution and run again.[20] The name Ficha Limpa (clean slate or clean record) was the inspiration of Marlon Reis, a judge who was one of the movement's leaders.[21]

At the outset, few were optimistic that the MCCE could collect so many signatures. The movement, through the vast networks of its CSO members and the Catholic Church, including legions of volunteers, systematically built mobilizing capacity and engaged citizens through trainings, grassroots meetings, dissemination of information about Ficha Limpa, debates, public lectures in churches and schools and at NGOs, and street actions.[22] The support of the Catholic Church proved to be vital. Its social authority was a counterweight to the institutional authority of the Congress, and its reach extended throughout the country, particularly in rural and more remote areas. Information and communication technologies (ICT) were also used extensively to communicate, debate, and exchange information.[23] As importantly, the MCCE cultivated allies within the Congress—politicians supportive of Ficha Limpa who would later prove to be instrumental eyes and ears for a digital resistance campaign.[24]

In less than one and a half years, the MCCE surpassed the required 1.3 million signatures. On September 29, 2009, the Ficha Limpa bill, together with 1,604,794 handwritten signatures, was submitted to the Congress.[25] The movement made history, and the first victory was won.

Avaaz, Digital Resistance, and a Flying Cow

The MCCE's leaders understood that without massive civic mobilization, it was unlikely that Ficha Limpa would ever be passed. Opposition to it was fierce; once enacted, the bill would disqualify close to one-third of the entire Congress from serving. Legislators could also try to weaken it and use myriad stalling techniques to indirectly quash it, such as keeping the bill under review in committees for years. One politician commented, "It is easier for a cow to fly than this initiative to get approved in Brazil" (*É mais fácil uma vaca voar do que esse projeto ser aprovado no Brasil*).[26]

The MCCE had already been in contact with Avaaz, a worldwide digital movement with the goal of bringing "people-powered politics to decision-making everywhere."[27] Now, at this critical juncture, the groups decided to join forces.[28] According to Graziela Tanaka—at the time an Avaaz campaigner based in Brazil—Ficha Limpa was an ideal anticorruption initiative. "It had a clear goal, clear input, it was easy to cut to the issue, and was something bold that people would want to join."

Strategies

Facing an uphill battle with the Congress, Avaaz identified three strategies for its overall campaign. In order to create political will for the legislation to be passed, it had to turn Ficha Limpa into an issue that no one could dare oppose. Their approach was to use sustained, overwhelming public pressure on the one hand and positive media attention on the other, which in turn would also generate pressure. Second, building support—genuine or pragmatic—from within the Congress during the legislative process was also essential, in order to overcome efforts to thwart and delay the bill's passage. "When thinking of campaign strategy, you need to think of how there's a two-way benefit for people in power," said Tanaka.

The upcoming October 2010 general elections became the vehicle for this interchange. Once the campaign began to reach a critical mass and go viral, backing for the bill grew as politicians grasped the political advantages of coming out in favor of it even before a vote. Finally,

Avaaz sought to reinforce the movement's discourse and legitimacy that the MCCE had cultivated: the struggle was led and owned by regular citizens, who—initially through the documented, handwritten signatures, and now through mass digital and nondigital actions—were demanding that their elected representatives uphold Brazilian democracy by carrying out the people's will.

Recruitment

Avaaz campaigner Tanaka credits the MCCE with having done the hard part—building a national civic alliance, activating people on the ground, developing relationships with honest politicians and other powerholders, and cultivating the media. When Avaaz joined the struggle, citizens had already reached the point of wanting to participate. Avaaz's strategy was to tap and multiply this people power by adapting to the Brazilian context its online model of recruitment and mobilization. This consisted of sending out regular alerts with specific calls for action, and asking recipients to spread the alerts throughout their social networks—via Twitter, Facebook, Orkut (another social networking site), and "old-fashioned email"—to the extent that sharing becomes exponential and seemingly takes on a life of its own. That is, it goes viral. "It's the power of people spreading and owning the campaign," Tanaka explained.

At the outset of the campaign Avaaz had 130,000 members in Brazil. By April 2010 this number had grown to 650,000 and then climbed to 700,000, most of whom were multipliers, circulating Avaaz alerts to their social networks. While not all were equally active, Avaaz has found that the longer a person stays on the alert list, the more active that person becomes. Tanaka reports that they had no challenges maintaining member interest in Ficha Limpa and, more generally, in corruption. "People were disillusioned with the political system and because the same politicians always had power." It was seen as another form of *coronelismo*, a term referring to big landowners associated with rural elite dominance and vote buying. "People wanted to see corrupt politicians out of elections," she added.

"Sign to End Corruption"

Avaaz sought to build people power momentum to push the Ficha Limpa bill through the entire legislative process, all the way to a final vote in the Chamber of Deputies and Senate, ratification by the president, and a Supreme Court vote over the constitutionality and validity of the law.[29]

The pace of the online campaign picked up in February 2010, when the bill began winding its way through congressional committees. Building upon the MCCE's signature drive to submit the bill, Avaaz launched an online petition with the goal of obtaining 2 million signers, although Tanaka acknowledged that the total seemed "far off" at the outset.

The petition went viral, which Avaaz used to garner media coverage. Media interest was so great that Ficha Limpa was landing on the front pages of the biggest newspapers on a weekly basis, reported Tanaka. This, in turn, piqued public interest in the movement, the bill itself, and the legislative process—driving more and more citizens to Avaaz, which then reaped further media attention. The interplay between the campaign and the media resulted in an ever-increasing, mutually reinforcing cycle of attention and pressure. By May 3, 2010, the petition reached the 2-million mark.[30]

Minicampaigns

From approximately February through April 2010 Tanaka coordinated one to two such rapid-response campaigns almost every week. The MCCE tracked the movement of Ficha Limpa through committees in real time, thanks to congressional allies it had cultivated over the previous two years. These legislators would inform the MCCE—day by day, sometimes even hour by hour—about what was going on, what was being said, who was opposed, who was undecided, who was supportive, and so on. In turn, the MCCE conveyed this information immediately to Avaaz, which was able to send out action alerts quickly with status updates to hundreds of thousands of members to take action, including

- E-mailing messages to specific legislators straight from Avaaz's website.
- Directly phoning the offices of targeted politicians involved in the Ficha Limpa committee, which broke new people power ground in Brazil, as literally thousands of citizens flooded offices with calls. People were asked to register their call through a live chat tool, which Avaaz used to tally numbers.
- Signing the e-petition, and tweeting and posting the alerts to Facebook and Orkut.

Through the emails and phone calls, citizens conveyed collective demands to individual lawmakers at critical junctures in the legislative process. Avaaz's time-sensitive asks were directed at committee members who did not publicly disclose their opposition but behind the scenes were using watering-down and delaying tactics. "We showed them that we had a presence online and a real presence," said Tanaka.

Additional Tactics

In conjunction with Avaaz's campaign, the MCCE created a video on increasing social action that was used to create political awareness in civil society.[31] Another tactic was the prominent use of online information feeds to generate excitement among citizens as well as media interest and coverage. This included tweets and e-petition names appearing on the Avaaz website in real time. Finally, on May 4, 2010—the day the Chamber of Deputies was scheduled to vote on Ficha Limpa—Avaaz organized a rally at the National Congress. Rich with symbolism and visuals that garnered extensive national media coverage, Avaaz submitted a complete list of the names of the 2 million citizens who signed the e-petition in favor of the bill. Supporters, including some politicians, engaged in street theatre, humorously cleaning the site by washing the steps with pails of water and brooms.

Communications and Media

The MCCE's core message, reinforced by Avaaz, was that Ficha Limpa was a Popular Initiative bill—demanded, initiated, and driven forward by the Brazilian people. What claimed media attention during the online campaign was the movement's legitimacy and numbers, and the novelty of digital resistance. After the legislation was successfully submitted to Congress, Tanaka reported that they did not receive much attention from journalists at first. "It was only when we got close to a million e-signatures and the mass calls to congressmen started that we became interesting to them." Positive media coverage surged as Ficha Limpa became one of the top-trending Twitter topics. According to Tanaka, journalists and congressional representatives later voted Ficha Limpa the most important political issue of 2010.

Backfire

By March, Congress started to block messages that citizens were sending from the Avaaz website tool. Avaaz shifted gears straightaway. It used alternative email addresses, switched servers, and rallied people to send messages from their own accounts. In any case, the blocks went into effect after the first thousands of emails reached the designated inbox, so many emails still made it through. The congressional move backfired, perceived as an affront to citizens. Rather than stymieing them, it spurred higher levels of commitment and action. Moreover, the MCCE publicized the developments to the media, gaining valuable coverage.

Campaign Attributes

Organization and Coordination

Avaaz defies definitions. It is charting a new form of citizen engagement, civil resistance, and people power that transcends national borders and the virtual-physical divide. Although Avaaz is not a conventional international nongovernmental organization (INGO) or CSO with fixed headquarters, it has a hierarchical structure for decisionmaking. Nor is it a regular social movement where the leadership and strategists operate out of a physical space and interactions both among core activists and with citizens occur largely in the real world. Its stated mission is to "organize citizens of all nations to close the gap between the world we have and the world most people everywhere want."[32] Avaaz's overriding objective is to empower "millions of people from all walks of life to take action on pressing global, regional and national issues, from corruption and poverty to conflict and climate change."[33]

Consisting of a small core team working virtually from points around the world, meeting occasionally in person at strategy and planning sessions, Avaaz is now completely member-funded. Tanaka, the digital group's only campaigner in Brazil, interacted remotely with the core leadership. For Ficha Limpa, she regularly coordinated with one of the leaders of the movement, Judge Marlon Reis. At the time, it was a unique partnership for Avaaz, and Tanaka believes it was effective, due in part to the good collaborative process established with the MCCE.

Tactical Planning and Sequencing

Digital resistance lets a movement see in real time how people react to online calls for action by their "click rate," and how they in turn spread appeals to others. Such monitoring allows the campaign to measure public interest; quickly assess and hone strategies, tactics, and messaging; and create new actions and media outreach efforts; for example, Avaaz created an online Twitter button and focused strongly on Twitter after noticing that the petition started to go viral through it. This approach had never been undertaken before. Avaaz also coordinated public pressure with media outreach coordinated by the MCCE. "So the Members of Congress got hit by the media and our pressure," explained Tanaka.

Breaking Down Barriers
The Avaaz action-alerts empowered citizens to become engaged in the legislative process, all the way down to the committee level, and communicate with lawmakers by providing contact information as well as tips about what to say and how to interact with congressional staff. These exchanges started to break down the entrenched boundaries between the ruling elites and regular people. "In a way," reflected Tanaka, "the campaign was strengthening the democratic process because Members of Congress weren't used to getting calls from voters, and voters were not used to following the legislative process, and calling and making demands of Members."

Unity
The MCCE and Avaaz both strategically cultivated unity of goals and people—in their messaging and tactics. The Popular Initiative bill was by nature grassroots and dependent on citizens' sharing Ficha Limpa's objectives and translating support into tangible actions, first and foremost, through handwritten signatures with voter identification. Tanaka recounted that Avaaz's action alerts always contained a movement-building message that "reinforced that people were a part of something bigger, that the campaign's strength depended on how far people spread the messages, and that it depended on us to keep the pressure and show Congressmen we were watching them," she added. The live chat tool also built unity; Tanaka explained that people could share messages of encouragement as well as excitement for the campaign, showing that this movement was a truly collective power.

Outcomes

Ficha Limpa Passage
The law was ratified by a majority in the Chamber of Deputies on May 4 and unanimously in the Senate on May 19. It was subsequently approved by then-president Luis Ignacio da Silva on June 4, 2010. One of the MCCE leaders, Daniel Seidel, executive director of the Brazilian Commission for Justice and Peace, proclaimed, "I say, the cow flew!"[34]

Soon after this people power triumph, corrupt interests launched efforts to undermine the new law, resulting in a confusing application for the 2010 elections and ongoing legal battles all the way to the Supreme Court by candidates who won their seats but were ruled ineligible to take office by lower electoral courts. Avaaz launched a digital resistance, powered by citizens, during the Ficha Limpa vote in the Supreme Court.

On March 23, 2011, the Supreme Court issued a decision that Ficha Limpa could not be applied to the 2010 elections. Consequently, those candidates who won but were barred from taking office would now be eligible to claim their seats.[35] On February 16, 2012, the Supreme Court ruled that Ficha Limpa was constitutional and would be enforced in the October municipal elections that year.[36]

Cleaning Up the Corrupt

In September 2012, regional election courts banned 317 mayoral candidates from running in the municipal elections.[37] Some politicians are reported to have stepped down due to public pressure, even before the bill was ratified. Joselito Canto, who was under investigation for suspected involvement in at least thirty transgressions involving embezzlement of public funds, resigned from office. He tweeted, "Today I announce the end of my political career. Ficha Limpa, mix-ups in the ALEP [Legislative Assembly of Paraná]. Enough! I stopped."[38] In addition, a local campaign in the state of Rio de Janeiro heralded the unanimous passing of a Ficha Limpa law in the State Legislative Assembly.[39]

The MCCE is still making strides. It launched an electoral reform campaign and wants to initiate new grassroots efforts targeting graft in the health and law enforcement systems, thereby addressing forms of corruption that are not only widespread but particularly harmful to citizens in their everyday lives. The MCCE is also deliberating on how to initiate a broader societal debate about reforming the country's political system.[40]

Bottom-Up Democracy

The Ficha Limpa movement has changed the way Brazilians view themselves, their democracy, and their capacity to make their collective voice heard. "What's happening now is part of this new democratic process," reflected Tanaka. "People are excited that they can exercise their civic duty, that they can be engaged with their democracy." This shift in public consciousness—from cynicism and apathy to outrage and empowerment—is reflected in a variety of ways:

Both Avaaz and the MCCE detect a fresh level of *political engagement* in the society. According to Tanaka, "People are paying more attention to their democratic system. They know who is their congressman, who are the candidates, and they want to make sure that those who commit crimes are remembered at election time." In a survey conducted a week after the October 2010 presidential elections, 73 percent out of a 1,300-person sample stated they took Ficha Limpa into consideration when choosing a candidate.[41] Seventy percent of candidates accused of Ficha Limpa violations lost their elections.[42] As well, websites and blogs are focusing on electoral democracy, including the MCCE's own site and the Movimento Voto Consciente, which focuses on the Legislative Assembly of São Paulo.[43]

Digital engagement has increased. Between 2009 and 2011 Brazil's Facebook use grew by a factor of 38 (3,832 percent).[44] During the first quarter of 2011, the country ranked third in the world for Twitter reach at 23.7 percent of the population.[45] As of November 1, 2011, of the 10 million people who made up Avaaz globally, Brazil had the largest community, with over 1.2 million members. The next biggest was France, with almost 1.1 million members, while the United States had under 789,000 members.[46] Since the Ficha Limpa movement, digital activism is now expanding to remote areas, allowing people to become part of political and social activism even when they cannot physically connect to groups. According to Tanaka, during 2011, more protests were organized through social media, including Facebook, than ever before.

The Ficha Limpa movement changed Brazil's culture of *citizen advocacy* from a traditional reliance on civil society specialists to mass popular pressure. In addition to organized civic action to fight corruption, regular people are taking their own initiative. "People now want things to do," observed Tanaka. They use Facebook and Twitter for political purposes—to post their reactions to political events and developments, to find out about campaigns and actions, and to link up over shared concerns. For instance, Mapa Coloborativo da Corrupcao do Brasil is an online, interactive, open-access corruption map created by Rachel Diniz, a journalist and filmmaker. The map is designed to be built by citizens, who can post corruption cases that have been documented in the press in their localities or nationally. Diniz also connected to the Ficha Limpa community by sharing information and links on its Facebook wall, which elicited comments.[47]

Rather than peter out, people power pressure has continued, over both local corruption and political machinations to overturn Ficha Limpa. The mobilizations are uniting citizens from different walks of life and civic organizations, and are identifying linkages between corruption, poverty, violence, and democracy. At the end of May 2010 in Natal, students organized two rallies through Twitter over alleged mayoral corruption and mismanagement. Their actions morphed into an occupation and protest camp inside the city council on June 7. According to a news report, the group presented a series of demands, and after negotiations, twenty-one councilors signed an agreement and the occupation was dismantled. That same month, protests were launched in thirteen cities in Paraná over corruption, including embezzlement of public money in the state Legislative Assembly. A participant said, "What really works is the involvement of society. If [society] doesn't make a demand, politicians will keep on doing what they want."[48] Finally, a digital civic campaign in the state of Rio pressured the state legislature to pass its own Ficha Limpa bill.[49] The unanimous vote was held in November 2011.

When Ficha Limpa was being challenged by appeals submitted to the Supreme Court, and scandals rocked President Dilma Rousseff's cabinet, thousands of people took part in nonviolent actions during autumn 2011, organized through social media rather than by political parties or unions. On September 7, Brazil's Independence Day, protests were held in the capital, Brasilia, and twenty other cities. They were supported by the country's College of Lawyers, the Brazilian Press Association, and the National Bishops Conference, which jointly issued a statement: "Corruption in our country is a pandemic which threatens the credibility of institutions and the entire democratic system."[50]

Several days later, on September 19, Rio for Peace, a local CSO, surprised residents with a visual dramatization on the famous Copacabana beach; 594 brooms, representing the members of the Congress, were planted in the sand. "The purpose of our initiative is to make people aware of the extent of rampant corruption and to demand greater transparency in the management of public funds, since the deviation of funds is responsible for the death of thousands of Brazilians," said Antonio Carlos Costa, a social activist, theologian, and the group's founder.[51] Since June 2013, Brazil is regularly making international headlines as mass mobilizations over government spending priorities, public service cuts, and corruption are pressuring powerholders.[52] Avaaz launched another grassroots digital campaign to pass legislation, sitting in the Congress since 2006, to end the dubious practice of "secret voting." Digital resistance involving the largest online petition in Brazilian history (1.6 million names) and a nude protest pressured lawmakers in the Chamber of Deputies, who unanimously voted in its favor in early September 2013.[53] The legislation then headed to the Senate. While it was up for vote, Avaaz reported, "Right now, senators' telephones are ringing off the hook as Avaaz members across Brazil use our online calling tool to directly tell them to stop this corruption—experts say a win is likely in days!"[54] A partial victory finally came on November 26,

2013, when the Senate approved a weakened version of the House legislation. Avaaz vowed to continue the struggle.[55]

Changing Powerholder Culture

Tanaka and MCCE activists assert that the culture of impunity among powerholders is changing in Brazil. "Today we have a national discussion about our politics thanks to this law, and the voter is analyzing the quality of candidates based on new parameters to see if the candidate has the requirements to represent him or not," said Luciano Santos, a lawyer with the MCCE.[56] "The language of Ficha Limpa is being incorporated into the political discourse, and candidates are now trying to show voters that they aren't corrupt," reported Tanaka. Political elites of differing ideologies are contending they must alter their ways. Around the center, Alvaro Dias (Partido da Social Democracia Brasileira, Paraná) predicts changes will be a "natural consequence" of Ficha Limpa. On the right, Antonio Carlos Jr. (Democratas, Bahia state), said that parties will become more careful about candidate selection and will need to reeducate members and draft ethical codes.[57] Some political parties, such as the leftist Partido Socialismo e Liberdade, have even taken the step of implementing the "clean record" criteria into their ranks. As with the case of the Citizens Alliance for the General Elections (CAGE) 2000 in South Korea, in the long run, this dynamic may prove to be as significant as the actual legislation—by stimulating the internalization of public standards of integrity and accountability among institutions, the political system, and powerholders in society.

Transnational Inspiration

Other countries and the international community are looking at Ficha Limpa as a model for new anticorruption legislation. According to Brazilian officials, some civic actors in Bolivia are observing its implementation as they want to strengthen a similar but weaker law in their country.[58] Avaaz adapted the "Clean Record" concept to the 2011 general elections in Spain. Partnering with the Indignados movement, Avaaz launched an online and offline campaign demanding that political parties drop from their lists for the local and regional elections candidates indicted or convicted of serious crimes and offenses, and to select individuals "with a well-known track record of responsible public service."[59] "Theatrical stunts" were combined with an online petition that was short of the 125,000-person target (108,524 signatures).[60] They triggered a public debate, but their immediate demands went unheeded, perhaps a reflection of its short-lived and much, much smaller scale of mobilization than the strategic, well-organized, and planned Ficha Limpa movement.

Case Analysis

Institutionalizing Accountability
Political corruption is a common target of bottom-up civic initiatives, from CAGE 2000, the Dosta! youth movement in Bosnia-Herzegovina (see Chapter 10), and the DHP (Dejemos de Hacernos Pendejos) movement in Mexico (see Chapter 10). Ficha Limpa brings a new strategy to the struggle. Rather than pressure political parties to drop corrupt candidates or inform voters about them during elections, both of which require recurrent civic campaigns, a legal mechanism was created to institutionalize exclusion from the political process—hence, to gain accountability for malfeasance. One could argue that Ficha Limpa cannot prevent all corruptors from seeking public office. Some have not been caught and tried by more than one judge, or they can get associates to run in their place, as did Joaquim Roriz, whose wife, Weslian Roriz, stepped in when he was blocked in the 2010 race.[61] However, it fundamentally disrupts the corrupt status quo, creates incentives for integrity, supports—and, one could argue, even rewards—honest politicians, and tackles impunity without having to directly target each and every corruptor.

Tipping Points
At the moment when enough citizens say "this is enough," digital resistance can provide an alternative recruitment method that quickly channels people's anger toward mitigating the injustice and oppression via tangible objectives and demands, and it can tap into their desire to act through multiple online and real-world nonviolent tactics. Avaaz tries to identify "tipping point moments" in struggles, when powerholders are faced with a monumental choice and "a massive public outcry can suddenly make all the difference."[62] It sees these instances as briefly open windows of both crisis and strategic opportunity, as "crucial decisions go one way or another depending on leaders' perceptions of the political consequences of each option."[63]

For Avaaz, tipping points go hand in hand with a "good ask," a demand that Tanaka characterized as "ambitious and inspiring enough for people to take action." A good ask has the dual strategic function of encapsulating tangible requests for powerholders while appealing to or resonating with citizens. Online rapid-response alerts issued at key junctures conveyed a sense of urgency that enhanced unity, ownership in the struggle, and excitement to be involved. For instance, a message sent prior to the vote on Ficha Limpa declared, "Dear Brazilian Parliamentarians, We urge you to support the Clean Record Law Proposal (PLP 518/2009). We expect you to vote for clean elections, in which political candidates who have been convicted of serious crimes such as murder and mismanagement of public funds are ineligible for office. Our votes in October will depend on your actions in this critical moment for Brazilian politics."[64]

From Minicampaigns to Going Viral

Through information and communication technologies (ICT), the process of civil resistance can be broken down into rapid-response minicampaigns, sometimes on a daily basis. These smaller campaigns can quickly create a sense of momentum among citizens, provide positive reinforcement for taking action, and produce modest, incremental victories.

The Ficha Limpa movement—on the ground and online—demonstrated how thousands of individual actions, even of a modest nature, can be combined into a powerful collective force. In this respect, Avaaz's online members can be considered the equivalent of on-the-ground movement activists, taking action and engaging fellow citizens in a variety of nonviolent tactics that generate people power. Just as the MCCE gained numbers and strength through the networks of the forty-four civic organizations in the coalition, Avaaz's ever-growing number of Brazilian members tapped into their own social networks to involve others. The difference was in magnitude. "The effectiveness of online campaigning is that you can reach a scale where you are not interacting with individuals but with hundreds of thousands of people who don't expect personal interaction but are ready to act upon receiving alerts," explained Tanaka.

Avaaz's online campaign was the largest in Brazil's history, with an unparalleled scale of mobilization, including the petition with 2 million signatures, 500,000 online actions, and tens of thousands of phone calls to legislators.[65] Together with the MCCE's efforts, the Ficha Limpa movement took on an air of people power omnipresence. "Congressmen couldn't run away from it," said Tanaka. "They were constantly hearing about Ficha Limpa from the media, email messages, and phone calls from citizens in the thousands." It was the country's third-top-trending topic in 2010. An MCCE poll conducted prior to the 2010 general elections found that 85 percent of respondents supported the legislation—indicating a profound shift away from public cynicism and complacency with the corrupt status quo to the demand for clean, accountable governance. Avaaz also received anecdotal feedback from politicians. Tanaka recounted that upon meeting legislators, they would make such

comments as, "Oh, so you're the group behind all those emails!" Together with the MCCE's efforts, this "created the political will for the
legislation to be passed," she said.

Partnerships

Avaaz strategically assessed both its own and the MCCE's strengths and
limitations. Each brought what the other generally lacked: Avaaz had a
track record of rapid response and scaling-up mobilization, while the
MCCE excelled in winning allies from within the corrupt system, intel-
ligence gathering, grassroots organizing and action, and media outreach
and communications. Avaaz didn't want to duplicate the MCCE's efforts and decided not to get involved until it could add value to the
struggle. That point came when the Ficha Limpa bill was introduced to
Congress. Digital resistance could generate swift, even instantaneous
pressure, when timing was absolutely critical and it wasn't possible to
mobilize people quickly on the ground.

Digital resistance blurs the boundaries between internal and external actors. Although Avaaz is a transnational network with global campaigns, it also launches national campaigns within countries. In Brazil,
Avaaz's campaigner Tanaka set the civic initiative in motion and coordinated with the MCCE. She developed campaign strategy and planning
along with input from Avaaz's global team.

Beyond the Online-Offline Dichotomy

Avaaz's Ficha Limpa campaign demonstrates that the debates about digital versus real-world activism and social change are flawed. First, they
tend to conflate the medium (digital realm) with tools (ICT such as
Twitter, Facebook, SMS, emails, blogs, and website links) and the nonviolent tactics derived from ICT tools (for example, viral messaging and
e-petitions). This leads to confusion about what is actually being de-
bated; the terms "Internet," "social media," and "social media tools" are
often used interchangeably. But disputing the value and impact (or lack
thereof) of the digital sphere is different from debating the value and
impact (or lack thereof) of social media tools, which are a subset of ICT
tools in general.[66]

Second, the debate tends to be framed through absolute questions:
for example, "Do social media make protests possible?" or "Have the
new tools of social media reinvented social activism?" or "Do social
media lead to democracy?" Such queries are based on a faulty assumption—that there are direct, linear relationships between the realm of
struggle (digital) and tools (ICTs such as social media) on the one hand,

and outcomes (democracy, freedom, accountability, justice) on the other hand. In the field of civil resistance, the overwhelming conclusion among scholars and activists is that there is no formula or consistent matching up of objectives, strategies, tactics, and outcomes. Sociologist Lee Smithey notes that civil resistance takes place on a cultural, social, political, and economic landscape.[67]

A more fruitful line of inquiry involves the examination of power relations, strategies, tactical choices, and people power dynamics in the digital sphere. For example, the above questions can be reframed as follows: How does the digital sphere expand the struggle arena? How do digital tactics (derived from ICT/social media tools) wield people power? In what ways are ICT/social media tools changing social activism and civil resistance? How does digital resistance shift power equations that can lead to political, economic, and social change?

Third, the boundaries between the online and offline worlds are blurring. As the Ficha Limpa movement demonstrated, on-the-ground and online civil resistance shared the same grievances, objectives, and demands, while creating synergies. Moreover, tactics can no longer be neatly categorized as digital versus real-world; they can actually combine both realms. A case in point is when thousands of citizens received an alert via ICTs asking them to phone a lawmaker's office to voice a concerted demand regarding Ficha Limpa (a daunting and unfamiliar action for regular Brazilians). Many overcame their reticence; the response was a flood of calls. Was this purely social media or real-world mobilization? And when these people subsequently used ICT tools to tell others in Avaaz and their social networks about their action, they in turn spurred more citizens to follow suit. How was this different in intent and desired outcomes to providing an on-the-ground movement with a list of personal contacts to approach or inform about their activities in order to engage them in the struggle?

Lessons Learned

Digital Resistance

Digital resistance is a form of civil resistance, and it can wield people power. The decision to struggle through this medium or on-the-ground or some combination of both depends on the objectives, strategies, and capacities of the civic campaign or social movement, and the realities of the particular struggle arena. Tanaka reported that during the vote, even some legislators who were not supportive of the bill acceded that they could not ignore the will of 3.6 million Brazilians who demanded the passing of Ficha Limpa. The reactions of these powerholders and the media are telling. They did not make a distinction between the 1.6 million handwritten signatures and 2 million online petitioners. Nor did they discount the authenticity of civic mobilization through the digital realm and the mass actions executed through ICTs/social media.

Another lesson is that online activism can shift power relations and translate into real-world actions. The Avaaz campaign broke new ground, as evidenced from the thousands of citizens who boldly called the offices of congressional representatives and Supreme Court members. This action was revolutionary in a society where political power-holders hold formidable social authority and interactions with citizens are infrequent, circumscribed, and hierarchical.

Finally, digital resistance is complementary to on-the-ground civil resistance but not necessarily a substitute for it. Grassroots organizing builds a strong, united base of groups as well as citizens, which, in the case of Ficha Limpa, was essential to collect over 1.6 million handwritten signatures. Only through on-the-ground interactions and relationships can allies be cultivated from within corrupt systems, and negotiations be conducted. Then again, digital resistance enables immediate communication; quick, even instantaneous responses; rapid mobilization without the time, organization, and resources needed for on-the-ground efforts; and opportunities to experiment with tactics and tweak actions and messages in real time with minimal resources.

Intangibles

ICTs/social media can foster a genuine sense of ownership and collective identity, two key intangible qualities of bottom-up civic initiatives. The blogosphere was reported to have "embraced" the Popular Initiative bill. Some bloggers created their own online banners. Others issued calls to action. One wrote, "It's time to fight the 'good fight.' Time to forget the ideological differences and to shine in a new era of national politics." Another tweeted, "Let's put pressure on the deputies reaching two million signatures to show that if they don't vote for 'Ficha Limpa,' we won't vote for them."[68] When the bill was passed, a Brazilian member of Avaaz wrote, "I have never been as proud of the Brazilian people as I am today! Congratulations to all that have signed. Today I feel like an actual citizen with political power."[69]

Digital resistance also provides an added dimension of movement ownership and social identity through an ongoing narrative that can be powerful either on its own or in combination with on-the-ground civil resistance. Tanaka explained that online civic initiatives are particularly effective in creating a narrative that people can closely follow, day by day, as the campaign or movement develops. In Avaaz's case, on a weekly basis while the Ficha Limpa bill was in committee, citizens "were given action opportunities that by the approval of the law, they could feel that they were a key part in it, truly own the campaign movement, and know that their actions were fundamental at every step of the way." The narrative is a powerful way of involving people in the whole campaign—from committees, to the vote, to presidential approval, to Supreme Court validation, she concluded.

As well, whether digital resistance gone viral or mass on-the-ground resistance, the scale of citizen participation enhances the credibility of the movement and legitimacy of its demands. "To tackle something big [corruption]," said Tanaka, "we needed to make it [Ficha Limpa] bigger than us. It needs to be publicly owned. This is the protection."

Wielding People Power

The Ficha Limpa case illuminates four lessons about people power. First, successful digital resistance involves the same people power dynamics as on-the-ground civil resistance: disrupting the unjust, unaccountable status quo; shifting loyalties among powerholders and within institutions; and winning people toward the movement or campaign, irrespective of their motives.

Digital resistance also offers economies of scale. While this alone is not a determinant of success, it can provide a strategic advantage under some circumstances and at critical points in a struggle. "Instead of going to meetings and planning rallies, in two hours we can send an email to 200,000 which can spread," noted Tanaka. Third, digital actions expand the repertoire of nonviolent tactics but are not inherently superior or more effective than on-the-ground actions, and vice versa. Lastly, whether civil resistance takes place in the digital or real-world realms, the elements of success are the same: shared grievances; unity of goals and people; collective ownership of the campaign or movement; skills, strategies, and planning; tactical creativity, diversity, and strategic sequencing; effective communications and messaging; and a strict commitment to nonviolent methods.

Notes

1. Political scientist Daniel Zirker defines liberation theology as a "philosophical and theological worldview that calls for the active role of Catholicism

in the temporal sphere on behalf of the rights and needs of the poor"; Daniel Zirker, "The Brazilian Church-State Crisis of 1980: Effective Nonviolent Action in a Military Dictatorship," in *Nonviolent Social Movements: A Geographical Perspective*, ed. Stephen Zunes, Lester Kurtz, and Sarah Beth Asher (Malden, MA: Blackwell, 1999), 260–261.

2. Ibid., 259–278.

3. Adrian Karatnycky and Peter Ackerman, *How Freedom Is Won: From Civic Resistance to Durable Democracy* (New York: Freedom House, 2005), 29.

4. Juan de Onis, "Brazil Presidency Won by Reform Candidate: Neves Chosen by Electoral College as Civilian Rule Returns After 21 Years of Military Regimes," *Los Angeles Times*, January 16, 1985, http://articles.latimes.com.

5. "Sarney Takes Oath as Neves' Replacement," *Los Angeles Times*, April 23, 1985, http://articles.latimes.com.

6. James Brooke, "Huge Rally Demands Brazil Chief's Impeachment," *New York Times*, September 20, 1992, www.nytimes.com.

7. "Factbox: Brazil's General Elections," Reuters.com, October 3, 2010, http://www.reuters.com.

8. CIA, "Country Comparison: Distribution of Family Income—Gini Index," *The World Factbook*, www.cia.gov (accessed October 3, 2013).

9. "Custo da corrupção no Brasil chega a R$ 69 bi por ano," FIESP, May 13, 2010, www.fiesp.com.br.

10. Luiza Mello Franco, "Brazil's *Ficha Limpa* (Clean Record) Legislation: Will It Run over Corruption or Will It Run out of Steam?" Council on Hemispheric Affairs, July 19, 2010, 1, www.coha.org.

11. "Brazil's Congress, Cleaning Up: A Campaign Against Corruption," *The Economist*, July 8, 2010, www.economist.com.

12. Ibid.

13. Janet Gunther, "Brazil: A Clean Slate?" Catholic Aid for Overseas Development (CAFOD) blog, March 24, 2010, http://blog.cafod.org.uk.

14. "Brazil's Congress."

15. Gunther, "Brazil."

16. "CNBB felicita Marcus Faver por idealizar a Lei Ficha Limpa," Colegia Permanente de Presidentes de Tribunais de Justiça, August 10, 2010, www.colegiodepresidentes.jus.br.

17. "Brazil's Elections: One Messy Clean Slate," *The Economist*, October 3, 2010, www.economist.com.

18. Mello Franco, "Brazil's *Ficha Limpa* (Clean Record) Legislation."

19. MCCE website, http://www.mcce.org.br/node/125 (accessed July 20, 2010).

20. Mello Franco, "Brazil's *Ficha Limpa* (Clean Record) Legislation."

21. "The Campaign: Popular Participation in Brazilian Politics," Poder Legislar, http://poderlegislar.com.br/en; "The Role of the Catholic Church: Popular Participation in Brazilian Politics," Poder Legislar, http://poderlegislar.com.br/en.

22. "The *Ficha Limpa* in Brazil," *Active Citizens, Accountable Governments: Civil Society Experiences from the Latin America Partnership Programme Arrangement*, UKAid, 9, www.aidsalliance.org.

23. Jovita Jose Rosa, "Interview: Popular Participation in Brazilian Politics," Poder Legislar, http://poderlegislar.com.br/en.

24. Débora Bressan Mühlbeier, "*Ficha Limpa*: Politicians in Brazil Must Have Clean Criminal Records," Infosurhoy, June 22, 2010, www.infosurhoy .com.

25. "Clean Record: Popular Participation in Brazilian Politics," Poder Legislar, http://poderlegislar.com.br/en.

26. "Ficha Limpa," Poder Legislar, http://poderlegislar.com.br.

27. "About Us," Avaaz, http://www.avaaz.org (accessed October 3, 2013).

28. This chapter is based on SKYPE interviews plus subsequent written communications with Graziela Tanaka, then a Brazil-based Avaaz campaigner, during September–October 2010 and October 2011.

29. The section title was the message heading for the Avaaz alert to sign the e-petition; Assine Para Acabar com a Corrupção/Sign to End Corruption e-petition, Avaaz, n.d., www.avaaz.org (accessed May 20, 2010).

30. Ibid.

31. "The *Ficha Limpa* in Brazil."

32. "About Us," Avaaz.

33. Ibid.

34. "Grandes questões sociais fazem parte do Encontro de Pastorais, Organismos e Regionais da CNBB," Conferência Nacional dos Bispos do Brasil (CNBB), www.cnbb.org.br.

35. Priscilla Mazenotti, "Supreme Decision Means Losers Are Now Winners in Brazilian Congress," Brazzil.com, March 27, 2011, www.brazzil.com.

36. Sarah de Sainte Croix, "Brazil Anti-Corruption Act Upheld," *Rio Times*, February 17, 2012, http://riotimesonline.com.

37. Lucy Jordan, "Ficha Limpa Bans 317 Candidates in 2012," *Rio Times*, September 11, 2012, http://riotimesonline.com.

38. Mühlbeier, "*Ficha Limpa.*"

39. "Vamos Aprovar o Ficha Limpa Estadual!" Meu Rio, www.meurio .org.br.

40. Information can be found at www.reformapolitica.org.br.

41. Carlos Pereira and Matthew Taylor, "Clean Slate Law: Raising Accountability in Brazil," Brookings Institution, December 22, 2010, www .brookings.edu.

42. Mazenotti, "Supreme Decision Means Losers Are Now Winners."

43. Ficha Limpa website, www.fichalimpa.org.br; Movimento Voto Consciente website, www.votoconsciente.org.br.

44. Nick Burcher, "Facebook Usage Statistics 1st April 2011 vs. April 2010 vs. April 2009," blog entry, April 5, 2011, www.nickburcher.com.

45. "The Netherlands Ranks #1 Worldwide in Penetration for Twitter and Linkedin," press release, Comscore, April 26, 2011, www.comscore.com.

46. "About Us," Avaaz.

47. Jose Domingo Guariglia, "When People Are Mad, They Start to React to Corruption," Inter Press Service, August 20, 2011, http://ipsnews.net.

48. Mühlbeier, "*Ficha Limpa.*"

49. "Vamos Aprovar o Ficha Limpa Estadual!"

50. "Brazilians Rally Against Corruption," BBC News, September 7, 2011, www.bbc.co.uk.

51. "Hundreds of Brooms in Rio's Beaches to Protest Brazilian Rampant Corruption," Merco Press, September 20, 2011, http://en.mercopress.com.

52. "Brazil Protesters Disrupt Rio Military Parade," Al Jazeera, September 7, 2013, http://america.aljazeera.com.

53. "Brazil Says NO to Corruption, YES to 21st Century Democracy!," Avaaz, http://www.avaaz.org/en.

54. Ibid.

55. "Brazil Senate Approves End of Secret Ballot," NewsDaily, November 27, 2013, http://www.newsdaily.com.

56. Gabriel Elizondo, "Brazil's Groundbreaking Step to Halt Corruption," Al Jazeera, Americas Blog, September 6, 2010, http://blogs.aljazeera.net.

57. Débora Zempier, "Brazil's New Anti-Corruption Law Scares Politicians and Jurists," *Brazzil Magazine,* July 5, 2010, http://brazzil.com.

58. Ibid.

59. "Spain: Kick Corrupt Politicians Out!" Avaaz, n.d., www.avaaz .org/en.

60. "Highlights," Avaaz, www.avaaz.org/en (accessed March 7, 2013).

61. Weslian Roriz subsequently lost.

62. "The Avaaz Way: How We Work," Avaaz, www.avaaz.org/en (accessed June 9, 2011).

63. Ibid.

64. Sign to End Corruption e-petition.

65. "Success Stories from the Avaaz Movement Worldwide," Avaaz, www.avaaz.org/en (accessed October 4, 2013).

66. Among the well-known minds in these debates are authors Malcolm Gladwell, Evgeny Morozov, and New York University professor Clay Shirkey. Digital activist and researcher Mary Joyce offers an alternative, nuanced exploration of the digital realm and the application of ICT to civil resistance (see Joyce's blog meta-activism.org). For references, see Malcolm Gladwell, "Small Change: Why the Revolution Will Not Be Tweeted," *New Yorker*, October 4, 2010, www.newyorker .com; Malcolm Gladwell and Clay Shirkey, "From Innovation to Revolution: Do Social Media Make Protests Possible?" *Foreign Affairs*, March/April 2011, http://sites.asiasociety.org.

67. Lee Smithey, "Social Movement Strategy, Tactics, and Collective Identity," *Sociology Compass* 3, no. 4 (2009): 658–671.

68. Paola Goes, "Brazil: Blogosphere in Support of Anti-Corruption Bill," *Global Voices*, April 7, 2010, http://globalvoicesonline.org.

69. "Success Stories from the Avaaz Movement Worldwide."

5

Citizens Protect an
Anticorruption Commission:
Indonesia

B y the 1990s the Indonesian people's dissatisfaction with the brutal
regime of General Suharto was increasing.[1] Political and military repression was relentless, and Suharto's extravagant enrichment of himself and his family members and cronies, related economic scandals,
and overt malfeasance angered many Indonesians. During this decade, a
new generation of human rights and prodemocracy groups began to develop. They established ties with student organizations and found common cause with other sectors in society, including displaced peasants,
suppressed workers, and community leaders.[2] In 1997 election-related
fraud and brutality reached new heights, adding to popular discontent.[3]
When the Asian financial crisis hit in 1998, the kleptocracy was ill-
prepared to cope. The Indonesian currency, the rupiah, plummeted in
value. Inflation soared, hitting regular people particularly hard as prices
of basic goods became exorbitant, the national banking system collapsed, the industrial sector declined, and unemployment escalated.[4]

On May 21, 1998, after thirty-two years in power, General Suharto
was forced to resign. His downfall was the result of a civic alignment involving student groups and religious organizations; months of student-
led protests around the country in what became known as the *Reformasi*
(reformation) movement against "corruption, collusion/cronyism and
nepotism"; and internal pressure from political elites.[5] One year later,
multiethnic Indonesia began a new chapter of governance when the first
free parliamentary elections were held since 1955.[6] The fledgling
democracy inherited a multitude of ills not unlike those of postwar contexts, from widespread poverty to a thirty-year armed conflict in Aceh
that resulted in close to 15,000 deaths, dysfunctional state institutions,

security force impunity, and endemic corruption. The latter was embedded into the power structures of government institutions, security forces (military and police) and public administration, and the economy and social fabric of the country.

Context

Into this thorny mix was born the Corruption Eradication Commission (Komisi Pemberantasan Korupsi), best known by its acronym, KPK. In 2002 the Indonesian House of Representatives passed the KPK law, instituting the legal basis for its creation. This marked a milestone for the country's post-Suharto Reformasi—namely, the effort to bring forth political and institutional change and to consolidate democracy. The anticorruption body became operational in 2003, armed with several crucial capacities. It has the authority to investigate, prosecute, and convict wrongdoers in its own anticorruption courts independent of the attorney general's office.[7] It has quite broad jurisdiction, encompassing all branches of the government, police (excluding military), and the private sector when coaccused in public sector cases. Finally, the KPK has surveillance and investigative powers, namely, the ability to conduct wiretapping, intercept communications, examine bank accounts and tax records, issue hold orders, enforce travel bans, and even make arrests.[8]

While many anticorruption commissions are dismissed as window dressing to satisfy donors and multilateral institutions, a few are at the forefront of fighting corruption and gaining transparency. The KPK is one of these trailblazers. It has exposed corrupt behavior and relationships in the national and subnational government, Parliament, the administration, the private sector, and the police, the latter having a particularly negative reputation with the public. According to Transparency International Indonesia's biannual Corruption Perceptions Index, in 2006, 2008, and 2010, the police were considered to be the most corrupt institution.[9] From 2004 onward, the KPK achieved a 100 percent conviction rate, including cabinet ministers, provincial governors, judicial figures, legislators, Election Commission members, ambassadors, and business executives.[10] As a result, the KPK overcame the public's initial cynicism and earned its respect and admiration. People saw it as "the hope to fix a broken country," said Illian Deta Arta Sari, an anticorruption activist and the public campaign coordinator of Indonesia Corruption Watch.[11]

By impacting the entire tangled system of influence and graft involving the executive and legislative branches, judiciary, central bank, and private sector, the KPK soon became a target. This shift included police criminalization of some of its activities, bomb threats, a Constitutional Court ruling in 2006 that the law establishing the KPK and the counterpart Corruption Court was unconstitutional, and subsequent parliamentary attempts to cut the institution's budget and authority, as well as to alter the Corruption Crimes Courts. These attacks are ongoing.[12] The situation came to a head in 2009, in the wake of the KPK's investigations of embezzlement in the infamous Bank Century bailout.[13] Wiretapping unveiled attempts by the police's chief detective, Susno Duadji, to influence legislators' decisions and unfreeze Bank Century accounts.[14] Another KPK case launched that January involved Aulia Pohan, the deputy governor of the central bank, who is also the father-in-law of President Susilo Bambang Yudhoyono's son. In June 2009 the Corruption Court sentenced him to four and a half years in prison.[15] Later that month, the president signaled his displeasure with the commission. He said, "The KPK holds extraordinary power, responsible only to Allah. Beware!"[16]

Not surprisingly, efforts to weaken if not destroy the commission intensified. On May 2, 2009, the police arrested the KPK's chairman, Antasari Azhar, for a murder conspiracy in a love triangle.[17] Exactly two weeks later, while in detention, he alleged that two deputy commissioners, Bibit Samad Rianto and Chandra Hamzah, were involved in extortion and corruption.[18] None other than Chief Detective Susno produced the handwritten testimony. Without delay the police launched investigations. On September 11 they began questioning Bibit and Chandra, and on the fifteenth of the month formally declared them suspects.[19] On September 21 President Yudhoyono issued a decree to temporarily dismiss Bibit and Chandra, requesting a presidential team to recommend new commissioners.[20] The removed officials fought back by challenging the decree in the Constitutional Court.[21]

Campaign

Objectives and Strategy

That July, well before Bibit and Chandra were arrested, a core group of civil society leaders already "saw the signs," recalled Deta Arta Sari. Many of them had been young activists for democracy and human rights during the 1990s and then veterans of the Reformasi movement against the Suharto regime. They met informally and decided it was necessary to proactively develop a strategy and plan to protect the

KPK—the institution, its mandate, and its authority—before it was too late. "It's now a very dangerous time for the KPK. Whether it's the police, attorney general's office, or parliament, there is a systematic agenda to destroy the KPK," asserted Teten Masduki, a prodemocracy veteran who was the executive director of Transparency International Indonesia at that time.[22] They concluded that the only way to defend the commission was to apply extrainstitutional pressure. That pressure, according to Deta Arta Sari, was people power. "We realized that no government institution would protect KPK, so the people had to protect it."

The campaign's overall strategy was to generate firm political will to safeguard the KPK through overwhelming popular pressure on President Yudhoyono, who had decisively won a second term in office based on a strong anticorruption platform. Initially, activists demanded that the president publicly take a stand in support of the commission and force those intent on destroying it within the police, attorney general's office, and Parliament to back down. As unforeseen events unfolded, the campaign made specific requests: the establishment of an independent commission to quickly examine the case and legal proceedings against the two anticorruption deputy commissioners, their reinstatement at the KPK, and urgent reform of the attorney general's office and the police.

Coalition Building

An early step was to build a strong coalition from the civic realm. At the core were the members of the Judicial Monitoring Coalition (KPP). It was made up of key civil society democracy guardians: Indonesia Corruption Watch (ICW); the Centre for Policy and Law Studies (PSHK); Indonesia Institute for Independent Judiciary (LeIP); Indonesian Legal Aid Foundation (YLBHI); Indonesian Legal Roundtable (ILR); Indonesia Transparency Society (MTI); Jakarta Legal Aid Institute (LBH); the National Law Reform Consortium (KRHN); and Transparency International Indonesia.

Deta Arta Sari and Emerson Yuntho, a fellow anticorruption activist and a law and justice monitoring coordinator with ICW, reported that campaign planners approached organizations and initiatives around the country to enlist their support, including women's groups, human rights nongovernmental organizations (NGOs), student groups, the religious communities, local civic anticorruption initiatives, and organized labor. Among the civic entities were KontraS (Commission for "the Disappeared" and Victims of Violence), a major human rights organization; RACA (Institute for Rapid Agrarian Conflict Appraisal), which mitigates agrarian conflicts; and FAKTA (Jakarta Citizens' Forum), focusing on the urban poor. A few unions, on the left of the ideological spectrum, also joined the coalition. Over one hundred groups came on board, some at the national level and others at the provincial and local levels.

Gecko vs. Crocodile

The civic leaders officially launched the Love Indonesia, Love Anti-Corruption Commission (CICAK) campaign on July 12, 2009, through a *deklarasi,* a public declaration supported by several respected national figures, including Abdurrahman Wahid, the first elected president in 1999, and two former KPK commissioners, Taufiqurrahman Rukie and Erry Riyana Hardjapamekas. They chose a Sunday so that more people could come to the launch, which also featured a huge draw, the famous rock band Slank. The name "CICAK" has a dual meaning. It's an acronym for Love Indonesia, Love Anti-Corruption Commission (Cintai Indonesia Cintai KPK). It also refers to the gecko lizard, turning a police insult into a symbol of defiance. In an April interview with a major news magazine, Chief Detective Susno said he knew the KPK was investigating and wiretapping him, but added, "It's like a gecko challenging a crocodile," the latter referring to the police.[23] His comment angered the public, as he made no effort to veil his contempt for both the antigraft body and the overall struggle against corruption, which allowed those in power to benefit while the average person was cheated.

In the ensuing weeks through to September, CICAK groups formed in twenty of the country's thirty-three provinces. Indonesian students studying in Cairo even established a diaspora branch.[24] Well-known statesmen, celebrities, artists, and religious figures took a stand in support of the anticorruption commission. The CICAK organizers were ready to channel popular anger into mass civic mobilization—to a level unprecedented since the Reformasi movement against Suharto.

Meanwhile, the situation was growing more and more ominous for the antigraft body. In August the media reported that the country's chief prosecutor, Hendarman Supandji, boasted that if the police and attorney general's office joined forces on the Bank Century case, there would not be a crocodile but a Godzilla.[25] Nevertheless, the KPK was not cowered. It intensified inquiries and announced on September 9 the investigation of Chief Detective Susno in multiple corruption cases. Shortly thereafter, it made a daring move, leaking wiretappings to the media, implicating him and other police officials in corrupt activities, including attempts to manipulate legislators' decisions and unfreeze Bank Century accounts.[26] The police announced that Deputy Chairman Chandra was a suspect of power abuse and extortion on August 26, followed by Deputy Chairman Bibit on September 15. Two weeks later, the KPK hit back, filing corruption charges against Chief Detective Susno, recalled Dadang Trisasongko, a civic anticorruption leader and veteran of the Reformasi movement.

Interim Demands

On October 29 the police arrested Bibit and Chandra on charges of abuse of power. The arrests came a day after President Yudhoyono ordered an investigation into the KPK's wiretapped telephone conversations involving a senior attorney general's office official, in which one of the speakers alleged that the president supported efforts to suppress the KPK. On October 30 the president gave a televised address, stating that he would let the police continue with the case. He argued that the arrests of Bibit and Chandra needed to move through law enforcement procedures and the judicial process, finally reaching the courts. Given that all three institutions involved—the National Police, the attorney general's office, and the judiciary—were corrupt and part of what was commonly known as the "judicial mafia," CICAK's leaders demanded the establishment of an independent commission to examine the arrests of the KPK deputy commissioners. The police had a flimsy case, the activists asserted. They also insisted that this inquiry be conducted within a short time frame in order to prevent stalling tactics, indefinite incarceration of the two men, and irreparable harm to the antigraft institution.

Upping the People Power Ante

People were furious with the police and embittered with their leader, who had won a landslide reelection based on an anticorruption platform. The repression against the KPK deputy commissioners backfired. Usman Yasin, a young university lecturer conducting postgraduate studies, took the initiative to create a CICAK Facebook group called "A Million Facebookers in Support of Bibit-Chandra." It soon played a role bigger than anyone imagined.[27] Twitterers used the hashtags "#dukungkpk" or "#support KPK" to express solidarity and views.[28] People were urged to change their Facebook profile picture to the CICAK symbol. The Facebook group grew so quickly that television news ran hourly updates of the numbers. Within several days it reached the 1.4-million mark, becoming a key tool through which to communicate with and rally citizens.

Popular singers added their support and composed an anticorruption song, with the refrains, "Gecko eats crocodile" and "KPK in my heart." Citizens could download the song and ringtones free of charge.[29] Campaigners organized actions in Jakarta. Local chapters, civil society organizations (CSOs), university students, and high school students, supported by their teachers, initiated their own events across Indonesia's far-flung archipelago. Some university students built a tent in front of the KPK and went on a hunger strike. In East Java and Central Java, teenagers held competitions to throw small stones at alligator puppets. While the latter tactic may not sit well with principled nonviolence adherents, these actions were symbolic, signifying that regular people were no longer fearful or intimidated by the police, who were considered to be corrupt and deserving of punishment. At one high school in Jakarta, pupils fashioned a banner in support of the KPK and 1,000 classmates signed their names on it, while at another, students drafted a joint statement that was also posted on the blog of one of the teachers.[30]

Campaign tactics included petitions, leafleting, hanging banners, sit-ins, gathering in front of police stations, concerts, street theatre, and stunts, such as dressing up like mice. Thousands adorned themselves with pins, stickers, black ribbons symbolizing the death of justice, and T-shirts with the CICAK logo. Bandanas proclaiming "I am gecko" reportedly "spread like wildfire."[31] An account by an Australian scholar observed, "Bibit and Chandra—who, with the gecko, are stars of millions of posters and T-shirts."[32] Campaign leaders also worked with mural painters and singers, resulting in eye-catching street graffiti still visible in Jakarta and the aforementioned popular anticorruption songs.[33] The campaign also created attention-grabbing acts they termed "happening art," which often involved humor and garnered national media coverage—for example, jumping off the KPK building with parachutes to symbolize that the KPK faced an emergency and needed protection.

Street actions grew across the country with each passing day. The sites were deliberately chosen, explained Trisasongko. In some cities, they were police stations. "This was solidarity against injustice and the corrupt police, and to support the movement and KPK," he said. In Jakarta, protests were held in front of the presidential palace in order to tell President Yudhoyono that "he had the authority to stop the criminalization of the KPK," Trisasongko added. On November 2, approximately 3,000 people massed together and then marched to the presidential palace. Activists assert that the mobilization stunned the government.

That very same day, CICAK achieved its first victory. The president acceded to the campaign's demand to create an independent commission tasked with investigating the legal proceedings and the case against Bibit and Chandra. Known as the Team of Eight and led by a respected lawyer and law reform advocate, the commission had two weeks to make its determinations.[34] Then came the bombshell. On November 3, during live broadcast hearings over Bibit and Chandra's temporary dismissal, the Constitutional Court played four hours of wiretapped conversations strongly indicating that a conspiracy was under way to frame the deputy commissioners and undermine the KPK.[35]

Millions around the country heard senior prosecutors from the attorney general's office, a bigtime businessman, and police officials plotting against the KPK. Chief Detective Susno was mentioned numerous times.[36] There was even a suggestion that Deputy Commissioner Chandra could be murdered once in detention, and an unidentified woman was heard saying that the president supported the plan.[37] The public uproar was immediate. By midnight, Chandra and Bibit were released from prison, although the charges were not dropped. Chandra avowed, "Let's take it as strong momentum to improve the fight against corruption, because in this situation, the loser is the country and the winner is the corruptor."[38] The next day, approximately 500 people rallied in front of the Constitutional Court and along Thamrin Street, a major thoroughfare. They demanded that Susno be fired. CICAK used SMS, Twitter, and Blackberry Messenger to mobilize citizens overnight, said Trisasongko.

On November 8 the campaign organized its biggest action to date, again utilizing social media such as Facebook and Twitter. The date was chosen for practical and symbolic reasons. It was a Sunday and one of the city's festive "Car Free Days," which not only facilitated a mass convergence but was a day associated with fitness and well-being. Approximately 3,000 to 5,000 people gathered from early morning—including a special CICAK Facebook group contingent—for a rally and concert with the billing, "For a Healthy Indonesia, Fight Corruption." Starting with a mass group exercise for the country's well-being, the action combined humor, entertainment, and appearances by public figures.[39] Slank performed a concert. Speakers included Usman Yasin, the CICAK Facebook group creator; Effendi Gozali, a TV personality and University of Indonesia lecturer; Yudi Latif, chairman of the Center for Islam and State Studies, and media commentator; and former KPK deputy commissioner Erry Riyana Hardjapamekas.[40]

Meanwhile, in Yogyakarta city, local activists held a concert featuring traditional Javanese music.

Campaign Attributes

Unity

Citizens of all ages, socioeconomic groups, and religions participated in the campaign. CICAK leaders reported that the upper-middle and middle classes joined in street actions; professionals reportedly took time off from work and could be seen standing together with students and poor people. According to Yuntho and Deta Arta Sari, it was highly unusual for the upper classes to participate, but "they realized the KPK was in danger and we needed to save the KPK to save Indonesia from corruption." Many prominent figures from different walks of life affirmed their support, from Bambang Harymurti, a leading journalist and head of the investigative news magazine *Tempo*, to Akhadi Wira Satriaji (otherwise known as Kaka), the lead singer of Slank.

Senior clerics of Indonesia's five faiths and respected public figures paid solidarity visits to the KPK. Former president Abdurrahman Wahid (Gus Dur) urged the KPK and citizens to question the arrests.[41] He declared, "I came to add more support for their release from detention. I am prepared to put my name on the line in this case."[42] Jimly Ashiddiqie, a former Constitutional Court chief justice, publicly expressed support and advised the KPK to hand over wiretaps to the Constitutional Court rather than to the police.[43] In Malang in the East Java province, academics and a network of human rights and state administrative law lecturers publicly prevailed upon President Yudhoyono to stop the "criminalization" of the KPK officials.[44]

Leadership and Organization

CICAK formed through the cooperation and coordinated efforts of a small group of civil society activists, lawyers, and law scholars. "They came together to make a grand strategy," recalled Deta Arta Sari. The core organizers, constituting the leadership of the campaign, were based in the capital. They met on a daily basis to plan, organize, communicate, and carry out activities, all while maintaining their professional and personal responsibilities. They worked out a division of labor based on expertise and capacities. Generally, their efforts fell under two complementary categories: (1) legal analysis and activities; and (2) civic actions, campaign messaging and communication, media outreach, and behind-the-scenes contact with government officials among the police, attorney general's office, and president's staff.

Decisions were made through consensus. The key organizing entities were Indonesia Corruption Watch (ICW) and the Indonesian Center for Law and Policy Studies (PSHK), although they did not direct the campaign nor were they the face of it. "We wanted to be separate from ICW and others, in order to get broader involvement and support," said Deta Arta Sari. The campaign had no leader—another strategic move to build citizen ownership. Rather, it was led by "cicaks," the little lizards symbolizing regular people, who together could peacefully overpower the mighty crocodile (police).

CICAK's leadership group also deliberated over how to quickly expand the campaign to the national level, not an easy feat considering Indonesia's geography of far-flung islands as well as multiple cultures and ethnicities. They decided on a strategy of decentralization. Pooling their considerable contacts and networks cultivated since the Reformasi movement, they cooperated with grassroots civic actors to initiate, expand, and sustain local mobilization and nonviolent actions around the country. According to Trisasongko, regional and local activists went on to "do their own thing, and we just distributed Jakarta's press releases to them." In tandem, the Jakarta core also contacted and coordinated with student groups in universities across Indonesia.

The campaign was based on voluntary participation. Activists, legal experts, and citizens contributed their time and even money. Street actions were characterized by spontaneous acts of generosity. For example, during the November 3 march to the presidential palace, which took place on a particularly hot day, protestors collected money from one another in order to buy water for those in need.

Strategic Analysis and Information Gathering

The Jakarta core conducted a strategic analysis of parts of the president's cabinet and the judicial mafia. They mapped the National Police and high-ranking personnel of the attorney general's office in terms of who was clean and who was corrupt. This mapping was shared with some honest interlocutors inside the system. Throughout the campaign, the civil society network invited experts from universities to analyze legal issues concerning the KPK in order to provide legal interpretations that could be offered to officials and lawyers in the antigraft body, as well as related government institutions. This activity underscores two often overlooked yet essential dimensions of civil resistance movements: the need for ongoing education and information gathering, and empowering those within the system who support accountability, honesty, and justice.

Communications

CICAK's communications strategy had three main components: objectives, messaging, and medium. The objectives were to ignite public concern, convey a sense of urgency, mobilize citizens, and attract media coverage. Communications were also designed to build unity of grievances, people, and goals. Core messages included, "I'm a gecko, fight corruption"; "Don't stay silent"; and "Say no to crocodiles." Together, the campaign's acronym of CICAK (gecko) and full name (Love Indonesia, Love Anti-Corruption Commission) brilliantly encapsulated the struggle: the problem (corruption), the positive target (KPK), the objective (save KPK), the protagonists (cicaks, symbolizing regular citizens), and motivation (love of country).

Trisasongko said that the emphasis was on the institution rather than on Bibit and Chandra, although their safety took on primacy after the arrests. "We tried to keep the personal side out of the messages," he said. "Implicitly we protected the two deputy commissioners because the police wanted to crack down on the KPK through them." Campaign activists utilized multiple methods through which to convey messages. They spread news and information for nonviolent actions through the media, Facebook, SMS, and the Internet. Messages were also conveyed through graffiti, posters, leaflets, songs, ringtones, and even individuals in the thousands, who became walking billboards through special CICAK T-shirts, pins, and bandanas.

A concerted effort was made to get media coverage. Organizers sent notices for press conferences, street actions, and "happening art" to journalists through SMS. They reported that the media were very supportive. Deta Arta Sari and Yuntho acknowledged that they weren't sure why. "The KPK is a newsmaker. Whoever hits the KPK is a good news story," they hypothesized. The struggle between the corruptors and the antigraft body, and the escalation of public action—through social networking as well as on-the-ground tactics—resulted in an unfolding story, replete with twists and turns, drama, and suspense. In part, given their proximity to Indonesian and international journalists, Jakarta events were meticulously planned, from advance PR to speakers, posters in Bahasa and English, press conferences, and distribution of leaflets, T-shirts, pins, and stickers.

International Dimension

Campaign leaders sought international attention and support. First, as Indonesia is a signatory to the UN Convention Against Corruption (UNCAC)—which recognizes the role of the civic realm in state accountability—activists approached the relevant body in Jakarta, namely, the United Nations Office of Drugs and Crime (UNODC). While most Global South capitals have numerous missions representing international institutions, they are not necessarily cognizant or appreciative of grassroots anticorruption initiatives. The UNODC office in Jakarta stands in contrast. To its credit, it did not dismiss the overture.

Instead, on September 16, CICAK's leaders met with Ajit Joy, the country manager, and asked him to inform UNODC headquarters that Indonesia has problems implementing UNCAC, particularly "maintaining and ensuring the independence of the anticorruption authority," said Trisasongko. Following the session, the activists held a press conference in front of the UNODC office. On November 10 the campaigners held another press conference, announcing they would raise the attack on the KPK at UNCAC's Third Conference of States Parties that just began in Doha. CICAK capitalized on the UNCAC conference's timing, gaining even more media attention. As the KPK crisis raged during UNCAC's round of negotiations, the campaign sent daily press releases about the grassroots mobilization to the Indonesian journalists covering them in Doha. "We would get into the headlines," he recalled.

Repression

Notwithstanding the institutional and legal efforts to harm the KPK and detentions of senior officials, no overt repression took place against the CICAK campaign, its organizers, or its protestors. According to Trisasongko, "It would have made things worse." However, anticorruption activists involved in the civic initiative had experienced harassment in the run-up to CICAK. In January 2009 the attorney general's office reported Yuntho and Deta Arta Sari to the police for defamation after they pointed out a multitrillion-rupiah gap in the institution's annual budget and demanded an investigation.[45] Nothing happened for months; then suddenly in October, during the throes of CICAK, they received a summons from the police. They avoided the order over a technicality: the letter had a mistake in the wording of Indonesia Corruption Watch.[46] Eventually, the police dropped the case.

Outcomes

The CICAK campaign succeeded in protecting the KPK from a concerted plan to harm, if not destroy, the institution and its anticorruption capacities. A summary of events during the crisis is as follows.

• On November 2, President Yudhoyono established the "Independent Fact-Finding Team on the Legal Proceedings of the Case of Chandra M. Hamzah and Bibit Samad Rianto," aka the Team of Eight. It had two weeks to conclude its inquiry. The two deputy commissioners framed for corruption were released from prison on November 3.

• On November 17, the Team of Eight publicly announced that there was no evidence that the two officials had engaged in corrupt activities. It formally recommended that the case be dropped and called upon the president to punish "officials responsible for the forced legal process."[47]

• Chief Detective Susno subsequently resigned from the National Police, along with Abdul Hakim Ritonga, the deputy attorney general, who was also implicated in the wiretaps.[48] A couple of months later, Susno testified that the police force had a special team in place to target KPK commissioners Antasari, Bibit, and Chandra.[49] Susno has since gone on to expose corruption involving police, the attorney general's office, and businesspeople involved in money laundering and tax evasion.[50]

• On November 23, President Yudhoyono ordered the police and prosecutors to settle the case against the KPK deputy commissioners out of court, publicly affirming that reforms were necessary within the National Police, the attorney general's office, and the KPK.[51] While taking a stand against corruption, he nonetheless equivocated.[52] First, he didn't call for the case to be dropped. Second, at that juncture, it was odd that the antigraft body was considered to be in need of reform, alongside the very same state institutions involved in a plot to damage it. Civic anticorruption advocates saw this as a sign that social pressure must be sustained on the president as well as the judicial mafia of corrupt police, prosecutors, and judges.

• The attorney general's office officially dropped the case against the KPK deputy commissioners on December 1. Bibit and Chandra resumed their positions on December 7, following a presidential decree.[53]

• On December 30, 2009, President Yudhoyono appointed a two-year Judicial Mafia task force.[54] Its responsibilities consisted of "advising, monitoring, and evaluating reform and supervision measures by all law enforcement institutions."[55]

Civic leaders remain vigilant against new attacks on the KPK. At the Fifteenth International Anti-Corruption Conference in November 2012, Trisasongko described how a new campaign was launched to counter parliamentary delays in approving the KPK's budget, including funds for a new building. Dubbed the Public Donation for KPK Building, the civic initiative collected symbolic amounts of money and construction materials from citizens around the country from June to October 2012. As a result of the collective pressure, the parliament finally passed the budget. That same October, the Save KPK campaign carried out a nonviolent intervention. Citizens conducted an overnight vigil to block the arrest of an investigator looking into traffic police corruption.[56] Digital resistance through Twitter, coupled with real-life protests, questioned President Susilo Bambang Yudhoyono's silence. Shortly thereafter, he announced that the KPK should conduct the investigation.

Anticorruption activists also exert pressure on the KPK itself in order to keep it clean and accountable. For instance, in February 2010 CICAK submitted an ethics violation report to the KPK concerning one of its officials. When no response was forthcoming, campaigners staged a "happening art" silent protest in front of the building. Chandra Hamsah, the KPK deputy commissioner targeted by corruptors, said the commission would question its staff about the incident.[57] Nothing happened immediately, but a few months later some officials were replaced; the activists surmise it was a result of their nonviolent action.

All in all, the CICAK campaign shook up the horizontal system of graft involving state institutions and the private sector. It "forced the government to scrutinize indictment procedures and prosecutors," observed Trisasongko. People power pressured Indonesia's leader to take specific measures targeting corruption and impunity. It encouraged transparency and won a degree of accountability from government and economic powerholders. After CICAK, the Bank Century case was investigated by the Parliament. The findings and recommendations sent to the president were also made public. Finally, CICAK put the systemic transformation of law enforcement institutions on the national agenda, creating a degree of political will to push for serious internal reform of the judicial mafia.

In a country that in previous decades had suffered violence from genocide, political repression, armed insurgency, and ethnic strife, anger and outrage were productively channeled through civil resistance. Through CICAK, citizens overcame cynicism and apprehension to raise their voices against corruption and impunity. "I am a gecko and am not afraid to fight a crocodile," was a common refrain.[58] By participating in the campaign, they refused to be observers and victims of the machinations of powerful political and economic families, officials, legislators, and bureaucrats. They rediscovered their collective power in the largest social mobilization since the anti-Suharto movement. Through this process, citizens became actors in their democracy. For Masduki, "The pillar of democracy is people power, so without it, democracy could not work for the people."[59]

Case Analysis

Intangibles

CICAK transformed public anger toward the police into grassroots solidarity against injustice. "We wanted to cultivate a sense of ownership," recalled Trisasongko. Through this sense of collective responsibility to save the KPK, ordinary people experienced a shared social identity—that of empowered "cicaks"—which became a strong motivator of civic action. "We tapped the sentiment of being victims of corruption and violence and directed it toward protecting the KPK, which many knew about and supported," he stated.

CICAK's leadership strategically infused the campaign with humor for several reasons. According to Trisasongko, "Humor is a universal language here for people. . . . It also cuts across social and economic classes." Thus, humor is an effective way to communicate with citizens. It also mitigates a common form of powerholder repression in Indonesia—accusations of defamation made by state institutions and lawsuits initiated by individuals. Through humor, messages can be shared that would otherwise put people at risk. Finally, humor separates outrage from anger, preserving the former and transforming the latter from a negative into a positive—saving the antigraft institution through nonviolent action. "We don't just have to show anger to protest something," he added.

Neutrality

CICAK's organizers deliberately chose to maintain a nonpolitical, nonideological character, and did not approach political parties for support. According to a Harvard report, "Distrust of politicians is so deep and widespread that one gets the sense that any politician who had attempted to identify him- or herself as a gecko would have been laughed off the political stage."[60] In any case, there was no danger that any would jump on the anticorruption bandwagon. "All of the political parties were silent because they all have cases in the KPK," commented Yuntho.

Backfire Phenomenon

The CICAK campaign constitutes a compelling example of how an injustice can be made to backfire. According to nonviolent action scholar Brian Martin, powerful perpetrators of injustice—such as corruption—typically use one or more of five methods to reduce public outrage.[61] First, they cover up their actions, as nearly all corrupt operators do—including the Indonesian police, who tried to keep their plotting out of the public eye. Second, perpetrators try to devalue their targets and critics, exactly what the police did in seeking to discredit the KPK by charging and arresting its leading figures. Third, perpetrators reinterpret events by lying, minimizing the effects on targets, blaming others, and reframing the narrative. The state's narrative—namely, its reinterpretation of events—consisted of an intransigent KPK, dishonest officials, and delivery of justice through administrative and legal measures. Fourth, powerful perpetrators of injustice use official channels to give an appearance of justice without the substance. This normal operation of the corrupt judicial system served this purpose. The KPK was the exception, being an honest and effective official channel, and hence was seen as a serious threat to powerholders. Fifth, powerful perpetrators attempt to intimidate targets, their supporters, and witnesses, as did the police.

The police used all five methods to reduce public outrage over corruption, but on this occasion their efforts were unsuccessful. Campaign organizers intuitively countered each of the police's five outrage-reduction tactics. With the aid of KPK wiretaps, they exposed the police plot, countering the cover-up. They validated the KPK targets, countering devaluation. They emphasized the injustice of the attack on the KPK, countering reinterpretation. They mobilized public support, avoiding ineffectual and time-wasting official channels. Finally, they nonviolently resisted in the face of intimidation.

The result was that the attack on the KPK backfired on the police. The planned effort to quash the antigraft body, culminating in the arrest of senior officials, backfired as a result of a nonviolent civil resistance campaign. Not only was this plot thwarted, there were negative consequences for some of the most visible attackers.

Digital Resistance

The CICAK Facebook group played multiple roles in the campaign. It was used to win public sympathy and transmit information, news, and calls to action around the country, thereby contributing to the formation of a national initiative that overcame geographical and socioeconomic barriers. Second, street actions around the country were organized through Facebook. Third, the social media platform created a sense of unity and enthusiasm as members became part of a group that grew from 0 to 1.2 million in just ten days (from October 30, the day of the Bibit and Chandra arrests, to November 8, the day of the big demonstration and concert).

CICAK members had at their fingertips an instantaneous method of communicating with one another that reinforced a sense of shared outrage and collective identity. "If KPK is being put to death, that's really nice for the corruptors who are clapping as they see what has happened," said a posting.[62] Finally, online tactics—for instance, changing one's profile photo—were translated into street actions, such as the organized Facebook contingent in the November 8 rally.

Unconventional Allies

The involvement of artists, such as street muralists and singers, had multiple benefits. Strategically, such popular figures contributed to unity because their association gave the campaign credibility and created excitement among regular people, explained Danang Widoyoko, coordinator of Indonesian Corruption Watch. Tactically, the artists enabled the campaign to reach the masses, because their support of the KPK and involvement in CICAK were covered by entertainment media, such as TV programs, gossip magazines, and fan websites.

Lessons Learned

Civil Resistance

The CICAK campaign provides a clue as to why research has found that civil-resistance transitions from authoritarianism are more likely to result in democratic governance and civil liberties than violent or elite-led, top-down changes. Leaders and activists of nonviolent social movements develop close-knit bonds and often go on to become the (unsung) defenders of democracy in their countries. Most in the Jakarta leadership group were veterans of the Reformasi movement. These civic actors, some having experienced imprisonment and abuse under the Suharto regime, have since 1998 worked tirelessly—as individuals and through CSOs—to advance the reformasi process. Over the years they have maintained an effective, informal network of communication and coordination. While each organization has its own mandate, they collectively function in a complementary manner.[63] Their shared objectives resemble a strategic blueprint for consolidating democracy in Indonesia: dismantle the venal authoritarian system, transform the corrupt military and keep it out of politics, reform the constitution and the justice system, gain powerholder accountability, improve human rights, tackle widespread poverty in a country bestowed with vast natural resources, and prevent sectarian strife.

CICAK also affirms a central tenet of civil resistance scholarship: systems of graft and oppression, incorporating state and nonstate institutions and actors (pillars of support for the system or oppressor), are not monolithic. One can identify allies and supporters, shift loyalties, and quietly communicate with them, as did the CICAK campaign with individuals in the National Police and attorney general's office. Masduki encapsulated this approach:

> I believe not all government officials are corrupt. The anticorruption movement should be decided by collective action, by people, the government, and also the business sector. It is very important for me that anticorruption [work] includes confidence building among and inside government, business, and the whole of society. Everyone involved should also be aware of and reap the benefits of anticorruption work. Without these, we could not get support from the population.[64]

Corruption Dynamics

The CICAK campaign offers valuable lessons regarding how systems of corruption function. First, the plan to delegitimize and irreparably weaken the KPK illustrates, in real terms, the machinations of a system of corruption that spans across multiple realms—in this case, various state institutions, the executive branch, the private sector, families, and enablers in the professional realm, such as lawyers. The myriad malfeasant relationships in Indonesia's judicial mafia had mutually dependent interests, thereby revealing how such relationships are not always between a corruptor and corruptee but between two or more corruptors who are all deriving benefits by abusing their power and authority.

In order to change a corrupt system, such as Indonesia's judicial mafia, Trisasongko highlighted the lesson that a "dual track" is necessary: extrainstitutional demand for change coupled with internal reform measures and implementation capacity.

Finally, corruption breeds corruption. Not only are systems of graft and abuse unlikely to reform from within, they are prone to growing ever more venal because more and more graft is needed to maintain vested interests and the crooked status quo.

Unity and Civil Resistance

Unity is understood to be an essential element of civil resistance, as documented by scholars in the field. Why it is so critical (beyond citizen mobilization) and how it plays out in nonviolent campaigns and movements—that is, its dynamics—have received less attention. The CICAK campaign offers instructive lessons.

In addition to unity of people, grievances, and goals, there must be a shared sense of outrage and a common adversary, reflected Trisasongko. In the case of CICAK, there was overwhelming and widespread dislike of the police, which was necessary for mobilization and, as importantly, for long-term momentum and civic pressure to achieve real reform of corrupt institutions and systems.

Unity often involves coalitions of various sorts, comprising groups and prominent individuals in the particular struggle context, that afford higher levels of participation, protection through numbers (of people), credibility, and legitimacy. Such alliances are also a font of creativity, ideas, and talent, as well as increased resources, relationships, and contacts—all of which can be utilized by the civic campaign or movement. A third lesson is that unity also increases diversity of expressions of dissent, from tactics to messaging and even the channels through which messages are communicated. For instance, the involvement of popular singers and street artists led to innovative nonviolent actions, such as anticorruption songs and ringtones, and reached an untapped swath of the public through entertainment media outlets.

CSOs that already have well-developed, on-the-ground networks and relationships with local community-based organizations (CBOs) and citizens bring the added value of grassroots ties. Such CSOs have done the painstaking work of establishing trust and credibility with locals. Thus, their endorsement and involvement in a civic campaign or movement can pull into the fold small-scale, bottom-up civic initiatives and mobilize people who would not have otherwise been reached. According to Trisasongko, some of the CSOs in the CICAK coalition already had ties to local Muslim CBOs through cooperation on civic projects, such as budget advocacy, internal accountability, and anticorruption. As a result, through the CSOs' network of on-the-ground community groups, the campaign was able to rally citizens across the country.

Organization and Strategic Planning

The CICAK campaign demonstrated that an effective division of labor is essential for civic initiatives, particularly ones involving a coalition or alliance of multiple groups. Leadership groups can methodically plan divisions of labor that minimize duplication, maximize resources and capacities, and maintain a well-functioning, harmonious endeavor.

As well, leadership is more than the strategies and decisions of individuals heading a civic initiative. For Trisasongko, "It is important, not just in terms of persons but of ideas." His insight adds a new dimension to a fundamental element of social movement formation—movement discourse—which civil-resistance scholar Hardy Merriman defines as "the narratives, cognitive frames, meanings, and language" of the movement or campaign."[65]

Balancing is an ongoing consideration for civic initiatives, including what is planned versus what is spontaneous, what is centralized versus what is decentralized, who makes strategic decisions and represents the campaign at the core versus the periphery, and what degree of independence there should be between the core and local groups and activists. As with Addiopizzo in Italy, CICAK's leadership group took care to strategically address such issues rather than ignore them or allow them to haphazardly unfold on their own accord.

Fourth, the CICAK campaign offers another demonstration of the critical roles that information gathering and education play in civil resistance. The Jakarta core invited legal experts from universities to conduct interpretations of laws and proceedings. For example, the police said it was illegal for two out of five KPK commissioners to be making decisions, thereby having an excuse to impede the institution's functioning. CICAK and legal scholars countered with legal opinions and arguments that foiled the police's plans, and as importantly, gave KPK officials confidence to continue working.

Tactics

Humor can bring multiple benefits to a campaign or movement. It can function as a low-risk tactic in some contexts, communicate serious messages, and dispel fear. Humor often cuts across social and economic divisions, thereby building social identity and enhancing unity.

Street actions such as protests, rallies, and marches are not merely symbolic actions, but strong tactics as well. They can generate social pressure on powerholders. In CICAK's case, "The government had to consider them; otherwise they would keep getting bigger and bigger," said Widoyoko. "It was like 1998 [Reformasi movement]; they started small and when there was no response, they grew."

As with Ficha Limpa in Brazil, information and communication technology tools were used to foster a sense of ownership and social identity. Online activism, even through participation in an enormous Facebook group, is a digital form of citizen mobilization that, coupled with on-the-ground actions, can create formidable social pressure.

Third-Party Actors

In contrast to systems of graft—comprising overt and covert sets of corrupt relationships embedded with vested interests—the CICAK case shows how nonviolent social movements and campaigns can build alternate systems of cooperative relationships based on unity of people, grievances, shared outrage, objectives, and a common opponent(s). This insight points to a fundamental lesson, namely, that such interconnected people power systems cannot be manufactured or stimulated by external third parties, including well-intentioned anticorruption and development actors and human rights advocates. Nonetheless, external actors can provide solidarity, as did the UNODC mission in Jakarta when it received CICAK leaders to discuss Indonesia's compliance with the UNCAC.

Second, the dynamics of unity and the organic emergence of people power systems through civil resistance have critical advice for external third parties interacting with internal CSOs and CBOs:

- Do not ignore networked, often low-profile CSOs in favor of elite-based NGOs, as the former have credibility, networks, and relationships with the grass roots.
- Do not create situations whereby such CSOs find themselves in competition with one another, as this can harm essential relationships, cooperation, potential unity in a civic initiative, and systems of people power.

In the next two chapters, I move from finite campaigns to ongoing social movements that have both long-term transformative goals and shorter-term objectives, such as the youth-led Addiopizzo movement in Palermo, Italy, and the citizen-empowering 5th Pillar in India.

Notes

1. Naming customs in Indonesia are complex, and people commonly have only one name.

2. Adelburtus Irawan Justiniarto Hartono, "State-Business Relations in Post-1998 Indonesia: The Role of Kadin" (PhD thesis, University of Groningen, 2011).

3. Suharto came to power in 1965, part of the military's intervention against President Sukarno, the previous authoritarian ruler who originally galvanized defiance against Dutch colonial rule. The country essentially lurched from a left-wing autocracy to a right-wing military dictatorship. When Suharto took power, an estimated 500,000 to 1 million people belonging to fully legal leftist and communist groups were killed from 1965 to 1966 in what scholars deem a genocide, and over 1 million were imprisoned without trial, from writers, artists, and poets to teachers and regular citizens; see *Derailed: Transitional Justice in Indonesia Since the Fall of Suhaerto*, ICTJ and Kontras, March 2011, http://ictj.org.

4. Hartono, "State-Business Relations in Post-1998 Indonesia."

5. Ibid., 58.

6. I. N. Bhakti, "The Transition to Democracy in Indonesia: Some Outstanding Problems," in *The Asia-Pacific: A Region in Transition,* ed. Jim Rolfe (Honolulu: Asia Pacific Center for Security Studies, 2004), 195–206; Adrian Karatnycky and Peter Ackerman, *How Freedom Is Won: From Civic Resistance to Durable Democracy* (New York: Freedom House, 2005).

7. Dadang Trisasongko, a veteran of the Reformasi democracy movement and a civil society leader, explained that the Anti-Corruption Court Act of 2009 mandated that the Supreme Court establish anticorruption courts in all districts of the country (over 400) and in all thirty-six provinces. As of May 2012, anti-corruption courts have been established in the capital cities of thirty-three provinces.

8. Emil Bolongaita, "A New Model for an Anti-Corruption Agency? Indonesia's Corruption Eradication Commission" (presentation at the Symposium on the Fundamentals of an Effective Anti-Corruption Commission, Asian Institute of Management, Makati City, May 6, 2011).

9. "Attacks After Reports on Police Corruption in Indonesia," Deutsche Welle, July 20, 2010, www.dw-world.de.

10. Bolongaita, "New Model for an Anti-Corruption Agency?"; Tim Lindsey, "Indonesia's Gecko-Gate," *The Australian*, November 20, 2009, www.theaustralian.com.au.

11. The case study on CICAK is based on interviews conducted in April 2009 with Dadang Trisasongko, then with Kemitraan and presently executive director of Transparency International Indonesia, and Illian Deta Arta Sari, Danang Widojoko, and Emerson Yuntho of Indonesia Corruption Watch, who were all directly involved in the campaign. They spoke with me in a personal capacity, not reflecting their institutional affiliations.

12. For example, in the wake of its ruling, the Constitutional Court gave the Parliament until 2009 to create a new law establishing the KPK and the Corruption Court. Representatives delayed passing new legislation, which was seen as an attempt to extinguish it. In September 2009 an anticorruption bill was drafted that would have severely curtailed the KPK's powers by abolishing its authority to conduct wiretaps and prosecute corruption suspects. As of August 2011, efforts to pass a KPK provision bill continued. According to Transparency International Indonesia, "The initiative has been much criticized as unnecessary and a move to strip the KPK of its authority"; Ilham Saenong, "Indonesian NGOs Protest an Unnecessary Revision of Anti-Corruption Laws," Transparency International, http://www.ti.or.id/en; Norimitsu Onishi, "Corruption Fighters Rouse Resistance in Indonesia," *New York Times*, July 26, 2009, www.nytimes.com; Christian von Luebke, "The Politics of Reform: Political Scandals, Elite Resistance, and Presidential Leadership in Indonesia," *Journal of Current Southeast Asian Affairs* 29, no. 1 (2010): 79–94.

13. The government spent US$710 million in a rescue of Bank Century, a small bank reportedly comprising shareholders and depositors from among the country's wealthiest families. The collapse was due to embezzlement of funds. The bailout amount—ultimately five times greater than what the Parliament had authorized—was not used to recapitalize the bank but was distributed directly to shareholders and depositors; Tom Allard, "President Swept Up in Indonesian

Corruption Scandal," *Sydney Morning Herald*, November 21, 2009, www.smh
.com.au.

14. Von Luebke, "Politics of Reform."

15. Irawaty Wardany, "SBY's In-Law Aulia Pohan Gets 4.5 Years for Corruption," *Jakarta Post*, June 17, 2009, www.thejakartapost.com; on August 17, 2010, Indonesia's Independence Day, President Yudhoyono gave a remission and pardon to Pohan, who ended up serving less than two years of the four-and-a-half-year sentence, which had already been reduced to three years. "Govt to Cut Graft Convicts Prison Terms for Idul Fitri," *Jakarta Post*, September 9, 2010, www.thejakartapost.com.

16. Michael Buehler, "Of Geckos and Crocodiles: Evaluating Indonesia's Corruption Eradication Efforts" (presentation, CSIC/USINDO, Washington, DC, November 23, 2009), http://csis.org; "Released KPK Officers Bibit and Chandra Overwhelmed by Public Support," *Jakarta Globe*, November 4, 2009, www.thejakartaglobe.com.

17. Antasari was an ambiguous figure in the KPK, seen by some as an anti-corruption champion but found to engage in questionable practices, such as meeting outside his office with witnesses under investigation. Indonesia Corruption Watch objected to his appointment in 2007. In November 2009 a police precinct chief, Williardi Wizard, testified that he was ordered to take part in a conspiracy to frame Antasari. Nevertheless, in June 2010 the former commissioner was sentenced to eighteen years in prison. In February 2012 the Supreme Court rejected a case review request. The murder victim's own brother previously testified that there were irregularities in the accused former antigraft chief's conviction; Haryanto Suharman, "Supreme Court Turns Down Antasari's Case Review," *Indonesia Today*, February 13, 2012, www.theindonesiatoday.com; Rangga Prasoka, "Brother of Victim in Antasari Trial Tells the Court About His Doubts," *Jakarta Globe*, September 23, 2011, www.thejakartaglobe.com; Andreas Harsono, "The Gecko vs. the Crocodile," *Reporter's Notebook: Indonesia, Global Integrity Report*, 2009, http://report.globalintegrity.org; "Antasari 'Framed,'" *Jakarta Post*, November 11, 2009, www.thejakartapost.com; Illian Deta Arta Sari and Emerson Yuntho, Indonesia Corruption Watch, interview, April 2009.

18. In Indonesia, Susno Duadji is referred to as Susno, Antasari Azhar as Antasari, and Bibit Samad Rianto and Chandra Hamzah as Bibit and Chandra. This chapter refers to them in this customary manner.

19. Arry Anggadha and Desi Afrianti, "Bibit dan Chandra Diperiksa Sebagai Saksi," vivanews.com, September 15, 2009, http://korupsi.vivanews.com.

20. Harsono, "Gecko vs. the Crocodile."

21. Ibid.; Suhartono, "Ternyata, Perppu No. 4/2009 Ada Penjelasannya," KOMPAS.com, September 24, 2009, http://nasional.kompas.com.

22. Onishi, "Corruption Fighters Rouse Resistance in Indonesia."

23. Ibid.

24. Rusian Burhani, "Number of 'Facebookers' Supporting KPK Reaches One Million," Antara News, November 7, 2009, www.antaranews.com.

25. Pandaya, "Gecko, Crocodile, Godzilla, and the Politics of Brute Force," *Jakarta Times,* August 11, 2009, www.thejakartapost.com.

26. Von Luebke, "Politics of Reform."

27. Usman Yasin was at the Muhammadiyah University in the province of Bengkulu on Sumatra.

28. Carolina Rumuat, "Indonesia: Criminalizing the Graft Fighters," *Global Voices*, November 3, 2009, http://globalvoicesonline.org.

29. The artists were the band Slank as well as Fariz M, Once From Dewa, Jimo Kadi, Cholil, and Netral; Rina Widiastuti, "Indonesian Artists Create a Song to Support KPK," *TEMPO interactive*, November 4, 2009, www.tempo interactive.com.

30. The teacher's blog was from the Senior High School of Northern Jakarta (SMA 13 Jakarta); Retnolistyarti's Blog, "Pernyataan Sikap Antikorupsi Siswa SMAN 13 Jakarta," blog entry, March 4, 2012, http://retnolistyarti.wordpress .com.

31. Anthony Saich, David Dapice, Tarek Masoud, Dwight Perkins, Jonathan Pincus, Jay Rosengard, Thomas Vallely, Ben Wilkinson, and Jeffrey Williams, *From Reformasi to Institutional Transformation: A Strategic Assessment of Indonesia's Prospects for Growth, Equity, and Democratic Governance* (Boston: Harvard Kennedy School Indonesia Program, 2010), 147.

32. Lindsey, "Indonesia's Gecko-Gate."

33. I saw some of the graffiti at major intersections while doing field research in Jakarta during April 2010.

34. The lawyer was Adnan Buyung Nasution.

35. A portion of the wiretap recordings was originally leaked to the media on October 29, but the contents were not made public until November 3.

36. The businessman was Anggodo Widjojo (also spelled Widjaja). His brother Anggoro, who escaped to Singapore, was under a KPK investigation for bribing forestry department officials over contracts and in order to cut down protected mangrove forests in South Sumatra for a seaport development. Harsono, "Gecko vs. the Crocodile."

37. Allard, "President Swept Up."

38. "Released KPK Officers Bibit and Chandra Overwhelmed by Public Support."

39. Videos from the rally can be found at www.engagemedia.org/search ?SearchableText=cicak.

40. Prodita Sabarini, "Thousands of People Rally for 'CICAK,'" *Jakarta Post*, November 9, 2009, www.thejakartapost.com.

41. Indonesia has the largest Muslim population of any country in the world. It also recognizes the following religions practiced in the country: Buddhism, Confucianism, Christianity, and Hinduism.

42. Jafar Sidik, "Gus Dur vouches for Two KPK Deputy Chiefs' Innocence," Antaranews.com, October 31, 2009, www.antaranews.com/en.

43. Irawaty Wardany and Erwida Maulia, "Support Mounts for Arrested KPK Deputies," *Jakarta Post*, November 1, 2009, www.thejakartapost.com.

44. Ibid.

45. The defamation article in the Indonesian Penal Code is used by officials to clamp down on activists and reformers, and to restrict dissent and freedom of expression. For additional information about various cases, including those of Yuntho and Deta Arta Sari, see Urgent Appeals Programme and Indonesia Desk, "Indonesia: Two Activists Are Accused of Criminal Defamation by the Attorney General After Questioning Gaps in His Annual Budget," Asian Human Rights Commission, November 4, 2009, www.humanrights.asia.

46. There are other cases of intimidation and violence toward anticorruption activists and journalists. In 2010 the office of *Tempo*, a leading investigative newsmagazine, was firebombed. An ICW activist was also hospitalized following an ambush by four assailants with metal rods; Bagus Saragih, "Joint Team to Investigate Assault," *Jakarta Post*, July 13, 2010, www.thejakartapost.com.

47. "'Gecko vs. Crocodile,' 2009," *Jakarta Post*, November 24, 2009, www.thejakartapost.com.

48. Karishma Vaswani, "Indonesia Fights Corruption with People Power," BBC, November 6, 2009, http://news.bbc.co.uk.

49. "Susno: Police Had Special Team to Target Antasari, Bibit, Chandra," *Jakarta Post*, December 11, 2010, www.thejakartapost.com.

50. "An Unlikely Indonesian 'Hero,'" *Asia Sentinel*, April 5, 2010, http://alicepoon.asiasentinel.com.

51. Von Luebke, "Politics of Reform"; Harsono, "Gecko vs. the Crocodile."

52. For an in-depth examination of President Yudhoyono's contradictory signals and actions vis-à-vis the KPK, see Buehler, "Of Geckos and Crocodiles."

53. Von Luebke, "Politics of Reform."

54. Bagus BT Saragih, "Until the Bitter End, SBY Mum on Task Force," *Jakarta Post*, December 31, 2011, www.thejakartapost.com.

55. At the very end of 2010 President Yudhoyono indicated he would extend the tenure of the task force for two additional years. However, he did not. Assessments of the Task Force's impact are mixed. For an analysis, see Rendi Witular, "Judicial Mafia Task Force: The Unsung Crusader," December 29, 2011, www.thejakartapost.com.

56. Footage of the "Save KPK" nonviolent intervention can be viewed at http://vimeo.com/51039023.

57. Arghea Desafti Hapsari, "Zero Tolerance for 'Judicial Mafioso': CICAK," *Jakarta Post*, February 24, 2010, www.thejakartapost.com.

58. Pandaya, "Gecko, Crocodile, Godzilla."

59. Teten Masduki, "A Conversation with Teten Masduki," part 3, *Voices*, ANSA-EAP Online Channel, February 13, 2011, http://voices.ansa-eap.net.

60. Saich et al., *From Reformasi to Institutional Transformation*, 147.

61. Brian Martin, *Justice Ignited: The Dynamics of Backfire* (Lanham, MD: Rowman and Littlefield, 2007); Brian Martin, April 20, 2013, personal communication with the author.

62. Achmad Sukarsono and Agus Suhana, "Indonesians Hit Facebook, Streets to Protest Anti-Graft Arrest," Bloomberg.com, November 1, 2009, www.bloomberg.com.

63. Among the reformasi organizations, all founded in 1998, are Indonesia Corruption Watch, the human rights group KontraS (the Commission for "the Disappeared" and Victims of Violence), the National Law Reform Consortium, and the Indonesian Center for Law and Policy Studies (PSHK).

64. Teten Masduki, "A Conversation with Teten Masduki," part 2, *Voices*, ANSA-EAP Online Channel, February 6, 2011, http://voices.ansa-eap.net.

65. Hardy Merriman, "Forming a Movement" (presentation at the Fletcher Summer Institute for the Advanced Study of Strategic Nonviolent Conflict, Tufts University, June 20, 2011).

6

Nonviolent Resistance Against the Mafia: Italy

N onviolent resistance to the Mafia in Italy is not a new phenomenon. Many readers are familiar with the campaigns of Danilo Dolci, the activist, educator, social reformer, writer, and poet. Over the course of the second part of the twentieth century, Dolci strove "to break the closed circle of poverty" in Sicily.[1] Known as the Italian Gandhi, he targeted the Mafia and corrupt, conniving government and clerical power-holders, linking their malfeasance to the grinding destitution, hunger, and violence he witnessed on the island. His nonviolent tactics included fasts, demonstrations, manifestos, alternative social institutions, sit-ins, radio broadcasts disrupting the government's monopoly of the airwaves, strikes, and a reverse strike or "work-in" that garnered international attention.[2] Dolci and his followers—from illiterate villagers to trade unionists and intellectuals—challenged acquiescence to the exploitative system, pressured the state to support local development (including the construction of a long-awaited dam and access to clean water), and fostered community empowerment and cooperation. In spite of these collective efforts, the Mafia's grip on Sicily remained tight. But in the first decade of the new century, a group of young people resumed the unfinished struggle.

Context

Corruption and the Mafia

For Edoardo Zaffuto, one of the founders of the youth anti-Mafia movement Addiopizzo (Good-bye, protection money), corruption and organized crime are two illicit sides of the same coin.[3] In his hometown of Palermo, "[Corruption] is managed by the Mafia; they are the monopoly of the corrupt system."[4] The link between the two is not exclusive to Sicily; corruption and organized crime essentially go hand in hand.[5] The most common forms of collusion are between crime syndicates and corrupt officials at all levels of government.[6] As well, ties can exist between organized crime and political parties, members of Parliament, and various parts of the private sector, media, and organized religion.

Corruption can be a catalyst, facilitator, or by-product of organized crime. First, endemic corruption impedes growth, development, and legitimate economic and political activities. This situation creates an environment ripe for organized crime to emerge, as wealth can most easily be generated through illicit means, and a ready pool of disadvantaged and disaffected people, often youth, is available to be recruited.[7] Second, corruption can facilitate organized crime because criminal organizations need state complicity in order to avoid punishment and prosecution; engage in trafficking, smuggling, and money laundering; gain protection; and infiltrate the legitimate economy. Consequently, "Corruption provides criminal groups the opportunity to operate under relatively safe circumstances."[8] Finally, where organized crime flourishes, corruption also increases as such groups step up their efforts of collusion in order to facilitate their operations.

By the early 1990s, the long-established Cosa Nostra Mafia operated throughout Sicily, killing at will—including Libero Grassi in 1991, a Palermitan businessman who publicly refused to pay extortion money, and in 1992, two judges, Giovanni Falcone and Paolo Borsellino. Popular outrage over these assassinations sparked protests. Residents hung sheets with anti-Mafia slogans from balconies. But in these instances, people reacted to an external event, explained Zaffuto. "The problem was that when the shock went down, the movement disappeared."

As a result, the Mafia changed tactics. In what is described as the Corleone II phase, it kept a low profile and refrained from such brazen acts of violence in order to minimize public anger. Nevertheless, according to Zaffuto, the Mafia actively infiltrated the economy and sought new allies within the political class locally and nationally. An estimated 58 percent of Sicilian businesses overall, and 80 percent of those in Palermo, had in the previous decade paid protection money—known in the local slang as *pizzo*, referring to a bird's beak pecking here and there.[9] A 2007 study by Antonio La Spina, a University of Palermo professor who examined confiscated *pizzo* ledgers, calculated that in Sicily alone, the Mafia took in US$260 million. However, public resentment lingered below the surface, and more importantly, a new generation was beginning to question the status quo.[10]

Obstacles and Challenges

The biggest obstacle for grassroots resistance to the Mafia was people's mind-set. In Sicily there was a pervasive climate of fear coupled with apathy. The public generally felt powerless that things could be different or that they themselves could be drivers of such change. Traditionally, an anti-Mafia stance was seen as a legal battle, delegated to experts. Additionally, the Mafia had a system of control, enrichment, and power to which people were accustomed. Paying pizzo was not only the norm, it was a habit. As those who singularly rebelled were inevitably punished, they were considered foolhardy by the populace.

As time went by, Addiopizzo discerned other challenges, what they came to call "hidden opponents." These included the commercial and professional organizations, which in the past discouraged their members from speaking up or going to the police, in part because so many had ties to the Mafia or were paying pizzo. When Grassi defied the Mafia, he was abandoned and even criticized by the Sicilian branch of Confindustria, the Italian employers' confederation.[11] Finally, the political establishment was viewed as an obstacle. Traditionally, politicians were quite hesitant to speak out against organized crime. Some have been found to have ties to the Cosa Nostra; more recently, some politicians bluster anti-Mafia rhetoric in order to gain popularity but do not follow through with actions, stated Zaffuto.

From Sticker to Social Movement

Origins

"In the beginning there was a sticker."[12] Resembling a traditional Sicilian obituary notice affixed to neighborhood lampposts, it read, "An entire people who pays pizzo is a people without dignity." On the morning of June 29, 2004, when the residents of Palermo, Italy, ventured out of their homes, they found their town plastered with these stickers. A spontaneous act by seven friends set in motion a chain of events that gave birth to a powerful anti-Mafia movement that is inspiring others. The youth had come together to talk about opening a pub when one said that they should not forget about having to pay pizzo. That distasteful realization prompted their defiance. The response from the townsfolk, however, took them by surprise. Rather than the usual silence, people began to react. According to Zaffuto, "It was a shock. It forced people to think about what was taboo." In the coming days, the group brought more friends together and decided to create a website, which garnered more support from others who wanted to become involved.

During the first year, the youth remained anonymous, but they concluded that they had to come forward if they expected fellow citizens to do the same. Several went public together, to show that the group had no leader and also to protect themselves, as the Mafia's proclivity is to attack lone dissenters. During 2005 they launched several daring nonviolent actions. Taking inspiration from the 1992 sheet protests, they hung their own with anti-Mafia slogans on the railings and bridges of the city's ring road. At a soccer match they unfurled a sheet that said, "United Against the Pizzo," along with their website address, which garnered more support, including from Giorgio Scimeca, the owner of a village pub who had refused to pay extortion money and subsequently lost his customers. Upon learning about his plight, Addiopizzo rallied around him. In February and March of that year, every Saturday night a group of youth traveled to the countryside to patronize the establishment, showing the locals that people in Palermo supported the owner. Consequently, the villagers surmounted their fear and came back. The bar was saved, and the Mafia has since left it alone. Scimeca became the first business owner to formally take the anti-pizzo pledge.

Vision, Mission, and Early Strategies

While engaging in these nonviolent tactics, the group began strategizing and planning about how to harness this outpouring of attention and energy. Their vision is to wrest Sicily from Mafia control and, above all, to gain freedom. "For us living in Palermo, the Cosa Nostra is a power more similar to a dictatorship," said Zaffuto. "They control the economy, politics, even the way people think. They influence our everyday life even when we don't realize it." As an example, he cited poor neighborhoods under Mafia control, which he said are deliberately kept depressed so that people remain dependent on the mob. Even public funds—taxpayers' money—go to the Mafia; through a combination of corruption and intimidation, organized crime influences public tenders. "This fight, for these things, is to free ourselves," he said.

To this end, Addiopizzo's mission is to "push people to stand up to Mafia domination."[13] The young strategists astutely reasoned that it was impossible to confront the Mafia in its entirety, which is a vast, layered, mostly covert network. Nor could Addiopizzo focus on every type of illicit activity. Thus, they decided to stick to their initial target of pizzo for a number of reasons:

- It serves as a symbol of an economy twisted and controlled by organized crime.
- Pizzo is the most visible aspect of the oppressive system, and is real rather than abstract.
- Pizzo affects the entire community, either directly or indirectly.
- Pizzo is easily understood by regular citizens.
- The injustice runs counter to people's sense of fairness.
- It stunts Palermo's economic development.[14]
- Pizzo is the principal method through which the Mafia exerts domination over citizens and territory.[15]
- Extortion is an important source of income and is used to support the Mafia structure. They use pizzo to pay the "wages" of extortionists and other lower-level operatives, cover the fees of lawyers defending accused mafiosi, and provide financial support to families of jailed mafiosi.

An initial insight was that Addiopizzo had touched a nerve that had not been disturbed in the past: collective shame. However, this feeling needed to be fused with a sense of collective responsibility in order to mobilize citizens. To this end, the movement's founding propositions were as follows:

- If you live in a town that pays protection money, you are part of the system and helping the Mafia.
- The time has come to get over the idea that the anti-Mafia fight is delegated to others, that people themselves cannot do anything about the Mafia.
- Everyone has a responsibility to do something.
- Every single person in Palermo who agrees can be part of this movement.

Inspired by fair-trade products, ethical purchases, and consumer boycott campaigns, the youth came up with the idea of "ethical consumerism"—bringing together two major sectors in Palermo: businesses that refuse to pay pizzo and consumers who support them. To launch this initiative required cumulative steps, as shop owners were frightened and locals felt disempowered.

Not to be daunted, Addiopizzo came up with an interim strategy: identify people who would pledge to patronize future pizzo-free businesses. Addiopizzo painstakingly collected and published the names of 3,500 Palermitans. Zaffuto reported that, for the city, "It was a big deal!" The tactic was not only bold and unusual, it constituted the movement's first collective act of anti-Mafia resistance involving regular citizens. Through the list, Addiopizzo demonstrated power in numbers, which they understood was essential in order to defy organized crime. The list also became a potent tool for the second step of their strategy: convincing businesses to publicly refuse to pay pizzo. "We showed [the owners] all these people won't leave you alone," recalled Zaffuto. The movement argued that, in the past, those who rebelled—such as Libero Grassi—were on their own and were actually deserted by their fellow entrepreneurs. Thus, it was easy for the Mafia to silence them, just as an individual worker can be suppressed with more ease than a collection of workers in a union. But now, Addiopizzo and thousands of Palermitans would stand by those who refused to obey the crime syndicate, and not only provide visible solidarity but also economic support as consumers. In one year, through great effort, Addiopizzo succeeded in getting one hundred businesses on board.

According to Aldo Penna, the owner of Il Mirto e la Rosa restaurant, there are three types of owners who join the movement: those who open a business and don't want to pay from the outset (often young entrepreneurs), those who are paying and want to stop, and those caught by the police because their name was in a confiscated pizzo ledger. Once involved, a chain reaction is activated as each business not only becomes an example to others but the owner actively recruits new members. For Penna, associating with Addiopizzo "provided the way to keep the Mafia away."[16] Ultimately, his vision is for "a normal city without violence and fear."

Consumo Critico (Ethical Consumerism)

On June 29, 2006, at a major press conference, Addiopizzo officially launched the Consumo Critico campaign, the keystone defining method of the movement. The first objective of the campaign was to shift public awareness about collective responsibility and power. The movement drove home the following message: "In Palermo, 80 percent of the shops pay pizzo. When I buy something, I indirectly finance the Mafia. I am part of the 'entire people without dignity.' What can I do, what is my power? I am a consumer. I can choose." That citizens can play a role in the struggle through simple daily acts such as shopping was a revolutionary notion, said Zaffuto. The campaign created catchy slogans encompassing these messages: *Contro Il Pizzo, Cambi I Consumi* (Against pizzo, change your shopping habits) and *Pago Chi Non Paga* (I pay those who don't pay). The campaign was based upon two complementary tactics—businesses refusing to pay pizzo and a reverse boycott, whereby consumers support those establishments that are Mafia-free. These civic actions undermined the crime group through civil disobedience (disobeying the Cosa Nostra), power of numbers (active moral and economic solidarity with those who disobeyed, thereby encouraging defiance and making repression more difficult), and disruption (of the crime group's system of control and enrichment).

A set of supplementary tactics was developed in the ensuing years to bolster the initiative, including

- Special stickers on windows of pizzo-free shops, which can be seen on the streets of Palermo today.
- Pizzo-free yellow pages.
- Product labeling.
- Website and e-newsletters.
- Maps with locations of the businesses.
- Annual three-day "Pizzo-Free Festival" in May, including stalls, food, performances, music, workshops, and above all, the opportunity for the anti-Mafia businesses and citizens to meet one another en masse.
- Music and theatre skits.
- Pizzo-free emporium opened by a movement member.
- Sports—following the suggestion of an athlete, Mafia-free shopkeepers sponsored a semiprofessional basketball team, Addiopizzo Basket, which garnered media attention from local television and sports newspapers. The objective was to demonstrate how sports can also incorporate ethical practices, as there have been cases of fake athletic sponsorships for tax evasion.
- Pressuring public institutions and the municipality to adopt the practices of ethical consumerism in their procurement and contracting activities. The movement only had occasional success with this tactic, with a few schools and some public events that needed goods and services, such as catering.
- Joint rallies and demonstrations with other civic groups—for example, to demand the resignation of Salvatore Cuffaro, then governor of Sicily. He stepped down in January 2008, after being convicted of passing state secrets to a Mafia godfather while in office. He was finally jailed in January 2011 after losing a final appeal.[17]

In order to prevent Mafia infiltration and check the veracity of business owners who sought to join Addiopizzo, the youth set up a volunteer subgroup to conduct inquiries. Through this effort, Zaffuto remarked that they have cultivated good contacts with some of the police and have developed "a variety of expertise."

Retaliation and Backfire

At first, according to Zaffuto, the Mafia didn't take Addiopizzo seriously. But by 2006, as the movement was eroding the mob's reign of fear over Palermo and the number of businesses openly defying extortion grew to 230, the Cosa Nostra retaliated.[18] On July 31, 2007, it set fire to the warehouse of a painting and hardware distribution company owned by Addiopizzo member Rodolfo Guajana. The movement faced an existential test. The youth knew that they had to rally support and help Guajana get back into business. "If he failed, we would all fail because it would have shown that we cannot protect people who reject the Mafia," explained Zaffuto. Rather than cower, the movement made the Mafia's violence backfire. It rallied support from citizens, who collected money for the unemployed staff. The youth worked behind the scenes and demonstrated on the street to secure a new and bigger warehouse from the Sicilian government through anti-Mafia compensation laws. A few months later, Guajana was back in business, and two men were convicted for the arson, Mafia boss Salvatore Lo Piccolo and one of his thugs.[19]

Addiopizzo youth are also in the field to protect honest officials and rebellious shopkeepers. They conduct sit-ins and send letters to local and national newspapers in solidarity with judges, and supporting businesspeople who denounce the Cosa Nostra. In a case that sent shock waves through Palermo, Vincenzo Conticello, the owner of the oldest restaurant in Palermo, Antica Focacceria San Francesco, publicly identified his extortionist in court in October 2007. He said later, "The moment I arrived at the court, I saw a huge crowd. Many young people with the 'Goodbye Pizzo' T-shirt. The presence of all these people really gave me strength. I realized that it wasn't just my personal battle; it was the battle of an entire city."[20]

Tactical Diversity

Addiopizzo conducts a host of actions that are strategically derived to further short-term or longer-term objectives. It has an on-the-ground presence in Palermo in order to directly engage citizens, communicate messages, build support, and keep the anti-Mafia rebellion visible. The youth commemorate the loss of "anti-Mafia martyrs" by cooperating with other civic groups such as Fondazione Falcone on events or holding their own actions. In 2008 and 2009 they organized a bike march from the location where Libero Grassi was murdered to symbolic landmarks where victories have been won against the Cosa Nostra. More recently, a special effort is being made to reach out to young people in general, who, Zaffuto says, "are eager to be involved, but they want someone to push them." As a result, Addiopizzo is organizing socially oriented events in pizzo-free spaces such as bookstores and restaurants.

Systemic Approach

The movement grew to realize that focusing only on organized crime wasn't enough. A system of linkages exists between it and other parts of society, consisting of interdependent relationships, common interests, and mutual gain. For Zaffuto, "That is why it's been so hard to beat the Mafia." The movement now sees the struggle as having three components—first and foremost the economic realm, but also the social/cultural and the political realms—all of which require ongoing tactics designed to disrupt the entire system.

Unity

To this end, the movement began to strategize over how to build a broad social consensus and undermine the ties between organized crime and various parts of society. "Year by year we try to ally with new sectors," said Zaffuto. For example, a committee has been established to reach out to the influential Catholic Church establishment, which traditionally has been quiet about the Mafia. In addition to engaging university students and professors, Addiopizzo established contact with higher education administrations. For instance, since 2005, in the administrative letter sent to each student at the beginning of the academic year, the University of Palermo includes a statement of support for the movement and a form that students can complete and mail back to become "Addiopizzo consumers." As well, the movement has developed good relations with the anti-Mafia branches of the police and judiciary. Ignazio De Francisci, a senior investigative magistrate in Palermo, sees them as the most inspiring symbol of the new fearlessness of the population.[21]

Ethics and Accountability

"The history of the Mafia is connected to official power," observed Zaffuto. To weaken these ties, Addiopizzo devised a twofold strategy. First, the movement works—often in cooperation with other civic groups—to expose political collaboration (regardless of party affiliation) with the Cosa Nostra and to pressure public institutions and politicians to adopt policies and bills that undermine these links and increase accountability. Tactics include joint street demonstrations with other civic groups and support for honest politicians and officials. Second, the movement seeks to build public awareness that even voting can help maintain the Mafia's hegemony, and citizens can thus wield power through their votes to demand integrity and withdraw support from those who collaborate with organized crime. Prior to local, regional, and even national elections, the movement conducts "name-and-shame communication campaigns." They release information about candidate backgrounds and Mafia ties while building awareness about the consequences of vote buying and Mafia corruption.

However, the impact has not been invariably successful. For example, during the 2007 mayoral elections in Palermo, Addiopizzo attempted to get all five candidates to promise in writing to take specific measures against the Mafia if elected. The incumbent and eventual winner, Diego Cammarata, refused. This was a lesson, according to Zaffuto, that "Addiopizzo needs to be louder and stronger on the political side without losing its nonpartisan reputation."

Education
Quite early on, the civic initiative recognized that to transform Palermitan society, it was necessary to begin with children, so that the next generation would have a different mind-set about the Mafia and corruption. As early as 2004, the youth began conducting informal meetings and talks at schools. They soon were approached by elementary, middle, and high school teachers, university student groups, and even professors. They developed a multifaceted program to engage and educate young people.[22] The objectives, explained Francesca Vannini, who runs the projects, are to re-create the dynamics of Addiopizzo in the schools, motivate children to think about the problems caused by the Mafia, set goals for activities and develop strategies to reach their goals, and encourage students to work together in a "creative and grassroots way."

The program has evolved over the years and is adapted for different grade levels. Addiopizzo volunteers facilitate all the activities in cooperation with teachers. In 2007 the movement launched Addiopizzo Junior, which are clubs starting at the elementary level. Children organize events, such as sending out notices to the movement's e-list of ethical consumers, and getting together at a Mafia-free *gelateria* (ice cream café), where they can meet the owner and ask questions. One group even composed an anti-Mafia rap song and performed it for Giorgio Napolitano, the president of Italy. That same year, the national Ministry of Education learned about the program, which led to financial support for educational activities. Also in 2009, children in twenty-three schools conducted surveys about attitudes toward the Mafia in their localities, including in economically deprived neighborhoods associated with organized crime. Accompanied by a teacher and a movement volunteer, children asked fifteen questions of locals, from their own parents to neighbors and shopkeepers. A video and book were released out of the collective experience. By 2010, seventy-three schools were involved in the educational program, of which twenty-five had allocated a special room for meetings called Fortino de la Legalità (legality fort).

Strength Through Expansion and Diversification
While the movement's focus is on the Cosa Nostra in Palermo, the youth believe that their struggle has no boundaries. As word of their actions grew, inquiries and requests for talks began to come in from across Italy. Other people in the country wanted to take part in the struggle, and the youth could gain valuable allies and support as well as increase participation in the movement, generate funds, bring in new business for pizzo-free enterprises, and inform the public. As a result, two new initiatives were born in 2009. The first is Addiopizzo Community. Its strategic objective is to build a "social network that can be a tool for supporters of the civic initiative to meet and discuss," reports Zaffuto. Members pay a modest EUR 10 fee to join and can also purchase T-shirts, both of which contribute funds for the movement. By 2011, there were approximately 1,000 members, including non-Italians. The second is Addiopizzo Travel; this commercial arm organizes educational and recreational pizzo-free tours of Sicily in Italian, English, and German. For tourists, Addiopizzo Travel conducts a range of organized tours as well as Mafia-free tourism options for independent travelers. "We want people to discover the real Sicily and show them that not all Sicilians are mafiosi, but also educate them about the anti-Mafia struggle," said Zaffuto. School trips are designed for different age groups, providing "cultural awareness through firsthand experience of a living revolution."[23] They combine sightseeing with on-the-ground learning about the anti-Mafia struggle, including meetings with activists and veterans, such as those who struggled in earlier decades alongside Danilo Dolci.

In June 2011 another dimension was added to the educational tours: cooperation with universities. As part of an ongoing relationship between Addiopizzo and the Terrorism, Organised Crime, and Global Security MA degree program at Coventry University, twenty-four students took part in a study trip to Sicily.[24]

Movement Attributes

Image

The movement cultivated three strategic attributes concerning its image:

- *Youth*, not only in terms of age, but also in spirit. According to Enrico Colajanni, president of Libero Futuro, an antiracketeering association, for those in the older generation this attribute has been particularly important to revitalize the anti-Mafia struggle.[25] He said that for too long it had negative associations, such as sadness, murder, and dry legal strategies. The movement brought new life and a sense of hope to the struggle. Zaffuto echoed these impressions. He said, "With us there is joy. People see that anti-Mafia is no longer something sad."
- *Rebellion*, channeled into action against what Addiopizzo views as "the most authoritarian power in Sicily, the Mafia."
- *Freedom* from the Mafia, for Palermo and its citizens.

Organization, Leadership, and Finances

The movement's structure evolved over time. Under Italian laws, in order to operate, it needed to have a legal identity. Consequently, on May 18, 2005, the group officially created a nonprofit association called the Comitato Addiopizzo. The movement has a core of about sixty young volunteers, many in their twenties, mostly university and high school students. Some of the original founders have now reached their thirties. From the outset, they decided to be open and transparent. The leadership is shared, both because of the collective nature of the movement and to avoid giving the Mafia targets. Addiopizzo has two decisionmaking bodies: the Direttivo, a core group of six elected members who have the authority to make quick decisions; and the General Assembly, composed of all members, in which decisions are taken by democratic vote.

Within the movement are working teams, each with its own focus—for example, business owners, the wider Addiopizzo community, the legal group staffed by young lawyers, educational programming, and institutional matters. Membership is fluid, both joining and leaving, said Zaffuto. Addiopizzo developed a procedure for involvement, whereby new recruits are quickly integrated through placement into the working teams. They are considered "rookies" and do not immediately have the right to vote. In 2011 Addiopizzo had ten staff persons through the

Servizio Civile Nazionale (National Civil Service), a state program that offers young adults (ages eighteen to twenty-eight) a twelve-month work opportunity in the civic realm.

As the movement has grown, so has it developed creative approaches to funding, such as the aforementioned Addiopizzo Travel. Yet it began and remains a voluntary organization, made possible through the time, skills, and efforts of its members, who initially pooled their own resources to cover outlays. It also accepts donations through its website. In 2007 the youth secured an apartment through the anti-Mafia compensation laws, which they converted into an office. In 2009 they received EUR 70,000 from the Ministry of Education, for the youth education initiatives involving cooperation with local schools. That year they applied for support in the amount of EUR 1,168,264 from the Ministry of the Interior for several activities, including the introduction of a "pizzo-free discount card" for consumers. The application was approved, and the funds were released in 2011.

Communications

The movement uses traditional and unconventional methods to channel its messages. It taps the ideas and energy from its own activists and the larger Addiopizzo community. Messages are delivered through stickers, sheets and banners, T-shirts, websites, web banners, social networking (Facebook, YouTube, blogging, Internet mailing lists, e-newsletters), leaflets, advertising (billboards), children's rap songs, poster contests in partnership with Solidaria (a civil society organization supporting Mafia victims), theatre skits, and media coverage and interviews. The overriding message has not changed since an impetuous group of friends plastered Palermo with stickers: "An entire people who pays pizzo is a people without dignity." But now, that sentiment has been balanced by a new, positive slogan: "An entire people that doesn't pay pizzo is a free people." Over the years, the movement has had two main targets:

- *Consumers:* Messages are designed to cultivate a sense of shared responsibility and participation in the struggle, through the notion that change can only happen through the cooperation of all in society.
- *Business owners:* Messaging seeks to make them feel comfortable with the idea that the time has come for change. Moreover, refusing to pay pizzo is not only ethical but financially beneficial, and now it is possible to be protected from the Mafia.

The communications strategy is undergoing an evaluation. Zaffuto acknowledged that they have not had a long-term strategy, and efforts have been largely event-driven. The youth are in the process of developing a "wider framework for communication."

Outcomes

By the end of 2012, there were 1,000 businesses in the network that publicly refuse to pay pizzo, mostly in Palermo and Catania.[26] "The Mafia doesn't ask for money from these businesses because they are a *camurria*" [Sicilian slang for a pain in the derrière], reported Zaffuto. When a detained mafioso used this term to slight the movement, activists took it as a compliment and a confirmation that their strategies and actions were working.[27] In fact, when Palermo's Deputy prosecutor of the Anti-Mafia Directorate, Calogero Ferrara, listened to police wiretaps, he heard mafiosi ordering their henchmen not to target an Addiopizzo store because they won't be paid and they fear getting arrested.[28] By 2008 the list of consumers grew to 10,000. At that point, they decided it was no longer necessary to maintain the list because public consciousness had shifted and "people didn't need to sign anything anymore," said Zaffuto.

Another outcome was Libero Futuro. The name has a double meaning—a "future with freedom" and a "future in the name of Libero [Grassi]." Established by "oldies" in 2007, this apolitical, voluntary civic group is a "strategic instrument," founded to complement Addiopizzo, said Colajanni.[29] It added a heretofore missing element to the struggle and the people power dynamic of disruption—encouraging business owners to testify to the police and the courts against extortionists. While the youth movement emboldens businesses to refuse to pay pizzo and mobilizes citizens around them, Libero Futuro increases the risk for the Mafia to demand extortion money.[30] It accomplishes this objective by working individually with businesspeople to go through the denunciation (*denuncia*) process, which Colajanni states is the only way to cut ties with the Mafia once extortion has begun. Libero Futuro provides legal, economic, and psychological support and services every step of the way. Once the judicial track is over, it encourages the entrepreneurs to join the civic initiative and take the anti-pizzo pledge. Libero Futuro has forty members and, since its founding, has helped over 150 shopkeepers and entrepreneurs. As with Addiopizzo, Libero Futuro sees its power coming from the grass roots. Colajanni explained, "We need to start from the bottom so we can push.

We have to organize a community of people against the Mafia, so when someone denounces a mafioso, they are not alone."[31] For Zaffuto, Libero Futuro and Addiopizzo are "two faces of the same strategy." "We complete each other," he reflected.

A third outcome was denunciation cases. In 2007 Addiopizzo had a breakthrough when it was approached by a businessperson already paying pizzo who wanted to stop and break free from the Mafia's clutches. It was an affirmation that the movement could offer protection— through people power—that did not exist in the past. In 2008 the movement and Libero Futuro convinced several owners, whose names were found in a confiscated pizzo ledger, to testify against the Mafia. Between 2007 and 2010 Zaffuto reported that fifty shopkeepers denounced, or in his words, "rebelled" against the Mafia.

The youth movement also inspired new civic initiatives beyond Palermo. When the Addiopizzo stickers were launched in 2010, it posted a free download on its website to encourage others to resist the Mafia. The stickers soon started appearing in other parts of Sicily. Thanks to the antiracket association FAI (Federazione Nazionale Antiracket), an ethical consumerism campaign was launched in Naples.[32] The campaign spread to the towns of Catania and Messina.[33] The impact can be felt all the way in Germany. In 2007, after the Ndrangheta Mafia went on a murder spree, killing six Italians one night in Duisberg, Laura Garavini, an Italian German, took direct inspiration from Addiopizzo. Together with some Italian restaurant owners, she founded Mafia Nein Danke (Mafia no thanks) in Berlin. Many more soon joined, and all were required to take a written pledge "not to employ any person maintaining contact with Mafia groups and to report every attempt of blackmailing to the police."[34] In December of that year, after dozens of Italian restaurant owners had been threatened and one establishment set on fire, forty-four businesspeople reported the extortion to the Berlin police.[35]

Finally, a breakthrough outcome concerned shifting complacent or complicit sectors. Addiopizzo and Libero Futuro's efforts to change policies and practices among the commercial and professional associations continue. On August 29, 2010, the groups achieved an important victory. Ivan Lo Bello, president of the Sicilian branch of Confindustria, the Italian employers' association, asserted that it had expelled all members who had contacts with the Mafia, including those who payed extortion money. He also extended an apology to Grassi's widow for their "abandonment of her husband," declaring, "the moral responsibility of the assassination is ours."[36] In addition, the Sicilian regional branch of Confcommercio, the main entrepreneurs' association in the fields of trade/sales, tourism, and services, began cooperating with Addiopizzo in 2010, resulting in 140 of its member businesses joining the movement.

Case Analysis

Expanding and Reframing the Struggle
"Addiopizzo added a new actor to the anti-Mafia struggle—the citizen," reflected Colajanni. Any Palermitan can be a part of the community that wants to reclaim its dignity and gain freedom from organized crime. Even children are viewed as players and are engaged through educational programs and creative tactics, such as neighborhood surveys. While the geographical focus is Palermo, the struggle arena has no boundaries. Regular people, inside the country and internationally, can participate through the Addiopizzo Community and Addiopizzo Travel. The movement deliberately set out to reframe the struggle from a legalistic, law enforcement approach removed from people's daily lives. The youth cultivated a sense of rebellion that combined a feeling of shared responsibility with individual acts of resistance, from refusing to pay pizzo to patronizing Mafia-free shops. They invigorated the struggle by balancing the negative—oppression and suffering—with the positive—collective empowerment, hope, and change through incremental victories.

Deconstructing the Racketering System
In order to effectively fight the Mafia, Addiopizzo, later with Libero Futuro, needed to understand how it functioned on the ground. While they, of course, did not have intimate knowledge, it was nevertheless possible to examine what made the mob strong and devise actions to change this. Three key, complementary strategies evolved that cumulatively increased disobedience to the Cosa Nostra:

1. *Disruption of the extortion system on the ground.* However complex the entire system of racketeering is, one crucial pillar upon which it rests is business owners complying with extortion threats. Hence, once a sizeable number of them begin refusing to pay, the system is disrupted and starts to weaken.

2. *Increasing risk.* Encouraging and supporting people willing to say no to the Mafia through testimonies against extortionists heightens the overall risk for the mob. As importantly, it increases risk for its foot soldiers, whom the criminal "godfathers" rely upon to intimidate businesses and collect pizzo.

3. *Replicating Mafia functions*. However dreadful it is, the Cosa Nostra carries out various functions. Addiopizzo and Libero Futuro understood that in order to impact the crime group, in some respects they have to beat it at its own game. The mob provides protection—from itself—through pizzo. Thus, this anti-Mafia front offers its own form of protection through people power. For some in Palermo, the Mafia engenders a sense of authority and collective identity; the movement cultivates an alternative collective community based on nonviolent resistance and dignity. The mob sponsors athletics—albeit as a front for money laundering. Addiopizzo supported a team, but through transparent contributions of clean money from extortion-free businesses. The Cosa Nostra has its network of legal enablers—such as lawyers, accountants, and unfortunately, even politicians—who are a source of know-how and resources. Libero Futuro provides business owners with legal, financial, and even psychological counsel, while Addiopizzo mobilizes citizens through reverse boycotts, which leads to sales—that is, resources and economic benefits—for those who refuse to pay protection money.

Provide a Way Out

A fundamental tenet of civil resistance is that not everyone associated with the oppressor is equally loyal. Through people power, switching loyalties and producing defections are possible, which also applies to the organized crime context. Whether they like it or not, those who pay pizzo are linked to the Cosa Nostra. However, many owners are complicit in the system because they fear the consequences of disobeying and cannot get out alone. Addiopizzo, Libero Futuro, and the collective actions of Palermitans present a safe way out of this venal, exploitative, and violent system. Offering a path for those within the illicit system to escape initiates a chain reaction. Each time someone is free of the mob, the movement gains an incremental victory that emboldens others to defect. Consequently, the anti-Mafia front doesn't need to motivate everyone at once in order to make progress.

Engagement

Where it fit with the movement's strategies and yielded benefits, youth engaged with the state. It cleverly made use of the legal system and anti-Mafia mechanisms by taking part in court cases and lawsuits against the Mafia and to gain reparations for businesses. As mentioned, it also secured confiscated Mafia properties for its office and replaced the torched warehouse of an Addiopizzo member. Finally, it identified and cultivated allies from within the school and university systems, Ministry of Education, law enforcement, and the judiciary.

Lessons Learned

Benefits of Grassroots Participation

Citizens have multiple talents and resources that civic initiatives can discover and nurture. They can be a source of creative strategies and tactics; their vigor, ideas, and skills can be encouraged and tapped, whether they are activists or regular people in the larger community. Colajanni observed, "Citizens bring a missing element and resources to the struggle. . . . If you organize people, you discover wonderful people, but when wonderful people are alone, their qualities don't come out."

In order to maximize people power, movements and campaigns need to develop multiple paths and an array of actions through which the public can participate. In the case of Addiopizzo, that included tapping existing civic organizations and fostering new initiatives. It launched diverse, innovative tactics, many of which were low-risk mass actions, such as patronizing Mafia-free businesses and fairs and attending basketball games. It systematically seeks to find new ways to appeal to and engage citizens, including youth.

Youth are often catalysts for change, not only because of their energy and creativity, but because they impact others around them, particularly the older generation. As an illustration, Zaffuto cited an outcome from their elementary school activities. A girl asked her father, a shopkeeper, whether he paid protection money. He was so ashamed to answer her that he contacted Addiopizzo. "His decision to rebel [against the Mafia] began with that question," recalled Zaffuto.

Strategic Considerations

Three strategic lessons can be gleaned from Addiopizzo. First, winning people over from within the corrupt system not only weakens the illicit status quo and removes support for oppressors; it can yield practical and even tangible benefits for the movement or campaign. Civic initiatives often overlook the latter point in their strategic deliberations. In this case, Addiopizzo cultivates contacts and cooperative relations with state institutions, law enforcement authorities, and professional organizations, in spite of the Mafia's links throughout the local society. The movement reaps benefits, such as the acquisition of information needed for its background checks on business owners who want to become part of the Mafia-free business community.

Second, Addiopizzo and Libero Futuro carefully studied the strengths, weaknesses, allies, enablers, attributes, and practices of the

Cosa Nostra, to the extent possible given its covert nature. Through this knowledge they were able to develop innovative tactics, compelling messages and symbols, and effective strategies, such as replicating particular Mafia functions and providing an escape from the illicit system.

Third, without realizing it, Addiopizzo put into practice a key insight of Mohandas Gandhi: "Even the most powerful cannot rule without the cooperation of the ruled."[37] They applied the concept not to a dictator or occupier but to a crime syndicate and its system of oppression, extortion, and corruption over the townspeople of Palermo.

Intangibles

Synergy—whereby various aspects of the movement (including strategy, tactics, targets, objectives, messages, and alliances) are complementary or mutually reinforcing—helps build unity, maximize resources, generate people power, and improve prospects for longevity.

As well, dynamism—encompassing ongoing review, assessment, and adaptation—is an integral attribute of effective civil resistance. It fosters sharp strategic deliberations, tactical diversity, and compelling messaging that contribute to a civic initiative's innovation, resilience, and ascendancy in the struggle.

Finally, as the efforts of a small group of activists evolve into an ongoing campaign or social movement involving hundreds if not thousands of people, leadership and organizational challenges can emerge. Finding a balance between dynamism and fluidity on the one hand, and a functional yet unencumbered structure and decisionmaking system on the other, can be critical to the civic initiative's sustainability.

Notes

1. Joseph Amato, "Danilo Dolci, A Poetic Modernizer," *Worldview*, December 1973, 32.

2. The latter was a form of civil disobedience whereby 200 jobless men repaired a road without compensation in defiance of police orders to desist. Seven were arrested. The action dramatized Sicily's pervasive unemployment, and the ensuing court case was used to test the right to work enshrined in the Italian constitution; Joseph Amato, "Danilo Dolci: A Nonviolent Reformer in Sicily," *Italian Americana* 4, no. 2 (Spring/Summer 1978): 215–235; "Danilo Dolci Leads Fast and Reverse Strike for Employment, 1956," Global Nonviolent Action Database, Swarthmore University, http://nvdatabase.swarthmore.edu.

3. There are many definitions of organized crime. A holistic definition is as follows: criminal activities for material benefit by groups that engage in extreme violence; corruption of public officials, including law enforcement and judicial officers; penetration of the legitimate economy (e.g., through racketeering and money laundering); and interference in the political process (Marie

Chêne, "U4 Expert Answer: Organised Crime and Corruption," U4 Anti-Corruption Resource Center, May 28, 2008).

4. This chapter is based on interviews with Edoardo Zaffuto, one of the founders of the Addiopizzo anti-Mafia movement in Palermo during June 2010, plus subsequent written communications, and a video presentation and Power-Point presentation (Clinton School of Public Service Speaker Series, University of Arkansas, April 27, 2009), www.clintonschoolspeakers.com.

5. Chêne, "U4 Expert Answer."

6. Ibid.

7. Ibid.

8. Ibid., 6.

9. Zaffuto, presentation.

10. *Italy: Taking on the Mafia*, PBS *Frontline* World Documentary (Boston: WGBH, 2009), www.pbs.org.

11. "Libero Grassi, Confindustria chiede scusa Ivan Lo Bello: 'Nostre responsabilità morali,'" *Il Fatto Quotidiano,* August 29, 2010, www.ilfattoquotidiano.it.

12. Zaffuto, presentation.

13. Ibid.

14. As an illustration of the scale of the economic distortion, a 2003 study by Indagine Censis-Fondazione estimated that if southern Italian businesses had not paid protection money from 1981 to 2001, the region's per capita GDP (gross domestic product) would have reached that of northern Italy.

15. Pizzo is the entry point through which the Mafia begins to take control of a business or sector. First come threats, which can escalate to overt intimidation, vandalism, and physical violence. Once pizzo is established, more demands are often made—for example, one-off pizzo; payment-in-kind; imposed staff, suppliers, subcontractors, sources of credit, or business practices; restrictions on the business; and partnerships, which finally can lead to expropriation.

16. Aldo Penna, pizzo-free restaurateur, Palermo, Italy, June 2010, interview with author.

17. Associated Press, "Governor of Sicily Quits After Conviction," *Seattle Times*, January 27, 2008, http://seattletimes.nwsource.com; "Sicily Senator Salvatore Cuffaro Jailed in Mafia Case," BBC News, January 23, 2011, www.bbc.co.uk.

18. Associated Press, "Sicilian Businessmen Openly Defying Mafia in Rebellion Shaking Cosa Nostra to Its Core," Katu.com, January 14, 2008, http://www.katu.com.

19. Katrina Onstad, "A New Way to See Sicily," *New York Times*, May 6, 2011, http://travel.nytimes.com.

20. *Italy: Taking on the Mafia.*

21. Joshua Hammer, "In Sicily, Defying the Mafia," *Smithsonian Magazine*, October 2010, www.smithsonianmag.com.

22. Francesca Vannini, Palermo, Italy, June 2010, interview with author.

23. Addiopizzo Travel, http://www.addiopizzotravel.it.

24. Ibid.

25. Enrico Colajanni, president, Libero Futuro, Associazione Antiracket Libero Grassi, Palermo, Italy, June 2010, interview with author.

26. Adrian Humphreys, "Beating the Mafia at Their Own Game: After Years of Paying a 'Protection Tax,' Palermo Businesses Came Together to Fight Back," *National Post*, January 23, 2013, www.addiopizzo.org.

27. Associated Press, "Governor of Sicily Quits After Conviction."

28. Humphreys, "Beating the Mafia."

29. Colajanni, interview with author.

30. Penna, interview with author.

31. Colajanni, interview with author.

32. Comitato Addiopizzo, www.pagochinonpaga.org/.

33. Rosaria Brancato, "'Pizzo Free,' a Messina inizia la campagna per il consumo critico 'pago chi non paga,'" *Tempostretto*, October 31, 2013, www.tempostretto.it.

34. Laura Garavini, "The Story of Mafia Nein Danke," http://www.garavini.eu.

35. Ibid.

36. "Libero Grassi."

37. Quote from Mohandas Gandhi, in Peter Ackerman and Jack DuVall, *A Force More Powerful: A Century of Nonviolent Conflict* (New York: Palgrave, 2000), 62.

7

A Citizen Pillar
Against Corruption: India

Every citizen can rise to be part of the 5th Pillar to make sure the
other four pillars of democracy are working properly for people.
—*Vijay Anand, president, 5th Pillar*

Changing an entrenched system of corruption embedded in the government, private sector, and other societal realms can seem daunting
if not impossible. The sheer dilemma of where to begin given so vast a
challenge, and the seeming difficulty of melding near-term visible
change with long-term societal transformation, can hinder civic initiatives before they even start. The burgeoning 5th Pillar movement in
India is charting a path through this conundrum by building upon the
legacy of a trailblazing forebear, the Right to Information movement,
and through a set of innovative, complementary nonviolent methods.

Context

The Right to Information movement began as a bottom-up struggle linking access to information with government transparency, powerholder
accountability, and the basics for survival, such as wages and food. At
the forefront was the grassroots social movement organization (SMO)
Mazdoor Kisan Shakti Sangathan (Union for the Empowerment of Peasants and Laborers), otherwise known as MKSS.[1] The national struggle
grew out of a civic initiative in a destitute village of approximately forty
families in Rajasthan in 1997.[2] What began as an antipoverty effort of
laborers to receive minimum wages due to them took a turn. "We determined that the underlying problems affecting working conditions and

137

wages in Rajasthan during this time were corruption and nepotism," said MKSS veteran Sowmya Kidambi.[3] In order to counter powerholder claims that the laborers had not completed their work assignments, MKSS began demanding access to local administration records, such as time measurement books, labor lists, copies of bills, and vouchers.[4] When the authorities refused, the Right to Information movement was born.

Over the years it conducted numerous people power campaigns involving a multitude of tactics, from hunger strikes and *dharnas* (short and extended sit-ins) to leafleting, picketing, street theatre, songs, truck *yatras* (journeys), and the Ghotala Rath Yatra (Chariot Rally of Scams), a traveling spoof of political campaigning. MKSS is perhaps best known for creating the *jan sunwai* (public hearing). The movement was a source of inspiration for Integrity Watch Afghanistan's community-monitoring initiatives (see Chapter 8), and its nonviolent methods were adapted by Muslims for Human Rights (MUHURI) in Kenya and neighboring African countries (see Chapter 10). In 1998 the movement achieved its first large-scale victory: consultations with the newly elected Rajasthani government to draft a provincial Right to Information Bill. In 2000 the bill was passed. Concurrently, in 1996, members of the MKSS core were instrumental in founding the National Campaign for People's Right to Information, which fought for a citizen-centered national Right to Information Act (RTI) through engagement with powerholders, nonviolent action, and networking with civil society organizations (CSOs) and civic groups.

The historic legislation was passed in October 2005. Shekhar Singh, a civic activist and academic, encapsulated the impact: "Usually the laws are for the government to control the people, but this law [India's Right to Information Act] turns all that around: it's for the people to evaluate the government."[5] It grants India's citizens access to information in any form held by public authorities, such as documents, logbooks, emails, contracts, or legal opinions.[6] Information can also be sought about nongovernmental organizations (NGOs) receiving funding from the state. The law's stipulations are astoundingly user-friendly, a reflection of the Right to Information movement's bottom-up input into its content. There is no official form. Citizens can request information on a sheet of paper from a government department by asking one or more questions.[7] With the right questions—therein lies the key—it's possible to document fraud, overcome corruption, hold officials accountable, and ultimately foster good governance.[8] In spite of incessant efforts to weaken the law and create obstacles for regular people, such as increasing RTI filing fees, a 2011 global rating of access to information laws ranked India's act the third strongest in the world.[9]

During the two and a half years after the RTI became law, an estimated 2 million applications were filed, 400,000 from rural locales and 1.6 million from urban settings.[10] A report from the province of Karnataka found that the number of RTI petitions and appeals jumped from 10,485 in 2005–2006 to 177,259 in 2009–2010.[11] While this growth is encouraging, research from 2008 indicates that an even greater potential exists for public awareness and use of the law to curb corruption and gain accountability. A civil society study focusing on ten states and the Delhi National Capital Territory found that 45 percent of randomly selected urban respondents and only 20 percent of focus group participants in 400 villages knew about the RTI.[12] A report commissioned by the Indian Department of Personnel and Training found that 33 percent of urban dwellers and 13 percent of rural residents were knowledgeable about the legislation.[13] It concluded that "the Act has not yet reached the stage of implementation which was envisaged."[14] Since 2005, numerous civil society efforts and even government-civic partnerships have sprung up around the country to raise public awareness and encourage regular citizens to use the RTI Act to fight state malfeasance. And then there is 5th Pillar, which has integrated RTI into a larger movement empowering regular people to thwart corruption.

The 5th Pillar "Eruption Against Corruption"

Origins
In 2001 Vijay Anand was an IT entrepreneur in the Washington, DC, area.[15] Concerned about social conditions in India, he and other like-minded NRIs (nonresident Indians) created the AIMS India Foundation, a charitable organization to foster socioeconomic development through projects on rural education, infrastructure, and health care. Over the next three years, as the urban, university-educated Anand began visiting rural areas during trips home, he started to realize that the dire conditions many of his fellow citizens faced were not simply because they lacked a school, well, or clinic. Corruption was a core obstacle to genuine socioeconomic improvements. "I found that several elements of society were not allowing development to happen," he recalled. There was not a culture of people making demands of powerholders, nor did many civil servants have a sense of responsibility for their jobs and duty to

their obligations. "It made me think that government officials need to be made accountable in order to get long-term change."

In 2004 Anand connected with M. B. Nirmal, a social entrepreneur and activist, who earlier had been formulating an informal anticorruption group in Chennai called 5th Pillar. Anand was taken by his ideas and formally launched 5th Pillar in the state of Tamil Nadu, along with a US-based nonprofit international headquarters, to encourage participation and funding from the Indian diaspora. Its name is derived from the four pillars of democracy. In addition to the legislature, executive branch, judiciary, and media, a healthy democracy needs a fifth pillar: an active, engaged citizenry striving for a country free from corruption. Anand moved back home in 2007 in order to build the civic initiative and start fieldwork. "I wanted to do more on a large scale and came back to India work in social activism," he said.

Vision, Mission, and Overall Objectives

5th Pillar's vision is, quite simply, to realize freedom from corruption.[16] The struggle is viewed as a continuation of the Indian independence movement. Anand avows, "India won freedom from the British occupation, and now it must win freedom from corruption." Its mission statement reads, "Encourage, enable, and empower every citizen of India to eliminate corruption at all levels of society."[17] The civic initiative's overall objective is to create a national culture of civic responsibility and intolerance of graft. It sees its efforts as a "second freedom movement after decades of independence."[18] "Everyone can be freedom fighters of India through noncooperation, nonviolence, and self-defense against bribery," explained Anand.[19]

Initial Challenges and Strategies

5th Pillar's leadership core faced a number of critical, existential challenges at the outset. First, they wanted to build an ongoing social movement rather than a finite campaign. Second, they did not want to sacrifice the movement's overarching vision of societal transformation, yet they understood it would be impossible to fight the entire venal system and take on all forms of corruption. Thus, the group had to find a way to distill tangible objectives from maximalist, long-term aspirations; narrow down the struggle arena and targets to a manageable size; link corruption to common grievances and injustice in order to mobilize people; articulate clear demands; and strive for visible, incremental successes. 5th Pillar also had to tackle three psychological barriers: cynicism about the government, hopelessness that things could change, and fear of corruptor reprisals, the latter a reality for activists as well as regular citizens.[20] Last, 5th Pillar leadership wanted to lay the foundation for systemic change down the road. "If we collectively as a nation say no to bribe, eventually it will end," Anand said. By pulling the plug on bribery, the entire system of corruption would start to unravel.

To this end, 5th Pillar adopted a dual-track strategy that emanated directly from its vision and mission statement:

1. *Motivate regular citizens to confront corruption through awareness-raising, direct assistance, practical education, nonviolent tactics, and tools (both extrainstitutional and institutional).* What kind of corruption? The core members understood they had to identify a form of graft that was not only pervasive but also that touched the lives of the majority of the population. They decided to zero in on bribery. For the regular person, extortion by civil servants, government officials, and the police is a tangible grievance—a direct source of oppression that results in the denial of rights, public services, and state entitlements, which for the poor can impact their very survival. Two defining methods around which nonviolent tactics revolved came to underscore this strategy: RTI empowerment and the zero-rupee note.

2. *Strive for long-term change by instilling anticorruption ethics in youth and postsecondary students, who will become India's future workforce, civil servants, decisionmakers, and leaders.* The cornerstone is the Freedom from Corruption campaign.

RTI Empowerment
5th Pillar is a progeny of the MKSS, the Right to Information movement, and the passage of the RTI Act. 5th Pillar is fulfilling MKSS's vision that regular citizens may use the legislation as a tool to access information and curb corruption as it affects them in their everyday lives. The movement has designed a defining method (a set of complementary activities) with three objectives. The first is to maximize the legislation's use in order to impede graft and stop bribery. The second is to enable people to obtain public services (for example, water and electricity), entitlements (such as tax refunds and pensions), and antipoverty assistance (including rural employment schemes, education scholarships, and ration cards). The third objective, Anand said, is to make RTI "known and used by as many people as possible in the shortest time."

Education is one of 5th Pillar's main RTI tactics. The group seeks to provide training in submitting RTIs as widely as possible. It started initially in its home state of Tamil Nadu; has branched out more recently to Andra Pradesh, Karnataka, and two districts in Rajasthan; and aspires to cover the entire country. Six days a week at its Chennai headquarters and Coimbatore branch, it convenes free RTI clinics that provide immediate assistance; every Saturday, training-of-trainers workshops are conducted at those two locations.

In conjunction with its youth Freedom from Corruption campaign and student chapters, 5th Pillar conducts workshops at colleges and universities, while district coordinators throughout Tamil Nadu organize sessions in rural towns and villages, including with marginalized communities. The content covers the RTI process, the steps for filers to take, information collection and site inspections, penalties for corrupt officials, and a strategic approach to asking questions. "The act is to get information, so you need to use creativity and strategy to ask the right questions to stop corruption," explained Anand.

For example, a below-poverty-line mother is unable to obtain her food ration card unless she pays a bribe. In an RTI petition she could ask such questions as, What is the name of the official handling my ration card application submitted on X date? How many ration card applications were pending as of that date? How many ration card applications have been processed since that date by that official? On what date can I get my ration card?

5th Pillar helps people write and submit RTI applications, which are invaluable services for the illiterate, semiliterate, the elderly, and other vulnerable groups. As importantly, the movement files RTIs on behalf of citizens who are too intimidated to approach the relevant state office or who fear reprisals. Such considerations are common among government whistle-blowers—honest officials who want to expose graft within the system—as well as among the poor, tribal groups, marginalized groups in the caste system, and rural communities generally, where there is less anonymity than in urban settings. For grand corruption perpetrated by higher-level officials or police forces, 5th Pillar developed a network of volunteer RTI filers around the country. According to a former team member, they are often retired civil servants disgusted by avarice, who are far removed from the scene and thus cannot be easily tracked down or attacked by the corruptors. The movement also offers assistance to those who wish to approach the state government's Vigilance Department or the Central Bureau of Investigation's (CBI) Anti-Corruption Bureau. It educates people about how to make a report about extortion to the Vigilance Police for a sting operation, and offers psychological support if the person is fearful. 5th Pillar will even contact the Vigilance and Anti-Corruption Commission on behalf of citizens who want to make reports or launch a sting operation.

In many instances, reported Anand, simply filing an RTI generates enough pressure, as the possibility of an investigation and disciplinary action inhibits corrupt officials. 5th Pillar posts "success stories," including tough cases, on its website and in its monthly Tamil-language magazine, *Maattram* (Change). When an initial RTI petition does not lead to a rectification of the matter, the movement often launches RTI appeals for citizens.

Zero-Rupee Note

In 2001 an acquaintance of Anand, University of Maryland physics professor Satindar Mohan Bhagat, came up with a novel tool to sensitize Indians and the diaspora about corruption and to counter bribery demands when he traveled back to India. He created the likeness of a fifty-rupee note, but with a difference. It had no denomination and proclaimed, "Eliminate corruption at all levels." 5th Pillar's core team adapted the pseudo-currency, translated it into five of the country's

Front and Back of the Tamil Version of the Zero-Rupee Note

Source: "Zero Rupee Note," 5th Pillar, www.5thpillar.org. Used with permission.

major languages (Hindi, Kannada, Malayalam, Tamil, and Telugu), posted it on the movement's website, and created a secondary site (zerocurrency.org) that offers downloadable and printable zero-currency bills for virtually every currency in the world.

The zero-rupee note has multiple purposes. First, it serves as a "nonviolent weapon" for ordinary citizens to refuse to pay bribes, explained Anand. When extorted, citizens give this instead of the actual banknote. At the same time, the note sends a message of "nonviolence and noncooperation to corruption," he added. The flip side of the zero-currency note provides information about 5th Pillar. This strategic decision about the design shows corruptors that the citizen is not alone but is part of a larger movement that will hold the official accountable. Such solidarity in turn alleviates people's fear to oppose corrupt officials, thereby emboldening them to refuse to pay bribes.

Movement members hand them out at busy public spaces such as train stations, bus stops, cinemas, government offices providing services to citizens, and even weddings—the latter considered to be particularly auspicious occasions. Anand estimated that up until mid-2012, they had disseminated zero-rupee notes and movement materials at over two dozen marriage celebrations in Chennai and various districts. The district coordinator covering Coimbatore has systematically blanketed Tamil Nadu's second-largest city with the zero-currency note. 5th Pillar also disseminates the anticorruption currency at its events, workshops, and street actions. Since 2007, over 2.5 million notes have been distributed throughout Tamil Nadu, in Andhra Pradesh, Kerala, and Rajasthan, as well as the Delhi capital area and Mumbai.[21] In its 2011 Annual Report, 5th Pillar stated, "Thousands of citizens have handed out the Zero-Rupee Note under circumstances of demands of bribe and have found to their pleasant surprise that the erstwhile corrupt official/employee yields instantaneously to their request without the bribe."[22]

Youth Engagement

5th Pillar directs much of its outreach to youth in general, particularly targeting postsecondary students. "The general idea," explained Anand, "is to empower them to obtain their fundamental rights when they turn eighteen without paying bribes. Then when they leave college they know they have power and can use that power to obtain rights and state services without a bribe." In March 2009 the group formed a Students Against Corruption unit that conducts campus outreach about 5th Pillar to support establishment of campus chapters and to empower students to fight corruption. It also developed a pamphlet for schoolchildren. Students are involved in many of its street actions. The ongoing Freedom from Corruption campaign consists of comprehensive workshops on college and university campuses across Tamil Nadu, and more recently in other states. Originally launched in 2007 it cumulatively has reached over 1,600 colleges and universities.[23] Each workshop encompasses mutually reinforcing elements:

- *Anticorruption awareness presentation.* Focusing on India's greatness versus limitations, why Indians need to fight corruption, causes of malfeasance, consequences of it, and reasons for targeting bribery.
- *Zero-rupee note.* Discussion of its meaning and power over bribe-demanders, followed by distribution to participants.
- *Essay contest.* As a lead-up to a 5th Pillar visit, student chapters often hold anticorruption essay contests, with the winners announced at the event.
- *RTI Act presentation.* Overview of the legislation and how citizens can use it.
- *Recruitment drive.* Invitation to participants to raise their hands if they are interested in giving a similar presentation to students and other groups.
- *Small-group exercise.* Participants are divided into groups of five, and they identify questions they either want to ask of 5th Pillar representatives or want to answer themselves. Each group then shares its results with everyone.
- *Pledge.* Toward the end of the workshop, students are invited to take an anticorruption pledge. In unison, they declare, "I promise to neither accept nor take [a] bribe, and to encourage, enable, and empower every citizen of India to eliminate corruption at all levels of society."
- *Signature.* Very often a large banner of the zero-rupee note is unfurled and students affirm their commitment by signing their names on it.

Discourse plays a central role in the youth initiatives. The 5th Pillar team emphasizes three themes. First is *freedom.* Indians may be rid of British colonial rule but they are still oppressed by corruption. For example, during a workshop at the Vellore Institute of Technology (VIT) in April 2010 Anand exhorted, "You are the freedom fighters of India. We were slaves to the British for 190 years, and we are now slaves to corruption." *Patriotism* is the second theme. If people want to show their love for India, they need to fight corruption; India cannot achieve her full potential and greatness as long as endemic corruption exists. "It's in our hands to free ourselves," Anand declared at the event. Third is to *be the change*. Building upon the quote attributed to Mohandas Gandhi, "Be the change you want to see in the world," the workshops emphasize that it's up to its youth to change India. At VIT, Anand exhorted the students, "We need you! Sixty percent of India is younger than thirty years. If you take a stand you will make India take a U-turn for the better!"

At campuses where a 5th Pillar student chapter already exists, movement representatives spend time with the group prior to the workshop. Together, they also meet with selected faculty and senior administration officials, thereby cultivating their support and gathering input about how corruption impacts the education sector. Along with the workshops, 5th Pillar supports the establishment of new campus chapters, recruits members to the movement from campuses, and more recently, participates in major campus events. For instance, in May 2011, movement members had a prominent role at SRM University's Technology Management Festival in cooperation with the institution's administration and student body. 5th Pillar, a few other civil society organizations, and students held an anticorruption rally. The movement had a stand in the duration of the four-day gathering, provided input and speakers for a panel discussion, recruited 150 new student members, signed up 500 youth for the e-newsletter, and made plans with students to return later in the year to establish a new chapter on campus. "We want to start this as a silent revolution," Anand said. The long-term objective is to "keep it going ten to 20 years," he added.

Nonviolent Tactics

In the five years since 5th Pillar was launched, the Chennai core has regularly carried out a variety of nonviolent tactics, many of which complement or build upon its ongoing Freedom from Corruption campaign, the two defining methods of RTI empowerment, and the zero-rupee note. The tactics include the following:

• *Human chains.* Twice a year 5th Pillar stages high-profile mass actions at Marina Beach in Chennai, mobilizing anywhere from 500 to 1,500 postsecondary students, civic actors from other CSOs, Scouts, people from the National Service Scheme and Youth Red Cross, and regular citizens. According to K. Banukumar, a retired senior civil servant and 5th Pillar's executive director, they engage in a series of activities from fun stunts, such as kicking the corruption ball and hugging the anticorruption ball, to leafleting, distributing zero-rupee notes, signing names on giant zero-rupee banners, and taking an anticorruption oath.

• *Dharna.* This nonviolent tactic, steeped in cultural resonance, is described as "peaceful agitation." It can consist of sit-ins—employed frequently by the Right to Information movement—but also, said Banukumar, "nonviolent exhibition and protest with slogan shouting." For example, in early 2009 a dharna was held in front of the Tamil Nadu government guest house to save the RTI Act from being weakened and to change a corrupt commissioner in the State Information Commission, the agency authorized to carry out the RTI Act.[24] 5th Pillar earned widespread media coverage and the governor's attention. Another dharna made a direct appeal to Tamil Nadu's chief minister and the State Information Commission to increase punishment for corrupt officials and, once again, to save the RTI Act.

• *Flash street corner meetings.* Movement activists or student chapters set up a mini-table at a busy public intersection, gather a crowd, talk for ten minutes, hand out leaflets and zero-rupee notes, and then disband.

• *Signature collections.* Either in tandem with dharnas or at other nonviolent actions, 5th Pillar encourages regular people to sign their names to zero-rupee banners alongside specific anticorruption appeals and demands.

• *Commemorations.* 5th Pillar's leadership core and local chapters across Tamil Nadu annually observe the International Anti-Corruption Day on December 9. In 2010, street actions were carried out in Chennai, Cuddalore, Dharmapuri, Erode, Pondicherry, Madurai, Mannargudi, Tirunelveli, Tuticorin, Vellore, and Villupuram.

• *Tie-ins.* 5th Pillar often cooperates with social service camps conducted in rural areas in Tamil Nadu, either through colleges, universities, or the National Cadet Corps. Postsecondary students adopt a village for a week of community service. At some of the camps, the movement's district coordinators or the Chennai core convened one-day anticorruption trainings for villages.

• *Cultural activities.* The movement stages plays with an anticorruption theme in Chennai. Audiences up to approximately 1,000 people include supporters, volunteers, and the general public. Suhasini Maniratnam, a popular Tamil actor and director, performed a one-woman play at a diaspora fund-raiser in Washington, DC. 5th Pillar has also held anticorruption poetry contests, and student members have held plays at college festivals or cultural programs. Anand reported that during spring 2012, students from the Digital Film Institute in Chennai created an anticorruption video and song highlighting 5th Pillar.

 • *Phone hotline.* At the Chennai headquarters, the movement runs a hotline that anyone can call to report instances of corruption, ask questions, or get information.

 • *Anticorruption gear.* In addition to the zero-rupee notes, on occasion, when the movement has the financial capacity, it gives out special 5th Pillar items such as T-shirts, water bottles, and reusable shopping bags. It also produced a user-friendly RTI Act manual and a traffic-fine awareness pamphlet, which members hand out to regular people on the street, in lines, and at weddings—the latter through donations from relatives of the bride or groom.

District branches and local chapters, often launched by youth, also conduct their own "self-designed, self-motivated" tactics, said Anand. The actions are marked by creativity and daring, as social stratification and intimidation can be stronger in rural settings, which have less anonymity than urban centers. A few chapters set up information awareness booths at weddings and gave out zero-rupee notes to guests. T. Jayaselvan, administrative manager at the Chennai headquarters, recalled how another local coordinator leafleted ordinary people standing in a long queue. Every Monday the public can submit complaints to the district collector that either directly or indirectly pertain to corruption— for example, delayed state services, difficulties in receiving disability or old-age pensions, and issues with land titles.[25] As approximately 200 aggrieved citizens waited their turn, the activist gave them brochures and zero-rupee notes. Another rural area coordinator conducted a public meeting in the town of Radhapuram, then launched a procession on the same day to Ooralvaimozhi, a nearby village. Locals walked nineteen kilometers with placards, handed out zero-rupee notes, convened a public meeting, and held an anticorruption pledge-taking session.

Private Sector and Civil Society Outreach

The Chennai core frequently conducts anticorruption presentations to the business community through Lions Club and Rotary Club chapters across Tamil Nadu and more recently in Bangalore (Karnataka), as well as at Chambers of Commerce, including the American Chamber of Commerce–India Tamil Nadu chapter.[26] The content is largely tailored to middle-class, middle-aged businesspeople and entrepreneurs. As with the youth workshops, Anand and his colleagues begin by addressing how graft is holding back India's development, overall greatness, and international stature. They directly tackle the fear factor, prevalent in the private sector. Businesspeople not only face lower-level bureaucratic malfeasance but even extortion demands from more senior officials and the police, who threaten to harm their enterprises if they do not comply. Often generating a lively exchange with groups, 5th Pillar teams encourage people to share their experiences as well as voice their concerns about filing RTIs and the efficacy of the zero-rupee note.

The Chennai activists also discuss the negative impact of middle-class complicity in bribery. Addressing one such group, Anand explained, "The person who can afford to bribe affects one hundred people who cannot afford this, as this reinforces the bribe-demander and increases the cost of bribes." Finally, the activists encourage participants to become members of 5th Pillar, and they appeal for help, including monetary support; advertisements in movement publications; in-kind donations, such as equipment, printing, and professional services; and contacts with other business groups and postsecondary institutions in order to increase outreach and awareness.

As with the Freedom from Corruption workshops, discourse is central to these presentations. The core messages are as follows:

- Those who want to fight corruption, including businesspeople, are not alone. They are part of a larger movement [5th Pillar] that will help them and stand by them. "Together we can achieve change."
- The private sector can say no to graft—with simple, practical solutions, such as RTI petitions and zero-rupee notes.
- The state is beholden to its citizens. The people put powerholders in positions of power, and government employees are there to serve the citizens, not vice versa.

5th Pillar also teams up with other CSOs and civic initiatives on anticorruption efforts—for example, India Against Corruption and Transparency International India. "Our model is to partner with different organizations for different areas of change," said Anand. In April 2011, 5th Pillar co-convened with Transparency International India the All-India Anti-Corruption Summit in Delhi. In August 2011 the movement held numerous activities in Tamil Nadu in solidarity with the Gandhian activist Anna Hazare and joined his national mass mobilization for the Jan Lokpal (citizens' ombudsman) bill for the creation of an independent anticorruption body to investigate corruption cases.[27] In Chennai, Coimbatore, Cuddalore, Erode, and Pallavaram, 5th Pillar held several one-day fasts, symbolizing Hazare's hunger strike, and the more challenging "relay fasts," where individuals fast in blocks of three to five days. The Pondicherry branch held a daylong rally on August 16. In Coimbatore, Anand went on a hunger strike for twelve days, from August 17 to 28, in solidarity with Hazare. He was followed by Rajkumar Velu, who was then the head of the city's 5th Pillar branch, and Kesavan, an executive committee member. They began on August 20 for a dozen days. Coimbatore was also the site of two mobilizations.

In conjunction with the commencement of the hunger strike, a daylong citizens' rally was held, featuring music, anticorruption pledges, symbolic fasts, and an evening candlelight vigil. On August 24, approximately 5,000 students from thirty-six colleges formed a three-kilometer line on both sides of a road.[28] Others took part in one-day fasts, and activists collected signatures for a petition to the prime minister demanding implementation of the Jan Lokpal bill. 5th Pillar's Chennai core and India Against Corruption rallied an estimated 6,000 people for a Jan Lokpal march along Chennai's Marina Beach, recollected Anand. Candlelight vigils were held in both Chennai and Pondicherry.[29]

Movement Attributes

Duality and Discourse

5th Pillar has a dual nature. On the one hand, it is projected as a social movement, amassing India's second wave of freedom fighters. It emphasizes that people have the collective power to gain freedom from corruption, which is the enemy within rather than an external invader. On the other hand, 5th Pillar presents itself as an organization that serves as a partner and resource for the "common man," the expression used in India to denote regular citizens—hence, the RTI trainings and assistance activities, such as submitting RTI petitions for those who are too scared or lack the wherewithal to do so. "We want people to think of 5th Pillar as the equivalent of the Red Cross for natural disasters," reflected Anand. "We want them to feel confident and assured they can come to us if they want to say no to bribery."

The movement's discourse cultivates a sense of collective ownership in the struggle, from its eponymous name, 5th Pillar, to its mission statement, to slogans, such as "You are all 5th Pillar. You take the initiative and we'll stand by you"; "5th Pillar—Corruption Killer"; "5th Pillar—All of us who want a corruption-free nation"; "Be the Change—Together We Can"; and "It's up to us to gain our freedom."

The messages carry through on its website, placards at street actions, leaflets, and the ubiquitous zero-rupee note, which has many incarnations, including the pseudo-banknote, T-shirts, water bottles, and massive banners on which hundreds can sign their names to pledge against bribery. The anticorruption struggle is also infused with patriotism. From T-shirts to videos to public events, the movement conveys two core messages: India can never fulfill its potential to be a superpower while plagued by corruption, and to love India is to fight corruption, individually by refusing to demand or take bribes, and collectively by acting together to "eliminate corruption at all levels."

Ownership is built into 5th Pillar's two defining methods: filing RTI petitions and using the zero-rupee note to say no to bribery. Backed by the power of numbers, both methods revolve around regular people carrying out individual acts of defiance. At the same time, these acts are empowering because they can produce visible outcomes for those who engage in them, as when a police officer or civil servant refrains or backs off from bribe demands.

Unity

For 5th Pillar, unity is bound together with ownership of the struggle. The movement is not built upon an alliance of organizations but upon what Anand described as a "coalition of citizens"—volunteers, members, and regular people who through 5th Pillar are filing RTI petitions, using the zero-rupee note, and changing their mind-set about corruption. At the same time, the Chennai core recognized that it must strategically involve particular sectors in society, hence its deliberate targeting of

- *Youth and university students.* A generational change of attitudes and practices is needed to diminish corruption.
- *The private sector.* Given their influence, connections to powerholders, and frequent encounters with horizontal corruption.
- *Rural communities.* Oppressed by graft in their daily lives.
- *Indian diaspora.* As many nonresident Indians have tasted life without endemic corruption and have become less tolerant of it.

Nonetheless, Jayaselvan reported that at the local level, 5th Pillar coordinators do organize meetings with community-based organizations in order to create awareness about the RTI Act and the zero-rupee note. As previously mentioned, the movement has, on a case-by-case basis, joined forces with other civic initiatives both in Tamil Nadu and nationally, to protect the RTI Act and push for a strong Jan Lokpal anticorruption bill's passage in Parliament.

Digital Technology

5th Pillar's website serves multiple objectives: as a resource center on civilian-based action to curb corruption, from learning about the RTI Act and filing an RTI petition, to checking official fees for public services, obtaining contact information for Vigilance Offices across India, and using the zero-rupee note against bribery demands. The site also serves as the digital face of the movement for target constituencies, including regular people, students, media, and the diaspora. As of June 1, 2012, it had 581,510 visitors. Anticorruption videos and segments from events are cross-posted on 5th Pillar's website and YouTube.

According to Anand, the movement also maintains a blog, as well as a 45,000-person e-mail list, a 900-member Yahoo! group, and Facebook groups in various languages and parts of the country. The latter has multiple purposes. First, Facebook offers an online forum for discussion. Second, members can post problems, share success stories, and report incidents of corruption. Third, Facebook enables efficient communication and information sharing across various chapters. By June 2012 there were approximately 18,000 to 20,000 Facebook members in total. Information and communication technology tools are maintained by volunteers, with the exception of one paid staff member working part of the time on the website. "Specific individuals are the 'owners' of each online tool," explained Anand. For instance, a Washington, DC–based member in the leadership core handles the blog and the online version of the *Change* publication.

The Chennai core also linked up with kiirti.org, "a technology platform to enable collection and aggregation of governance issues through phone, SMS, email, and the Web." The plan was to create a digital tool that provided citizens with multiple low-risk methods through which to post instances of corruption and poor governance. However, the effort did not take off. When asked why, Anand said there wasn't funding to run the platform, volunteers with digital skills are already helping with other ICT efforts, and there are bandwidth limitations. In the meantime, Janaagraha, a civic organization in Bangalore, launched something similar: ipaidabribe.com. It has taken off in India and is inspiring new applications in countries around the world.

Leadership and Organization

In order to operate in India, 5th Pillar has the legal status of a trust registered in New Delhi, with operational headquarters in Chennai.

Overall strategy and decisions are made by a twelve-person executive committee. Its members communicate and brainstorm via email and social media (for example, SKYPE, Google Groups, and voice conference calls) and usually make decisions unanimously. In total, there are six paid staff—four in Chennai and two in Coimbatore. They handle general administration and management, RTI activities, the Freedom from Corruption campaign, fund-raising, and coordination of 5th Pillar chapters and local coordinators. At this juncture, all other staff are volunteers.

Over time, the movement has developed a process to recruit local coordinators. Candidates must first join as members and become involved in local activities. After the core observes someone's performance, that person may be invited to be a local coordinator. "We tell people to come, volunteer, and after six months we'll evaluate you," Anand explained. Those invited to become local coordinators must also go through training before they can become "office-bearers" of 5th Pillar. The Chennai team even convened a public speaking workshop for volunteers.[30] It also organizes an annual event for local coordinators, cleverly coinciding with a high-profile public outreach effort. Various activities are held that day, to which citizens are also invited. 5th Pillar brings in special guests, including anticorruption activists from other parts of India and overseas; in 2008 an RTI activist from Mumbai targeting police corruption was featured.

5th Pillar's international and national branches, as well as local district and Students Against Corruption chapters, act autonomously. As a result, some branches and chapters are more active than others. "They decide what they want to do, and 5th Pillar Chennai headquarters supports them as requested," explained Banukumar.[31] Such support can include training in using the RTI Act, cooperating on events and street actions, teaming up for coordinated mobilization involving multiple chapters, funding, and distributing anticorruption items. "Initially we wanted strict guidelines and policies for local chapters, because other NGOs have had problems with staff or coordinators who jeopardized the reputation of the organization," recalled Anand. "But as time passed, the people who joined 5th Pillar were different than others who go to work for NGOs for personal objectives, which happens a lot in India."

The movement is made up of members, many of whom are active volunteers, who all must sign 5th Pillar's anticorruption pledge. For in-country individuals, the fees are 200 rupees for new members and 100 rupees for annual renewal. There is also a category of nonpaying members, for those of very limited means. Nonresident Indians contribute a yearly fee of US$50. In sum, by June 2012, there were over 1,500 members. Citizens are recruited through myriad activities and street actions, referrals, media coverage, word of mouth, and the official website. Anand estimated that approximately 75,000 to 80,000 people were affiliated with 5th Pillar at that time.

The movement is funded through donations, modest membership dues, in-kind contributions, advertising in *Maattram* (Change) magazine, and for the first few years, Anand's personal savings. It faces a constant monetary challenge.

Perhaps because Anand himself was part of the Indian diaspora, he recognized the potential roles this constituency could play in the homegrown civic initiative. Hence, involving NRIs was an early priority, beginning with the aforementioned establishment of the Washington, DC, base for international activities. It focuses on fund-raising, networking, and spreading the anticorruption message across the diaspora. "NRIs are more willing to support and fund [5th Pillar]; their level of confidence [in fighting corruption] is higher because they live in a developed country," he surmised. Also, they may not be as vulnerable to reprisals from corruptors.

In the ensuing years, new chapters have been formed in Basel, Eindhoven, Dubai, New York, the United Kingdom, and Zurich. Each NRI group decides what it wants to do. The Eindhoven contingent, for example, engaged its contacts to start up a local chapter in the state of Uttar Pradesh. 5th Pillar in the United States also joined the global Dandi March II, a diaspora mobilization that organized street actions on March 26, 2011, in conjunction with activities in India to support the Jan Lokpal anticorruption bill. It was inspired by Gandhi's 240-kilometer Dandi March in 1930 against the British salt tax.[32] The Washington group held a march with a dharna in front of the Indian embassy.

Solidarity and Outreach

5th Pillar has not cultivated support from public figures and celebrities, thus far missing a potential source of solidarity, media coverage, and public exposure. However, one endorsement it garnered is from the actor Maniratnam, who considers herself a "well-wisher of 5th Pillar." A video interview with her, available on the Internet, garnered 12,465 hits as of October 11, 2013, far more than any other video on the movement's website and YouTube channel.[33]

5th Pillar does not have a distinct communications strategy and plan. Over the years, it has tried to maximize the channels through which it conveys messages, given its modest resources. In April 2010 a Tamil media coordinator was hired to develop strategies for local print and visual media, and who serves as editor of the movement's monthly magazine. Anand reported that he personally handles the international media, along with Shobila Kali, the head of the Washington, DC, office. They have received significant coverage from major Indian newspapers such as *The Hindu* to *The Economist* magazine and *National Geographic*. Anand is the international face of the movement. He has been a speaker at the Fourth Conference of States Parties (CoSP) to the United Nations Convention Against Corruption (UNCAC) and the Fourteenth International Anti-Corruption Conference (IACC).[34] In the digital realm, he presented at Pop Tech 2010; TEDxVelemaal on February 9, 2010; and TEDxLeeds on February 12, 2012.

Maattram magazine is printed monthly and is also available online. Launched in May 2009 its stated aims are "to convey the activities of the organization to the people; to make bribe-takers realize that it is not anymore possible to receive bribe; to create confidence among the people that things could be done even without bribe."[35] Approximately 60 to 70 percent of the content is informational, from pointers on how to say no to bribery to news of arrests of corrupt officials, RTI Act and zero-rupee note success stories, forthcoming activities, and general information about how to become a member or develop a chapter. A special student section contains reports from chapter coordinators, poetry about corruption, and interviews with new student members. Finally, an innovative feature of the magazine offers step-by-step guides to interacting with various state offices for common procedures—for example, registering recently purchased property and obtaining land titles and ration cards. An online English-language magazine, *Change*, was attempted, but has been defunct since February 2011 due to funding constraints. Anand reported that in spring 2012, a member volunteered to start translating *Maattram* into English for non-Tamil speaking individuals on the e-mail list.

5th Pillar's newest venture is a one-hour, prime-time television talk show with Makkal TV, a popular Tamil channel. *Vizhithezhu Thamizha* (Wake Up, Tamilians) aired every Sunday for six months, from September 2013 to February 2014. According to 5th Pillar's website, each program covered "one government department or area of governance, the procedures citizens should be aware of, the actual fees for each certificate or service, the details of where to complain in case of bribery, corruption, delayed governance."[36] It featured panels of experts and relevant government officials responding to comments and questions from the audience. Designed to empower citizens with information and advice, while not exactly a *jan sunwai*, the shows offered the potential to wield social pressure and gain accountability since the powerholders must answer to the public via the audience.

Outcomes

Zero-Rupee Weapon

5th Pillar encourages feedback from people who use the zero-rupee note. Anand stated that they have received hundreds of letters, phone calls, and emails reporting positive results, but keeping track once the pseudo-currency goes into circulation is impossible. At this juncture they only have anecdotal evidence, but he maintains that they have not received a single reported instance in which the official did not relent.

Success Stories: Zero-Rupee Note

Mr. Ashok Jain got his car towed in Chennai. When he went to the C1 police station, he was asked Rs 800 as fine. He was ready to pay the amount in return for a receipt, which they were not willing to give. After much talking and convincing, he called his friend Vinod Jain. When Vinod came to the station and saw what was going on, he handed a zero-rupee note to one of the policemen who was asking for bribe. They realized that he was a part of the 5th Pillar organization and without any further questions they asked him to pay the marked fine of Rs 150 and handed him the receipt immediately. The zero-rupee note reminds people of an organization that is willing to back them up in a dire situation relating to corruption, which motivates them to stand their ground when faced by corrupt officials.

One such story was our earlier case about the old lady and her troubles with the Revenue Department official over a land title. Fed up with requests for bribes and equipped with a zero-rupee note, the old lady handed the note to the official. He was stunned. Remarkably, the official stood up from his seat, offered her a chair, offered her tea, and gave her the title she had been seeking for the last year and a half to obtain without success. Had the zero-rupee note reached the old lady sooner, her granddaughter could have started college on schedule and avoided the consequence of delaying her education for two years.

In another experience, a corrupt official in a district in Tamil Nadu was so frightened on seeing the zero-rupee note that he returned all the bribe money he had collected for establishing a new electricity connection back to the no longer compliant citizen.

Source: "Success Stories," 5th Pillar website, http://www.5thpillar.org.

He believes a key reason is that corruptors rely on the public's fear. "When they actually face nonviolent defiance from citizens—backed by a grassroots civic initiative—they in turn become scared, because bribery is a crime." Prosecuted civil servants face punishment, including suspension, fines, and even imprisonment. 5th Pillar's website, *Maattram* magazine, brochure, and blog all publicize victories.

An information technology recruiter from Coimbatore started using the zero-currency each time he had to deal with state agencies. In an instance involving a tax official who refused to process documents without a 500-rupee "fee," he recounted, "I handed over the zero-rupee note, which I always keep in my pocket. She was afraid and didn't want to take it. She completed the job immediately and said she was sorry and asked me not to take it forward."[37]

An unanticipated outcome of the zero-rupee note has been its use by honest officials. Anand recounted how some civil servants have taken to prominently displaying the zero-rupee in their office to signal that they do not extort, nor do they want people to offer them bribes.

Wielding the RTI Act

The Chennai core makes known individual success stories that are shared with 5th Pillar, but "there are practical difficulties to track everything," said Jayaselvan. However, 5th Pillar can assess the outcomes of RTI petitions it has filed on behalf of citizens. Anand reported that 90 percent of cases the movement takes on reach a "successful conclusion." The following two instances are illustrative not only of the power of the RTI Act but the innumerable ways in which endemic corruption is linked to impunity and debasement of the rule of law at the local level, and their impact on regular people.

From Individual to Incremental Victories

Each time corruption is thwarted through the zero-rupee note or the RTI petition process, a person or a community experiences a visible victory and gains tangible justice—such as government services and documents to which they are entitled, observance of rule of law in local affairs, and accountability of state authorities—creating a sense of empowerment that propels further action. For instance, after approaching 5th Pillar, a software professional working in Chennai filed an RTI petition to obtain his income tax refund, which had been pending for three years. He was successful. Thus emboldened, he then used the legislation to obtain information about the delay in road construction outside his workplace. "To his surprise, the road was laid immediately in the days following

> ### Illegal Sale of Property Using Forged Documents Was Rectified by Filing RTI Petition
>
> Samuthiraraj from Karisalkulam village in Kovilpatti Taluk of Tuticorin District was robbed [of] his family property by miscreants in cohesion with corrupt government official, Rajendran who apparently registered the forged documents and sold it to another person. Similar crime was committed with 10 other people from the same village and its surroundings. Samuthiraraj and the other victimized approached the District Registrar, Taluk officer and Sub Registrar of Kovilpatti Taluk, pleading with them to intercept the wrong doings, and return their rightful property. Their pleadings were brushed aside as they were reluctant to take action against their fellow official Rajendran, who had recently been promoted as the District Registrar of Periyakulam. Samuthiraraj, who came to know about our organization, sought our help to solve this issue.
>
> 5th Pillar Chennai office filed an RTI (Right to Information) petition on behalf of the victim Samuthiraraj on January 12, 2010. The forged documents and the sale of the property were cancelled on 1st February 2010. Not only Mr. Samuthiraraj, but all the other 10 affected villagers' forged sale documents were cancelled. This is a remarkable success to the RTI Act itself. Our RTI coordinators directed the next step of reclaiming their documents with their name, by guiding them through the next step of procedure to follow. This is a very motivating incident for the residents of this village, and has instilled confidence on the RTI Act. The only sorry side of this story is, both the rightful owner as well as the buyer are cheated whereas the middle men loot away.
>
> *Source:* "Success Stories," 5th Pillar website, http://www.5thpillar.org.

his RTI petition," reported Anand. What is more, the man then became involved in the movement. He started as a (volunteer) public relations coordinator and promoted 5th Pillar to peers and colleagues. "He is now working for the same company but from the Japan office, and is still in touch, actually using RTI repeatedly from Japan, taking advantage of online tools and the Chennai HQ team," he added.

The Chennai core understood that change could not happen in one fell swoop. Incremental victories lay the path toward systemic transformation of systems of corruption. For 5th Pillar, these smaller-scale successes are essential, as they bring visible change at the grass roots. Anand recounted one instance in which a district coordinator, Adhi Narayanan, created a flyer comparing the official fees versus bribe prices for government services. He made 1,000 copies and

---

Encroachment of Public Road Was Remedied by Demolishing the Construction

Mr. Tamilselvan from Tirupattu accosted 5th Pillar Chennai Office to file an RTI (Right to Information) petition, to [confront] an influential person who had started construction of his building by encroaching the public mud road. Local residents filed complaints to local and higher authorities, but no action was taken and the construction was going ahead on full swing. An RTI petition was filed on behalf of Tamilselvan from 5th Pillar, for which we got a reply, acknowledging the encroachment, but no actions were implemented to stop the construction. An appeal to the previous RTI petition was filed by the RTI coordinators of 5th Pillar, addressing the situation with direct questions regarding encroachment, and the time frame for the implementation of the rectifying measures. We received a reply, and the building was demolished to the relief of all the local residents.

Source: "Success Stories," 5th Pillar website, http://india.5thpillar.org.

---

leafleted the area outside the Regional Transportation Office, which issues licenses, vehicle registrations, permits, and vehicle "fitness" certificates. The commissioner of this office called him for a meeting, asked him to stop, and told him to submit a formal petition with his complaints to Tamil Nadu's Regional Transportation Department. Narayanan responded that he wanted to make a point: everyone knows what's going on, and the commissioner should take action to stop bribery in the office. The outcome was remarkable, Anand recounted. Regular people were able to enter the Regional Transportation Office, when before only so-called brokers went in—an illegal yet well-established practice. Moreover, citizens could exercise their prerogative to fill out and submit forms and directly interact with civil servants.

As 5th Pillar grew, it began to receive anonymous reports and even leaked information concerning government graft. This information is suspected to have come from whistle-blowers within the corrupt system who are too frightened to go public. The Chennai team conducts inquiries and follows up if wrongdoing is apparent. Follow-up often consists of filing RTI petitions in such a way that the wrongdoer learns that his or her graft is no longer a secret and has been leaked. This creates fear in the wrongdoer, who then reverses the illicit activities—for example, in contracts—so as to avoid punishment.

Global Inspiration

Interest in 5th Pillar's strategies and activities is growing around the world. In November 2013, officials from the Malaysian Anti-Corruption Commission (MACC) visited the movement's Chennai headquarters for a briefing and knowledge-sharing session about the zero-currency note.[38] Anand reported that the World Youth Alliance Latin American team and a Ghanian CSO also contacted 5th Pillar about the zero-rupee note. Mariam Andan Al-ariqi, a young Yemeni activist, was one of the 2012 International Anti-Corruption Conference (IACC) Social Entrepreneurs award winners. She and other youth have since launched a campaign to give out 5,000 "honest-riyal" notes in schools and universities.[39] In 2007 Pro Public, an anticorruption and accountability NGO in Nepal, printed out and distributed the Nepali version of the zero-currency note.[40]

Case Analysis

Noncooperation

The Gandhian tenet of noncooperation with oppressors lies at the heart of 5th Pillar's strategies and tactics. Gandhi's insights originally applied to governments and occupiers; 5th Pillar has extended the strategy. Systems of corruption cannot function smoothly unless the people in it go along with the prevailing behavior. In the context of bribery, this behavior can include demanding or even offering bribes, paying them, or turning a blind eye to such illicit practices. When regular people renounce corruption and no longer acquiesce to corruptors' demands, the system is not sustainable. 5th Pillar started this process and seeks to build a national noncooperation movement consisting of citizens who say no to bribery in their daily lives. This approach is embodied in the movement's anticorruption pledge to "neither accept nor give [a] bribe."

The movement's noncooperation strategy is expressed through the defining methods of the zero-rupee note and RTI petitions. Both tools—one extrainstitutional, one institutional—empower citizens to resist extortion, disrupt the corrupt status quo, and overcome abuse of power and impunity. 5th Pillar seeks to turn their usage into mass nonviolent actions. What is unique is that these tactics are carried out individually under varied circumstances rather than en masse in a coordinated or synchronized manner. Nevertheless, each individual action is backed by the power of numbers, emanating from 5th Pillar and the thousands of members, volunteers, and fellow citizens who make up the movement.

The movement conducts a diverse range of nonviolent initiatives in tandem, including the Freedom from Corruption student campaign and street actions designed to build public awareness and pull people to its side. Anand and the Chennai core identified, beyond the general public, key groups in society to target and engage—namely, postsecondary students and youth, rural poor, and the private sector.

Holistic Approach

The movement takes a comprehensive approach to social change based upon the following elements:

• *Awareness-raising* is built into all 5th Pillar activities. Its 2011 Annual Report states, "We see awareness campaigns as a way to reduce citizen apathy to corruption and hence educate the general public with ways to combat corruption."[41]

• *Values regarding integrity and attitudes toward corruption* are targeted alongside illicit practices.

• *Generational change* is deemed necessary in order to achieve far-reaching systemic transformation. To this end, 5th Pillar made a strategic decision for several reasons to target youth. "More innovation and practical, results-oriented ideas come from the young generation," Anand pointed out. Second, young people are generally less set in their ways than the older generation. "Students, because of their enthusiasm, are prepared to accept a new way of thinking about corruption straight away," explained Banukumar. Third, youth can influence the older generation around them. Finally, postsecondary students are future power-holders; they can either become upholders of integrity or corruptors. "After ten years the students of today will become bureaucrats and politicians," observed Anand. "If we impact them now, 50 percent of corruption won't be there. To reach 100 percent, we need ten more years." Thus, 5th Pillar presently seeks to transform people before they assume positions of responsibility. In doing so, it draws the present and future together in the struggle.

• *Behavior change* is sought both on the part of those perpetrating corruption and those oppressed by it.

• *Incremental victories* are achieved at multiple levels, from individual acts of noncooperation (via the zero-rupee note) and disruption (through RTI petitions), to movement victories, such as curbing corruption exposed by whistle-blowers and systematic mass outreach and empowerment.

Intangibles

The one prevailing characteristic of 5th Pillar is synergy. Recruitment, defining methods, tactics, and messages function in harmony with one another, thereby making the movement greater than the sum of its parts. A case in point is the Freedom from Corruption campaign. While having a long-term goal of seeking to build integrity among tomorrow's officials and decisionmakers, 5th Pillar also has short-term objectives. It encourages young people to use the zero-rupee note, file RTI petitions, and train fellow citizens. Concurrently, during these campaign activities, it recruits members and fosters the establishment of new college chapters, thereby growing the movement and furthering longevity. As for the current generation of adults, the movement's strategy of individual empowerment—through the pseudo-currency, RTI process, and 5th Pillar support and solidarity—undermines corruption in the present.

Virtually every tactic is linked to other tactics. For instance, street actions invariably involve handing out the zero-rupee note and encouraging people to contact 5th Pillar for help filing RTI petitions. RTI workshops also introduce citizens to the zero-rupee note. Signature collections are taken on giant banners with the image of the zero-rupee currency. The anticorruption pledge made by students, volunteers, and members is one and the same as the pledge on the pseudo-currency. Anticorruption paraphernalia, such as placards, T-shirts, and water bottles, bear the note's image. Core messages—whether dharna slogans, presentations, or short online videos—invoke freedom, patriotism, and collective power. As a result, the movement's various components are complementary and reinforcing, creating momentum, synergy, and parsimony, as precious time, resources, and opportunities are maximized rather than squandered.

5th Pillar deliberately maintains a balance between negative and positive overtones, from its discourse to defining methods to various nonviolent tactics. When referring to corruption, the group does not shirk from using strong language, images, and even symbolic actions, such as kicking the corruption ball. However, balance comes from positive associations, affirmations, and symbolic actions, such as hugging the honesty ball. At movement events, Anand and fellow activists emphasize that the struggle is not about targeting individuals or exacting revenge but about ending corruption and gaining freedom. 5th Pillar's approach calls to mind a key element of Kingian nonviolence, which expands upon the Gandhian insight that means ultimately determine ends. Under conditions of oppression, Kingian practitioners explain that aggression is a common impulse. If that aggression is directed toward the oppressors, it can produce violent behavior and continue the negative status quo. Nonviolent struggle channels societal aggression away from physically harming or seeking revenge on the perpetrators toward constructively changing the unjust system. While justice should be sought and the behavior of the perpetrators is not accepted, Kingian practitioners maintain the necessity of treating them as human beings.[42]

Empowering Honest Powerholders

Civil resistance scholarship maintains that not all those on the oppressor's side are equally loyal; when applied to the anticorruption context, not all those within a corrupt system are equally venal, and in fact, many wish to behave with integrity. This dynamic is evident in the 5th Pillar context. The movement inadvertently provides officials and frontline civil servants a way out of corrupt systems. It affords them protection, stemming from the power of numbers, when they display the zero-rupee note at their worksite or leak documents and information to 5th Pillar.

Moreover, retired or former civil servants and state officials—such as Aruna Roy, cofounder of the MKSS and a leader of the Right to Information Movement, often play significant roles in civic anticorruption initiatives, giving them more authority. 5th Pillar's Banukumar is a retiree who, in spite of his formal responsibilities, initially volunteered and then began to draw a modest salary well below that of his past professional level (joint director of agriculture) in Tamil Nadu. When asked why he devotes his time to the movement, he said, "I want a clean India. I witnessed how rural activities and the ownership of rural land are soaked in corruption. It's a distortion of the rule of law." This cohort—those who are still working within the state and those who have retired—offers a source of knowledge, skills, resources, and people power so far largely untapped. 5th Pillar has not yet strategically assessed how to maximize this latent source of noncooperation, increase avenues out of corrupt systems, empower honest officials and civil servants, or overcome their fears to take action.

Leadership and Organization

Anand's vision, drive, international exposure, and personal devotion to the cause have made him the face and de facto leader of 5th Pillar. Although low-key and modest, he exudes a depth of conviction that captures media and public attention and has brought benefits to the group. He is able to generate trust, enthusiasm, respect, and support—all necessary to build a strong internal team and corps of volunteers, as well as win support and new recruits for the struggle. On the other hand, reliance on a charismatic leader can have drawbacks. In Anand's case, back in 2010 he seemed pulled in many directions and involved in minutiae, which can distract a leader and claim time that could be spent on strategic priorities. Charismatic leaders are vulnerable to attacks aimed at discrediting them and the civic initiative. A physical attack on Anand would probably backfire, generating outrage and aiding the movement. While such an attack fortunately has not happened, the more corruptors are threatened by 5th Pillar, the greater the possibility of such reprisal. As well, civic initiatives too closely bound to a leader may become rudderless and potentially face collapse, should the person no longer be able to sustain this role. Perhaps more importantly, charismatic leaders may cause others to display less initiative because they follow rather than innovate. The history of civil resistance has successful movements with and without charismatic leaders.

Anand reported that he has recognized and addressed this challenge. By 2012, regular day-to-day activities and recruitment of new leaders, coordinators, and volunteers were being conducted without his involvement or influence. He was freed to direct his energies to larger movement issues and focus on interactions with the Chennai headquarters and the executive committee, while meeting with regional coordinators and leaders during the half-yearly team meetings.

Social Movement or SMO?

5th Pillar defies categorization. Like Addiopizzo in Palermo, it established a formal identity recognized by the state. This status was necessary to operate and to collect contributions; it also created an organizational infrastructure through which the civic initiative could function on a long-term basis. In this respect, 5th Pillar can be considered a social movement organization (SMO). On the other hand, its nature and activities are those of a social movement, built upon a base of volunteers, citizen mobilization, and a variety of nonviolent actions to wield people power. This dual nature carries no contradiction; rather it illustrates the many shapes and forms that civic initiatives take in reality.

Challenges

Unlike many civic initiatives that focus on a specific aspect or manifestation of corruption and are of a finite duration, 5th Pillar's struggle seeks transformative social change and thus has an indefinite time frame. As a result, the leadership core has identified two major challenges: sustainability and funding. Both are critical because, as Anand remarked, "We can't change corruption overnight." Sustainability—how to maintain people's involvement—is an ongoing challenge with several implications. Without new recruits coming in, building numbers is impossible, as some people inevitably become less active or leave, in turn impacting the movement's resilience, resources, creativity, and capacity to wield people power.

Funding is an ever-present concern. Donors often overlook effective social movements and SMOs because they don't fit the traditional model of an NGO or CSO that conducts finite projects.

Lessons Learned

Societal Transformation

Social movements—with maximalist goals to break apart endemic systems of corruption—can be conceived along a series of six interrelated dimensions. First is *time frame*, which refers to short- and long-term objectives, strategies, and tactics. Achieving visible, short-term victories that feed into long-standing goals is essential. As 5th Pillar demonstrated, nonviolent actions may be directed upon immediate victories, future gains, or even both simultaneously. The second dimension is *targets,* including corrupt powerholders, corruptees, honest powerholders, citizens, and particular cohorts (for example, youth). The third dimension is *social mores*, with a focus on changing values about integrity, attitudes toward corruption, and norms of appropriate behavior held by powerholders and regular people. Another dimension is *behavior,* namely, changing the conduct of powerholders and citizens. Next is *people power dynamics,* which involve noncooperation, disruption, and winning people over to the movement. The final dimension relates to the *power equation,* that is, altering the relationship between powerholders and the grass roots.

Societal transformation also involves education. Like Integrity Watch Afghanistan's community-monitoring initiatives (see Chapter 8) and MUHURI's social audits in Kenya (see Chapter 10), education can be a source of empowerment. 5th Pillar incorporated training for regular people and youth to use the RTI Act and workshops designed to inoculate postsecondary students—future powerholders and civil servants—from corruption by impacting their values about integrity and attitudes toward corruption.

Mobilization and Tactics

The 5th Pillar movement provides five valuable lessons regarding mobilization and tactics. To challenge endemic corruption, public awareness–raising is a necessary component. As with Addiopizzo in Italy (see Chapter 6) and Egyptians Against Corruption (see Chapter 10), a consistent lesson is that effective awareness-raising depends on discourse that resonates with regular people and emanates from their sociocultural context.

Second, awareness-raising on its own, however, does not necessarily lead to change. 5th Pillar combined it with citizen empowerment and mobilization incorporating a host of nonviolent tactics. Third, to mobilize citizens and to win support, effective nonviolent actions need to be relevant to the local context, including culture, social norms, and even history.

Similarly to Addiopizzo, 5th Pillar provides ways for people to say no to extortion—in this case, public sector bribery. Thus, a key lesson for anticorruption advocates is that tactics of noncooperation with the oppressive system—for example, the zero-rupee note—can harness the power of no.

Finally, when identifying societal groups to target, one important consideration is the multiplier effect, namely, the capacity of a cohort to impact others around them or society at large. Thus, in many societies youth have a multiplier effect by influencing adults in their immediate circles or social settings. At the societal level, it could be religious figures or a group of highly respected or popular personalities, from retired statesmen and women to athletes and pop stars.

Top-Down and Bottom-Up
In the civil resistance realm, though, the focus is normally on the empowerment of regular people. Anticorruption movements such as 5th Pillar point to the importance of developing additional strategies that support honest powerholders and tactics empowering them to refuse to engage in corrupt practices.

A final lesson is that India's trailblazing RTI Act presents a new paradigm for anticorruption legislation, rules, and regulations—top-down measures that empower regular people to disrupt corruption, challenge impunity, and gain accountability. In contrast to traditional institutional mechanisms to combat corruption, which are usually punitive in nature and rely on state power to exert control, these methods involve bottom-up power and transform the relationship between the state and citizens.

Notes
1. A social movement organization (SMO) is a nonstate entity that is part of a social movement. It can provide multiple functions to the movement,

such as identity, leadership, strategizing, and planning, but the movement is not bounded by the SMO; nor are SMOs essential for social movements to flourish.

2. For an excellent case study of the Right to Information movement, see Sowmya Kidambi, *Right to Know, Right to Live: Building a Campaign for the Right to Information and Accountability* (Minneapolis: Center for Victims of Torture, 2008), www.newtactics.org.

3. Ibid., 6.

4. Ibid.

5. Lina Khan, "India Makes Remarkable Strides Towards a More Perfect Democracy," www.huffingtonpost.com, April 2, 2010, 3.

6. Ibid.

7. "How to Use the Right to Information Act," 5th Pillar, n.d., handout.

8. For information about the RTI application process, see "Right to Information Act," 5th Pillar, http://www.5thpillar.org.

9. "Global Right to Information Rating," Center for Law and Democracy, September 28, 2011, www.rti-rating.org.

10. "Safeguarding the Right to Information: Report of the People's TI Assessment 2008," RTI Assessment and Analysis Group (RaaG) and National Campaign for People's Right to Information (NCPRI), New Delhi, October 2009, 7.

11. Karnataka Information Commission, Third Annual Report, 2009–2010, 29.

12. "Safeguarding the Right to Information."

13. PriceWaterhouseCoopers, "Final Report: Understanding the Key Issues and Constraints in Implementing the RTI Act," Department of Personnel and Training of India, 2009.

14. Ibid., 4.

15. This case study is based on interviews with the following 5th Pillar members during April 2010: Vijay Anand, cofounder and president; K. Banukumar, executive director; T. Jayaselvan, administrative manager; as well as subsequent written communications with Anand. The section title is a slogan printed on a 5th Pillar brochure.

16. 5th Pillar brochure, April 2010.

17. Mission Statement, 5th Pillar website, http://india.5thpillar.org.

18. 5th Pillar brochure, April 2010.

19. Vijay Anand, personal communication with author.

20. A 2011 study released by the Asian Centre for Human Rights asserts that RTI activists who are not part of an organization "are among the most vulnerable human rights defenders of India." Furthermore, a civil society assessment of RTI usage found that 40 percent of rural respondents cited harassment and threats from officials as the most important constraint from filing RTI petitions, while 15 percent of urban respondents stated that harassment from officials and lack of cooperation were the most significant constraints (*RTI Activists: Sitting Ducks of India* [New Delhi: Asian Centre for Human Rights, 2011], 1).

21. Ibid.

22. 5th Pillar Annual Report of 2011 to the UNCAC (United Nations Convention Against Corruption) Coalition, copy provided to the author.

23. I witnessed a Freedom from Corruption workshop at the Vellore Institute of Technology University on April 7, 2010.

24. Not surprisingly, after the RTI Act was passed, efforts to dilute it began, from increasing the number of government agencies and departments exempt from the legislation to increasing the filing fees, thereby making it more difficult for poor people to submit petitions.

25. The district collector is the head of the district administration. There are thirty-two districts in Tamil Nadu.

26. I witnessed a 5th Pillar presentation at a Rotary Club chapter in Chennai on April 9, 2010.

27. "What Is the Jan Lokpal Bill, Why It's Important," NDTV, August 16, 2011, www.ndtv.com.

28. 5th Pillar Annual Report of 2011 to the UNCAC.

29. In January 2013 Anna Hazare rejected the new draft of the Jan Lokpal bill put forth by the central government. Soon after, he launched a Janatantra Yatra, an eighteen-month campaign around the country to rally people to pressure powerholders for the passage of a strong bill (D. S. Kumar, "Anna Hazare's Janatantra Yatra Reaches Roorkee," *Times of India*, April 17, 2013, http://timesofindia.indiatimes.com; "Anna Hazare Rejects New Lokal Bill Draft Proposed by Government," *Hindustan Times*, January 31, 2013, www.hindustantimes.com.

30. 5th Pillar, "Effective Public Speaking Workshop for 5th Pillar Volunteers," blog entry, September 24, 2007, http://blogs.5thpillar.org.

31. Naming customs in India are complex, and people commonly have only one name.

32. The Dandi March is also known as the Salt Satyagraha or Salt March.

33. Suhasini Maniratnam, 5th Pillar TV, May 7, 2007, interview by Vijay Anand, http://www.youtube.com/watch?v=HLb4qZUyfJc.

34. Anand was invited to speak at a People's Empowerment Special Session that I coordinated.

35. 5th Pillar's *Maattram* (Change) magazine, 5th Pillar website, http://india.5thpillar.org (accessed May 12, 2012).

36. 5th Pillar, http://www.5thpillar.org/programs/vizhithezhu-thamizha.

37. Yasmeen Mohiuddin, "Zero-Rupee Note Tackles India's Corruption Culture," *Daily Telegraph,* February 10, 2010, www.telegraph.co.uk.

38. E-mail announcement from 5th Pillar, October 31, 2013.

39. "Beating Bribery: Small Change," *The Economist*, December 7, 2013.

40. "Anti-Corruption Day Observed with Fanfare," Propublic, n.d., http://www.propublic.org.

41. 5th Pillar Annual Report of 2011 to the UNCAC, 1.

42. Bernard Lafayette Jr. and David Jensen, *The Nonviolence Briefing Booklet* (Galena, OH: Institute for Human Rights and Responsibilities, 2005).

8

Community Monitoring for Postwar Transformation: Afghanistan

In many ways, corruption in Afghanistan is a bigger detractor to stability and progress than the insurgency. Many Afghans face violence at the hands of the insurgency. But every Afghan experiences corruption, sometimes at the hands of government officials, whom they are expected to trust over the insurgents.
—*NATO secretary-general Anders Fogh Rasmussen,*
"NATO-ISAF Takes Steps to Prevent Corruption"

Corruption in war-torn Afghanistan is now considered a clear threat to peace and development.[1] It is undermining government legitimacy as well as national and international efforts for reconstruction, poverty reduction, and the provision of basic public services. A survey conducted in 2008 found that 64 percent of Afghans believed that aid efforts were tainted by corruption.[2] In August 2011 a special Pentagon task force estimated that $360 million in US contracting funds ended up in the pockets of the Taliban, criminals, or power brokers with ties to both.[3] Corruption is also enabling a flourishing drug trade that is a source of revenue for warlords as well as the Taliban, according to a confidential communication, with the Taliban exchanging drugs for weapons.[4]

For citizens, it adds a persistent burden. In a 2010 poll, 83 percent of Afghans said corruption affects their daily lives.[5] A 2013 report from the United Nations Office of Drugs and Crime (UNODC) stated that while some progress has been made, Afghans considered corruption to be the second most important issue for their country after insecurity.[6] Not surprisingly, the Taliban is recruiting new members from among the marginalized population oppressed by unrelenting graft, poverty, and unaccountability. Mafia networks, often intertwined with the state and insurgents, operate on the ground.

Context

In 2002 a French student, Lorenzo Delesgues, came to Afghanistan to conduct political science research. He already spoke Dari and since 1996 had traveled extensively through Iran, Pakistan, and Central Asia. In October 2005 Delesgues together with Yama Torabi, a former university classmate, and Pajhwok Ghoori, a young civic actor, founded Integrity Watch Afghanistan (IWA), the first civil society organization (CSO) focusing on corruption. Its overall mission is to "put corruption under the spotlight by increasing transparency, integrity, and accountability in Afghanistan through the provision of policy-oriented research, development of training tools, and facilitation of policy dialogue."[7] It seeks to enhance in-country research capacity, empower citizens to hold public institutions to account, and contribute to the formation of a coherent civil society movement, Delesgues explained.[8]

By 2006 the young men concluded that they wanted to go beyond producing reports while sitting in Kabul. They decided to involve those most affected by the dire conditions—everyday people—and the way to start was at the local level. "This is where things are happening and things can change," Delesgues observed. He and Ghoori began going into rural settings and listening to the locals. They heard many grievances, such as not being consulted about what they need, witnessing bad-quality development projects but feeling powerless to do anything, not having a chain of communication with the government, feeling afraid to speak with officials, and nongovernmental organizations (NGOs) being unresponsive to their input and demands. As importantly, Delesgues and his colleagues found that people wanted to go beyond the corrupt "collusion network" in their area and play a "citizen's role," but didn't know how in such situations.

Delesgues took inspiration from a variety of sources, including the pioneering social audit strategies and tactics of the Mazdoor Kisan Shakti Sangathan (MKSS) Right to Information movement in India, the achievements of nonviolent social movements, and the social accountability initiatives developed by the Aga Khan Foundation. The Afghan National Solidarity Programme, created in 2003 by the Ministry of Rural Rehabilitation and Development, also pointed to the role of communities in upholding integrity. At that time, the program was, according to Delesgues, "one of the few successes of reconstruction." Ghoori and Delesgues brainstormed. They held some informal conversations with an international civil society expert on accountability in reconstruction. Through these efforts, they drew the parameters of a new citizen empowerment and community-monitoring initiative, born out of Afghanistan's conflict environment.

Civic Initiative

Vision, Objectives, and Definable Outcomes

Through citizen empowerment and action, the young civic leaders envision a society where the interaction between the state and the people is not one of ruler and subject but one in which the state is an ally of the people and a regulator for the common good. Their overall objectives were to make aid and service provision accountable to citizens, give them a say over the reconstruction of their communities, and bring together the key parties involved in postconflict development—namely, the populace, government, and international community. They outlined two clear outcomes: in the short term, to prevent corruption and improve projects that were being monitored by communities; in the medium term, to develop a model that could be carried out in other parts of the country.

Strategic Analysis

In examining why the reconstruction effort has fallen short of expectations, Delesgues asserts that traditional, top-down efforts did not perceive much of a role for grassroots civil society, and donors initially thought they could achieve change by building state institutions. "In countries where the state is weak and the 'top' has little credibility, top-down doesn't work so well," he commented.

A detailed strategic analysis was conducted from the outset, including investigating the following factors:

- Social, political, and economic conditions.
- Those who would support and those who would be against them.
- Who could be potential "conflict engines."
- Sources of possible violent conflict.
- Risks and repression.
- Challenges to engaging citizens, such as fear, lack of skills, and illiteracy.

• How to best mobilize people.
• How to interest donors in the initiative and be transparent about projects that would come under community scrutiny.

The young leaders realized that if the citizen initiatives were characterized as anticorruption, they would fail for several reasons. Because project information and site access were needed, doors would have closed on them, and those benefitting from graft could retaliate, even with violence. Moreover, as rule of law is weak, identifying all the corrupt players and seeing them tried and jailed are impossible. "Weak governments can raise objections, create obstacles, not release information, and repress, but they have trouble enforcing the law," noted Delesgues.

In these contexts, corruptors can be more susceptible to social pressure than a punitive approach. The villagers needed to increase the (social) costs for being corrupt—something one organization or a few cannot do, but that requires pressure from many. Consequently, community monitoring was strategically framed in terms of getting projects done according to plan and making development efforts and donors accountable to the people's needs. IWA could approach and negotiate with the various players involved in reconstruction—donors, multilateral development institutions, governments, military, the confusing mix of international and Afghan contractors and subcontractors, NGOs, and the national and provincial governments.[9]

Finally, the linchpin of their strategic plan was that the entire effort be community-driven—civic initiatives led by regular citizens who decide whether their village will participate, who will conduct the monitoring, and which projects will come under scrutiny. They made demands, performed surveys and inspections, interacted on the ground with various project interlocutors and state reconstruction officials, and engaged in other nonviolent tactics to exert people power.

Local ownership of the initiatives was critical to overcoming obstacles and resistance from powerholders, including the government and some donors and multilateral aid agencies. For example, Delesgues reported that when a provincial governor raised objections, arguing that NGOs should not examine reconstruction projects, IWA justifiably countered that it was the citizens—the intended beneficiaries—who were engaged in monitoring.

Planning
Efforts began on two fronts: securing a minimal level of government acquiescence and setting up a pilot program. The first turning point unex-

pectedly came in May 2008, when an official from the Ministry of the Economy, who had some responsibility for monitoring reconstruction, agreed to cooperate with IWA, thereby enabling the CSO to state that the program had support from the authorities. Establishing contacts with other government agencies and overcoming the apprehension of villagers to take action were extremely important. At the very least, IWA's nominal agreements with state institutions were enough to create leverage for the grassroots initiatives, bolster demands for project-related information, embolden citizens, and expand civic space—that is, the arena for public expression and dissent.

Ghoori and Delesgues initially made contact with communities in the general vicinity of Jabulsaraj (approximately one hundred kilometers from Kabul), which was neither the toughest nor the easiest scenario. This area did not have the overwhelming security problems that plagued other parts of the country, and it was the target of significant aid efforts. Yet citizens were poor and frustrated, as reconstruction was not bringing what was promised or what they needed. Locals were not civically engaged, and they lacked hope and confidence that they could bring forth change. Still, they were not completely downtrodden. According to Delesgues, they were ready to try something but needed someone to make a convincing proposition. Ghoori played a key role in these interactions. "He was there on the ground. He understood how the corrupt system was working, could put players together, and could mobilize people," said Delesgues. The second turning point of the entire program came toward the end of 2007 and early 2008, when ten villages decided to participate in community-monitoring initiatives and IWA subsequently launched the pilot in the district of Jabulsaraj, Parwan province.

Defining Method

Delesgues considers community monitoring a derivative, rather than a replica, of social audits. In the civil resistance realm, community monitoring is also a defining nonviolent method, a series of sequenced nonviolent actions that together wield people power, consisting of a principal tactic around which a host of nonviolent tactics revolve. Each community-monitoring initiative lasted for the life cycle of the development project, normally one year, and encompassed the following steps:

• *Election.* Election of two local volunteer monitors for each monitored project. The voting process was determined solely by each locality. Initially, some monitors wanted to be paid, but IWA told them they would receive no compensation other than for modest out-of-pocket expenses incurred while conducting their duties. This approach ran counter to the prevailing donor-and-NGO culture that had developed, where people expect to be reimbursed for whatever they do.

• *Education.* IWA trained the local monitors, providing skills, standards, and tools for monitoring, conducting site inspections, and so on. The volunteers also signed a code of conduct outlining the way they would execute their work and underscoring their commitment to the community to report findings regularly, refuse bribes, and maintain integrity.

• *Project selection.* Each community chose the project that was important to it. IWA developed basic selection criteria in order to facilitate this process, including priority for ongoing infrastructure projects, rather than less demonstrable outcomes, such as carpet weaving. IWA also provided a list of donor projects slated for the community, based on information obtained from provincial planning departments. However, the people had the final say, and in some instances they picked projects not on the list. Schools, roads, clinics, irrigation channels, and flood walls were common targets of scrutiny.

• *On-the-ground information collection and assessment.* Local monitors collect project documents; make weekly site visits; document the reconstruction process, inputs, and outputs; engage with the project engineers and other implementers; and present their information and findings to their community, project implementers, and powerholders. Over time, these interactions with authority figures often led to productive relationships, even friendships, that won support for communities. In one case, a village gathered household donations and asked the contracting company to undertake extra measures in order to improve the project.

• *Weekly community forums.* Local monitors subsequently presented their findings every Friday at a community forum, often associated with the weekly gathering at the mosque for prayer. This setup built accountability into the monitoring process and promoted enthusiasm and unity among fellow citizens.

People Power

When the monitors found problems, the communities demanded changes. First they would use dialogue to come to a resolution. If that didn't work, they would ratchet up the pressure. This often involved expanding sources of input and monitoring. For instance, in 2009, to put pressure on a recalcitrant contracting company building a school near

Jabulsaraj, locals convinced both an official engineer from the provincial government and the donor's (UNICEF) engineer to check the project. The civic initiatives also tried to garner support from outside the community, such as state authorities, clerics, donors, and elected representatives. A third tactic was inviting project implementers or state officials to community meetings or site visits, which creates social pressure and can win over people from within the corrupt system. Finally, locals flexed their civil resistance muscles through other collective actions, such as protests, speaking in assemblies, petitions, letter writing, and garnering media coverage. In the very first campaign in Jabulsaraj, when monitors discovered low-quality bricks were being used to build a school, villagers launched a sit-in at the construction site and refused to budge until the company brought in new, higher-quality bricks.

Community members also directly provided support to local monitors, often in the form of technical know-how, facilitating contacts, and joining site visits. "The communities got involved, used their own knowledge, and went to others who had expertise they lacked. This was not about two local monitors working in isolation," said Delesgues. He cited an example of a local monitor who could not read and got literate villagers to help him for the duration of the initiative.

Tactical Innovations

Delesgues came up with the idea of having the villages conduct *community-led surveys*, which he called a "strategic instrument" designed to gain cooperation from the various development actors. IWA developed a set of thirty standard questions. Following the election of local monitors, a village representative would canvas a representative group of approximately 10 percent of households. They produced directly relevant data that donors did not collect in their own evaluations, could be used by the media, and often served as a source of leverage with disobliging state authorities.

After the pilot program, the young civic leaders realized that they needed to foster dialogue among the various actors involved in the projects being monitored. They fashioned an innovative solution—provincial monitoring boards—where people can meet regularly to talk about project problems, visit reconstruction sites, and find solutions. All decisions and commitments are recorded to ensure follow-up. Board members include representatives from the Ministry of the Economy, relevant reconstruction departments, donors, contractors, local monitors, and the media.[10] The first one was established in 2009, and others are now functioning in Balkh, Herat, Nangarhar, and Parwan.

Civic Initiative Attributes

Multiple Actors
The community-monitoring initiatives were composed of the following
sets of actors:

- Communities.
- Local monitors (two volunteers per village).
- Community notables, such as elders, mullahs, mayors.
- State representatives.
- Reconstruction implementers (donors, contractors, subcontractors).
- Provincial monitoring boards.
- IWA local representatives.
- IWA Kabul.

IWA has a locally recruited staff person in each district, which
encompasses approximately ten to fifteen projects. The local representatives function as a direct link between IWA and the communities, creating strong bonds and stimulating mobilization. Delesgues
explained, "If Afghans come from the city, they are respected. But if
the person is a local, someone they can relate to, he'll get an audience
that makes things happen." They serve as a focal point for the communities, meeting weekly with the volunteer monitors and trou-
bleshooting any emerging difficulties. IWA thus ensures that the
monitoring is conducted properly and volunteers are following the
code of conduct. The local representatives also function as an on-the-
ground resource for the communities—arranging appointments with
project players and powerholders, forwarding project documentation
and photos to IWA Kabul for safekeeping, solving problems with the
state, and raising concerns with IWA Kabul when resolution seems
difficult.

In the early stages, Ghoori and Delesgues were the main contact
persons with the communities. Although based in Kabul, they spent
much time on the ground, learning from the villagers and talking together with them as equals. Hence, they earned the locals' respect and
trust. Although foreign and an initial curiosity to people, Delesgues
was accepted due to his familiarity with Afghan society and fluency in
Dari. He believes that being an international was not automatically a
disadvantage, given the partnership with Ghoori. "We were complementary; we played upon each other's strengths in the eyes of the people," he said.

IWA's Role

From the outset, Ghoori and Delesgues saw IWA as an animator and enabler of citizen empowerment and action. "There is a distinction between trying to nurture community capacity versus controlling or directing it," said Delesgues. The CSO's decisionmaking focused on overall strategy, while the villages had control over monitoring initiatives and took their own decisions on the ground. IWA's only requirements were that the initiatives stay nonviolent and that monitoring activities be documented.

In many respects, IWA served as a coach to the communities, providing tangible as well as intangible support. Tangible elements included

• *Creating the overall plan.*

• *Developing a monitoring methodology and tools* that could be used by rural and peri-urban Afghans, who often were underprivileged, lacking in formal education, and relatively isolated.

• *Education and capacity-building*, through the volunteer monitors' training.

• *Access to information from donors and powerholders*; in order to conduct the monitoring, communities need to obtain the project's "statement of work," which consists of detailed information such as blueprints, budgets, donors, contractors, and so forth.

• *Placing a locally hired staff person on the ground*, to serve as a liaison, troubleshooter, and resource.

• *Creating a bridge among all interlocutors*, by facilitating contacts and direct dialogue and cooperation among the communities, the donors and military, the national government, and the provincial government—informally and formally, as is the case with the provincial monitoring boards.

• *Overcoming powerholder obstacles*—for instance, when a provincial government tries to thwart monitoring by sending low-level or unsuitable interlocutors to deal with the local monitors.

• *Fostering exchanges among local monitors from different villages.* After the pilot project, in addition to the regular trainings, IWA began bringing new monitors together with veteran monitors in order to add another dimension to their education. "You get someone who has done it and can explain things in a way that [new monitors] can relate to and isn't abstract," said Delesgues. As well, these gatherings allow monitors to exchange experiences, learn from one another, and build ties across communities.

• *Providing a centralized repository to store and make available all information collected by the communities.*

Intangibles were equally important to the tangible elements such as

• *Surmounting people's doubts*, and fears of reprisals, rejection, and failure.
• *Building confidence in people's abilities and self-worth* so they could interact with educated professionals and state authorities.
• *Encouraging a sense of agency*—that people have the power to change their circumstances.
• *Fostering unity* through collective objectives and responsibility for the monitoring initiative. Through its close interactions with communities, IWA was able to discern social divisions and thus take steps to overcome possible obstacles to unity. For example, it organized meetings in places where many people gathered. IWA's local representatives kept tabs on local leaders to ensure that they were gathering the bulk of their communities together for meetings and votes. IWA tried to get women involved, but given the highly patriarchal and traditional nature of Afghan society, it was difficult. However, the CSO conducted surveys to get their views. A few women were elected as local monitors, but they felt uncomfortable on construction sites. Women voted for local monitors, often attended community forums, and even spoke up. Last but not least, they participated in the aforementioned school sit-in.

Nonviolent Discipline

IWA continuously emphasized the need for communities to be nonviolent, which was also a key point of the local monitor trainings. In this postwar environment, the civic leaders were concerned that violence could quickly escalate from a small altercation, which would damage the entire monitoring program and result in blacklisting. However, through close interactions with the villagers, Ghoori and Delesgues found that people readily understood the arguments for nonviolent discipline. "Coming out of a postconflict context where violence was so prevalent, people knew its consequences and they are more reluctant to engage in violence," said Delesgues. However, the civic leaders also understood that they needed to show people that nonviolent methods would yield results. "To be nonviolent in a violent environment, you need to be effective," he added.

Communications

IWA also developed a communications strategy and plan. The objectives were to target the actors involved in reconstruction and win them over to the notion of community monitoring. The targets were donors, the Afghan state, communities that could potentially join the initiative, civil servants, and parliamentarians. Rather than focus on the negative (corruption and impunity), the principal message was positive: transparency in reconstruction is beneficial because it allows communities to scrutinize projects, thereby helping to ensure that projects are completed successfully, aid is spent properly, and recipients actually benefit from reconstruction efforts.

The provincial media is particularly important as it garners local publicity for the civic initiative, increases transparency, and indirectly pressures powerholders and other top-down players. IWA undertook a concerted effort to engage with the provincial media, making a strategic decision to invite journalists to attend and cover the provincial monitoring board meetings. In general, the national and international media were viewed more as a means to amplify people's voices to powerholders and the public in donor countries. It also helped external actors understand the power of the grass roots. In some cases, foreign coverage abetted cooperation from disinclined Afghan officials and international actors.

International Support

IWA was fortunate to have hard-core support from Making Integrity Work (TIRI) and the Norwegian Agency for Development Cooperation (NORAD), which was flexible enough to allow the allocation of a modest amount (US$30,000) for developing and planning the initiative and launching the pilot with ten villages. Following the pilot's success, other donors became interested, which enabled IWA to both meet grassroots demand among communities and to expand in different provinces. By 2010 the community-monitoring program's budget increased to US$120,000. In order to maintain neutrality, IWA does not accept money from the international military, although it cooperates with them so that communities can monitor their reconstruction projects.

IWA was one of the CSOs involved in setting up the Network for Integrity in Reconstruction (NIR), originally launched in 2005 by the international NGO (INGO) Integrity Action (then called TIRI [Making Integrity Work]). It fosters exchange and in-country visits among civic actors. Delesgues reports that the network is a valuable source of ideas, information, approaches, practices, and encouragement.

Outcomes

What began in 2007 with ten villages had expanded to almost 400 civic initiatives in several provinces by 2013: Badakhshan, Balkh, Bamyan, Panjshir, Parwan, Nangarhar, and Shindand, the latter two with particularly grave security problems.[11] The first wave of monitoring was done solely in rural settings. In the second and third waves, communities on the periphery of urban locales also took part.

Delesgues estimates that in approximately one-third of the civic initiatives, the problems were solved through strong community pressure. For example, between 2010 and 2011, the Majbura Abad Shura community launched a monitoring campaign for the construction of a new building for the overcrowded Nangarhar high school (8,000 students), funded by the Turkish International Cooperation and Development Agency (TIKA). In spite of "rigorous" donor monitoring, serious problems were detected, including exposed electrical wiring and lower-quality bricks, which were rectified.[12] The latter would not only have reduced overall longevity by 80 percent, but would have impacted structural soundness, a concern given that the area has been struck by earthquakes, most recently in 2009. In about another third of the cases, locals didn't find problems or the project implementers were open, accessible, and cooperative in settling issues. Consequently, in two-thirds of the localities, change was accomplished through civic action. Among the remaining third, success was not forthcoming. Either the problems weren't detected, access to the project site proved impossible to secure, or the communities were not organized and mobilized enough to wield people power on powerholders or implementers blocking the monitoring.

A network of over 600 local monitors voluntarily serves as resources after their term, including a few from peri-urban areas with professional backgrounds—for instance, in Nangarhar, a medical student and a teacher who graduated in computer science. According to Delesgues, IWA is working on pulling such people together to meet and exchange with one another, and to mobilize new communities.

According to IWA, communities that have gone through the civic monitoring initiative become more autonomous and effective in problem-solving and less dependent on local powerholders.[13] A local monitor in Nangarhar said, "It was a good experience to create collaboration. It belongs to us. It is up to us to make a good country."[14]

New forms of community monitoring are being launched in other realms rife with corruption: justice (monitoring courts), budgets (tracking expenditures), and mining (companies pledging social investments).

The World Bank and IWA initiated an innovative form of cooperation. They came to a monitoring agreement whereby in July 2011 the CSO opened a field office in the province of Badakshan, in order to begin empowering interested local communities to monitor World Bank–funded reconstruction projects.[15] IWA is also developing a com-

prehensive educational package nicknamed the Integrity Box. Delesgues reports that the plan is to "put all the tools together for other
groups to use."

Case Analysis

People Power Dynamics

Even in a violent conflict setting with limited institutional capacity and
state authority, people power can generate surprising pressure on powerholders, state and nonstate, by

 • Acts of disruption of the corrupt status quo (for example, information gathering and site inspections).
 • Gaining a modicum of support and cooperation from powerholders (through formal and informal agreements, public pledges, or institutional cooperation via IWA's provincial monitoring boards).
 • Winning people over from within the corrupt system (including
donors and officials who can wield institutional power even if they
themselves are not considered senior powerbrokers).
 • Cultivating social legitimacy—of the cause, actors (local citizens),
and nonviolent methods (monitoring, mobilization, and dialogue). Legitimacy in turn can enhance social pressure and help minimize reprisals and
repression from the tangled web of overlapping, interconnected corrupt
state and nonstate interests. IWA's community-monitoring initiatives accomplished legitimacy through the strategic framing of the grievances,
unity of the people and objectives, and grassroots ownership of the campaign. The community-monitoring program changed power relations between the grass roots and elites. Through monitoring, mobilization, site
visits, and the provincial monitoring boards, regular citizens raised their
voices and made demands directly to powerholders. For many locals, who
are accustomed to being marginalized, this change in the power equation
was revolutionary. To grasp this transformation, one only needs to picture
a board meeting at which a village volunteer first presents proof of inferior construction to government officials, International Security Assistance Force (ISAF) personnel, engineers, and the media, and then goes on
to make recommendations that these powerholders actually adopt.

Intangibles

Ghoori and Delesgues deemed it essential that communities feel ownership over the civic initiatives and strategically took measures to instill

it. "We were just planting the seed and creating the conditions for the seed to grow," said Delesgues. As a result, each civic initiative developed its own character, depending on, for example, the personalities and capacities of the volunteer monitors, the manner in which the villagers organized themselves, local leadership, and approaches to problem-solving. IWA's community-monitoring program was created out of the social and cultural realities of poor communities and the conflict conditions on the ground, instead of the application of standardized social accountability approaches or the replication of campaigns and movements from other countries. As a result, the community-monitoring initiatives resonated with citizens and fostered their participation.

Strategic Considerations

The young civic leaders understood that they needed to start small. Overambitious goals at the outset would have led to failure. Thus, they began with a modest pilot program and outlined a series of steps and accomplishments along the way that would set a precedent, slowly build a winning record of success, and gain credibility for the overall initiative. They applied this same strategy with the provincial monitoring boards. After succeeding to establish one, they pointed to it when approaching powerholders in other provinces.

IWA's strategic assessment identified the various powerholders impacting reconstruction: relevant national ministries and agencies, provincial departments, donors, the military, contractors and subcontractors, and the media. Within these pillars they assessed who had decisionmaking authority as well as those who had institutional power that could be tapped. The civic leaders wanted the overall program to gain strong allies and momentum before corruptors understood its impact, attempted to thwart it, or retaliated. Hence, the initial focus on donor projects was a deliberate move. It enabled IWA to minimize objections from national and provincial authorities and to maintain that IWA's involvement would benefit the state. Communities began monitoring state reconstruction projects in 2009.

The process of wielding people power through community monitoring calls to mind the Kingian (nonlinear) six-step strategy for developing a nonviolent campaign, namely, personal commitment, education, information gathering, negotiation, direct action, and reconciliation—the latter reflected in how donors and even some government officials began to recognize the valuable role of organized citizens in reconstruction and development.

Lessons Learned

Empowerment

IWA's community-monitoring initiatives offer several lessons for citizen empowerment and action. First, grassroots anticorruption initiatives build democracy from the bottom up, not in the abstract, but through practice, in this case, through informal elections, citizen-led surveys, and regular reporting activities on the part of volunteer monitors that instilled their accountability in their fellow villagers.

Consistent with the civil resistance literature, not all within the corrupt system are equally loyal to it—that is, not all are venal or equally wedded to maintaining the status quo. Thus, securing dialogue and cooperation with some powerholders and mobilizing external actors to apply top-down pressure can reinforce the voices and capacities of local communities and complement bottom-up pressure.

Third, NGOs and CSOs can catalyze civic initiatives, but "there's a distinction between trying to nurture community capacity versus controlling or directing it," noted Delesgues. While they are not substitutes for civic campaigns and social movements, such nonstate actors can empower the grass roots through education and training, developing methodologies and tools regular people can use, fostering grassroots networks, brokering contacts with powerholders and external actors for strategic dialogue and negotiation, and sourcing external and top-down pressure to complement people power.

Another lesson is that IWA understood the difference between imposing externally designed projects to stimulate civic engagement versus on-the-ground immersion and partnership with communities that cultivated know-how, problem-solving skills, and autonomy. IWA did not attempt to formalize social accountability, that is, people power. What was consistent was the set of standards and tools for the monitoring process, which were derived bearing in mind the users (Afghan villagers and peri-urban dwellers), the powerholders, and the sociocultural context in which they would be used.

Fifth, the grass roots—communities and citizens—have traditionally been viewed as subjects of donor projects and passive recipients of top-down anticorruption programs designed by experts, namely, elites and external actors. The impact of the community-monitoring initiatives demonstrates how regular people, even in deprived, violent, and often isolated settings, can become drivers of accountability, sources of information and insights, and partners in development.

People Power Building Blocks

Presented as a mathematical equation, one could say that unity plus ownership equals legitimacy. Unity is essential not only for gaining numbers (citizen participation) but for the legitimacy of the campaign or the movement's cause and its tactics. In turn, legitimacy can help mute repression, make it backfire if it occurs, sow doubts, shift loyalties, and win support among those within the corrupt system.

Another lesson is that the community-monitoring initiatives were built upon the existing social infrastructure—the social structures, social relationships, and culture of Afghan communities—rather than on "foreign" social systems interposed by external actors.

External Actors

In reconstruction and peacebuilding settings, a plethora of top-down actors can result in confusion, replication, and working at cross purposes, however unintentionally. By holding top-down actors to account, strong, organized, and strategically planned people power initiatives can be a balancing counterpoint.

Similarly, mobilized communities can be the eyes and ears of reconstruction and development efforts, as well as a source of information and practical recommendations. These communities can play a particularly vital role in conflict, postconflict, and natural disaster scenarios, where rule of law and institutions are weak and corruption is endemic.

Finally, third-party actors involved in development and peacebuilding can enhance prospects for civic campaigns and movements to emerge organically without impinging on them. This activity can involve

- Flexible support for CSOs to pilot new initiatives that require modest funding. In this way, CSOs can see what works and what needs fine-tuning, how best to expand (if at all) in order to have a lasting impact, and how to meet capacity-building needs.
- Reconceptualizing the management of small grants and developing new patterns of interaction with the grass roots that affirms its autonomy. The structure and administration of grants programs are often geared to big projects that entail high costs and top-down design and supervision. In such cases, donors don't know how to deal with independent civic initiatives and nonviolent campaigns.
- Access to information and transparency of reconstruction strategies, efforts, and interlocutors within the state and private sector.

Notes

1. Karen Hussman, "Working Towards Common Donor Responses to Corruption," OECD DAC Network on Governance—Anti-Corruption Task Team, October 18, 2009, www.oecd.org.

2. Yama Torabi and Lorenzo Delesgues, *Afghanistan: Bringing Accountability Back In* (Kabul: Integrity Watch Afghanistan, June 2008), http://relief web.int/sites.

3. Richard Lardner, "Official: US Dollars Ending Up in Taliban Hands," Associated Press, September 15, 2011, www.miamiherald.com.

4. Jerome Starkey, "Drugs for Guns: How the Afghan Heroin Trade is Fuelling the Taliban Insurgency," *The Independent*, April 29, 2008, www.indepen dent.co.uk.

5. US Embassy–Kabul, Facebook posting, http://www.facebook.com/topic .php?uid=34734118909&topic=15934 (accessed May 22, 2010).

6. *Corruption in Afghanistan: Recent Patterns and Trends* (Vienna: UN Office of Drugs and Crime and the Islamic Republic of Afghanistan High Office of Oversight and Anti-Corruption, December 2012).

7. "About IWA," Integrity Watch Afghanistan, www.iwaweb.org (accessed October 12, 2013).

8. This chapter is based on interviews, conversations, and subsequent written communications with Lorenzo Delesgues, cofounder, Integrity Watch Afghanistan, October 2010 and April 2011.

9. The term "military" in this chapter refers to NATO's International Security Assistance Force (ISAF). The UN Security Council approved the first resolution authorizing ISAF on December 20, 2001.

10. "Community Based Monitoring: For an Aid Effective and Sustainable Reconstruction," Integrity Watch Afghanistan leaflet, www.iwaweb.org.

11. IWA brochure, provided to author on October 3, 2013.

12. "Case Study: Community Mobilisation—Succeeding in Impacting Your Future," Integrity Watch Afghanistan, March 2011, www.iwaweb.org.

13. Ibid.

14. Ibid.

15. "CBM to Monitor World Bank Projects," *Integrity Watch Afghanistan Newsletter* 11, no. 7 (July 24, 2011), www.iwaweb.org.

9

Curbing Police Corruption Through Engagement and Disruption: Uganda

The idea to start the campaign originated with the citizens according to the complaints they raised against the police. . . . Citizens were much involved in the campaign, and they will never cease to deal with the police as it is there to protect their lives and property. The campaign came into being when the police itself were aware that citizens had lost trust and confidence in its work. So the campaign saved both citizens and the police.
                                                                    —*Joseline Korugyendo*[1]

Police corruption is a particularly destructive form of injustice and oppression that undermines the rule of law, human rights, and the legitimacy of the state. Police corruption harms the lives of regular people, creating conditions of fear and impunity in dictatorships and fragile states, as well as in emerging and established democracies. It is a source of violence, not only when police abuse their established authority and power to physically repress, but also when citizens lose confidence in the institution and take the law into their own hands through vigilante groups. The three broad types of law enforcement graft are street-level bribery and extortion, bureaucratic corruption within police forces, and criminal corruption that can involve organized crime collusion and infiltration.[2]

In spite of efforts to tackle such venality, by national governments and donors, it appears to be increasing. Transparency International's 2010 Global Corruption Barometer, involving respondents in eighty-six countries and territories, found that since 2006, payoffs to police are said to have doubled.[3] Daunting as it may seem, a grassroots civic organization based in southwestern Uganda decided to confront police bribery, extortion, and impunity, but with an unusual strategy of nonviolent action and engagement.

Context

The National Foundation for Democracy and Human Rights in Uganda (NAFODU) is a civil society organization (CSO) initially founded by youth in 2000. Its vision is for a "democratic Uganda where government is accountable to its citizens and in which all the citizens freely and willingly participate in the social, political, and economic affairs of the country." NAFODU's strategic objectives are to "strengthen and consolidate instruments, institutions, and the operation of democracy in Uganda, and to consolidate the respect and observance of human rights and tenets of good governance in Uganda."[4] In addition to documenting human rights violations and monitoring national, local, and village council elections, Joseline Korugyendo, the CSO's former head of programs, stated that by 2007 the group was promoting local awareness and enforcement of human rights in partnership with relevant law enforcement agencies and human rights groups. NAFODU also focused on political, social, and economic disputes and concomitant violence in communities—through public debates, workshops, general civic education, and institutional capacity enhancement. Corruption was increasingly understood to be linked to all these challenges. Consequently, NAFODU launched "Fight Corruption" radio programs; formed a network of volunteers trained in monitoring; and provided advice, support, and recourse to victims of malfeasance.[5]

In the course of its anticorruption activities, NAFODU found that complaints about police demands for "fees" (i.e., bribes) were widespread and increasing in three main areas: registering cases, which typically affect the poor; finding so-called lost or transferred case files; and payment for police bonds, which is actually a public service that incurs no monetary charge.[6] As a result, citizens in the region lost confidence in the authorities. "Police were feared by the general public as they had turned into armed robbers in uniform and police stations were converted into extortion and exploitation grounds," said Korugyendo. Rather than going to the authorities, people were approaching NAFODU and other CSOs to report criminal cases, including murder and rape. To the alarm of civic leaders, locals were resorting to mob violence to seek redress and justice. In September 2008 NAFODU conducted an Integrity Survey in southwestern Uganda. Not surprisingly, the survey found that the police were considered the most corrupt institution, followed by traffic police.[7]

The results dovetailed with a national report, released by the Inspectorate of Government in October of that year, that also identified the police as the most corrupt institution in the country.[8] The 2011 Transparency International East Africa Bribery Index found that the "Uganda police lead the pack of the most bribery-prone institutions in the region."[9]

Campaign

The impetus for the campaign thus originated from local people, out of which was born the NAFODU-Police-Community Partnership Forum. Deliberations and planning began in 2009, and the initiative came to a formal close at the end of 2010. NAFODU received a grant of approximately US$44,547 from the Partnership for Transparency Fund (PTF), which had previously provided the organization with modest funding for anticorruption projects. Notwithstanding this financial support, the campaign was made possible through the efforts of local volunteers and citizens.

Objectives and Initial Challenges

The overall objectives of the civic initiative were to improve police community service, reduce corruption, and build a culture of integrity among law enforcement in the southwestern region. These aims were derived from people's grievances and the public's loss of trust in police officials and overall confidence in the institution. The long-term vision is for law enforcement institutions in Uganda to fulfill their constitutional roles, which is considered necessary for the country to secure the rule of law and move forward.

The CSO's leaders understood that they needed to overcome several fundamental challenges from the outset. From the people's side, there was fear of the police, a sense of resignation that curbing their corruption was impossible, and the belief that extortion and bribery were actually "part and parcel of their work."[10] From the law enforcement side, there was mistrust about NAFODU's intentions—namely, fear that it wanted to confront the authorities combatively, interfere in their work, and make officers lose their jobs. A delicate balance was needed. The CSO discerned that change would not be possible without the readiness of citizens to engage in nonviolent action targeting corrupt forces, yet they felt that a minimal basis of police cooperation would be conducive to emboldening the public. What may at first seem incompatible—getting the police to acquiesce to citizen mobilization designed to thwart their own graft—was remarkably bridged.

Memorandum of Understanding

At the behest of the PTF, NAFODU pursued a memorandum of understanding (MOU) with law enforcement authorities, outlining the elements of cooperation. To this end, they first organized meetings with officials in all five districts (Kabale, Kisoro, Kanungu, Rukungiri, and Ntungamo), building upon contacts already established through previous police involvement in the CSO's workshops and other activities. During all these interactions, the group leveraged the solid evidence it had compiled of police corruption from the 2008 Integrity Survey, community meetings with victims of extortion, and citizen input about police corruption from call-ins to its *Iraka Ryawe* (Your Voice) radio program. People would call in with complaints even when this was not the topic of the show. "After a meticulous explanation about the project, they [police] welcomed the idea, and this was the beginning of the MOU," recalled Korugyendo. It was finally signed in all five districts in July 2009.

The agreement was the initiative's first interim success. The MOU included the following elements: police participation in community radio programs, community monitoring of police behavior, ethics training workshops for local police, and public information initiatives about law enforcement. Moreover, the memorandum empowered NAFODU and citizens. Whether every police officer was on board was immaterial; it gave the campaign an official stamp of approval, clearly authorized certain activities and measures, and made it more difficult for corruptors within the institution to thwart the initiative or intimidate NAFODU and locals.

NAFODU did encounter initial skepticism among some in the communities, who felt that the police were compromising the organization and the initiative. As a result, part of the campaign's communications included messaging about the benefits, principally promoting police integrity and curbing abuses against innocent civilians.[11] When asked whether it had been easy to interact with the police and get their agreement, Korugyendo smiled and said, "Of course it was difficult, but we kept going to them and didn't give up." When the time came to sign it, "So many questions and excuses came up; in other words, they wanted to participate without the agreement, but we insisted," she added.

If signing an MOU with law enforcement authorities had proved untenable, would the initiative have folded even before it got off the ground? When asked this, Korugyendo maintained that NAFODU was prepared to move forward in a partnership with citizens, while undertaking the civic initiative's other actions to engage with police at various levels as much as possible. NAFODU had already provided a platform for citizens to air grievances about graft, which constituted public evidence that the region's top brass found difficult to ignore completely, even in the absence of an MOU. NAFODU also observed differences between the top brass and the rank and file that could be utilized; the former were more willing to cooperate than the junior officers, who were most involved in bribe-taking from citizens.

Information Gathering

NAFODU conducted a baseline survey in the region in January 2010 by convening community meetings in the five districts. A total of 200 people were asked if they or anyone they knew had paid a bribe to the police in the past six months. NAFODU reported that of the 101 respondents who reported a police station experience, 86 had to pay for a bond (which should be free of charge), and 58 case files were transferred. Korugyendo explained that case file transfers are a common method through which additional bribes are extracted as each new officer involved in an investigation (often for trumped-up charges) will make a demand on the citizen.

The survey fulfilled multiple strategic objectives. Information gathering is essential for successful civic campaigns and movements. It provided timely substantiation of corruption that the authorities could not easily refute or ignore. It constituted a reference point that would be used to compare perceptions about police corruption after the campaign. In being systematically consulted, citizens could begin feeling a sense of ownership in the unfolding campaign, and their bond with NAFODU was enhanced. As importantly, the survey offered a low-risk tactic through which regular people could safely make their voices heard about the police, at a juncture when there was much trepidation. As such, the survey could be construed as one of the campaign's early expressions of people power, which in turn empowered NAFODU in its persistent interactions and negotiations with the police at the higher echelons and subsequently on the ground.

Police Engagement

Throughout the duration of the initiative, a variety of meetings were conducted with the top brass, street officers, NAFODU, and very often, citizens. After the MOU was signed, NAFODU conducted meetings with officers in their respective districts. The CSO found that quite a few among the police actually wanted to improve the institution's image and to address corruption—critical information for designing the civic initiative's strategy and tactics. These discussions also gave NAFODU the opportunity to convey people's grievances and in turn allay police suspicions that people wanted to go after them as individuals. NAFODU organized a regional meeting in Kabale for police commanders and other top officers from the five districts, held on February 17, 2010.[12]

The CSO also convened district forums in which top officials, the CSO, and local citizens came together. The objectives were to share experiences and views about police corruption, how authorities can build public trust and confidence, and next steps—all of which helped to cultivate a sense of ownership in the initiative. These interactions were quite unusual; senior authority figures and regular people do not normally communicate in a relatively egalitarian manner. Finally, NAFODU was invited to participate in community policing meetings; it was seen as a bridge between the two. Law enforcement authorities had previously launched this initiative, but it had not been particularly effective because citizens were apprehensive to attend. Consistent with its grassroots character, NAFODU's representatives at these meetings were district volunteers and volunteer monitors, invited through the police-community liaison office and local community leaders. They created a safe setting that helped to allay citizens' fears about speaking up directly to the police.

Strategically, these meetings began activating a key dynamic of civil resistance—winning people over to the campaign or movement, including from the oppressors' side. Their experience also confirms one of the tenets of civil resistance theory: support and allies can be drawn from within corrupt institutions and systems, and sometimes can become a source of information, access, and constructive negotiations.

Tactics

NAFODU designed a series of mutually reinforcing actions, in part built upon their previous experiences with radio broadcasts, public education, training, and public sector monitoring.

• *Radio*. Weekly one-hour programs on local stations in each of the districts, in which police officers were on hand to talk with and respond to callers. The programs had multiple aims: educating people about laws against police corruption, and raising awareness about the linkages between police behavior on the one hand, and justice, transparency, accountability, and social concerns on the other hand. The content included news headlines about police corruption; state and civic efforts to promote integrity; cases reported by the public on police abuses, and problems citizens face when they seek services to which they are entitled from law enforcement authorities; call-ins for listeners to ask questions of NAFODU or officers, comment on the cases, or share experi-

Police Integrity Pledge

We the Police Officers who have participated in this training workshop on Police Ethics organized by National Foundation for Democracy and Human Rights in Uganda (NAFODU) with the financial support from PTF

Bearing in mind that the Uganda Police force shall be nationalistic, patriotic, professional, disciplined, competent, and productive;

Acknowledging that the members of the Police Force in Uganda shall be citizens of Uganda of good character;

Recognizing that the Uganda Police force shall perform functions of protecting life and property, preserving law and order, preventing and detecting crime, and cooperating with the civilian authority and other Security organs established under the Uganda constitution of 1995 and with the population generally;

Now agree as follows

1. We shall not engage ourselves in any corrupt acts that are likely to tarnish our Images.
2. We shall ensure that our role of fighting corruption, promoting transparency and accountability in Uganda is upheld.
3. With immediate effect, we have stopped Police abuses of demanding bribes, demanding mobilization fees to register cases, misuse of the police bond, illegal frequent transfer of case files between Police Officers with the aim of demanding payment of extra fees by the complainants and continued loss of case files.
4. We shall continue to maintain higher ethical standards for Police Personnel in Uganda.
5. We shall respect the code of conduct for Police Officers in Uganda.
6. We shall work to address the factors negatively influencing Police ethics like changing moral standards, working environment, among others.
7. We shall work towards achieving necessary standards of Police integrity, having a policy of zero tolerance to corruption. And we agree to sign this resolution.

Source: Orishaba Bagamuhunda Justus, "Project Completion Report: Corruption Prevention and Saving the Integrity Within Police in South Western Uganda: NAFODU-Police-Community Partnership Forum," December 2010, www.ptfund.org.

ences about the police; and police responses and advice to callers; and reports regarding actions they took to address citizens' complaints from the previous week's show.

• *Police ethics trainings.* Conducted four trainings in each of the five districts. A total of 180 officers participated. The objectives were (1) to improve their understanding of codes of conduct, their responsibilities under the Constitution of Uganda, and their role in fighting corruption and promoting transparency and accountability in society; and (2) to elicit their responses about ethical behavior in various types of situations.

• *Police integrity pledge.* Signed at the end of the ethics trainings. The pledge was designed to create social pressure for ethical behavior and strengthen the sustainability of the initiative. Rather than presenting the police with externally developed codes of conduct, the campaign engaged them in the process, which built their sense of ownership in improving ethics and integrity within the corrupt institution.

• *Public information and advocacy drive.* Through the campaign's network of volunteers, it consisted of biweekly SMS messages encouraging NAFODU volunteers and citizens to report corrupt police.

• *Community monitoring of police through SMS.* The other half of the information and advocacy drive, citizens and volunteer monitors, on a biweekly basis, sent in SMS reports of incidents of police corruption.

Campaign Attributes

Mobilization

NAFODU tapped its network of 600 grassroots volunteers, consisting of local people who were recruited via the CSO's radio, district coordinators, and SMS outreach efforts, and trained to work in their communities. Training involved skills and knowledge to assist victims of police corruption and to monitor, document, and report such practices in communities. They convened local meetings in order to build support for the campaign; educate people about police duties and codes of conduct; get their input at regular intervals; sensitize them to the bigger picture of the relationship between law enforcement corruption and overall abuse, the rule of law, and rights; and as importantly, mobilize them to engage in monitoring tactics. As the civic initiative progressed, human rights activists and other CSOs became involved. "It happened naturally," said Korugyendo, "as the project went on successfully."

NAFODU targeted at regular citizens a communications plan consisting of public awareness, education, and mobilization. Radio and SMS were the main conduits of communication; the former is the most accessible form of media, and the latter an effective, low-cost medium to directly interact with people. The key messages were that people should report police corruption in their communities to NAFODU, and that help was available for victims of police corruption to get redress. The media was both a target for education and coverage, as well as a conduit for strategic messaging. Local newspapers and radio stations reported about the campaign. In addition to the regular NAFODU radio program, the group also ran announcements.

Education

Woven throughout the tactics of the civic initiative was education—of citizens, victims of corruption, and the oppressors (police). Education had the strategic objectives of empowering communities to take action, winning over elements of the public as well as oppressors from within the corrupt police system, and shifting law enforcement ethics and behavior.

Leadership and Organization

Leadership for the campaign came from NAFODU; decisions were made by consensus through meetings that included police and citizens. NAFODU established small local offices in four districts, each staffed by two local coordinators who ensured a "local presence."[13] Their roles were to interface with their respective communities, liaise with police in the district, attend the weekly radio call-in programs, participate in the community policing program, and—last but not least—handle complaints of police corruption and misconduct.

Outcomes

Citizen Empowerment

NAFODU shared the results of its monitoring with law enforcement authorities as well as publicly through its radio programs. They also followed up on any complaints that were raised. According to Korugyendo, by about the middle of the initiative, the messages started shifting from reports of police misconduct to those of honest behavior. Citizens were also texting their thanks to the police and NAFODU.

During the last week of broadcasting, focus group discussions were organized, consisting of thirty randomly contacted radio station listeners in each of the five districts. Of the 150 participants, 145 reported that they listened to at least one of the programs. All wanted the program to continue and requested that more time be allocated for listener call-ins to officers. The results indicate that, in this context, radio call-ins functioned as a low-risk tactic that generated social pressure for police accountability.

Through NAFODU's district offices, locals could safely lodge complaints about police personnel and misconduct, and seek redress. Not only was this a source of assistance for people, it provided valuable information about corrupt practices and served as an ongoing interface between the civic initiative and the grass roots. Citizens submitted a total of 321 complaints of police corruption. Eighty-one were lodged in the Kisoro district, of which local coordinators handled seventy-five to completion and six were referred to authorities such as courts, Legal Aid, the Uganda Human Rights Commission, and the director of public prosecutions. In Kanungu district, there were sixty-three complaints; NAFODU reported that all were successfully tackled by the coordinators. In Rukungiri, seventy complaints were made; sixty-two were handled and eight were transferred to other authorities. Finally, 177 complaints were received in the Kabale locality, of which 166 were dealt with and 11 forwarded to relevant authorities.[14]

Police Behavior

Korugyendo reported a perceptible change in police behavior during the course of the civic initiative, based on the radio call-ins, SMS monitoring, and citizens' input to NAFODU, including the district offices. In November 2010 NAFODU conducted a second survey to compare the results with the baseline survey. It convened a meeting in each of the five districts with volunteer community monitors. Of the 200 respondents, 167 stated that the "integrity and behavior of the police changed and that people now who visit the police stations find it easier interacting with the police." However, twelve monitors reported instances of police corruption. A significant weakness of the two surveys is that they were not conducted in the same manner and thus cannot be compared directly. The questions were different, and the respondents were not drawn from the same cohort.

Transforming Power Relations

Little by little, over the course of 2010, the civic initiative was shifting power relations between the police and the grass roots. Authorities were acknowledging people's complaints live on the radio and interacting on an equal footing with NAFODU, local coordinators, and citizens. As well, they were asked for and provided input about how to improve their own integrity and gain public trust. Finally, community policing meetings were improving. In follow-up interviews to assess the aforementioned regional commanders' consultation, officials "noted that it was their first ever meeting for them to interact and discuss their work and how it affects the community."[15]

An unanticipated turn of events provided the most telling indication that the civic initiative was not only impacting corruption but upending the power equation between law enforcement and regular people. As the campaign progressed, the police began to share with NAFODU their own grievances, such as low salaries, shortages of trained manpower, lack of computers and vehicles, and overall poor working conditions. They contended that due to inadequate budget allocations, the police force remained small in ratio to the population, resulting in their being overextended and overworked.[16] They made the often heard claim that corruption was linked to these poor working conditions.[17] Whether that is true is arguable. What is most salient, however, is that during autumn 2010, officers approached the CSO with an extraordinary query. According to Korugyendo, they asked for NAFODU's help and for citizens to "give police a voice and make recommendations to the government to enable the police leadership to improve the welfare and morale of the police force." Essentially, law enforcement officials, having experienced people power firsthand, turned to the grass roots to help overcome the problems and injustices police faced within the institution.

Case Analysis

Program or People Power

Several elements distinguished this civic initiative from NAFODU's past programmatic anticorruption activities. Previous efforts focused on the public administration and private sector rather than on the police. Volunteers were recruited and trained to become monitors, but regular citizens did not actively take part in disrupting the corrupt status quo beyond participating in radio call-ins. In the NAFODU-Police-Community Partnership Forum, people power was generated through the sustained actions of citizens—serving as community volunteers monitoring and reporting police corruption via SMS, and expressing their grievances and observations directly to senior officials.

NAFODU understood that citizens were the drivers of the civic initiative. "They were part of the partnership and had power and the will to curb police corruption as they are the real victims with experience in their daily encounters with the police," explained Korugyendo. Taken together, the citizen baseline survey, top commanders' meeting, community policing meetings, complaints desk, radio programs, and police ethics training workshops functioned as complementary forms of engagement among the three pillars of the campaign: NAFODU, citizens, and law enforcement (senior officials and street officers). Collectively, they provided opportunities—for winning people over to the campaign from the side of the police as well as from the public, wielding social pressure on the corruptors, and extracting accountability. Citizen monitoring of police corruption activated a second fundamental dynamic of civil resistance—disruption of the status quo, in this case, the system of bribery and extortion among law enforcement in the southwestern region.

Contention and Cooperation

The NAFODU-Police-Community Partnership Forum presents what may seem at first glance to be a paradox. The initiative clearly sought to change corrupt police behavior and institutional practices, yet it was a collaborative venture. On the one hand, the strategy rested on empowering the grass roots to challenge established authority; on the other hand, it included engagement with the oppressor. In nonviolent struggles, contention does not preclude cooperation. First, civil resistance entails "constructive confrontation"; that is, the conflict shifts from the negative to the positive. Second, civil resistance seeks to change power relations and undermine abuse rather than target particular individuals. Even in antidictatorship movements, the objective is not simply for the tyrant to go, but also to end the regime and transform the system of governance and relations between the state and citizens. Third, because those within oppressive systems and institutions are not all equally supportive of the status quo, interaction is often possible.

In this particular context, Korugyendo suggested that the police came on board partly because some top officials and rank and file genuinely wanted to address corruption and build public trust. One could hypothesize that others within the institution may have viewed the initiative as a public relations exercise rather than a meaningful effort, or they did not expect the campaign to take off, or they could not contemplate that regular people have the capacity to wield power. While it was beyond the scope of this project to research the motivations, deliberations, and strategies of the police, such a line of inquiry would provide valuable insights for the field of civil resistance in general and for its application to corruption in particular.

NAFODU viewed curbing police corruption in a holistic manner, to be embedded within a larger framework of law enforcement accountability through social pressure, systemic change, and building awareness of the relationships between police reform, democracy, rule of law, and social justice among the public and law enforcement.

External Support

The Partnership for Transparency Fund's engagement is an example of the constructive role external actors can play vis-à-vis a bottom-up initiative. PTF provided modest funding directly to local actors to turn ideas into action and amplified the voices of the protagonists by inviting NAFODU to speak about the campaign on a panel it organized at the Fourteenth International Anti-Corruption Conference. It was the impetus for the MOU, which proved to be a valuable element of the civic initiative in this particular context. However, in most cases, PTF funding is contingent on such formalized cooperation.[18] Notwithstanding the value of the NAFODU-Police MOU in this particular case, it is an example of an external actor directly influencing a grassroots civic initiative. (For further discussion of this issue, see Chapter 12.)

Longevity

In the ensuing months of 2011, after the initiative formally ended, Korugyendo reported that the partnership informally persisted. Locals are aware that local law enforcement pledged to stop engaging in corrupt practices, and the people now know "what to do to get police services without paying bribes," she said. Volunteer monitors continued scrutinizing police conduct in communities. Korugyendo has since left NAFODU, but police continue to pay her visits. They tell her how proud they were of participating in the campaign, how it has improved their image in their respective communities, and how they would like to engage in more partnerships with the civic realm. In the long run, without additional efforts, progress may backtrack, as some clean officers get transferred to other posts while new ones come into the districts, bringing with them the prevailing culture of corruption in Uganda's police forces. Integrity workshops are needed for newcomers while monitoring is essential to maintain people power pressure and thwart graft when it rears its head.

Lessons Learned

Extrainstitutional Pressure and Shifting Loyalties

The NAFODU case illustrates that security forces are not immune to people power and offers valuable lessons. First, citizens can play a proactive role to reform the police, reduce corruption, and increase accountability through the application of extrainstitutional pressure. NAFODU eschewed conventional street actions to engage regular people through a planned set of largely low-risk tactics such as community-based surveys, radio call-ins, complaint mechanisms, and SMS monitoring. Second, democratic policing concepts and practices can be introduced and cultivated through people power as well as through top-down, administrative measures.

Third, traditional approaches to addressing police corruption include building ethics and developing codes of conduct.[19] Such interventions tend to be top-down and often externally derived, and then imposed on the recipients. This initiative turned the process upside-down. The grass roots played the catalytic role, and the targets—police officers—were involved in designing their own integrity training, thereby building ownership of it.

While the process was not easy, the NAFODU case demonstrates how a grassroots civic organization was able to find allies within the police system and capitalize on differences within the ranks, which bears out the tenets of civil resistance theory that power is not monolithic. In the anticorruption context, not everyone within a corrupt system has the same loyalties to maintaining it. As well, it points to the importance of powerholder engagement in order to discern such allies, positions, and loyalties. Fifth, even within a corrupt institution, personnel can nevertheless have grievances. There can be strategic advantages for civic campaigns to address the legitimate complaints of those people, particularly the rank and file. This move can disrupt the status quo, reduce the propensity to target the public, win support for the civic initiative, and cultivate respect for citizens.

A sixth lesson is that negotiation proved useful to gain a baseline of cooperation, strategically strengthening the civic initiative by giving it an official stamp of approval, clearly authorizing certain activities and measures, and making it more difficult for corruptors within the police to ignore or thwart the initiative and intimidate NAFODU and citizens.

Legitimacy and Trust

Like Integrity Watch Afghanistan (IWA), NAFODU used a credible method to bolster the legitimacy of the civic initiative. In IWA's case, each community selected the development project it wanted to monitor (see Chapter 9). In NAFODU's case, the baseline survey had the strategic benefits of corroborating citizens' grievances, providing credible documentation that was used to engage police officials, creating leverage to secure cooperation with the authorities, systematically interacting with citizens, fostering their sense of ownership in the initiative, and bolstering the civic group's credibility to be an intermediary between an inimical public and abusive police.

As well, NAFODU was ensconced in local communities, serving as a resource for people's problems. The CSO was seen as a trusted interlocutor both by communities and the police, which in turn emboldened citizens to challenge the form of corruption most egregious to them.

In spite of positive feedback from citizens and law enforcement, and actual demand for additional police integrity trainings, NAFODU has not been able to maintain momentum after the Partnership for Transparency grant. Unfortunately, in the ensuing years, the status of the CSO and its activities is not clear. Whatever the reasons in this particular situation, sustainability of positive outcomes is a challenge for civic anticorruption initiatives that aim to curb actual corrupt practices and transform cultures of malfeasance within institutions. The key question for civic actors, policymakers, and external actors is no longer whether citizens have the power to impact graft and abuse; it is how to preserve and amplify hard-won change.

The next chapter highlights the five civic initiatives that complement the in-depth case studies examined thus far. I illustrate the applicability of people power to diverse contexts and forms of corruption, as well as the adaptability and creativity of nonviolent methods, from digital resistance to surveys, monitoring, low-risk mass actions, humor, and street tactics.

Notes

1. This chapter is based on a personal conversation and email communications with Joseline Korugyendo, formerly the head of programs for NAFODU, in November 2010 and from March to June 2011.

2. Marie Chêne, "U4 Expert Answer: Anti-Corruption and Police Reform," U4 Anti-Corruption Resource Centre, May 31, 2010, www.u4.no.

3. *Global Corruption Barometer* (Berlin: Transparency International, 2010), www.transparency.org.

4. Joseline Korugyendo (panel presentation, Fourteenth International Anti-Corruption Conference, November 11, 2010, Bangkok).

5. Orishaba Bagamuhunda Justus, "Project Completion Report on NAFODU II Rwanisa Oburibwenguzi (Fight Corruption) Project," NAFODU, 2009, http://ptfund.org.

6. Police bond refers to the guarantee to citizens to not pay a fee if they have been arrested; they are entitled to be released while the authorities conduct their investigation or when they close the case. This link is to a posting on a Ugandan newspaper website, in which a citizen traumatically recounts how he was forced to pay a bond: http://www.sunrise.ug/opinions/letters/2398-i -though-police-bond-was-free.html.

7. Korugyendo, panel presentation.

8. "Third National Integrity Survey," *Inspectorate of Government Final Report* (Kampala: Republic of Uganda, October 2008), 119, www.igg.go.ug.

9. "East African Bribery Index (EABI) 2011 Launch: Burundi Most Corrupt Country in East Africa as Uganda Police Heads List of Most Bribery Prone

Institutions," press release, Transparency International, October 20, 2011, www.transparency.org.

10. Korugyendo, panel presentation.

11. Ibid.

12. Turinawe Cleophas, "PTF Quarterly Report 2010—Jan, Feb, March," NAFODU, 2010.

13. Orishaba Bagamuhunda Justus, "Project Completion Report: Corruption Prevention and Saving the Integrity Within Police in South Western Uganda: NAFODU-Police-Community Partnership Forum," December 2010, www.pfund.org.

14. Ibid.

15. Ibid., 6.

16. According to official figures from 2007, the ratio of police officers to population was approximately 1 officer per 1,880 inhabitants, but there are variations by district, ranging from 1:100 in the capital city, Kampala, to 1:8,000 in some outlying districts ("Uganda: Overview of the Police Force, Including Structure, Size, and Division of Duties; Police Militarization; Existence of Police Complaints Authority and Recourse Available to Individuals Who File Complaints Against the Police," Immigration and Refugee Board of Canada, June 3, 2008, www.unhcr.org).

17. Debate is ongoing in the anticorruption world about whether a linkage exists between low remuneration and corruption in the public sector, including law enforcement. The Ugandan Inspectorate of Government's Second National Integrity Survey in 2003 concluded, "A main cause of corruption is still attributed by all those interviewed to low salaries and delay in payment of salaries." However, research from other countries casts doubt on a causal relationship. For instance, a study from Indonesia found that public officials can be comparatively well paid at the lower end of the scale (close to three-quarters of all civil servants), even though there is widespread corruption in the public sector. See www.u4.no./themes/health/healthsalaries.cfm.

18. "Concept Note Guidelines," Partnership for Transparency Fund, http://ptfund.org/apply-grant/concept-note-guidelines/.

19. Chêne, "U4 Expert Answer."

10

Highlights from Five Cases: Bosnia-Herzegovina, Egypt, Kenya, Mexico, Turkey

C hapters 3–9 presented seven in-depth case studies of how nonviolent civic initiatives and social movements have impacted graft and abuse with remarkable results. In the course of this research project, so many other examples came to light—all innovative and rich with lessons. This chapter summarizes five such cases. The One Minute of Darkness for Constant Light campaign (Turkey), shayfeen.com/Egyptians Against Corruption, Dosta! (Bosnia-Herzegovina), and DHP* (Mexico) all began at the same starting point. A small group of citizens—youth, women, professionals—decided to take action. Like 5th Pillar (India), they wanted to tackle the systemic corruption and impunity that were destroying their countries. But their existential dilemma was to ascertain where to begin when facing something so nebulous and pervasive. In contrast, Muslims for Human Rights (MUHURI) in Kenya—like Integrity Watch Afghanistan and NAFODU (Uganda)—specifically focused on empowering communities. Both shayfeen.com and MUHURI created grassroots monitoring tactics, the former at the national level and the latter at the local level.

Weakening the Crime Syndicate in Turkey

It's called the crime syndicate. It refers to the links between the Turkish state and organized crime—more specifically, a nationwide network involving politicians, elements of the police, *gladios* (paramilitary groups connected to state security institutions), the mafia, and the private sector.[1] By 1996 the country was beleaguered by this nefarious, intertwined underworld, which was exerting influence throughout the state.[2] Corruption was endemic, an "entrenched pillar of a system that makes billions of dollars for 'deep state' personages who influence both the economy and the politics of the country," according to filmmaker and civic activist Ezel Akay.[3] Extrajudicial murders were common, either linked to mafia battles or political in nature. "Everybody suffered from this in Turkey: the working class, the financial sector, and the ordinary people—because this gladio-mafia combination affected all walks of life," said Ergin Cinmen, a prominent lawyer.[4]

The gravity of the situation came to a head through an unexpected turn of events. On November 3, 1996, a speeding luxury car collided into a truck on a highway between the Aegean coast and Istanbul, near the town of Susurluk. The passengers in the car were

- Sedak Bucak, a parliamentarian allied with the Right Path Party (which at the time was the coalition partner in the government) and the leader of a large landowning Kurdish clan in the southwest of the country.
- Huseyin Kocada, a police chief and police academy director.
- Abdullah Çatl, an escaped criminal, hit man, and drug smuggler associated with gladios, classified as "most wanted" by the Turkish courts, Swiss police, and Interpol.
- Gonca Us, a former beauty queen and Çatl's mistress.

Çatl was found with a fake diplomatic ID signed by Mehmet Ağar, the minister of internal affairs and a member of Parliament with the Right Path Party, who had previously authorized the document when he was chief of police. The car contained cocaine, arms, ammunition, silencers, and a horde of cash. The sole survivors were Bucak and Hasan Gökçe, the hapless truck driver. Only Gökçe was arrested.[5] After the news broke, students spontaneously protested around the country. They were harshly repressed—the government's usual reaction to citizen dissent. In fact, that same day another group of students was standing trial for having broken the Demonstrations Law because they held up a banner in the Parliament concerning their right to education. They were sentenced to fifteen months in prison.

Ağar resigned from his ministerial post but held on to his legislative seat, which afforded him parliamentary immunity. Thus, the Susurluk crash was not merely a symbol of the crime syndicate. It was a real, tangible manifestation of it—from actual individuals to the interrelationships among the state, gladios, and the mafia; to corruption, abuse of power, and impunity; and finally to the perversion of justice.

Establishing the Building Blocks: Strategy and Planning

All over Turkey, people were outraged and began to talk independently about what to do. That December in Istanbul, a group of fifteen professionals and activists who personally knew one another decided that the scandal provided an opportunity to overcome citizens' fear and apathy, tap public disgust, mobilize people to action, and push for definable changes that would expose and weaken the crime syndicate. Key members of the group included Ezel Akay, the aforementioned filmmaker and civic activist; Ergin Cinmen, a leading lawyer; Yüksel Selek, a professor of sociology; and Mebuse Takey, a lawyer. In spite of the repressive political climate, they began meeting regularly to strategize and plan. They formed an informal group called the Citizen Initiative for Constant Light.

Some weeks later, Ersin Salman, a public relations professional, came on board. Prior to the Susurluk crash, Salman's firm had won a contract from the National Broadcasters Association to repair its credibility and image. The mafia had started to gain control over a major broadcasting corporation through business links and manipulating legislation. In general, the mass media had been complicit in the expansion of the crime syndicate into its midst. Salman saw Susurluk as a focal point around which the media could assert its independence. The core message was, "Nothing will be the same after Susurluk!"[6] It ran from November 1996 to January 1997. "The [media] campaign called on people to meet their duties [as citizens], and then the [One Minute of Darkness for] Constant Light campaign was an answer," he observed.

Decisions were made by consensus, while different people chaired meetings. Salman recalled, "It was a big school for everyone. We had never worked in NGOs [nongovernmental organizations], only political parties or other organizations with a hierarchical order, but we had to function in a horizontal way." Rather than rushing to action, the group carefully planned the campaign through informal discussions. First, members identified clear objectives that were legitimate and legal, Akay reported, in order to "move the majority."[7] Their overall goals were to reveal crime syndicate and deep state relationships, to begin breaking them apart, and to accomplish these ends without undermining democracy. To this end, members identified three clear, definable objectives. First, they sought to remove parliamentary immunity, which provided corrupt cabinet ministers and lawmakers, such as Ağar and Bucak, with iron-clad protection from investigations and prosecution. Second, they wanted the founders of the criminal groups to stand trial and face justice. Finally, judges trying these cases should receive protection in case they faced reprisals.

Strategic choices were made from the outset. The group adopted a leaderless organizational structure to defend against reprisals and to underscore the message that the campaign was driven by citizens. Furthermore, the Citizen Initiative would be nonpolitical in nature, and regular people should feel a sense of ownership in the effort—in order to protect against smear attacks, build a broad alliance, and attract the widest possible base of the public in the mobilization. Some political parties wanted to support the effort. "We told them no, but you can join us as citizens," said Salman. Understanding the necessity to build unity, the group systematically forged an informal coalition by approaching nonpolitical organizations, including the Bar Association, the Istanbul Coordination of Chambers of Professions, unions, professional associations (such as pharmacists, dentists, civil engineers, electrical engineers, architects, and doctors), and civil society organizations (CSOs). According to Tekay, "For the first time, groups that had never joined forces before in Turkey found themselves participating side by side—from the business community to the slum-dwellers."[8]

The organizers mulled over how to harness the voices and aspirations of the public into a collective act of defiance that would generate overwhelming social pressure on powerholders and the political will to tackle the crime syndicate. Hence, they endeavored to create a nonviolent tactic that would overcome real obstacles, such as imprisonment, violent crackdowns, and public fear and feelings of powerlessness. The organizers had several strategic considerations. The action should be legitimate and legal, simple to carry out, and low-risk, and create a national sense of unity. "People didn't want to get involved in political action, so we chose something that couldn't get them in trouble but could be seen," explained Salman. Cinmen's teenage daughter came up with the idea of the synchronized turning off of lights. "It was something very simple for people to say that they didn't want to live like this anymore," he added. The next consideration was who would make the call to action. "We felt the campaign idea should appear to come not from an intellectual or an elite group but from a street person, a kid, an aunt on a pension, etc. The last one had a good ring to it," said Akay. The "anonymous aunt" became the symbol of the campaign enjoining every Turk to turn off the lights. Therewith came into existence the One Minute of Darkness for Constant Light campaign.

Time for Action

The Internet was not yet ubiquitous in Turkey, and of course, social media did not exist in 1997. Nevertheless, the group creatively maximized use of the technologies at hand. A chain of mass faxes got the word out and called every citizen of Turkey to action. The unifying message of the outreach measures was, "Listen to the voice of the silent majority!" The one-pagers were faxed to all the organizations in the informal coalition. They in turn sent them to their respective members, urging them to disseminate the message as widely as possible—to relatives, friends, neighbors, and others. As a result, the call to action went viral, so to speak. Moreover, the fax had a dual purpose. It not only got the word out, it incorporated a signature drive in support of the One Minute of Darkness for Constant Light campaign. To the delight of the organizers, within one week 10,000 people responded by signing their

---

The Citizens Initiative for Constant Light Manifesto and "Call to Action"

Sürekli aydınlık için 1 dakika karanlık!
[1 Minute of Darkness for Constant Light!]

Suç örgütlerini kuranların ve onlara görev verenlerin, mutlaka yargı önüne çıkarılması konusundaki kararlı isteğimi göstermek; [To show my determination to bring to justice the ones who assembled crime organizations and the ones who hired their services;]

olayı soruşturan kişi ve mercilere destek vermek; [to support the persons and authorities who investigate the events in question;]

demokratik, çağdaş, şeffaf hukuk devleti özlemimi duyurmak için, [to make my yearning for a democratic, contemporary, and transparent state of law be heard;]

1 Subat 1997 Cumartesi gününden başlayarak, [Starting Saturday, February 1, 1997;]

her gün saat 21.00'de ışığımı BİR DAKİKA süreyle karartıyorum. [at 9:00 pm every day I'll turn my lights off for ONE MINUTE.]

Ve bu ülkede yaşayan herkesi, bir ay süreyle, her gün saat 21.00'de ışıklarını karartmaya çağırıyorum! [And I call everyone who lives in this country for a one-minute blackout every day at 9:00 pm for one month!]

Bu çağrı, YURTTAŞTAN YURTTAŞA yapılmıştır. [This is a call from CITIZEN TO CITIZEN.]

Lütfen Yaygınlaştırın! [Please spread!]

Adı-Soyadı Mesleği İmzası [Name-Surname Profession Signature]
CITIZENS INITIATIVE For CONSTANT LIGHT
[Address, phone and fax numbers . . .]

Source: Ezel Akay and Liam Mahoney, *A Call to End Corruption* (Minneapolis: Center for Victims of Torture, 2003), 2.

name to the call to action and faxing it back to the campaign. In essence, it was the first grassroots mass action of the campaign. The next one, however, far surpassed everyone's expectations.

With Salman's expertise, the civic initiative also developed a communications plan that capitalized on the Susurluk public relations venture he previously led for the National Broadcasters Association, before having joined the civic initiative. One month prior to S-Day (Susurluk Day), February 1, 1997, they systematically researched and contacted, via personalized letters, almost sixty print columnists who appeared interested in the crime syndicate menace and sympathetic to citizen action to fight it. They sought and got maximum media exposure in order to spread the word of the campaign and mobilize citizens from all walks of life. As a result of the media's sensitization to Susurluk, many television channels started to hold countdowns before the appointed time of action. On January 15, organizers convened an unusual press conference. They staged a theatrical stunt of the car accident, and prominently displayed the names of the citizens who responded to the faxed call to action. There were no official spokespersons; different individuals answered journalists' questions. Yüksel Selek, the Citizen Initiative general secretary, commented, "It was the first press conference held by 10,000 individuals."[9]

At 9:00 p.m. on February 1, 1997, citizens began to turn off their lights for one minute. Each evening more and more across the country joined the mobilization. By the second week, people began adding their own flourishes. They banged pots and pans, flashed lights, honked horns at intersections, circle danced (traditional style), held candlelight vigils and neighborhood marches, and shouted slogans such as, "Don't shut up. If you shut up it will be your turn." As citizens overcame their fear and gathered together, residential squares took on a festive character. In some regions, local initiatives were launched. "People started to remember what they'd forgotten—that they were living in the same building, same neighborhood and city," Salman said. "It was very exciting for them to see their neighbors and people far away [through the media]." Not surprisingly, after the second week, as people power intensified, the reprisals began. Senior members of the ruling coalition attempted to undermine the legitimacy of the campaign and the integrity of all who participated. Their contemptuous, derogatory public statements, some rife with sexual innuendo and accusations of treachery, gravely backfired. Not only did citizens take offense at their insults, civil resistance was undeterred.[10]

What was not anticipated was that the military, which considers itself the defender of the post-Ottoman secular state, used the citizen uprising to withdraw its support from the government. According to Akay, the generals and other critics of the senior partner in the ruling coalition, the Islamist-leaning Refah Party, saw an opportunity to undermine it. On February 28, the National Security Council forced the coalition government to resign. The prime minister, Necmettin Erbakan, held his post until the Parliament approved the new government six months later. In spite of the political turmoil, the One Minute of Darkness for Constant Light campaign continued. "We tried to emphasize that the campaign was against the organized crime–state syndicate, not the government. The military wanted to steal the movement for their own purposes," asserted Salman. He added that the campaign held a press conference to disassociate itself from the intervention and published ads saying, "We won't let you steal our light." In fact, the military's move was counterproductive to the campaign's goals, which required a working government and sought overall change in the corrupt system, regardless of those who are in power at any given time. In retrospect, the organizers regret not having taken an even more direct stand. "If we had spoken out against what happened, it would have been better. At least the generals couldn't look us in the eye and say that their postmodern coup d'etat had the support of the citizen," Tekay conceded.[11]

The mobilization peaked in the latter half of February. Organizers estimated that approximately 30 million people, 60 percent of the population, participated throughout the country. The group decided to end the campaign at a high point rather than wait for it to peter out, thereby producing a sense of victory. They called off the mobilization on March 9. However, as powerholders, including Prime Minister Erbakan, used stalling tactics and legal loopholes to block inquiries, the group maintained pressure well into 1998 in two ways. First was a smaller-scale Constant Light mobilization, accompanied by white ribbons symbolizing the demand for a clean state, and a humorous toy called the "Susurluk Bugger" democracy machine. The campaign challenged the two competing political poles—secularists (backed by the military) and Islamists—with a third vision, encapsulated by the slogan, "Neither the shadow of the Sharia nor the roar of the tanks: For democracy only."[12] The second mode of pressure was a series of nonviolent actions, including a mass mail-in of "stolen" copies of the high court inquiries to all legislators; a signature campaign proclaiming, "I resign from being a slave. Now I'm a citizen!"; public presentation of a "Susurluk Citizen Report"; roundtables for a Civic Constitution Initiative; and a letter-writing effort.

Outcomes

In a short time span, the Citizen Initiative for Constant Light literally mobilized the majority of the population, wielding people power that shook up the corrupt status quo. "It was a civic uprising," avowed Salman. The campaign broke the strong taboo over confronting the crime syndicate, epitomized by its linkages with the state and corruption. It succeeded in bringing to trial suspects associated with Susurluk, including mafia leaders, police, military officials, and businesspeople. The next prime minister, Mesut Yilmaz, continued the case. He authorized an investigative committee that issued a report listing the names of each crime syndicate victim. The Parliament also created an investigative committee that revealed the crime syndicate's activities. Individuals at the tip of the iceberg of this venal system were tried, and verdicts were pronounced. Taken together, these unprecedented measures began exposing some syndicate figures and relationships.

In 2001 Sadettin Tantan, the interior minister, launched a series of investigations in cooperation with the Banking Regulation and Supervision Agency. Large-scale embezzlement was exposed, resulting in the arrests of several well-known businesspeople. The victory was not complete, because their collaborators in the Parliament and government were left unscathed. The next year, however, voters changed the profile of the Parliament, which may have been punishment against the existing political establishment as well as the military. In the November 2002 elections Akay reported that 70 percent of those elected were incumbents, the old-guard party leaders were voted out, and the new democratic Islamist AK (Justice and Development) Party won by a landslide. Mehmet Ağar, the former police chief and interior minister, continues to elude justice, though the net is closing in. Until 2007 he was protected from prosecution by parliamentary immunity, but in September 2011 he was sentenced to five years in prison "for forming an armed criminal gang involving state actors and mafia."[13] He won an appeal and is still free.

The Citizens Initiative never came to a formal end. Some of the organizers moved on; for example, Selek is the co-spokesperson of the Green Party. At critical junctures, the organizers joined forces with other civic organizations and the public to wield people power. After the devastating 1999 earthquake, they cooperated with the Human Settlements Association to build a civic coalition and organize citizens to provide disaster relief. In February 2003, another One Minute of Darkness for Constant Light campaign was launched to oppose Turkish collaboration with the US Army for the war in Iraq. With surveys indicating that

94 percent of the population opposed the war, the mass mobilization turned dissent into action. On March 1 of that year, by a slim majority, parliamentarians voted against a measure allowing US troops to use southern Turkey as a base for attacks—in spite of expectations it would pass.[14] The Constant Light mobilization has not faded from the public's memory. Fourteen years later, from May 1 to June 12, 2011 (general elections day), citizens raised their voices to candidates on a series of issues, including corruption in university entrance exams; privatization of water; construction of hydroelectric dams, nuclear reactors, and coal-fired power plants; labor rights; journalists' rights; and the assassination of Armenian-Turkish journalist Hrant Dink.[15]

The Citizens Initiative for Constant Light altered the relationship between Turkish citizens and powerholders. "The system changed; nobody could question the state before, nobody could question what the government does, what ministers do. Now even the generals are answerable to the people." Have the crime syndicate and deep state machinations completely ended? No. For Salman and the leaders of the original Citizens Initiative for Constant Light, the struggle for accountability, justice, and democracy is ongoing. But looking back, Salman reflected, "We rocked Turkey so that the rocks cannot be in the same place anymore."

From Outrage to Action: Women Launch Monitoring Movement in Egypt

Egypt's momentous January 25 Revolution in 2011 for democracy and justice did not happen in a matter of weeks. Contrary to widespread misconceptions, the nonviolent struggle against the almost thirty-year dictatorship of Hosni Mubarak began in 2003. First came the Egyptian Movement for Change (2003–2006) known as Kefaya ("enough" in Arabic), and then in defiance of a wave of ruthless regime repression, the April 4 youth movement (2008), the "We Are All Khaled Said" youth campaign (2010), and the ElBaradei campaign for reform (2010).[16] In the midst of this tumult emerged another grassroots force for change, shayfeen.com, which combines a play on the Arabic words "we see you" or "we are watching you" with the group's website address.[17]

On May 25, 2005, in what would infamously become known as Black Wednesday, female journalists and protesters were molested by unofficial regime forces during protests over a questionable constitutional referendum that in practice would make it difficult for candidates to run against President Mubarak. In spite of videos of the attacks on

YouTube and other websites, the government denied responsibility. When the global news outlet Al Jazeera broadcast on a split screen a press conference with the minister of the interior denying the attacks had occurred together with footage of these very incidents, people reacted with disbelief and outrage. In Egyptian society, the violation of the women became a matter of the victims' honor, and dishonor on those who did not stop the assaults. As the Association of Egyptian Mothers (Rabetat al-Ummahat) organized silent protests, another small group of women—including Engi Haddad, a public relations consultant; Bothaina Kamel, a popular television host in the region; and Ghada Shabender, an English-language university instructor—decided they had to take further action. Tapping the prevailing public sentiment that "we have turned a blind eye for so long that the government must think we are blind," the group founded shayfeen.com in August 2005. Their aim, according to Haddad, was to build a grassroots "people's monitoring movement."[18] "When elections are corrupt, we're watching you. When you rig votes, we're watching you. When you torture prisoners, we're watching you. This is our mission statement," declared Kamel.[19]

Low Risk, High Visibility

The women began by providing a phone number to which anyone could call or text and by launching a website to monitor government irregularities and provide citizens with a platform to register complaints. In this context, the website had multiple functions. It served as shayfeen.com's initial recruitment method; within one month, approximately 500 people signed up to the campaign.[20] Second, the website was the medium through which citizens could engage in a low-risk tactic. Rather than gather on the street, which would inevitably meet with violent repression, people en masse could publicly and safely expose regime abuse, impunity, and malfeasance. Finally, people could express their sentiments about it, a further nonviolent act of defiance in a country that crushed dissent. The women quickly found that corruption was one of the major grievances of citizens who contacted them. They strategized that each action chipped away at Mubarak's reign of fear and contributed to building a sense of collective responsibility for change. "Once they're rid of the fear they've had so long, change won't come suddenly; it will be step by step," explained Kamel. "Our first step was to open our eyes, to see where we are now and where we are going next, to see what our government is doing to us, and to understand what we are doing to our country," she added.

Their next step was audacious. The newfound activists decided to monitor the September 2005 presidential elections, although the regime denied requests for international election observers. They ran a campaign ad in *al-Masri al-Yawm*, an independent newspaper, announcing, "This is your election, you have eyes, you can see."[21] They listed over twenty types of irregularities on the shayfeen.com website and encouraged the public to report violations through text messages, phone calls, and the Internet. The response was overwhelming. By the second day of the polls, they improvised a tracking system to deal with the traffic and onslaught of information. Within three days they received 28,000 calls.[22] Even before the election was over, state-controlled television alleged that they were spreading rumors, and an official from the Ministry of the Interior called to complain. Undeterred, shayfeen.com subsequently released its findings along with criticism of the government. The group was inundated by local, regional, and international media.[23] It was their first victory. Every citizen who sent information played a role in exposing the fraudulent electoral practices to the entire world. Even the US State Department used the data for its 2005 annual human rights report.[24]

Eyes on the Parliamentary Elections
The group next set its sights on the December 2005 parliamentary elections. In the space of a few months the women executed a highly organized campaign to mobilize citizens to actively monitor the voting and expose wrongdoing. Once again, shayfeen.com developed creative, low-risk, mass-action tactics to raise awareness, gain visibility, and garner support. Approximately 100,000 tea glasses with the movement's logo were distributed, bringing the campaign into homes and coffee and tea houses around the country. The group printed more than 250,000 plastic bags carrying the slogan, "We see you, and at the elections we are observing you," which in Arabic happens to rhyme. The bags were used and reused so much that the minister of trade dubbed those carrying them the "supermarket activists."[25]

Prior to the elections, shayfeen.com implemented a meticulous monitoring plan. They outfitted cars with digital photography equipment, laptops, and GSM and trained members and volunteers to use them.[26] Two hundred monitors each received a packet containing badges, instructions, and a violations checklist. They fanned out across Egypt's governorates, meeting up with local movement coordinators. Their assignment was to film the three phases of the voting process, document fraud via video, and disseminate the images by uploading to websites in real time, as well as by sharing with the media and even projecting footage onto building walls in public squares. They cooperated with the aforementioned Kefaya movement, which distributed CDs of the videos. The polling was marred by police brutality, violence, and eleven deaths. Shayfeen.com recorded over 4,200 reports of violations, of which 80 percent concerned corruption, and women were the source of people power at the grass roots.[27]

"Long Live Justice!"

Undeterred, in spring 2006 the leaders sent the findings to the Supreme Election Committee, which refused to conduct an investigation, as well as to the Ministries of Interior and Justice, and the media.[28] Among the violations was judicial fraud. The report identified the eighteen judges allegedly involved in such activities, including an instance that Haddad witnessed. "I saw a judge change the results. I walked to the judge and said, 'What you're doing is wrong.' He said, 'You go out or I throw you in jail!'"[29] The leaders met with two honest judges, Hesham Bastawissi and Mahmoud Mekki, who then took up the findings within their professional association, the Judges Club (also known as the Judges Syndicate). They examined the eighteen cases and confirmed judicial fraud. Not surprisingly, the regime counterattacked and launched investigations against the two. The intimidation backfired. Shayfeen.com, Kefaya, and human rights and prodemocracy youth activists launched street actions, from rallies to a tent city outside of the Judges Club. The latter tactic is notable as it foreshadowed the occupation of Tahrir Square approximately six years later. Emboldened by their fellow citizens, by late April fifty honest magistrates maintained a three-day sit-in at the Judges Club. They were attacked daily, resulting in the hospitalization of Judge Mahmoud Hamza.

Out of these actions emerged the campaign for an independent judiciary and the demand for a new law to enshrine this fundamental liberty. Street protests continued in spite of violent repression. On May 25, on the anniversary of Black Wednesday, nonviolent actions were held in Egypt and around the world. In addition to shayfeen.com, youth and labor groups, Kefaya, the El Ghad (Tomorrow) Party, and the Muslim Brotherhood rallied around the judges. In Cairo, demonstrators cried out, "Have courage, judges. Rid us of the tyrants" and "Long live justice!" while 300 magistrates staged a silent protest. Shayfeen.com members took part, engaging with security forces and even interjecting themselves between the two sides to prevent violence. Kamel recalled telling them, "When you approach these kids, be gentle. They're Egyptians like you. We're one people, don't forget." Offering a sticker to riot police, her outstretched hand was displayed in news reports all over the world. In May of that year, Judge Mekki was cleared of charges. However, Judge Bastawissi was "reprimanded" and denied a promotion.[30]

Winning Support: Egyptians Against Corruption

The female activists strategized their next move. In September 2006 a new movement was created to complement shayfeen.com. While the website maintained a more daring profile, Egyptians Against Corruption broadened the struggle by creating an inclusive social platform designed to win over regime supporters and wide swaths of the public. In general terms, shayfeen.com activated the disruption dynamic of people power, while Egyptians Against Corruption focused on shifting loyalties and pulling people to its side. Indeed, they reported that members of Mubarak's National Democratic Party wanted to join. Egyptians Against Corruption reframed the struggle discourse, zeroing in on everyday matters that resonated with citizens by demonstrating the links between graft and tragedies resulting from calamities such as train crashes, contaminated food, and collapsed buildings. They developed communication strategies targeting both the public and various sources of support for the corrupt status quo, such as parts of the government, political and policy elites, and the media. The core messages were that

- Corruption is a societal problem that needs to be dealt with from the bottom up as well as from the top down.
- Every day, in every way, everyone is a victim of corruption.
- It's up to people to claim their rights.
- The movement is for any citizen who cares about and loves Egypt and believes he or she is entitled to justice, equality, and a life free from corruption.

They launched an innovative educational website, designed to target youth in particular, along with a civic education campaign called Claim Your Rights (Eksab Ha'ek). Imaginative mass actions were a hallmark of the civic initiative. Members sold the new badge in the thousands, mostly through one-on-one interactions. The tactic forged a sense of social identity with the movement, and the proceeds were used to fund activities. As importantly, in buying and wearing the pin, citizens joined thousands of others in a low-risk act of dissent similar to 5th Pillar's use of the zero-rupee note in India (see Chapter 7). "It is clear that a badge will not fix corruption," explained Haddad. "But by buying and wearing the pin, and the conversations that ensue, you are giving the other person a chance to enter into and generate a discussion. It is that dialogue that we are trying to achieve."[31] Before the end of the year, the activists initiated a popular anticorruption contest on December 9, International Anti-Corruption Day, whereby the public could vote for anticorruption heroes via SMS or on the movement's website. The tactic not only reinforced integrity but bestowed the honor through the collective actions of thousands of fellow Egyptians, which was broadcast before millions via Arab satellite television.

Countering Repression with Legal Instruments

By 2007, elements of the regime grew uncomfortable as shayfeen.com and Egyptians Against Corruption gained momentum. That March, security forces ransacked Haddad's public relations company. Shayfeen.com was charged with incitement, corresponding with a foreign entity, possessing documents challenging government policy (one of which was the Transparency International Toolkit), and propagating negative information about Egypt. They successfully sued the government by demonstrating that their activities were legal because Egypt was a signatory to the United Nations Convention Against Corruption (UNCAC). As a result, the government was forced to publish UNCAC in Egypt's official legal chronicle, which was essential to render it binding in courts of law.

The Anticorruption Legacy

In 2008 shayfeen.com was dismantled and Egyptians Against Corruption assumed the overall struggle. The next turning point came during the internationally criticized November 2010 parliamentary elections.[32] "What we witnessed was a charade; there was no legality to the Parliament," asserted Haddad. The anticorruption movement joined together with the April 6 youth movement, the We Are All Khaled Said campaign, the youth wing of the El Ghad party, labor, and democracy activists to mobilize people in a nonviolent insurrection against the dictatorship. As citizens rose up against the regime, Haddad and some colleagues launched efforts to freeze the ill-gotten gains amassed by the Mubarak family and its cronies. In 2013 they embarked on a new struggle to recover the country's stolen assets.

Haddad recently reported on another extraordinary development. In 2011, during the early days of the January 25 Revolution, shayfeen.com seemed to resurface. She discovered that a group of youth activists had adopted the name and updated the logo. They formally resurrected the movement in March 2011. The young people approached Kamel and her for help to monitor the first post-Mubarak parliamentary elections in November of that year. In 2012 the young people came back and asked to work with them on corruption. The women are now on the group's fifteen-member Board of Trustees, which is made up of nine youth and six elders. The youngsters, many of whom are affiliated with We Are All Khaled Said, have established chapters in each of the country's twenty-seven governorates. The new shayfeen.com, like its predecessor, is neutral in ideology. It wants to instill anticorruption values among its peers; empower them through educational initiatives such as workshops to use UNCAC; activate the public, for example, through a toll-free call center for reporting corruption; and disrupt graft and abuse of power through monitoring. According to Haddad, by August 2012 the new shayfeen.com had over 150,000 members. "It's now bigger than any political party other than the Muslim Brotherhood." Looking back, Haddad reflected, "There is a latent energy inside youth. We and other predecessors such as Kefaya helped to plant this consciousness in them to rise up and demand their rights."

In just a few years, the outrage and courage of a few women spawned two remarkable initiatives that took corruption out of the shadows and into the public domain, channeled people's anger and indignation into civil resistance, sparked a judicial revolt for independence, pressured authorities, and utilized the Internet and emerging social media to communicate, educate, mobilize, and directly disrupt corrupt practices. They not only dented the regime's reign of fear but turned the power relationship upside down. After twenty-five years of the state's monitoring the populace, citizens used nonviolent tactics to keep an eye on the regime.

Social Audits Pressure Powerholders: Kenya

Muslims for Human Rights (MUHURI) is a civil society organization based in Mombasa, Kenya, working at the grass roots with marginalized communities in the Coast province, as well as advocating for human rights, rule of law, and accountability at the national level. Its vision is "a just society anchored on human rights and good governance."[33] The organization's goal is the promotion of good governance that respects human rights and the rule of law.[34] Back in 2005, similarly to NAFODU's experience in Uganda, citizens began coming to MUHURI with complaints. In this instance, they told the group that money was being spent for development in their communities, but they were not being consulted, nor were they seeing any changes or benefits. "We were focusing on human rights, and people started asking, 'Why are we so poor?'" recollected Hussein Khalid, the youthful executive director.[35] By listening to those with whom they worked, MUHURI realized that the struggle for human rights was linked to tackling poverty, and graft was at the nexus. "In order to decrease poverty levels, we had to start fighting corruption and increasing accountability and transparency," he added.

Like Integrity Watch Afghanistan (see Chapter 8), the group initially had no program or funding to expand activities. It had to improvise. But MUHURI was committed to following up on the complaints because "they [complaints] were dear to the people," said Khalid. Most of the grievances concerned constituency development funds (CDFs), which are annual allocations of approximately $1 million to each member of Parliament (MP) for his or her district, ostensibly to conduct needed public works projects and improve the lives of residents. CDF is the result of a noble and fashionable idea in the development world; devolve power, and give communities resources for their own development schemes. However, without meaningful independent oversight and with endemic corruption, the end result is often mismanagement and graft, even if on paper the program is structured to involve local participation in the selection of development projects and management of funds.[36]

Origins of the Social Audit

Taking their lead from citizens, the civil society actors initially tried to find out more about the CDF-supported projects in the Coast province. Although Kenyan legislators list CDF projects on a website, the information is general and limited.[37] For over a year MUHURI sent letters and approached CDF offices and officials, but to no avail. Yet they refused to take no for an answer, and were even beaten by assailants, according to Khalid. All the while they began holding community forums on the CDF, to educate people about how it works, to collect their input about local needs, and to gather information about projects, such as whether they were completed, the quality of materials used, and so on. Equally important, these meetings were designed to overcome psychological barriers to action. "There was a general apathy. People were hopeless, corruption and impunity were at a maximum, and poverty levels were increasing," he recalled.

Their first break came in the Mvita constituency. MUHURI discovered that a well actually built by a wealthy individual was listed as a CDF project in an official report. Then they found another well on the list that was built through private sector support. Locals also informed the group that ten computers slated for district schools were instead acquired by the MP. The latter example epitomized the extent of graft and mismanagement; the children never received the equipment, and in any case, it would have been of little use since most of the schools do not have electricity. "It got us thinking: In how many other projects was this happening?" Khalid said, adding, "We realized this could be huge." MUHURI released the information and sent the MP a letter inviting him to a community forum. Through these preliminary activities, the parameters of the social audit were sketched.

In 2007, after two years of canvassing powerholders, MUHURI achieved a major breakthrough. The CSO convinced the MP of Changamwe to release the CDF records for his constituency, arguing that he would be the first legislator in the country to act with such transparency, which would enhance his public image at a critical time, given that it was an election year. The group only received a partial set of records, for fourteen projects that the Changamwe CDF Committee deemed the best. However, this proved more than enough for a start. A pilot social audit soon followed.

International Actors: Constructive Support

That same year the young civic actors were contacted by two international nongovernmental organizations (INGOs), the Open Society Initiative's East Africa program (OSIEA) and one of its partners, the International Budget Partnership (IBP). Through an OSIEA grant, in August 2007 MUHURI organized an intensive weeklong national CDF training for sixty participants from fifteen civil society organizations across Kenya. IBP brought a training team, including veterans from the Right to Information social movement in India, who were also affiliated with the Mazdoor Kisan Shakti Sangathan (MKSS; Union for the Empowerment of Peasants and Laborers), the civic entity that catalyzed this landmark nonviolent struggle and effectively utilized community monitoring in its arsenal of tactics.[38] The objectives of the workshop were threefold. First, organizers sought to build know-how about the CDF process, budgets, data collection, analysis and compilation of user-friendly information, and site visits. Second, they wanted to facilitate peer-to-peer learning. Finally, through practical experience, they endeavored to empower Kenyan civic leaders and activists to develop their own plans of action. During that week, participants conducted their first social audit using the fourteen Changamwe CDF reports. OSIEA also worked with the International Budget Partnership to produce an educational handbook on the CDF and social audit process.[39]

MUHURI's Six-Step Social Audit

Out of this innovative collaboration, MUHURI honed a defining nonviolent method in the six-step social audit:[40]

1. *Information gathering*. Gathering of records from the local CDF office. Trained MUHURI representatives are sent, because it is daunting for ordinary citizens to approach officials and obtain tightly guarded information.

2. *Training local people*. Training men and women to become community activists. They learn how to decipher documents and budgets, monitor expenditures, and physically inspect public works.

3. *Educating and mobilizing fellow citizens*. Educating about the CDF and their rights to information and accountability of powerholders. Concurrently with the second step, community activists and MUHURI attract attention, directly engage people, and encourage them to attend a "public hearing" through nonviolent tactics such as street theatre, trumpet and drum processions, community radio, and leafleting by volunteers. Information about CDF misuse and graft is shared, and people's reactions and input are gathered.

4. *Inspecting the CDF project site*. Citizen-activists conduct systematic, meticulous documentation, comparing records to the reality on the ground. They also use site visits to speak with residents in order to share CDF project records, generate interest in the social audit, encourage them to attend the public hearing, and gather additional information about corruption and abuse. For instance, an inspection of a market center built with CDF money revealed that inferior roof sheeting was used in contrast to what was recorded in CDF documents. Moreover, by talking with people in the area, activists learned that materials from the old market center were reused in the new structure, although the records stated that all new materials had been purchased.[41]

5. *Holding the public hearing*. Local CDF officials, members of the CDF committee, the MP, district administrators, and the media are invited. MUHURI's theatre team first leads a procession through the community, complete with slogans, chanting, and a youth band. It gathers adults and dancing, singing children as it goes along. "What do we want? We want our money!" they exclaim. Various MUHURI representatives open the forum by pointing out that the audit was done by local residents, that everyone there shares the responsibility of ensuring that CDF money is benefiting "our" communities, and that the goals of the audit are not political.[42] Once the session begins, local citizen-activists present the results of their investigations, CDF

officials are questioned by both the activists and attendees, and the community demands accountability of them. In full view of citizens, MUHURI first secures promises from the officials to address the problems and then obtains their signatures on an "accountability charter" outlining their commitments.

6. *Following up with officials.* MUHURI prepares a report of the community's findings and recommendations to members of the local CDF committee, and then checks on their implementation.

At MUHURI's first ever public hearing on August 26, 2007, conducted during the above-mentioned training workshop, approximately 1,500 to 2,000 residents of the Changamwe slum participated, many standing in the rain for much of the day because there were not enough seats. Even three opposition candidates showed up. Although not all invited officials attended, three from the CDF came, carrying fifty files. Faced with the community's documentation of mismanagement and apparent corruption, they soon made a frantic call to the MP, who quickly arrived. After a few hours, the MP finally agreed to register their complaints and charges against the concerned contractors. The two MKSS activists from the training reported,

> It marked the first time that CDF officials in that constituency (and probably in the entire country) had felt the need to present information on CDF-supported projects before the residents of their constituency at a forum that was initiated, organized, and supported by the local community members, at a time and venue chosen by them as opposed to a rally organized by the MP or his supporters.[43]

Creativity, Nonviolent Discipline, Countering Intimidation

MUHURI employs a variety of creative actions derived from local contexts to communicate messages, mobilize citizens, and wield people power during the social audit process. Humor is often used to lighten tension and address serious matters in a nonthreatening manner. Tactics from puppet plays to a ten-foot-tall masked man dressed in traditional attire garner attention, generate enthusiasm, and overcome people's fear to speak up and face powerholders. At the Changamwe public forum, MUHURI rolled out a fifty-meter-long cloth banner petition demanding the addition of accountability and transparency measures to the CDF Act and passage of the Freedom of Information law. The MP, known to oppose the law, initially refused to support it, but after all the people, including the opposition candidates, signed it (or stamped their fingerprints), he acquiesced to civic pressure and added his name.

Once MUHURI and citizens began to disrupt the corrupt status quo—that is, threaten vested interests—intimidation followed. The group refused to back down. It emphasized the peaceful nature of its struggle. Second, the CSO had taken proactive measures to maintain nonviolent discipline by training youth in what Khalid termed nonviolence: "Youth sometimes want to fight and then they can't be controlled in huge crowds. We learned that we need our own 'ushers' to prevent violence." Indeed, after receiving threats from a politician, ten young men began to guard MUHURI's office by sleeping there at night. One evening they were attacked. Khalid recounted, "They were trained to just sit down. They did, and they got a beating."

Finally, when they faced one of their gravest threats, they triumphed by making a violent attack backfire. In 2009, during the Likoni constituency social audit, two nights before the public hearing, MUHURI's office was ransacked by a gang of nine, and one of the guards was stabbed in the neck. They understood that the objective of repression was to generate fear and deter them from action. Exemplifying the general mood of defiance, Malfan, a young resident and activist, declared, "If they came to rob the documents we are having, it seems that there is something so big that they are hiding. In fact they are giving us more motivation for us to go for more information."[44] Rather than retreat in fear, the next day Khalid and Farida Rashid, another citizen turned activist, spoke out on a popular local radio station—a major platform through which to communicate with the public, as well as with those behind the attack. The activists avowed they would not be intimidated, and they emphasized unity and collective responsibility. Khalid told listeners, "They are attempting to scare us. . . . But when the people of Likoni arrived this morning, they said, 'We are determined to stay and protect this work, so that tomorrow we can present our findings at the public hearing.'" Finally, the two civic leaders turned the attack on its head. Khalid declared on air, "And until the citizens emerge and participate completely in the process—like coming to the meeting tomorrow at the Bomani grounds at 2:00 p.m.—until they emerge and show their purpose, and their desire to see changes brought forward, we the people will continue to hurt while the politicians continue to profit."[45]

Harnessing the Power of Numbers: Collective Identity, Recruitment, Mobilization

MUHURI, like Integrity Watch Afghanistan (see Chapter 8), views regular people as protagonists of change while its role is to empower communities. "The key actors were the communities, and we were backing them up," affirmed Khalid. As with Integrity Watch Afghanistan's community-monitoring initiatives, the social audits ran on the efforts of citizens—an essential element of people power that solidifies collective identity, collective ownership, and commitment to the cause. "The issues were owned by the communities; they asked us to assist them," he explained. Through its communications, outreach activities, and creative nonviolent tactics, the group sought to overcome regular people's apathy, hopelessness, and sense of inferiority vis-à-vis powerholders; foster collective responsibility to address grievances; provide needed information, training, know-how, and coaching; and offer innovative opportunities for citizen action, from serving as volunteer monitors to participating in community forums, the latter activating the power of numbers and helping to overcome fear. An International Budget Partnership report concluded,

> Both the MKSS and MUHURI have held social audits in hostile environments. Their experiences show that individuals that would otherwise feel intimidated to speak out against public officials are willing to do so in the context of a well-attended social audit forum—perhaps due to the strength they perceive from being part of a collective evaluation process.[46]

MUHURI is rooted in communities, and initiatives are jointly undertaken. When queried about the group's relationship to the communities, Khalid replied, "I don't know where one starts and the other ends. The communities are part of us, and we are a part of them." Thus, recruitment for the social audits was an organic exercise. The civic leaders had contacts at different levels in the communities and were part of informal local networks. Community members also identified potential citizen-activists. Once involved, these people tended to bring in others, he reported. Engagement in the social audits was sustained because citizens were the impetus for them and they participated on a voluntary basis, all of which fostered a strong sense of collective responsibility. "When they know it's for their own good, people find a way to do it, especially when they know others are counting on them and want them to be responsible," said Khalid.

Outcomes
Convincing parliamentarians and CDF officials to release records has been an uphill battle in the absence of a right to information law. Nevertheless, MUHURI did succeed on numerous occasions to gain access to documents. Consequently, over the next three years, it conducted

comprehensive social audits in ten constituencies in the Coast province. Through people power, malfeasance was uncovered and rectified. For example, in 2010 in Kisauni, the civic initiative learned that a dispensary for HIV patients had been indefinitely closed. The CDF committee contended that it was to be upgraded. In reality, citizen-activists discovered that no money had been allocated for this renovation and the land on which the clinic was built had been illegally sold. As a result of the social audit process, the land transaction was cancelled, funds were budgeted for the clinic, improvements were made, and it finally reopened.[47]

Not content with these successes, in 2010 MUHURI made a strategic decision to expand social audit initiatives while increasing the grassroots capacity to conduct them. The overall goal was to create sustainability by empowering others—CSOs, communities, regular people—to hold authorities and politicians accountable, independently of MUHURI. First, it shifted from conducting social audits together with communities to training CSOs and citizens to conduct their own civic initiatives. Second, it has developed the mini–social audit, whereby residents monitor a single project in their immediate locality rather than a large set of projects throughout a constituency.[48] This new defining method calls to mind Integrity Watch Afghanistan's community-monitoring initiatives. Not only is people power devolved to one of the most basic levels of society, each small victory builds confidence and yields a visible outcome that benefits residents in their daily lives. Third, MUHURI is now in discussion with government departments to explore citizen-led social audits conducted in cooperation with authorities.[49]

At the national level, MUHURI's advocacy combined institutional and extrainstitutional sources of pressure. Like DHP* in Mexico (see below), Ficha Limpa in Brazil (see Chapter 4), and the above-mentioned shayfeen.com in Egypt, MUHURI sought to make use of the judicial system. In 2009 it initiated a lawsuit in the Kenyan courts to challenge the constitutionality of the CDF legislation based on the role of MPs in the fund. While MUHURI did not win, the lawsuit was enough to send shock waves through the ruling establishment. Harnessing the power of numbers, activists from eight constituencies that conducted social audits joined together in a national campaign to change the CDF law. By June of that year, the Kenyan government set up a task force to review it.[50] The report, containing a number of reforms to the law, was finally released in July 2012.[51]

Social audits, generating bottom-up pressure, changed the relationship between powerholders and the public. Legislators and officials were pressured to interact with regular people as equals, who in turn began to see themselves in a positive light. Through nonviolent action and incremental victories, citizens cultivated a sense of agency, which Khalid believes can lead to even greater justice. "If people are able to be encouraged to go out, today it's CDF, tomorrow it's something else, and another day it's another thing. So CDF is an entry point to the realization of so many rights that people are not getting."[52] Like the community-monitoring initiatives in Afghanistan, the Kenyan social audits practice democracy from the bottom up. The IBP summarized this dynamic: they are "exercises in participatory democracy that challenge the traditional 'rules of the game' in governance."[53] Perhaps most revolutionary is that in some quarters of the Kenyan government, power-holders have begun to encourage civic action. In February 2013 the Ethics and Anti-Corruption Commission vice chair, Irene Keino, made the following public appeal: "We are asking Kenyans to be vigilant at the grass roots and report cases of corruption to our offices. . . . Kenyans should monitor leaders and how they manage funds. If they identify cases of misappropriation, they should not hesitate to report them to us."[54]

As for the Changamwe constituency parliamentarian who was the first to open CDF books to public scrutiny, there was a happy ending. In spite of corruption discovered through the social audit, he touted his transparency during the campaign, and it worked. He won the 2007 elections even though the majority of incumbents lost their seats. As MUHURI representatives were monitoring the constituency's vote count, a CDF official told them that at least 40 percent of the votes for the MP were due to his having cooperated on the social audit.[55]

Youth Say "Enough!" to President's
Abuse of Power: Bosnia-Herzegovina

Dosta! (Enough!) is a nonviolent youth resistance movement that emerged in 2006 after a small online chat group decided to meet in person rather than simply talk about politics and problems in postwar Bosnia-Herzegovina (BiH).[56] Like Mexico's DHP*, Dosta!'s overall goals are transformative. It aims to "promote accountability and government responsibility to the people, and to spark civic participation of all Bosnian citizens, no matter what religious or ethnic group," said Darko Brkan, one of the movement's founders.[57] In tandem, the youth identified three core problems to impact: passive citizens, government corruption and crime, and ethnic hatred stoked by political fear tactics.[58]

Dosta! strives to be informal, independent, and what Brkan described as "free-minded."[59] Initially, the young people simply wanted to protest, to air their concerns. In March 2006 they organized a demonstration against the increase in electricity prices by the energy regulatory commission. To their pleasant surprise, approximately 600 people—most over the age of fifty—gathered in what was then the biggest peacetime civic mobilization in the country. The novelty brought extensive media coverage but no response from officials. Nevertheless, the public's support confirmed that in spite of a variety of grievances, citizens shared a general dissatisfaction with how the government was running the country.[60] Dosta! understood that it had ignited a small spark of dissent.

In subsequent years, the youth movement became synonymous with grassroots organizing, civic activism, and transcending ethnic and religious divisions. It utilized a diverse range of nonviolent tactics, such as silent marches against corruption, petitions demanding the resignation of crooked local officials, a nonviolent blockade of Sarajevo to protest police brutality, cultural activities, and alternative social services. By 2010 it was well-known to the public, powerholders, and the media. As of August 2012 there were five active chapters. Just as important, Brkan reported that new organizations have sprung from the chapters, and they are active in most of the country across ethnic divisions.[61] The overall vision, strategy, and planning are driven by the Sarajevo-based Coordination chapter, but each chapter functions autonomously. Decisions are consensus-based. This structure evolved over time through trial and error. The movement has no running budget, paid staff, or formal organization. It is completely volunteer driven and funded.

From Abstract to Concrete:
A Prime Minister's Shady Apartment Deal

In early 2008 Dosta! decided that a new strategy was necessary to tackle endemic corruption. Similarly to the aforementioned Citizens Initiative for Constant Light, DHP* (Mexico), and 5th Pillar (India), the activists faced a seemingly insurmountable challenge. They pondered how to impact something so vast—where to start and what to do. Their conclusion was to link corruption to a tangible abuse and to make an example of a public figure rather than a particular form of corruption or institution. When asked why, Brkan explained, "We targeted individuals because with Bosnian institutions it's very hard to exact accountability. Government jurisdictions are unclear; there are lots of levels within the government, and it's easy for [powerholders] to dispute things, block decisions, or say it's not their responsibility."[62] The leadership core decided to focus on Nedžad Branković, the prime minister of the Federation of BiH, who Brkan asserted was infamous for malfeasance all the way back to 1994, when he served as director general of BiH Railways. "We connected him to the whole [corrupt] system," he elaborated. Likewise, the young activists reasoned that if one of Bosnia's heads of state could be held accountable for corruption, the success would impact powerholder venality, and citizens would be emboldened to continue the struggle.

The activists initially postponed the campaign in order to address deteriorating personal safety conditions in Sarajevo, epitomized by the murder of a teenager and callous indifference on the part of the prime minister of the Sarajevo Canton, Samir Silajdžić, and the Sarajevo mayor, Semiha Borovac. After months of civic mobilization in which thousands of people protested every week demanding their resignations, the movement scored another victory. In October 2008 Borovac lost the election and her party lost its majority, according to Brkan. Silajdžić was forced to resign after his party took a drubbing in local elections from which it never recovered, and it is now a small opposition party.

During the final quarter of 2008 the youth turned their attention back to the prime minister, deliberating over what to do. Early in 2009 they floated different corruption scandals to the public and attempted to engage citizens and the media, but to no avail. "Enormous amounts of money were being misused, but regular people could not relate to this," recalled Brkan. "The public was used to living with the corrupt system, and we needed to find a way for them to see it differently and get engaged." They zeroed in on an incident that finally resonated with the grass roots. In 2000, when Branković was director of Energoinvest, he acquired from the government, in record time, a large, luxurious apartment in one of the most exclusive parts of Sarajevo, for the equivalent of US$500.[63] These underhanded transactions literally hit home; families were still struggling to find lodging and reclaim property, while housing purchases were complicated by bribery and extensive red tape. "It was something that people could grasp, it was tangible, and everyone wants one [apartment]," recounted Brkan. "This connected people to the issue," he added.

A little-known 2007 article and online report by the Center for Investigative Journalism (CIN) originally revealed the arcane deal. The government and a state company bought the residence at huge taxpayer expense, transferred it onto a list of "excess apartments" created after the war for refugees, and then privatized it. Branković subsequently obtained it through cheap vouchers, all within several days.[64] Technically, each step in the nefarious process was "legal" but could not have happened without flagrant abuse of power. The story started spreading in 2008 when Dubioza kolektiv, a popular alternative band, released a song and video called "Šuti i trpi" (Shut up and take it). It featured spliced parts of CIN's interview with the prime minister claiming he couldn't remember how he bought the apartment but that "it was done legally."[65] However, not until the nonviolent youth movement took up the venal case did it balloon into a political issue finally undermining the prime minister and sweeping away remaining support from within his Party for Democratic Action (SDA).

Exacting a Cost for a Bargain-Priced Apartment

In planning the campaign, the leadership core made strategic decisions over timing, tactics, and communications. They decided to launch the initiative in January 2009 for several reasons. According to Brkan, the 2008 local elections were over, resulting in losses for the corrupt incumbent parties. It was also the middle of Branković's term, and he was starting to lose support from parts of his party. "We tried to use timing to our advantage," he said. Second, Dosta! made a strategic determination to take the struggle off the street and engage in digital resistance, in order to catch the prime minister and authorities off guard. "The campaign was the first totally online campaign in BiH, which came as a total surprise to the government, since by 2009, when it took place, they were used to protests from Dosta! and prepared for them," stated Brkan.[66] A third reason was to increase participation—that is, numbers—hence people power. "You need other actions for those who support you but don't necessarily come to the street actions," explained Brkan.

Sometime during the early hours of January 10, 2009, mysterious graffiti proclaiming, "Give back the apartment, you thief!" appeared on the building containing Branković's apartment. The prime minister was livid over this civic defiance. He publicly insisted on quick action from law enforcement, resulting in interrogations and arrests, patrols all over Sarajevo, and police protection outside the building.[67] Moreover, he called on the judiciary for swift proceedings against the perpetrators and for the Parliament to launch an investigation.[68] And in a gift to Dosta!, he accused the movement of molesting him, Brkan said. His heavy-handed reaction backfired spectacularly and created momentum for the campaign.[69] Not only did all of BiH hear about the graffiti, the shady apartment acquisition was elevated to national prominence, generating widespread outrage. The establishment media, not particularly known for taking venal powerholders to task, covered the action and characterized his response as arrogant.[70] The youth pounced on the opportunity.[71] The movement mobilized the public in the Federation of Bosnia and Herzegovina through imaginative, low-risk, humorous tactics all united by one demand: Branković's resignation.

Innovative Tactics

The resourceful activists created a Facebook group called, "I Wrote the Graffiti," which launched digital dilemma actions. Within two days, over 7,000 people joined, each posting a photo along with his or her name.[72] It was a phenomenal number for the small country. The Facebook group then encouraged citizens to flood police stations with phone calls and emails declaring, "Arrest me, I wrote the graffiti."[73] The authorities received over 4,000 electronic messages alone.[74] Consequently, they were put in an awkward, lose-lose situation, while the movement gained publicity and mobilized the grass roots. Meanwhile, through Facebook, thousands of citizen-members were communicating, sharing, and brainstorming. Out of the digital grass roots came a new dilemma action: billboard "advertisements." With Dosta!'s blessing, some Facebookers collected donations. "We looked at what we could rent with the money, and the company gave us four more because they liked us," said Brkan. On January 24, ten billboards in highly prominent spots around Sarajevo proclaimed, "Apartment for only KM 920! Get real estate in accordance to the law."[75] Within forty-eight hours the Cantonal government quickly ordered most of the billboards to be razed, maintaining that they were illegal and had been marked for removal the previous July, though Brkan reported they had been up for years.[76] As is common with dilemma actions, the authorities' efforts to muzzle dissent rebounded. According to Brkan, "All the media, even international, covered it, and they [the government] were totally disgraced."[77]

Around the same time, the movement added another dilemma action to the arsenal—clothing. Through its chapters, members distributed approximately 2,000 T-shirts emblazoned with the words, "I wrote the graffiti." They were so popular that many citizens fashioned their own, while personalities wore them on television, including the band leader of Dubioza kolektiv. "You could see people wearing them on the street," recalled Brkan. The activists also disseminated roughly 2,000 badges and 25,000 stickers, all with the same message.

As soon as the civic initiative was under way, the activists sought to maximize media coverage in order to reach and engage those who weren't digitally active, and to ratchet up social pressure. Brkan summarized, "Once it [the campaign] got started we established a communications strategy in terms of what media to approach and how to use the Internet. We set up a plan to be present as much as possible and get [media] focus on the graffiti and T-shirts. Also, we had a communications plan for [civic] groups on the ground and potential allies who could support us." Dosta!'s key messages were as follows: the prime minister is corrupt and misusing his position, he should resign, he should give back the apartment, and "I wrote the graffiti." The latter message, according to Brkan, "was the most important for public engagement." It was short, simple, and inclusive. Implying that any Bosnian could have written the graffiti built a sense of mutual outrage and collective identity.

Outcomes

As a result of the civic mobilization, Branković was left with few supporters within his own party. Its members worried about his negative impact on the October 2010 elections. In civil resistance parlance, they shifted loyalties. Consequently, at the May 2009 SDA congress, he was asked to resign. He complied one month later, a year and a half before the end of his term. Meanwhile, in April of that year, the prime minister, along with former prime minister Edhem Bičakčić (who signed off on the apartment scam while in office), were charged with abuse of office and authority.[78] They stood trial before the Municipal Court of Sarajevo but were acquitted in 2010 on the grounds that it was done "in accordance to the law," Brkan explained. "The law was meant for people to buy the publicly owned apartments which they had been living in, and not for the government to make an apartment 'public' by buying it in cash from an individual and then 'selling' it to the prime minister for 1 percent of its value a few days later," he said. Brkan doesn't dispute the ruling but sees this as an example of how the judicial system is flawed and is susceptible to abuse by those in power. "The judges were right that it was done 'in accordance to the law,' but exactly that fact that it could be done that way and that the guy who has everything used this to get the apartment actually forced him to resign in the end."

Dosta!'s campaign had two less tangible but equally important outcomes. For Brkan, it built up the movement's credibility and membership, thereby increasing its numbers and enhancing its sustainability. Second, civil resistance changed the nature of the relationship and the balance of power between the government and politicians, on the one hand, and the civic realm on the other. The young activist explained,

> It created different connections between civil society and citizens, civil society and politicians, and between citizens and the political

system. Once you accomplish something like this, this creates a new set of rules in the political system. By impacting the political system and basic structures in their [powerholders'] decisionmaking process, civil society and citizens have more power in society.

In conclusion, not only did relationships change, the campaign created a new, bottom-up link between powerholders and the people that is qualitatively different from elections, the traditional medium through which the populace exerts power and gains accountability. "They have to calculate this into their decisionmaking," he concluded. A potent example of this altered dynamic was soon evident. Two days after the new prime minister, Mustafa Mujezinović, took office, he showed up at a Dosta! protest "to talk with us and try to meet our demands," Brkan recollected. On the spot he invited Dosta! to join him on a television program to discuss his mandate. A Dosta! member, Demir Mahmutćehajić, was plucked from the street and went off with the prime minister to the TV station.

Changing Citizens to Change Mexico

Back in November 2008 a group of ten friends felt that they could no longer ignore the harsh reality: "México no va bien" (Mexico is on the wrong track), said Maite Azuela, one of DHP*'s founders.[79] Narco-violence was claiming the lives of thousands of civilians following President Felipe Calderon's so-called war on drugs. The global financial crisis had triggered a deep economic slump, the worst since the 1930s. Last but not least, powerholder corruption and impunity were endemic.[80] For example, some surveys have found that lower-income households spend 33 percent of their monthly income on bribes.[81] The group decided they needed to act to save their beloved country, and they could only do this together with fellow citizens who shared their concern. To gauge interest for a civic movement, they launched a chat on the website of *El Universal*, one of the most influential and widely read newspapers in the country. To their astonishment, 6,000 people participated. "We learned that people wanted to join, to do something, but they didn't know how to start," Azuela recalled.

They also tested a controversial name—Dejemos de Hacernos Pendejos (aka DHP*)—meant to be provocative and fun, yet serious and inclusive. While the literal translation is, "Quit being an ass/Quit being an idiot," the actual meaning is, "Let's stop fooling ourselves." She explained that the name itself is a "call to action" that connotes collective responsibility for Mexico's situation, as "pendejos" is phrased in both the first person and the plural. "There is a tendency in Mexico to blame the government, but we said that we citizens are not doing our work to fight corruption and improve our country," avowed Azuela. "What Mexico needs is for citizens to start organizing themselves."

The group quickly hashed out the parameters for the nascent movement. DHP*'s vision is to get Mexico back on track politically, socially, and economically. Its mission is to "produce an effective change in the way people understand their citizenship. Being a citizen does not imply only the exercise of our rights, it also means assuming responsibilities."[82] This encapsulates overcoming general public apathy and channeling citizen aspirations for change into organized action. DHP*'s overall objectives are to

- Generate civic initiatives that catalyze changes in the everyday life of citizens.
- Break the cultural paradigm of complicity, so that society rejects corruption, apathy, and irresponsibility.
- Channel anger over graft and impunity by empowering citizens to assume their responsibility to hold powerholders to account and ensure that public services, resources, and budgets are used in an honest, transparent, and effective way for the common good rather than for powerholder gain.
- Support efforts of state and nonstate institutions and organizations to foster citizen responsibility.

After having generated interest through the newspaper chat, the group started a Facebook page that quickly grew to 4,000 friends. Azuela recalled, "We thought that in Facebook people would spontaneously form smaller groups around the country and do their own campaigns. But people here are waiting to be told what to do. It's a paternalistic culture after decades of nondemocratic government." Hence, the original group of ten realized that abstract exhortations, what Azuela called "a beautiful discourse," in and of itself would not spur citizens. DHP* would have to be the catalyst for action. The group decided to zero in on legislators in the Mexican Congress, who are generally viewed as holding office to advance their political parties, special interests, and personal agendas rather than serving the people.[83]

They identified an issue—Christmas bonuses—that would not only rankle the public but symbolize the corruption and impunity embedded in the political system. Employees in Mexico customarily receive a holiday bonus equivalent to one month's salary, which is taxed as income.

Mexican deputies (members of Congress) also receive this benefit, but, unbeknownst to the public, abuse their authority to get a tax refund. After the 2008 bonus, only 4 of the 500 deputies returned their refund to the Treasury. First, DHP*'s leadership core examined the "Transparency and Access to Information" law to see if it could be used, but the fit was not right. A lawyer in the group then studied the Mexican constitution and discovered that citizens have the right to petition the state. According to Azuela, not only are public authorities obliged to respond within three months, they must also address the alleged wrongdoing or face sanctions. The lawyer concluded that the deputies' refund was illegal, and DHP* had the foundation upon which to utilize the Citizen Petition Law.

Testing the Waters

During December 2008 the core group planned its first campaign, named Operation DHP* 001. Its goal was to stop the Christmas bonus tax refund by combining institutional (legal) measures and extrainstitutional pressure—that is, people power. In addition to legal measures taken through the Citizen Petition Law, during January and February 2009, DHP* conducted a citizens' petition drive with a catchy, humorous slogan based on a colloquial expression—"Diputados coludos, ciudadanos rabones" (Long-tailed deputies, short-tailed citizens), meaning, "While the deputies take public money, the citizens lose it." In addition to using Facebook, the movement's website, and emails, it organized on-the-ground signature collections in Mexico City, while Facebookers in Guadalajara, Jalisco, Merida, Oaxaca, Puebla, Querétaro, Tuxtla, and Yucatán organized their own actions. The leadership core provided them with a one-page petition and guidelines on collecting signatures and "citizen language" to explain the campaign, said Azuela. The activists made a strategic decision to combine digital and on-the-ground resistance. First, it wanted to get the attention of traditional media, in order to broaden public dialogue and garner more support. Second, explained Azuela, "We needed to go out of Facebook to see if people wanted to do more than click." All in all, DHP* gathered a total of 4,000 handwritten and electronic signatures and submitted the petition to the Congress.

The next step was to ratchet up civic pressure. By then, the media had started taking notice, and DHP*'s team conducted radio and newspaper interviews. Adding an element of international pressure, they wrote an article for the online site of *El Pais*, the highly influential and largest-circulation daily newspaper in Spain. The activists produced an online guide for citizens—publicized through Facebook, its website, and in the media—on how to send e-mails and make calls to legislators about the Christmas bonus tax refund. Of the 150 emails and thirty reported calls, not one reply came back from a member of Congress.

In spite of efforts behind the scenes to thwart the petition and stall the process of inquiry, DHP* achieved what Azuela termed a "larger victory." Following the 2009 legislative elections, the incoming members of the LXI Legislature (2009–2012) stopped refunding themselves the Christmas bonus tax. "It was more important than a legal victory because we changed the corrupt practice," asserted Azuela.[84]

DHP* in Full Swing

As the Operation DHP* 001 campaign progressed, the budding movement joined a coalition of seventy civic organizations—the National Citizens Assembly—that called on voters to boycott the 2009 parliamentary elections on July 5 by submitting blank ballots. The purpose was to withdraw cooperation from the political system in which all the parties were viewed as corrupt. As a result, 5 percent of the ballots were annulled, she reported. The campaign sent a message that a sizeable number of citizens were dissatisfied with the political parties and no longer intimidated to collectively raise their voices. The experience proved invaluable for DHP*. It discovered shared concerns, established contact with many CSOs, and perhaps most importantly, helped to crystallize its priorities.

Impunity—defined by Azuela as "no consequences, no accountability, no punishment for wrongdoing"—characterizes both the executive and legislative branches of government, as well as state institutions. Rather than attempt to tackle the problem in its entirety, DHP* made a strategic decision to limit its focus on the Congress, for three principal reasons. First, there generally was more scrutiny of the president than the legislature. Second, the latter decides on the budget and spends public money. Third, all the major parties are represented in the Congress. Consequently, challenging politicians can impact the entire corrupt political system rather than one party, as would be the case with the president. In the ensuing years, DHP*'s campaigns have focused on

- Decreasing the publicly financed budgets of political parties.
- Empowering citizens to exercise their right to information about congressional activities and spending through tactics such as monitoring.
- Changing the Freedom of Information act to apply to political parties.

- Impeding political corruption.
- Holding legislators accountable.
- Instituting participatory democracy mechanisms into the legislative branch—for example, independent candidacies, federal referendums, and citizen-initiated legislation.

Attributes

Social media provides essential tools for DHP* to build unity, raise public awareness, and mobilize citizens. Facebook helped jump-start the movement. It provided an easy, inexpensive medium to reach people, which was particularly important for the emerging movement because it did not have access to traditional media. Twitter soon became indispensable for communication with the public and the media, including its capacity to share videos from nonviolent actions, which can increase citizen participation in real time. Humor has been a hallmark of the movement since its inception. Most of its campaigns incorporate catchy names, attention-getting stunts, and nonviolent actions characterized by levity and fun—a strategic decision on the part of DHP* to engage citizens, overcome fear, and balance somber messages about corruption, impunity, violence, and hopelessness. The movement's founding core is largely made up of young professionals, including a lawyer, an advertising and public relations expert, editors, a media intellectual, and graduate students and professors. The friends meet monthly in the capital to strategize, plan, and carry out actions. Decisions are jointly made. Local DHP* groups in other parts of the country operate semiautonomously. They develop their own initiatives while cooperating with the founding core on national campaigns.

Highlights

Since 2009 DHP* has carried out multiple campaigns, intended to incrementally build a nationwide discourse that citizens have the responsibility to save Mexico. The process has been one of experimentation and trial and error. Among the initiatives DHP* has conducted are the following:

Ya Bájenle (Right Now, Go Down). From October to December 2009, DHP* challenged legislators to cut the budget for political parties rather than funding for infrastructure and social services. The movement called on citizens to contact their legislator through the DHP* website; 3,000 e-mails were sent. Once again, not one person received a reply. Using Twitter and Facebook, the activists organized a twenty-four-hour activity at El Ángel, a prominent park and memorial site in Mexico

City. Called the Citizens Light, they hooked up a light on a stationary bicycle that would turn on when people pedaled. Azuela reported that there was a line of 200 people waiting to ride the bike when they started. People from other states around the country sent in messages of solidarity. Sympathetic journalists and a few members of Congress also joined the action to show their support. Some media coverage and DHP*'s live video, broadcast through their website and Twitter, brought out hundreds throughout the night. A deputy from the right-of-center PAN (National Action Party) took DHP*'s proposal to the Congress and secured a *transitorio* (temporary provision) stipulating that the amount of any reduction of the political parties' budget should be allocated to the infrastructure and social services budget. Two months later, a senator from the left-of-center PRD (Party of the Democratic Revolution) presented the movement's proposal to the Senate. In spite of these efforts, Azuela stated that nothing happened as the rest of the political parties did not support the measure.

Aventon Ciudadano (Citizen Ride). Building upon input from citizen meetings in the capital, Guadalajara, Tlaxcala, and Monterrey in January 2010, DHP* began planning a new campaign to decrease the budget of political parties. During April and May, DHP* volunteers began a hitchhiking trek toward Mexico City from four different parts of Mexico (north, northwest, southwest, southeast). Each group carried part of a letter addressed to the Chamber of Deputies, containing the movement's demands. They relied on citizens, asking for their assistance if they supported the initiative. Their journeys were filmed in real time and transmitted via mobile phones and Twitter. At a public gathering, the four groups met at El Ángel park, whereupon they put together the letter and presented it to the Chamber of Deputies. The campaign garnered significant media coverage and increased public support for DHP*.

Operación 003/500sobre500 (500over500). Focusing on the new Congress, in February 2010 DHP* initiated a monitoring campaign through an interactive platform on its website. Five hundred citizens were invited to "adopt" their respective deputy. The objectives were to empower regular people to track and evaluate their representatives' work, in order to improve congressional transparency and accountability. As well, DHP* sought to pressure legislators to respond to constituent email and phone requests for information about their activities, budgeting, and voting. Citizens were equipped with a special guide and instructions on requesting information through the digital platform. Azuela stated that over 2,000 people took part, four times the anticipated number. Initially, some deputies responded to constituents but soon reverted to business as usual—ignoring those they were supposed to serve.

Diputómetro. As a result of the deputies' disregard, the leadership core went back to the drawing board. It subsequently launched the Diputómetro, an interactive digital monitoring platform that aggregates information about legislative activities—for example, attendance at sessions and in committees, numbers of initiatives approved, and the quantity of committee meetings. Volunteers, mainly students recruited from universities, maintain the platform.

No al Chapulizano (No to the Jumping Crickets). Begun in August 2011 the campaign wants to change state and federal legislation and political party statutes in order to stop elected officials who have not finished their term from running for another office that would overlap with their current position. DHP* activists carry out highly visible and humorous stunts—for example, traversing the Senate wearing masks resembling the politicians who jump elected positions. They succeeded in generating media coverage and public awareness. "Nowadays, many people talk about the crickets," recounted Azuela.

Café DHP.* Initiated in January 2012, DHP* convenes monthly group discussions on such issues as active citizenship, civic responsibility, anticorruption, civil liberties, access to justice, and social networking. They are held in multiple locations, from the capital to Puebla, Querétaro, and Yucatán. Each local group organizes its own events and decides on the topics and format. The inaugural café in Mexico City focused on Internet censorship and included Senators Javier Castellon (PRD); Oscar Mondragon, the social media strategist for 2012 presidential candidate Andres Manuel Lopez Obrador; and Antonio Marvel, a digital activist.

Outcomes

DHP* is maintaining momentum, building a base of local chapters, and experimenting through creative campaigns to generate civic responsibility and citizen action for transparency, accountability, and participatory democracy. Azuela reported that citizens have started to shake off apathy—by 2010, regular people began taking the initiative to contact DHP* to report about corruption, and as importantly, to ask what they themselves could do to tackle problems. "It's an enormous achievement for us, that we are awakening citizens' minds to not let things go to the same old, corrupted way, but to want to change them and create new ways of acting," she said. DHP* chapters around the country are not only initiating their own actions, they are developing solutions for local problems. Last but not least was the Christmas bonus success. It serves as a potent example of how, when institutions—in this case the Congress and judiciary—fail citizens, citizens can still carry the day.

Conclusion

The five cases illustrate the many different approaches that grassroots, bottom-up initiatives can take to what ultimately are common challenges. The groups' objectives stem from how to undermine corruption when it is entrenched and pervasive, while the public is resigned, indifferent, and often fearful to express dissent. The long-term goals are usually transformative in nature, enveloped within a vision of a just society whereby citizens assume collective responsibility, recognize their inherent power, and wield it strategically in order to hold to account those at the top. While, on the surface, this approach may seem abstract or even utopian, in each instance these people power initiatives have made visible strides toward these ends.

In Chapter 11, I move from the individual cases to the wider application of people power to curb corruption and gain accountability, rights, and justice. I distill common attributes, general lessons learned, and noteworthy patterns that expand our understanding of civil resistance, people power, the practice of democracy, and citizen engagement.

Notes

1. The Turkish gladios are far-right, ultranationalist paramilitary squads. They were active during the civil war between the state and Kurdish separatists in the southeastern part of the country that began in 1984 and raged during the early part of the 1990s. The gladios and the mafia took control of lucrative drug-trafficking routes from eastern producers for the large European market. They grew in size and influence as they amassed huge, illicit fortunes (Ezel Akay and Liam Mahoney, *A Call to End Corruption* [Minneapolis: Center for Victims of Torture, 2003]).

2. This section is based on an interview with Ersin Salman, one of the leaders of the Citizen Initiative for Constant Light, on June 20, 2010, and the following resources: Akay and Mahoney, *Call to End Corruption*; Ümit Kıvanç, *Action for Constant Light: Turkey, 1997* (documentary film), http://www.gecetreni.com.

3. According to Salman, the "deep state" refers to a network that is part of the state but operates clandestinely to thwart genuine democracy, public debate of sensitive issues, and citizen dissent. It is said to engage in repression against whatever and whomever it deems a threat to its interests and nationalist agenda. Akay defined the "deep state" as "those in the establishment who use state power and authority illegally to maintain corruption and prevent reforms to-

ward democratization, the rule of law, transparency and accountability of the administration." A BBC report stated that Turks suspect that the deep state is composed of groups linked to the security forces, originally formed in the 1950s, to carry out illegal activities, including assassinations, in order to "protect" the republic. See Akay and Mahoney, *Call to End Corruption*, 6; Sarah Rainsford, "'Deep State' Trial Polarises Turkey," BBC World News, October 23, 2008, http://news.bbc.co.uk.

4. Akay and Mahoney, *Call to End Corruption*, 8.

5. Gökçe was the first to be tried in court, receiving a three-year sentence, which was later reduced to a fine, allowing his release; "Rally on First Anniversary of Susurluk Scandal," *Hurriyet Daily News*, November 3, 1997, www.hurriyetdailynews.com.

6. Akay and Mahoney, *Call to End Corruption*, 10.

7. Ibid., 9.

8. Ibid., 13.

9. Ibid., 2.

10. There was one fatality, due to police violence. Forty-five-year-old Celal Cankoru was out on an evening walk with his wife. Upon reaching Cumhuriyet Square, where a demonstration was under way, he asked a police officer what was going on. In response, he was hit on the head with a two-way radio and shoved into a minibus ("The Dangers of Being a Citizen," *Hurriyet Daily News*, January 17, 1998, www.hurriyetdailynews.com.

11. Akay and Mahoney, *Call to End Corruption*, 14.

12. Zafer Yoruk, "One Minute of Darkness—Back for Democracy," *Hurriyet Daily News*, April 4, 1997, www.hurriyetdailynews.com.

13. "World Report 2012: Turkey," Human Rights Watch, January 2012, 3, www.hrw.org.

14. Dexter Filkins, "Threats and Responses: Ankara—Turkish Deputies Refuse to Accept American Troops," *New York Times*, March 2, 2003, www.nytimes.com.

15. "Turkish Protesters to Hold 'One Minute of Darkness' on Various Issues," *Hurriyet Daily News*, May 1, 2011, www.hurriyetdailynews.com.

16. Sherif Mansour, "Enough Is Not Enough: Achievements and Shortcomings of Kefaya, the Egyptian Movement for Change," in *Civilian Jihad: Nonviolent Struggle, Democratization, and Governance in the Middle East,* ed. Maria Stephan (New York: Palgrave Macmillan, 2009), 205–218; Mansour, "From Facebook to Streetbook," webinar, International Center on Nonviolent Conflict, February 17, 2011, www.nonviolent-conflict.org.

17. This section is based on interviews with Engi Haddad, one of the founders of shayfeen.com and Egyptians Against Corruption, on November 12, 2009 (in person), and August 11, 2012 (via SKYPE), subsequent written communications, and the following resources: Shaazka Beyerle and Arwa Hassan, "Popular Resistance Against Corruption in Turkey and Egypt," in *Civilian Jihad: Nonviolent Struggle, Democratization, and Governance in the Middle East,* ed. Maria Stephan (New York: Palgrave Macmillan, 2009), 265–280; Sherief Elkatshas, *Shayfeen.com: We're Watching You*, Independent Television Service International film, 2007, www.itvs.org; Robin Wright, *Dreams and Shadows: The Future of the Middle East* (New York: Penguin, 2008).

18. Beyerle and Hassan, "Popular Resistance," 270; Elkatshas, *Shayfeen.com*.

19. Elkatshas, *Shayfeen.com*.

20. Wright, *Dreams and Shadows*.

21. Beyerle and Hassan, "Popular Resistance," 270.

22. Ibid.

23. Wright, *Dreams and Shadows*.

24. Ibid.

25. Beyerle and Hassan, "Popular Resistance," 271.

26. GSM phones are mobile devices using the global system for mobile communications.

27. Shayfeen.com website, http://www.shayfeencom.org/pageView.aspx ?pageid=4 (accessed January 28, 2013); Beyerle and Hassan, "Popular Resistance."

28. Elkatshas, *Shayfeen.com*.

29. Ibid.

30. Christine Spolar, "Egypt Court Rejects Appeal," *Chicago Tribune*, May 19, 2006, http://articles.chicagotribune.com.

31. Beyerle and Hassan, "Popular Resistance," 273.

32. "Egypt's Parliamentary Election a Farce: ElBaradei," BBC News, December 8, 2010, www.bbc.co.uk.

33. "Background of MUHURI," MUHURI website, http://www.muhuri.org /index.php (accessed February 1, 2013).

34. Ibid.

35. This section is based on an interview with Hussein Khalid, executive director, Muslims for Human Rights (MUHURI), on November 12, 2010, and the following sources: Vivek Ramkumar and Sowmya Kidambi, "Twataka Pesa Zetu (We Want Our Money): A Public Budget Hearing in Kenya," International Budget Partnership, n.d., www.internationalbudget.org; Damani Baker, *It's Our Money: Where's It Gone?* International Budget Partnership documentary film, www.youtube.com.

36. Ramkumar and Kidambi, "Twataka Pesa Zetu."

37. "Social Audits in Kenya: Budget Transparency and Accountability," International Budget Partnership Impact Story, 2008, http://internationalbudget .org.

38. For an excellent case study on the Indian Right to Information movement, see Sowmya Kidambi, *Right to Know, Right to Live: Building a Campaign for the Right to Information and Accountability* (Minneapolis: Center for Victims of Torture, 2008).

39. To download the handbook, see Wanjiru Kikoyo, *The CDF Social Audit Guide: A Handbook for Communities* (Nairobi: Open Society Initiative for Eastern Africa, February 2008), www.opensocietyfoundations.org.

40. The previously cited twenty-minute documentary on the MUHURI social audits captures on film this defining method, as well as parts of the 2007 CDF training.

41. Ramkumar and Kidambi, "Twataka Pesa Zetu."

42. Baker, *It's Our Money*.

43. Ramkumar and Kidambi, "Twataka Pesa Zetu," 3.

44. Baker, *It's Our Money*.

45. Ibid.

46. Manuela Garza, "Social Audits as a Budget Monitoring Tool," International Budget Partnership, Learning from Each Other Series, October 2012, 6, http://internationalbudget.org.

47. Rocio Campos, "Kenya's Muslims for Human Rights (MUHURI) Takes Its Success with Social Audits to the Next Level," International Budget Partnership newsletter, no. 58, January–February 2011, http://internationalbudget.org.

48. Ibid.

49. Ibid.

50. Baker, *It's Our Money.*

51. The delay was due to the groundbreaking new constitution ratified by voters in 2010, which enshrines the right to information and the right to petition for enacting, amending, and repealing legislation under Article 119. For information about the new Kenyan constitution, see "Countries at the Crossroads: Kenya," Freedom House, 2012, www.freedomhouse.org; Faith Muiruri, "New Law Guarantees Right to Information, Representation," *The Link*, Special Report, November 2012, www.kas.de.

52. Baker, *It's Our Money.*

53. Garza, "Social Audits as a Budget Monitoring Tool," 6.

54. Faith Ronoh, "Commission to Investigate Kenyan MPs over CDF Use," *The Standard*, February 3, 2013, www.standardmedia.co.ke.

55. "Social Audits in Kenya."

56. Bosnia was engulfed in the ethnic war in the former Yugoslavia from 1992 to 1995. The ethnically divided Bosniak, Serb, and Croat country is characterized by organized crime infiltration of the state, endemic corruption, politicization of the public sector, complex power-sharing structures, disjointed administration, and venal political elites that collude with criminal and informal economic networks that have persisted since the war. Marie Chêne, "Corruption and Anti-Corruption in Bosnia and Herzegovina (BiH)," U4 Anti-Corruption Resource Centre, November 23, 2009, www.u4.no.

57. Darko Brkan, recorded interview: Dosta! Movement, International Center on Nonviolent Conflict, June 24, 2010, www.nonviolent-conflict.org.

58. Darko Brkan, "Civil Resistance in Bosnia: Pressure by the People for Accountability and Social Change," PowerPoint presentation, June 24, 2010, www.nonviolent-conflict.org.

59. Brkan, recorded interview.

60. This section is based on SKYPE interviews with Darko Brkan, one of the founders of Dosta! on May 3, 5, and 19, 2011, and June 12, 2011.

61. For additional information about Dosta!'s activities, innovations, and outcomes beyond the campaign profiled in this chapter, see Brkan, recorded interview; Brkan, "Building a Movement in Bosnia and Herzegovina," Movements.org, Build Awareness post, n.d., www.movements.org.

62. Bosnia-Herzegovina's postwar constitutional and institutional structures were put in place through the 1995 Dayton Peace Agreement. It is confusingly complex, leaving governance open to corruption vertically within the executive and legislative branches and state institutions, as well as horizontally. The country comprises two entities, the Federation of BiH and Republika Srpska. They both have their own parliaments, and the Federation of BiH has ten cantons, each with its own parliament. In addition, there is the self-governing Dis-

trict of Brčko and an overall "House of People." Essentially, there are a total of fourteen parliaments—all for a population estimated at 3.8 million in 2012 (there has been no official census in the aftermath of the war). For further background, see "Background Note: Bosnia and Herzegovina," Bureau of European and Eurasian Affairs, US Department of State, March 15, 2012, www.state.gov; Brkan, recorded interview.

63. According to the Center for Investigative Reporting, which uncovered the graft, Branković paid 900 KM (BiH Marka) for the apartment, which had a market value of 500,000 KM. For further details, see "A Lucky Real Estate Deal," Center for Investigative Reporting, September 4, 2007, www.cin.ba; "Branković—From a Tenant to a Rich Man," Center for Investigative Reporting, December 22, 2009, www.cin.ba.

64. Rosemary Armao, *Covering Corruption: The Difficulties of Trying to Make a Difference* (Washington, DC: Center for International Media Assistance, National Endowment for Democracy, July 21, 2010), 9.

65. "Branković, Bičakčić Indicted," Center for Investigative Journalism, April 17, 2009, www.cin.ba. Youtube has the video: http://www.youtube.com /watch?v=oXobejzkijo.

66. Brkan, "Building a Movement in Bosnia and Herzegovina."

67. Ibid.

68. Armao, *Covering Corruption*; Brkan, "Building a Movement in Bosnia and Herzegovina."

69. After the furor subsided, no evidence emerged and there were no trials.

70. "Anatomy of a Resignation," Center for Investigative Reporting, July 15, 2009, www.cin.ba.

71. To this day, Brkan maintains he doesn't know who was behind the graffiti and Dosta! was not officially the instigator. This assertion doesn't preclude that someone or some individuals in or affiliated with the group took the action.

72. Brkan, "Building a Movement in Bosnia and Herzegovina."

73. Brkan, recorded interview.

74. "Branković Apartment Billboards Gone," Center for Investigative Journalism, January 30, 2009, www.cin.ba.

75. Ibid.

76. Ibid.

77. Brkan, "Building a Movement in Bosnia and Herzegovina."

78. "Branković, Bičakčić Indicted."

79. This section is based on interviews with Maite Azuela, a cofounder of DHP*, on February 11 and November 11, 2010, and email correspondence during December 2011.

80. "Mexico Country Profile," BBC News, July 4, 2012, http://news.bbc.co.uk.

81. Max Heywood, "Wanted: A Replacement for 'Petty,'" Transparency International, Space for Transparency blog, June 28, 2012, http://blog.trans parency.org.

82. DHP*, unpublished document, n.d.

83. The Mexican National Congress is bicameral, consisting of the Senate (Camara de Senadores) and the Chamber of Deputies (Camara de Diputados).

84. The legal track did not succeed. According to Azuela, the argument against the citizens' petition was that there wasn't enough evidence to prove the deputies were guilty. She stated that they went all the way to the Supreme Court and finally lost the case.

11

What We Have Learned

While it may seem paradoxical at first, the more deeply I ventured into the cases—their individual contexts, histories, founders, strategies—the more I found in common. Patterns emerged that contribute to our understanding of civil resistance, genuine democracy, and anticorruption strategies. Similar attributes were evident across varying situations, and from the multitude of lessons learned, recurrent themes jumped out. I summarize these findings in this chapter.

Notable Patterns

Corruption Breeds Corruption
Many of the civic leaders expressed dismay that endemic corruption never seems to taper off; it just gets worse. Why is this so? A systemic approach offers an explanation. In Chapter 2, I presented a systemic, macro definition of corruption as a system of abuse of entrusted power for private, collective, or political gain—that involves a complex, intertwined set of relationships, some obvious, others hidden, with established vested interests, that can operate vertically within an institution or horizontally across political, economic, and social spheres in a society or transnationally. The implications are twofold. Not only are systems of graft and abuse unlikely to reform from within, they are prone to growing ever more venal because more and more graft is needed in order to maintain vested interests and the crooked status quo.

Conditions Are Not Determinants

The cases add to the historical record and ever-growing body of scholarship illustrating that structural conditions do not play determining roles in the success of people power. The connotations for the anticorruption and development realms are clear; the time has come to set aside the myth that a set of conditions needs to be in place in order for citizens to have "voice," for the grass roots to mobilize, and for people power to have an impact (see Chapter 1). Bottom-up nonviolent campaigns and movements to curb corruption and gain accountability, rights, and justice can be found in virtually every part of the world and across the spectrum of governments, from democracies to dictatorships and various permutations in between. No particular region, racial or ethnic group, or religion has a monopoly on civil resistance efforts. They are prevalent in societies enduring poor governance, poverty, low levels of literacy, and severe repression, the latter perpetrated by the state, organized crime, or paramilitary groups. I would even contend that the most innovative, effective, grassroots civic initiatives now come from the Global South, not the Global North, where populations generally enjoy higher levels of civil liberties and rule of law. Citizens in mature democracies who are increasingly alarmed over the connection between corruption and a host of serious challenges—such as financial crises, special interest politics, and poor governance—would do well to learn from their counterparts who are making strides in far less congenial settings.

Bottom-Up Democracy

What distinguishes these people power manifestations from traditional antidictatorship or occupation movements is that the goals are not to remove an authoritarian government or an occupier, but to change an overall system of graft, abuse, and impunity—be it vertically within one entity or horizontally across multiple institutions and societal sectors. In some instances, a civic initiative may have an interim target, as was the case in Bosnia-Herzegovina, but this is couched within a broader struggle with far-reaching goals, and the immediate objective is to unsettle the status quo.

In transitions from violent conflict (Afghanistan, Bosnia-Herzegovina) or authoritarian rule (Brazil, Egypt, Indonesia, Korea, Turkey) to democracy and peace, we should not assume that corruption will dissipate. More often than not, venality persists. Many of the same players retain influence and power, and systems of graft and abuse reconfigure as vested interests adapt to the new situation. A civic leader and academic in Korea explained, "Politicians and institutional political parties have had a strong power to resist the reform and could continue to distort the reform itself to keep their status-quo interests untouched."[1] Thus, one of the greatest challenges to the consolidation of fledgling democracies is the persistence of such malfeasant, self-serving powerholder systems.

When voters have limited choices beyond obstructive politicians backed by corrupt parties, representative democracy alone cannot deliver accountability and justice, and can even lose legitimacy in the eyes of the people. Consequently, both top-down and bottom-up strategies are needed. "Political will means from the top. People power is from the bottom up. We need both if we want democracy," observed Dadang Trisasongko, one of the Indonesian civic leaders of the first Love Indonesia, Love Anti-Corruption Commission (CICAK) campaign (see Chapter 5).[2] Top-down strategies include building mechanisms, legislation, and capacity within state institutions. Bottom-up strategies maintain extrainstitutional pressure to create political will, support honest powerholders, back genuine reform efforts, and creatively disrupt the corrupt status quo. How long do transitions take? Reflecting on Indonesia's experience since the end of the Suharto regime, Trisasongko said, "We are still in a transition. It is not completed yet. It depends on the effectiveness of people power. If we have more pressure from people, the transition may be shortened."[3]

Anticorruption civic initiatives can either be the precursors to national democracy movements (Egypt) or the successors of them (Brazil, Indonesia, Korea). In the first instance, shayfeen.com gave birth to Egyptians Against Corruption and catalyzed the judges' campaign. In turn, Egyptians Against Corruption was one of the currents of organized civic dissent that merged into the mighty river of the January 25 Revolution that brought an end to the Mubarak regime. In the second instance, civic leaders—who witnessed how graft and abuse were hindering development, harming citizens, and undermining their hard-won victories—decided to take action. The Indonesian and Korean campaigns illuminate another factor that impacts democratic transitions. Leaders and activists of social movements develop lasting bonds through nonviolent struggles to end authoritarian rule. During what can be called the second phase, namely, the aftermath, they often remain activists and civil society leaders, committed to consolidating democracy, transforming the venal system inherited from the dictatorial regime, and building just societies. They continue to work together—sometimes formally, other times informally. When common threats are perceived, they activate long-standing relationships, networks, and organizations to fight corruption and impunity, and to mobilize their fellow citizens.

Civic anticorruption initiatives are incubators of democracy. First, they can build democracy at the grass roots through action—via informal elections (Afghanistan), surveys (Afghanistan, Uganda, Korea), reporting to fellow citizens (Afghanistan, Kenya), and even voting for anticorruption heroes (Egypt). Second, as witnessed in Afghanistan, Brazil, Kenya, Mexico, Korea, and Uganda, they are "exercises in participatory democracy that challenge the traditional 'rules of the game' in governance."[4] Through people power, citizens have the potential to hold politicians and state officials to account. Among the cases, methods included delegitimizing fraudulent elections (Egypt), pushing for accountability legislation (Brazil, India, Kenya), blacklisting "unfit" candidates (Korea), banning venal legislators from holding office (Brazil), and challenging corrupt practices (India, Kenya, Mexico).

Changing Power Relations

Civic campaigns and movements targeting corruption can redefine the relationship between the bottom and the top. The research found that regular people, even among the disadvantaged, moved from resignation to action. Instead of prostrating before malfeasant powerholders or shrinking in fear, people held powerholders to account through nonviolent actions (Afghanistan, Bosnia-Herzegovina, India, Kenya, Uganda, Korea) and disrupted the corrupt status quo (Brazil, Egypt, Indonesia, Italy, Mexico, Turkey). They invigorated representative democracies nonetheless plagued by corrupt politics (Brazil, Korea). The latter turned voting into an act of rebellion against having to choose from among unsatisfactory candidates selected by relatively unaccountable political parties. All in all, these cases redefined the role of citizens, who became active interlocutors vis-à-vis their governments and the state, thereby changing the power equation between the bottom and the top. The most profound example came from an unassuming spot—rural southwestern Uganda. Toward the end of a civic campaign to curb police corruption, local officers turned to the grass roots for help to overcome the problems and injustices they faced within their institution.

Through the lens of civil resistance, negotiation is a tactic that can be used both during and at the cessation of a civic campaign or movement. In the anticorruption realm, negotiation can help achieve interim goals and small victories, such as gaining access to information (Afghanistan or Kenya) or establishing a cooperative relationship with an institution plagued by corruption (Uganda). Negotiation can offer strategic benefits as well, even when the probability for gains is low (Korea). In this instance, it can build legitimacy for both the civic initiative and citizen action by demonstrating that an effort was made to engage with powerholders, which in turn can build support, engage the public, and delegitimize corruptors.

Unity

Civil resistance scholar Peter Ackerman points out that unity of people and goals is critical to citizen mobilization and successful nonviolent campaigns and movements. Anticorruption civic initiatives broaden our understanding of unity. First, they illuminate its psychological and emotional underpinnings. Unity is built upon widely held grievances, collective ownership of the struggle, and what sociologist Lee Smithey calls collective identity, defined as "a sense of 'we-ness' that derives or emerges from shared cognitions and beliefs."[5] Second, the cases shed light on the underlying dynamics of unity, which is fueled by a shared sense of outrage, and sometimes a commonly perceived source of the injustice or oppression—for example, the Mafia (Italy), police (Uganda), political parties/Parliament (Brazil, Mexico, Korea), the public sector (India), or the overall government (Egypt). Through these intangible yet essential elements, individuals can transcend differences—such as gender, age, rural-urban, class, ethnicity, race, religion—not only to feel a sense of sameness, but to take action in concert.

Common Attributes

Multidimensional Focus

Most of the civic initiatives targeting corruption were linked to other injustices and struggles, such as powerholder impunity and unaccountability (Bosnia-Herzegovina, Brazil, Egypt, Kenya, Mexico, Korea, Uganda), poverty (Kenya), development and reconstruction (Afghanistan), freedom from the Mafia (Italy), crime syndicate–state links (Turkey), attacks on honest officials and graft-fighting institutions (Indonesia), police intimidation (Uganda), and a demoralized citizenry (Mexico). Hence, corruption does not function in isolation.

Neutrality

All the cases were politically neutral in terms of their goals, membership, and broader mobilization efforts. The exception was Egypt, where the target was the Mubarak regime because it was considered the source of injustice, abuse, and graft. In this respect, shayfeen.com and Egyptians Against Corruption were not politically neutral. On the other hand, they directed their mobilization efforts to all Egyptians, including people within Mubarak's National Democratic Party, who were welcome to join and who, in many instances, became members of Egyptians Against Corruption. The logic is clear: when tackling endemic corruption involving the political establishment and the state, no one party has the monopoly on graft. The objective is to disrupt and transform the entire system. From a strategic standpoint, partisanship also hampers unity and undercuts participation as segments of the population can be alienated. Finally, as evident from Brazil, Kenya, Korea, and Turkey, neutrality is essential for maintaining legitimacy and inoculating against opponents' accusations of bias and interference.

Protagonists

Women (Brazil, Egypt, Mexico) and youth/young professionals (Afghanistan, Bosnia-Herzegovina, Italy, Kenya, Mexico, Uganda) played galvanizing roles in several cases. Veterans of nonviolent movements for democracy (Indonesia, Korea) also created and led national campaigns. Interestingly, lawyers (Brazil, Kenya, Turkey) and public relations experts (Egypt, Turkey) were among the core founders of campaigns and movements.

In virtually every case, the catalysts for the civic initiatives were either already connected to the grass roots or deliberately cultivated relationships with regular people through one-on-one interactions or social networking. In Afghanistan, Kenya, and Uganda, civil society organizations (CSOs) were immersed in marginalized communities—sharing experiences and witnessing their circumstances—which in turn approached the CSOs with their grievances and problems. These groups made painstaking efforts to establish credibility and trust, thereby building a foundation upon which to engage and mobilize people.

Strategic Approach

Across the board, the leadership core of these campaigns and movements engaged in strategic thinking, often at a highly sophisticated level. They linked overall goals to defining methods and nonviolent actions. They charted paths to overcoming obstacles and building unity. They deliberated over how to undermine the corrupt status quo, support honest powerholders, and win people over from within corrupt systems. Most of the movements seeking far-reaching change developed comprehensive, multidimensional approaches (Bosnia-Herzegovina, Egypt, Italy, India). The key elements were

- Awareness-raising in order to identify shared grievances and counter apathy.
- Changing attitudes toward the corrupt status quo and instilling values of integrity.
- Targeting youth because systemic transformation ultimately requires a generational change.
- Altering behavior of those engaged in corruption (corruptors, willing corruptees) and those oppressed by it.
- Achieving incremental victories at various levels, from overall movement successes to wins at the community and individual levels—for example, not paying a bribe.

Organization

Most of the cases—from finite campaigns (Afghanistan, Brazil, Indonesia, Kenya, Korea, Turkey, Uganda) to ongoing movements (Egypt, India, Italy)—engaged in extensive planning, organization, and trial and error to manage the overall initiative, mobilize citizens, and execute nonviolent actions. While, behind the scenes, the campaigns and movements had small leadership cores, only a few faces were highly public (Egypt, India, Kenya, Mexico). Indeed, the image associated with most of the civic initiatives was that of the people.

Civic initiatives can face a variety of leadership and organizational tensions, such as balancing structure and flexibility, core group planning versus decentralization, and core-group authority versus collective decisionmaking. The research reaffirmed the general finding in the civil resistance realm: there is no magic formula. However, almost across the board, small, core leadership groups engaged in much of the primary decisionmaking, strategizing, and planning. At the same time, they encouraged decentralization in terms of decisionmaking, planning, and local autonomy.

Several challenges were common among the twelve cases. For long-term movements with transformative societal goals, recruitment and sustainability required ongoing attention. Funding was an issue for virtually all the civic initiatives. However, equally significant is that these campaigns and movements were not constrained by their limited funds. In fact, because of their grassroots, voluntary nature, expenditures were modest. They employed creative methods to cover expenses, often pooled their own personal resources, and relied on monetary donations and other contributions from citizens. In a few cases (Afghanistan, Italy, Kenya), they had financial support from external actors or state institutions. In only one instance was a civic initiative completely dependent on donor support (Uganda). The outcome is instructive. In spite of remarkable success, the effort in Uganda came to an end after one year, partly because no second grant was awarded.

Intangible Qualities

If one overall quality can describe these civic initiatives, it is dynamism. In each instance, civic leaders, activists, and even regular citizens displayed creativity, ingenuity, and adaptability to changing circumstances. This was often accompanied by ongoing assessments; rapid responses to unexpected events, the latter an inevitable part of people power; and maximizing opportunities, large and small, that arose from such occurrences.

Success can be contagious, as witnessed in Afghanistan, Brazil, Egypt, and Kenya. It inspires new applications of tactics, overall defining methods, knowledge-sharing, and campaigns—domestically (Italy) and even across borders (India to Yemen, Palermo to Germany, Korea to Japan).

General Lessons Learned

Readers are urged to review the lessons learned at the end of each case study. While this section consolidates the material into fifteen general lessons, their breadth, applicability, and value to curbing corruption, gaining accountability, and, more generally, effectively wielding people power are more apparent in the longer discussions.

The first lesson highlights the multiple benefits of *unity*. Unity of people often involves coalitions of various sorts, comprising groups and prominent individuals. In addition to affording higher levels of participation, protection through numbers (of people), credibility, and legitimacy, such alliances are a font of creativity, ideas, and talent, as well as increased resources, relationships, and contacts—all of which the civic campaign or movement can use. Unity also increases diversity of dissent, from tactics to messaging and conduits through which messages are communicated. For instance, the involvement of popular musicians, street artists, television personalities, and others can lead to innovative nonviolent actions, such as anticorruption songs and ringtones, and reach an untapped swath of the public through entertainment media outlets covering celebrities. Finally, winning people over from within the corrupt system—a key people power dynamic that weakens the corrupt status quo and removes support for oppressors—can also produce practical and even tangible benefits for the movement or campaign, as was found in Afghanistan (access to project information and contacts), Brazil (tracking the Ficha Limpa bill's journey through Congress), Italy (background on Mafia extortion), and Kenya (access to information).

Second, clear, *definable objectives* are essential to engage citizens, produce visible outcomes, gain incremental victories, and build an overall track record of success. While identifying relatively tangible goals when targeting overall systems of graft and abuse may seem difficult, the twelve cases demonstrated that it is indeed possible.

Third, beyond the building blocks of nonviolent campaigns and movements—objectives, strategy, tactics, organization, and planning—this investigation demonstrated the impact of *intangible qualities* on people power and how they can be strategically cultivated:

• *Honest image.* The association of individuals or groups in society perceived as incorruptible and upright builds credibility and can stimulate support and participation.

• *Resonance.* Resonance of the civic initiative with regular people and their experiences. This involves shifting from abstract exhortations against corruption or legalistic and administrative jargon (too technical and removed from citizens' lives) to discourse, tactics, and objectives derived from the social and cultural realities of the grass roots in the particular struggle context.[6]

• *Collective responsibility.* The personal sense that "I am needed in this effort, and my efforts will contribute to our success."

• *Legitimacy.* Legitimacy of the civic initiative, in the eyes of the people as well as the corruptors. Legitimacy is vital to people power. It can counter smear campaigns by oppressors (Bosnia-Herzegovina, Korea, Turkey), prevent or thwart intimidation (Afghanistan, Bosnia-Herzegovina, India, Italy, Uganda), and make attacks backfire (Kenya, Turkey). As well, movements and campaigns emanating legitimacy can embolden honest individuals inside the system (Brazil, Egypt, India, Mexico), weaken the resolve of corruptors to maintain the status quo (Afghanistan, Bosnia-Herzegovina, Brazil, Kenya, Mexico, Korea, Uganda), and cumulatively garner support within venal systems as well as from the public.

• *Unity + credibility + ownership = legitimacy.* While legitimacy may perhaps be the most ephemeral of these intangibles, the twelve cases demonstrate there is no mystery to its cultivation. Legitimacy stems from unity of people, grievances, and objectives, plus credibility of the civic actors and collective ownership of the struggle.

Another general lesson is that successful bottom-up, civic initiatives targeting corruption are built upon the existing *social infrastructure*, that is, the social structures, social relationships, prevailing culture, and even history of the struggle context. Effective and credible strategies, tactics, discourse, and messaging derive from these home-grown settings, rather than from externally developed, formulaic approaches to citizen engagement.

Fifth, whether the civic action arena is as small as a single community, or a town-, region-, country-, or transnational-level effort, power comes from numbers relative to the particular setting. Thus, *mobilization* is essential. To win public support and engage citizens, three key elements play a role:

• *Framing the struggle*. Linking general concepts or abstract issues to widely held grievances and everyday concerns.
• *Using low-risk mass actions*. Actions that are accessible to many or can help to overcome fear in hostile environments (Bosnia-Herzegovina, Brazil, Egypt, Indonesia, Korea, Turkey, Uganda).
• *Emboldening individual acts of defiance*. Through the power of numbers—for example, handing a civil servant the 5th Pillar movement's zero-rupee note when extorted for a bribe (India), providing multifaceted support for each business that refuses to pay Mafia protection money (Italy), and creating collective settings for people to directly speak out (Facebook in Bosnia-Herzegovina and Indonesia, public forums in Afghanistan and Kenya, and radio call-in programs in Uganda).

The sixth lesson focuses on people power *dynamics* and moving from *strategy* to action. When corruption is viewed in a systemic manner, as discussed earlier in the chapter, one learns that it is impossible to discover all the venal interconnected relationships, eradicate the entire system (in the short term), and punish or "convert" to integrity all the corruptors and willing corruptees. The twelve cases demonstrate that people power offers an alternative to this colossal if not impossible feat. Social, economic, political, and psychological pressure exerted by significant numbers of individuals organized around shared grievances and goals, engaging in nonviolent strategies and tactics, can curb corruption through three dynamics. First is disrupting systems of graft and abuse. Second is weakening those systems from the inside by pulling people within the system toward the civic initiative—shifting their loyalties away from the status quo, and supporting those inside the system who want change but felt outnumbered and fearful to act alone. Cumulatively, this dynamic can produce defections—individuals and groups within the corrupt system who refuse to go along with it. When developing strategies and actions to activate this dynamic, citizens must recognize that not everyone within the corrupt system is equally wedded to perpetuating it. The third dynamic is applying nonviolent pressure through the power of numbers, namely, citizens raising their collective voice over shared demands, on corruptors who refuse to change the venal status quo.

Thus, a strategic approach to citizen empowerment and action involves several elements:

• *Harnessing the power of "no."* That is, noncooperation with corruption. The Gandhian precept of noncooperation with oppressors applies equally well to fighting graft and abuse. Such systems can only function smoothly if people do what they are supposed to do, whether demanding or even offering bribes, paying them, exchanging favors, turning a blind eye to illicit practices, not asking questions, or accepting things as they are. When enough people renounce corruption, refuse to go along with the status quo, and disengage from the system, it starts to break down.

• *Assessing the corrupt system.* To interrupt its smooth functioning in the present, and for social movements, to foster societal transformation in the longer term.

• *Designing nonviolent actions.* Actions that embody noncooperation, actively disrupt the corrupt status quo, or pull people (either out of the corrupt system or from the general public) toward integrity and accountability (the civic initiative).

The seventh lesson is that *tactical ingenuity* is essential for anticorruption civic initiatives. The creativity of nonviolent actions employed by these civic initiatives and social movements—both in the physical and digital worlds—was truly extraordinary. As evident from the twelve cases, tactical ingenuity can be critical to establishing a strategic advantage (Bosnia-Herzegovina, Brazil, Italy, Korea) or creating dilemmas for oppressors (Bosnia-Herzegovina). Certain types of tactics can also encourage participation by overcoming tough situations (Afghanistan, Egypt, Italy, Mexico, Turkey), apathy or cynicism (Afghanistan, Bosnia-Herzegovina, Egypt, India, Indonesia, Italy, Kenya, Mexico, Korea,

Turkey, Uganda), and fear of challenging powerholders (Afghanistan, Brazil, Egypt, India, Italy, Kenya, Turkey, Uganda). Through tactical ingenuity, social movements can make oppressor attacks backfire (Indonesia, Italy, Turkey) and can maintain resilience in the face of repression (Italy, Kenya, Egypt).

The eighth overall lesson concerns *tactical variety*. Civic anticorruption initiatives expand the overall tactical repertoire of civil resistance. While several ways are available to classify these actions in the civil resistance realm, I propose four categories that correspond to the functions of the tactics: disruption, engagement, empowerment, and an additional delineation for defining methods. The Appendix compiles all the nonviolent actions documented in the research.

Once tactics are classified in this manner, it becomes apparent that many nonviolent actions fall under more than one category. Depending on the struggle context at hand, a tactic can actually have multiple functions, which reflects the reality that tactics are not static; their functions and impact are derived from the struggle context. For example, public pledges can constitute tactics of disruption as well as engagement. Behavioral pledges to desist from corrupt activities can potentially disrupt the systems of graft and abuse. They also can produce engagement as the tactic involves close interaction with the public, gains support for the movement or campaign, and can increase recruitment. Taken together, several related lessons emerge.

Surveys, of one sort or another, are a tool that can yield strategically useful information for civic anticorruption initiatives (Afghanistan, Kenya, Korea, Uganda). On the one hand, they serve as a mechanism to gather people's views, which helps in planning the campaigns. On the other hand, they generate information that can be directed to powerholders, the media, or the public. Moreover, the process of conducting a survey constitutes a nonviolent tactic that can involve regular people as the information-gatherers, and provides opportunities for awareness-raising, active recruitment, and acquiring support from citizens.

Inventive civic initiatives take advantage of top-down, *institutional tools and mechanisms*—such as legislation, judicial processes, and anticorruption bodies—in order to secure information and repel attacks. They are often combined with nonviolent tactics in a complementary manner, thereby creating synergy between institutional and extrainstitutional forms of pressure. The cases included the Right to Information Act education in conjunction with Right to Information petitions (India), exercising constitutional rights for citizen-sponsored legislation together with a grassroots movement to submit it to Congress and digital resistance to pass it (Brazil), public accountability hearings in conjunction with legal efforts to change laws (Kenya), boycotting blacklisted candidates while voting in elections (Korea), and thwarting a government crackdown by invoking the United Nations Convention Against Corruption (Egypt) in court.

Monitoring constitutes an entire group of nonviolent tactics that can disrupt the corrupt, unjust status quo. It can take limitless forms, from digital scrutiny (Egypt, Mexico, Uganda) and blacklisting candidates (Korea), to ongoing, defining methods such as community monitoring (Afghanistan) and social audits (Kenya).

With imagination, commonplace activities can be turned into *low-risk mass actions*, which civil resistance scholar Maciej Bartkowski describes as "ingenious benevolent protests of everyday defiance."[7] Examples include turning lights on and off (Turkey), drinking tea and coffee (Egypt), regular shopping (Egypt, Italy), tourism (Italy), downloading mobile phone ringtones (Indonesia), wearing clothes (Bosnia-Herzegovina, Indonesia, Italy), and even voting (Korea).

Nine, effective tactics can offer inspiration to civic actors targeting corruption, not to be blindly copied, but to stimulate new ideas or serve as examples to be adapted and contextualized. Consequently, a critical lesson is that *tactics are not inherently effective or ineffective*—because their efficacy depends on the situation and the parameters of the struggle, such as objectives, strategies, unity, organization, overall tactical repertoire, social infrastructure, and intangibles (see Chapter 12). The distinction between transplanting versus adapting tactics was amply illustrated in the Afghan community-monitoring initiatives (see Chapter 8) and the Kenyan social audits (see Chapter 10).

As so vividly demonstrated by the Ficha Limpa movement in Brazil, the tenth lesson is that *digital resistance*—in which people power is wielded through actions involving information and communication technologies—does indeed exist (see Chapter 4). Digital resistance can shift power relations and usher in real-world outcomes. Online tactics can cultivate intangibles such as collective identity and ownership, provide an ongoing struggle narrative, expand the overall repertoire of nonviolent actions, and offer strategic advantages as well as economies of scale (Bosnia-Herzegovina, Brazil, Egypt, Indonesia, Mexico). However, across these cases, the astute combination of online and offline tactics created potent nonviolent pressure on powerholders.

Eleven, *information plus action equals power*. In some contexts, asking questions and requesting documents can function as nonviolent tactics and begin to disrupt the corrupt status quo (Afghanistan, India, Kenya). Acquiring information on budgets, spending, and powerholder assets can be an interim victory in the struggle. However, information on its own may not be enough to challenge corruption. For instance, a foundation manager shared observations that in some parts of Africa, donors have encouraged the practice of publicly posting school budgets. But school-related corruption continued when citizens, particularly parents, were disengaged or passive and did nothing with the information. In contrast, research in Uganda found that a key feature in the success of publicizing school budget information to reduce leakage of funds was the existence of parent-teacher groups at the village level that could engage in monitoring. In this case, "Parents were already organized and able to exert pressure. Mere publicity will not work in isolation."[8] The combination of information (access, collection, and dissemination) plus nonviolent direct actions—public forums, community meetings, monitoring, petitions, leafleting, stunts, street theatre, and creative, humorous, or fun mobilizations—can be a compelling source of people power.

The twelfth lesson is that bottom-up campaigns and movements can support those inside corrupt systems who are not necessarily venal through two overall strategies. First is generating the political will to *support powerholders who are inclined to push for reforms and change*, and bolstering integrity champions within state institutions and other entities who are actually attempting reforms and change. All too often, lone figures or agencies cannot challenge or dismantle entrenched systems of graft and unaccountability. Nonviolence academic Brian Martin has compared such attempts to the actions of political dissidents who stand in singular defiance before an entire undemocratic system and are therefore easily suppressed.[9] Such was the fate of John Githongo, a former Kenyan anticorruption chief, who fled the country in 2004 after threats to his life. Contrast this outcome to Indonesia, where the CICAK campaign mobilized citizens to successfully defend the Corruption Eradication Commission (KPK) and two falsely imprisoned deputy commissioners (see Chapter 5). Indonesian people power has on more than one occasion stimulated political will at the highest echelons, all the way to President Susilo Bambang Yudhoyono.

A second way to support those within corrupt systems who seek change is to *offer them a way out*. Not all individuals within horizontal or vertical systems of graft and abuse are dishonest, nor are they equally wedded to perpetuating the status quo. This dynamic expands upon the traditional civil resistance concept of shifting loyalties vis-à-vis the oppressor. Countless decent people are caught in the system, but individually they feel outnumbered and powerless and fear retaliation. If they act alone, their options are either to disobey (that is, refuse to engage in graft) or to expose corruption (become a whistle-blower). In either instance, as with honest powerholders attempting change, they are one standing against all the venal vested interests. Not surprisingly, they—and even their families—are likely to experience grave consequences, from harassment, demotion, and dismissal to violence and even death. Anticorruption campaigns and movements can empower honest insiders by offering them a way out of malfeasant systems (Italy), providing tangible support to resist or expose graft and abuse (India, Italy), publicly honoring their courage to speak up (Egypt), and rewarding their integrity at election time (Brazil and Korea).

In both of these contexts, grassroots campaigns and movements wield the *power of numbers*—people—so that individuals and even entities challenging corruption within the system are no longer sole dissenters facing a large cohort of corruptors. They, in turn, are backed by many from the public, making it more difficult for vested interests to harm them and subdue their efforts. And when corruptors do retaliate, their vile actions are more likely to backfire (Indonesia, Italy).

Thirteen, *planning and tactical sequencing* are essential elements to wielding people power, and this investigation reveals that anticorruption campaigns and movements are no exception. Even when a civic initiative jump-starts from an impulsive act (Italy) or through initial pilot activities (Afghanistan, Kenya), strategizing, planning, coordination, and sequencing are necessary to consolidate the civic initiative and maintain momentum.

Often neglected in nonviolent struggles, another lesson is that *education and training* are nonetheless vital to building capacity, resilience, and citizen confidence, courage, and hope. Education and training featured prominently among the twelve cases and varied from workshops (India, Kenya) to skills and capacity building (Afghanistan, Egypt, Kenya), overall programs targeting young people (Egypt, India, Italy), and last but not least, instruction in nonviolent discipline (Kenya, Korea).

Fifteen, well-developed *communications* are strategically important to build awareness, win support, and actively involve citizens. Depending on the audience(s) and goals of the messaging, there are multiple mediums of communication, ranging from traditional media outlets, music, street theatre, stunts, humor, graffiti, leaflets, clothing, badges, stickers, everyday objects (such as reusable shopping bags), websites, online videos, SMS, social media, and in the case of 5th Pillar, the antibribery currency called the zero-rupee note. A particularly innovative element of messaging is providing an ongoing, real-time narrative through information and communication technologies that people can closely follow, day by day, as the civic initiative unfolds (Brazil, Indonesia).

Finally, anticorruption struggles by nature involve a negative. Thus, a paramount lesson for civic initiatives is to *reframe the discourse* by balancing negatives (oppression, injustice, suffering) with positives (collective empowerment, tangible outcomes, hope, incremental victories, and affinity for one's community, country, or entities and groups fighting corruption and seeking accountability).

Conclusion

Twelve civic initiatives, millions of regular people in countries around the world, engaging in nonviolent actions, wielding people power, impacting corruption and impunity, and gaining accountability, rights, and justice. These cases expand the application of civil resistance to new arenas, enhance our understanding of the dynamics of people power, and demonstrate the linkages between curbing corruption, strengthening democracy, and redefining the relationship between governments and citizens. I propose five takeaways from this study:

1. Corruption is a form of oppression that harms people in their everyday lives. For the originators of these nonviolent civic initiatives, ultimately the struggle is for human rights, dignity, and freedom.

2. Regular citizens bring numerous capacities and a wellspring of courage and resolve to the anticorruption struggle. This includes the disadvantaged and marginalized, whose potential contributions should not be overlooked. "We believe that poor people think, and think as well as the literate do. In fact their ideas are rooted in a common sense from which literacy alienates the schooled, because the theory subsumes the reality very often," avowed Sowmya Kidambi, a veteran of the Indian Right to Information movement.[10]

3. People who are organized in civic initiatives, campaigns, and social movements have agency and the potential to wield power.

4. People power is a positive force that constructively confronts injustice while seeking engagement. It applies extrainstitutional, nonviolent social pressure on corruptors who refuse to change the venal status quo, disrupts systems of graft and abuse, and empowers integrity champions pursuing accountability, reform, and change from within the system.

5. External actors can support, defend, and enable homegrown ini-

tiatives in a variety of ways (see Chapter 12). But third parties are not the drivers of bottom-up change; nor can they produce genuine citizen engagement and action through monetary incentives and standardized projects. Citizens are the protagonists who chart the course, make the decisions, take the risks, propel the struggle, and own the victories.

Notes

1. Hee-Yeon Cho, "A Study on the Blacklisting Campaign Against Corrupt Politicians in South Korea—Focused on the 'Naksun Movement' in April 2000" (paper presented at the Civil Society in Asia, Today and Tomorrow conference, South Korea, December 5, 2003), 2–3.

2. Dadang Trisasongko, "After the Transition: The Role of People Power in Dismantling Entrenched Corruption, and Consolidating Democratic, Accountable Governance and Sustainable Peace" (presentation, Fifteenth International Anti-Corruption Conference, Brasilia, November 9, 2013).

3. Ibid.

4. Manuela Garza, "Social Audits as a Budget Monitoring Tool," International Budget Partnership, Learning from Each Other Series, October 2012, 6, http://internationalbudget.org.

5. Lee Smithey, "Identity Formation in Nonviolent Struggles," in *Recovering Nonviolent History: Civil Resistance in Liberation Struggles,* ed. Maciej Bartkowski, 31–47 (Boulder: Lynne Rienner, 2013).

6. "Discourse" refers to the narratives, cognitive frames, meanings, and language used by nonviolent movements and campaigns; Hardy Merriman, "Forming a Movement" (presentation, Fletcher Summer Institute for the Advanced Study of Strategic Nonviolent Conflict, Tufts University, June 20, 2011).

7. Maciej Bartkowski, ed. *Recovering Nonviolent History: Civil Resistance in Liberation Struggles* (Boulder, CO: Lynne Rienner, 2013).

8. Susan Rose-Ackerman, "The Challenge of Poor Governance and Corruption," Copenhagen Consensus 2004 Challenge Paper, Copenhagen 2004 Consensus Project, 2004, 18, www.copenhagenconsensus.com.

9. Brian Martin, "Whistleblowing and Nonviolence," *Peace and Change* 24, no. 1 (January 1999): 15–28.

10. Sowmya Kidambi, *Right to Know, Right to Live: Building a Campaign for the Right to Information and Accountability* (Minneapolis: Center for Victims of Torture, 2008), 8.

12

The International Dimension

Although civil resistance targeting corruption is, by its very nature, bottom-up and homegrown, it impacts foreign policy considerations, donor effectiveness, and overall anticorruption, development, democracy, and peacebuilding strategies. While this may first seem paradoxical, it becomes evident once people power is taken into consideration. Given the capacity of citizens, mobilized in nonviolent civic initiatives, to effectively wield power, the grass roots is by default part of the overall equation of political, social, and economic change. Moreover, as this research has found, successful civic anticorruption initiatives can be sources of transnational inspiration, strategies, and knowledge, thereby adding an international dimension to local and national struggles.

Ten Policy Implications
Taken together, the twelve case studies point to the following policy implications and development outcomes.

Enriched Analysis and Policy Development
The civic dimension is often lacking or minimally examined in country analyses. Thus, the foreign policy realm can acquire a fuller, more dynamic overview of political, social, and economic currents when the grievances of citizens and their capacities to shift the power equation are included. Telltale examples are the 2010–2011 manifestations of people power in the Middle East, and the nascent Russian democracy mobilizations, which took many governments, analysts, and journalists by surprise. While the complexity of multifaceted social phenomena

makes it impossible to identify a special set of precursor conditions or to predict when a civic initiative or social movement will emerge, one can ascertain where the likelihood exists by recognizing the building blocks of civil resistance. They include

- Shared awareness among people of tangible, often everyday concerns that are linked to corruption, impunity, abuse, injustice, and poverty.
- Collective feelings of being affronted by powerholders (state or nonstate).
- Emergence of cooperation and new alliances at the grass roots.
- Decreasing citizen fear to express dissent.
- Recurring small-scale or larger-scale nonviolent tactics (on the ground and digitally) expressed in an organized, collective manner.

The international reaction to post-Taliban Afghanistan provides lessons about the need to integrate the civic dimension into policy and peacebuilding. Notwithstanding the enormous challenges facing the country when the Taliban was violently deposed at the end of 2001, an earlier awareness, both of citizens as sources of positive power and the corrosive social impact of corruption, could conceivably have resulted in somewhat different strategies and priorities. Corruption has reached such epic proportions that it is now considered a clear threat to peace, counterinsurgency, reconstruction, and development.[1] Malfeasance is undermining trust in the government, adding a crushing burden to the overwhelmingly poor population and enabling a flourishing drug trade that is a source of revenue for warlords and the Taliban. In congressional testimony, then US secretary of state Hillary Clinton stated that "much of the corruption" in Afghanistan has been fueled by billions of dollars' worth of foreign money spent there, "and one of the major sources of funding for the Taliban is the protection money."[2] Afghans fighting corruption within the state and in the civic realm lament that early opportunities for systemic reforms were missed.[3] International and local civil society organizations contend that donor strategies were largely influenced by security concerns rather than people's needs.[4] Nor were citizens considered as players in the process.[5]

Practical Insights into Systems of Corruption and Development Challenges

By understanding what happens on the ground, the international anticorruption and development realms gain practical knowledge and insights about corruption patterns in countries, how they function and are manifested vertically and horizontally, and what the pervasive challenges are from a humanitarian perspective. Hence, substantive engagement and consultation with grassroots civic actors can contribute to identifying forms of corruption that matter to the public as well as developing accountability, economic, and social programs in tandem with governments receiving international assistance that are user-friendly for citizens. Engagement and consultation also inform the parameters and substance of policy reform and institution-building initiatives supported by the international community, and the prioritization of donor support and projects. Communication with grassroots civic actors helps incorporate people-centered concerns and mechanisms into top-down anticorruption initiatives at the national and multilateral levels. It can contribute to reduced corruption in development efforts, donor project subcontracting, and the political leveraging of donor aid by recipient country powerholders.

Civic initiatives have an inherent wisdom to them since they zero in on those forms of corruption most egregious to citizens. The international community and national decisionmakers can learn from those on the ground rather than deciding what forms of corruption they think should be tackled in order to improve the lives of the public. Ordinary people—often socially and economically disadvantaged and facing duress for expressing dissent—do not voluntarily give of their time and precious resources unless the graft and abuse they target truly matter. While these points may seem obvious, anecdotal input and research find they are not the norm. The Listening Project, which solicited 6,000 views about international assistance (humanitarian, development, peacebuilding, human rights, environment, etc.) in twenty societies, found that respondents wanted more ownership and opportunities to play an active role in their own development—to "discuss together, decide together, and work together."[6] Furthermore, corruption was one of their principal concerns, not only as practiced by powerholders in their countries, but also in aid and development efforts. An Afghan man characterized a common observation in this way: "The donor comes to an international NGO, the INGO comes to a local NGO, the local NGO comes to a contractor, the contractor to a subcontractor, and finally we receive nothing."[7]

However, there are promising signs of international engagement with grassroots anticorruption initiatives. For instance, in July 2011, Integrity Watch Afghanistan had meetings in Washington, DC, on improving the effectiveness of aid distributed by the United States Agency for

International Development (USAID), which included a briefing in the US Congress on corruption in Afghanistan.[8]

Enhanced Top-Down Anticorruption and Accountability Mechanisms

A general lesson emerging from the comparative examination of citizen engagement and accountability is that the involvement of credible collective actors in policy reform, notably from grassroots initiatives, can strengthen top-down "accountability functions."[9] A number of compelling cases are available for study, ranging from the role of the Sanitarista public health movement in the reform of Brazil's state health system to the impact of the Mexican women's movement for reproductive health in crafting participatory mechanisms.[10] In this study, potent examples include the development of India's landmark Right to Information law (see Chapter 7), implementation of the United Nations Convention Against Corruption in Egypt (see Chapter 10), and transparency in reconstruction and development projects in post–violent conflict settings (see Chapter 8).

Conditions Are Not Predeterminants

The misconception prevalent in the anticorruption and development realms that structural conditions are predeterminants for civic initiatives to develop and succeed can have a disempowering effect on grassroots initiatives. First, it can perpetuate top-down approaches to anticorruption and accountability when conditions on the ground are not perceived as being ideal for citizen dissent. More significantly, it can demotivate civic groups and citizens from taking collective action and divert campaigns away from appropriate goals. For example, Right to Information laws (RTIs) are undeniably useful to fight corruption. But even if there is no RTI in a country, change is still possible before an RTI is attained, and all civic efforts need not focus on getting such legislation passed. People power can be used to secure information even in the absence of legislation, which Kenya's MUHURI demonstrated (see Chapter 10). Finally, such civic pressure can also push for the enactment of people-centered RTI legislation, as was achieved by the Indian Mazdoor Kisan Shakti Sangathan (MKSS) movement. In a film interview, MKSS cofounder Aruna Roy explains, "In 1996, the MKSS sat in a forty-day sit-in in Beawar, and we were demanding the right to access records of the Panchayat, the smallest elected body in India. We involved the entire city and made it a people's campaign. We involved people from all over India, and the national campaign for people's right to information was born."[11]

Affirming Enabling Environments Versus
Interference in the Trajectory of People Power

Enabling environments is a valuable concept that is circulating in the development and anticorruption realms. From the civil resistance perspective, it offers an alternative to the notion of preconditions for citizen empowerment and action. The international community can play a role in affirming enabling environments for the emergence of home-grown anticorruption campaigns and movements. However, the challenge for external actors is to do so without imposing their own notions about what they consider acceptable forms of citizen dissent and nonviolent action. For the grass roots to wield power to gain reforms or change, a combination of tactics is needed: some that disrupt the status quo and some that engage people, groups, and institutions, shifting loyalties and pulling them toward the cause, including from within such corrupt systems.

A powerful illustration of how international actors played an enabling role can be found in the case of Santa Lucia Cotzumalguapa, a small town in Guatemala, where the nexus of corruption, impunity, and cross-border narco-trafficking created a horrendous situation akin to violent tyranny. In the aftermath of the civil war in 1996 this ongoing movement emerged to recover the community from the hands of drug lords and organized crime, maintain resilience in the face of violent repression, defend victories, and foster social and economic development. Their successes triggered severe counterattacks, including murders and electoral fraud. By 2007, eleven community leaders had been murdered, four attempts were made on an honest mayor's life, slandering and defamation cases were lodged, electoral fraud was orchestrated, and the police, prosecutors, and judges favored the drug cartels.[12]

Under such abysmal circumstances, how could the international community affirm the movement, thereby fostering an enabling environment for action and survival? Together with Guatemalan human rights defenders, international groups drew world attention to the struggle. The movement also garnered support for civic initiatives from the United Nations Development Programme (UNDP) and the Friedrich-Ebert-Stiftung. International observers and nonviolent accompaniment were provided to protect people at risk. Finally, Santa Lucia Cotzumalguapa became the host of national and international meetings, thereby sending a message to the corrupt powerholders—that the country and the world were watching and stood together with the townspeople.

A more complex example can be found with the aims and activities of the Partnership for Transparency Fund (PTF). A valuable international source of modest grants and, more recently, peer-to-peer exchanges, its stated vision is for societies in which "citizens succeed in making their government free of corruption."[13] As discussed in Chapter 9, PTF's support enabled the launching of the Police-NAFODU-Community Partnership initiative in Uganda. Nonetheless, it imposes its own notions and values about civic dissent onto the CSOs it funds. While there is no debate over its right to set funding criteria as it sees fit, there are implications for grassroots civic initiatives and people power.

The fund's website states, "PTF believes that in most cases collaborating with the public sector, while addressing a corruption problem, provides the greatest chance for long-term change. . . . The hypothesis is that consensus building and collaboration yield better and longer-lasting results than confrontation."[14] But what exactly is meant by consensus building, collaboration, and confrontation? These assertions suggest an underlying ambivalence and discomfort about citizen dissent. It considers some forms of nonviolent action—consensus building and collaboration—as more legitimate and effective than other forms. It appears to imply that when citizens raise their collective voice and exert nonviolent pressure—people power—they should behave in a nonchallenging manner. In a filmed interview, Rev. James Lawson, one of the leaders of the US civil rights movement, described nonviolent action as "your dignified, disciplined, confrontation of the wrong."[15] Thus, a distinction needs to be made between positive (constructive) and negative confrontation. Positive confrontation involves the refusal to continue acquiescing to malfeasance, combined with nonviolent action to curtail abuse, corrupt practices, venal systems, oppression, and injustice. Negative confrontation, in contrast, is characterized by indiscriminate belligerence or hostility directed toward individuals.

What are the implications of PTF's viewpoint? For CSOs and other grassroots groups, the internalization of such beliefs can be self-limiting. First, it could dampen the potential for bottom-up civic initiatives to emerge if civic actors or citizens themselves believe they need to enter into agreements with public entities in order to effectively target corruption. Second, those living under authoritarian regimes or facing unresponsive state entities might conclude that prospects for success are negligible and give up before even trying. Third, civic initiatives may not consider the full range of nonviolent tactics available in their context, because international actors may consider them to be confrontational and frown on them. This could include a variety of types of civil disobedience: public forums, street actions (protests, vigils, processions, marches, etc.), street theatre, stunts, visual dramatizations, cultural expressions (songs, poetry, ringtones), graffiti, displaying symbols, petitions, digital resistance, information gathering, publicly exposing corruptors and graft, citizen-generated blacklists, and disseminating information about citizen rights and public sector fees outside government offices.

Finally, PTF advises CSOs to obtain formal agreements. Its guidelines state, "Consequently, where support of a public entity is necessary for the success of the project, the applicant needs to line up the support from the municipality, government department, judicial structure, legislative body, university, etc., and confirm the public sector entity's willingness, preferably in writing."[16] This arrangement had strategic and practical benefits for NAFODU in Uganda. In other situations, however, there may be less to gain. One can take the case of 5th Pillar in India. Although operating within an established democracy, had they sought permission for volunteers to post official fees for documents and certificates outside public offices, it is doubtful they would have received it, and the time spent would have been a distraction. Moreover, a civic initiative entering into formal cooperation with a state entity may not be strategically wise. In some contexts, this could be viewed cynically or suspiciously by regular people and thus undermine a civic initiative's legitimacy and capacity to mobilize. In fact, NAFODU first encountered such negative sentiment among locals, but fortunately was able to overcome it.

Citizen Voice and Social Accountability
Involve People Power

While development practitioners and international donors understand that citizens have the capacity to impact corruption and are eager to support people's empowerment, there is limited knowledge about how citizens actually achieve such bottom-up change. They tend to view grassroots civic initiatives through the framework of citizen voice and social accountability, which neither offer an explanation about the process through which accountability is gained nor explicitly encompass the underlying dynamics of people power.[17] Traditionally, citizen empowerment was viewed as part of governance, which was considered a political issue and not an element of development.[18] As a result, social accountability emerged as a framework through which innovative development and anticorruption practitioners could get around this impediment and incorporate the notion of citizen-generated pressure into policymaking and programs.[19] In light of the paradigm shift under way in the development realm over the role of citizens in undermining corruption and oppression, the timing is right for the social accountability field to incorporate people power concepts and scholarship, in which three dimensions are key.

First, the *social accountability* framework, up until now, has not been able to articulate what actually produces change, relying instead on circular definitions such as, "a wide range of citizen and civil society organization actions to hold the state to account, as well as actions on the part of government, media, and other societal actors."[20] Social accountability at its core consists of empowered citizens generating social pressure, which shifts power imbalances; disrupts corrupt practices, relationships, and systems (vertically within an institution or horizontally across institutions and groups); and supports honest powerholders who attempt reforms but alone cannot stand against all the vested interests in the venal status quo. In other words, social accountability involves people power.

Second, as in any struggle, *negotiation* may play a role in interactions between the grass roots and powerholders. But on its own, negotiation is unlikely to yield favorable results if a power imbalance exists at the outset. People power has the potential to equalize the interaction and further negotiations by creating leverage for the civic initiative.[21]

Lastly, *donor-initiated or -sponsored efforts* to build social accountability into national development projects require permission or some form of acceptance from government counterparts, for example, the World Bank's Global Partnership for Social Accountability. While such initiatives do not appear to grow organically out of the grass roots, they seek citizen engagement and action, and ultimately have the potential to generate social pressure through which accountability is gained.

Hence, the social accountability field can benefit from accumulated knowledge about effective social movements, particularly the need for strategy, planning, organization and tactical innovation, diversity, and sequencing.

Bottom-Up People Power Initiatives Do Not Equal Top-Down Mechanisms Involving Citizens

A disquieting trend is emerging to institutionalize and scale up civic anticorruption and social accountability initiatives. While the embrace of citizen-led change is laudable, if it is translated into attempts to jumpstart, engineer, or standardize civic initiatives, the results may lead to disappointment and could be detrimental to the civic realm. The following points elaborate on this issue.

A randomized, controlled set of field experiments conducted in 608

Indonesian villages is illustrative of these hazards. The widely cited study intended to compare the efficacy of "top-down monitoring by government auditors and bottom-up monitoring through grassroots participation in the village monitoring process."[22] But what was construed as citizen engagement was designed by external actors and, not surprisingly, failed to yield significant outcomes. Each community was the recipient of a new road under a national infrastructure program. After the project design and allocations had been finalized but before materials procurement or road construction began, villages were subjected to one of three interventions: external audit, accountability meeting, or accountability meeting plus comment boxes. In the external audit intervention, communities were told that after the funds were awarded but before construction began, they would be audited by the state audit agency (BPKP), and the results would be reported to the central government and publicly presented at an open meeting. In a second experiment, villages were informed that "accountability meetings" would be held after the project, at which point officials would explain how they spent the funds. Invitations were distributed to approximately half of the households, apparently by village heads. In addition to the accountability meetings, in the third intervention, anonymous comment forms were attached to accountability meeting invitations given to community recipients. The forms could be left at drop boxes and would be summarized at the accountability meeting. The results were that external audits (intervention 1) reduced missing expenditures, but the accountability meeting scenarios (interventions 2 and 3) had little average impact.

The study concluded that "grassroots participation in monitoring" had a negligible effect on corruption. In fact, the research inadvertently demonstrated the opposite—namely, the limitations of externally driven, narrowly defined accountability initiatives projected onto citizens, who were assigned monitoring roles, responsibilities, and actions by powerholders. First, regular citizens did not have input about how to monitor the road construction projects. Second, citizens neither initiated nor organized the public accountability meetings. As importantly, they did not attempt to mobilize fellow residents to participate. Finally, the complex process of exacting accountability was reduced to attendance in one meeting—in some cases, combined with the option of filling out an anonymous comment form prior to the gathering. Thus, there was no local ownership of the development projects and accountability measures, let alone a sense of collective responsibility and even a shared goal of preventing corruption. In contrast, one can compare these artificial grassroots efforts with the successful outcomes of MUHURI's social audits in Kenya and Integrity Watch Afghanistan's community-monitoring initiatives (see Chapters 10 and 8, respectively).

When it comes to scaling up civic initiatives, effective civic campaigns and movements naturally inspire other communities and groups. For example, the Right to Information movement in India had a transcontinental impact in Africa and inspired the young founders of Integrity Watch Afghanistan. Domestically, each time an Afghan village successfully monitors a development and reconstruction project, other communities hear about it and want to embark on their own civic initiatives. Thus grew the original pilot program of ten villages in 2007 to 400 in 2013.

Externally driven efforts to encourage citizen engagement tend to simplify the complex reality of civic initiatives, limit the anticorruption arena to prescribed interactions with governments, and narrow the range of tactics. They can unintentionally create confusion about what constitutes citizen empowerment and action. Top-down accountability mechanisms (designed by states or donors) that include citizen input into government policy and activities are not the same as civic initiatives springing organically from the grass roots. The former's track record is mixed. One large literature review concluded, "No 'accountability effect' was in evidence in cases where voice mechanisms failed to facilitate the influential expression of civic voice."[23] In another analysis of public sector reforms, it was found that elites can hijack institutional opportunities to engage with policymakers. The authors concluded, "The 'success stories' are rooted in social movements and organizations which have built trust and mutual support among members."[24] And they caution donors to "not assume that accountability initiatives can be treated as mechanisms to be 'transplanted' in new contexts without considerable groundwork in building social and organizational support."[25]

While recognizing some donors' worthy objectives to support citizen empowerment and action, a potential danger exists that in seeking to multiply "demand-driven initiatives," they may unintentionally channel bottom-up civic impulses into structured social accountability projects, thereby hampering the emergence of other forms of citizen dissent, social mobilization, and people power.

People's Engagement and Civic Initiatives Are Not Formulaic

To expect to see a direct linear relationship between a tactic and an anticorruption or accountability outcome is unlikely. Civil resistance takes place in what sociologist Lee Smithey describes as a cultural, social, political, and economic landscape.[26] And that cultural, social, political, and economic landscape varies in each situation. The overwhelming conclusion among scholars and activists is that there is no such thing as a viable, effective people power formula or a replicable set of objectives, strategies, actions, and outcomes. Nor are particular tactics inherently good or bad. What works in one context would not necessarily work in another. In the anticorruption and development worlds, social accountability activities (many of which can be construed as nonviolent tactics in the people power realm) are commonly viewed as fixed variables. But to be effective, they need to resonate with the existing culture and values in the particular society, and provide motivational and emotional resources to those who engage in them and those who react to them. An example is Addiopizzo's creation of stickers resembling traditional Sicilian obituary notices that were affixed to walls and street lamps.

Thus, there is a difference between copying a nonviolent action and deriving inspiration from it. The efficacy of tactics depends on struggle context, social and cultural intangibles, and the parameters of the struggle, such as objectives, strategies, unity, organization, overall tactical repertoire, and social infrastructure. Nevertheless, effective tactics in one situation can offer inspiration to civic actors targeting corruption by stimulating new ideas or serving as examples to be adapted and contextualized. For example, the defining method of monitoring is a potentially powerful set of tactics. The key lesson is not that there is a formula for this method that can be reproduced and scaled up across settings. Rather, its potential efficacy derives from its capacity to disrupt the smooth functioning of the corrupt status quo. Hence, monitoring can take a variety of forms depending on the creativity of civic actors and the situation at hand.

As well, civic actions need to tap into shared identities and, on occasion, raise ethical dilemmas, as demonstrated by Addiopizzo's slogan, "An entire people who pays pizzo [extortion money] is a people without dignity."[27]

In sum, tactical creation and selection depend on the overall strategy, the local context, and their combination with other actions in a sequenced, complementary manner—that all come together in a coherent, organized campaign or movement that mobilizes people and maintains nonviolent discipline. How does this apply to a real case? Site inspections of public works projects are touted as a method to decrease corruption and increase accountability. Inspections have the potential to disrupt corrupt practices by documenting illicit activities or preventing them—when corruptors know they will be exposed. But the impact of this tactic depends on multiple factors—for instance, the credibility, reputations, societal positions or roles, and social perceptions of the individuals conducting the inspections; nonviolent tactics leading up to the site visit (for example, obtaining information from authorities); behavior during the site visit; tactics following the site visit to disseminate the findings; messaging and communications directed to the community or powerholders; support from other groups and sectors in the community, larger society, or external actors; potential support from sympathetic officials; timing of the action, and so on. In a strategic campaign, these multiple considerations are factored into the design of the tactic(s).

Adverse Consequences of Standardization Efforts

Standardized, prescriptive blueprints of tactics and tools promoted by third-party actors to in-country CSOs may not only lead to failure but can divert grassroots efforts from more effective paths, create disillusionment, and potentially put regular people in harm's way. In the latter case, what may be low-risk in one setting could be high-risk in another. Strategic planning includes risk assessments, which are always context specific and cannot be done by outsiders. Continuing with the case of monitoring public works, if some kind of inspection is planned, have the following questions been addressed: Is there a likelihood the monitoring activities could be thwarted? Would the citizens conducting the visit be attacked or face subsequent reprisals? Would the likelihood of interference be the same for people of different social sectors (for example, adult men or grandmothers or schoolchildren)? Are the people volunteering to take part aware of the risks and willing to continue? If the possibility of retaliation exists, what can be done to make it backfire? As a result, a host of other alternatives might be designed, thereby enabling a campaign to strategically consider different or complementary tactics to further the original objective.

In Bosnia-Herzegovina, Dosta! strategically decided to use social media tactics rather than traditional street protests, because the movement's leaders understood that corruptors were ready to thwart nonviolent direct action but were taken by surprise with digital resistance (see Chapter 10). Therefore, those who are involved in the civic initiative are the best placed to diagnose such situations, as well as to decide on the course of action—whether to assume risks and face potential negative consequences.

Constructive Support

International actors, donors, and development institutions can play positive roles and provide invaluable forms of support to bottom-up anticorruption efforts, including access to information; small, flexible grants; and opportunities for national and transnational peer-to-peer learning and dialogue (see the "Recommendations" section below).

The evolution and use of social audits in Kenya and community monitoring in Afghanistan demonstrate the positive confluence of bottom-up civic initiatives and external actors, directly through international NGOs and indirectly through donors. In both cases, tactics were adapted at the local level rather than copied from other campaigns and movements in the international arena. The origins of the six-step social audit developed by MUHURI in Kenya stem from the MKSS and the Right to Know movement in India, through the jan sunwai (public hearing) nonviolent actions in Rajasthan.[28] Two NGOs, the New Tactics Project of the Center for Victims of Torture and the International Budget Partnership, played catalytic roles in disseminating information and lessons learned from this movement. The New Tactics Project makes available online an outstanding case study authored by Sowmya Kidambi, a former MKSS activist. The International Budget Partnership facilitated a workshop in Mombasa that brought together MKSS activists, MUHURI, local citizens, and other CSOs in Kenya. The international dimension is further bolstered in that both the New Tactics Project and the International Budget Partnership receive financial support from foundations and development agencies. Other examples are the modest financial support provided by the Partnership for Transparency Fund to NAFODU in Uganda and TIRI and the Norwegian Agency for Development Cooperation's overall support to Integrity Watch Afghanistan, which allowed the CSO to allocate a small amount to pilot the community-monitoring initiative.

When grassroots CSOs and community-based organizations are considered counterparts rather than recipients of aid or conduits of externally driven programs, valuable synergies can emerge that build anticorruption into aid and development by harnessing the strengths and capacities of citizens wielding people power. A case in point is the innovative form of cooperation initiated between the World Bank and Integrity Watch Afghanistan. As mentioned in Chapter 8, they came to a monitoring agreement whereby in July 2011 the CSO opened a field office in the province of Badakshan, in order to begin empowering willing local communities to monitor World Bank–funded reconstruction projects.[29]

Guiding Principles for Third-Party Actors

Although third-party actors cannot bring grassroots civic initiatives into existence or direct them, the international community can develop a host of supportive policies and measures. The following general principles are presented as a guide to international engagement:

- *Affirm*, through solidarity and engagement, rather than interfere in the development and trajectory of civic anticorruption initiatives.
- *Enable* the emergence of citizen empowerment and action through efforts to improve challenging situations on the ground.
- *Empower* citizens and civic organizations through actor-oriented approaches that can include transfers of useful knowledge and skills, peer-to-peer learning exchanges, access to information, national and international networking opportunities, provision of modest grants, support for ICT development and new tools, and access to ICTs and infrastructure.
- *Recognize* that citizens have agency and power—generated through nonviolent, bottom-up initiatives and social movements. They are sources of change rather than simple recipients of peacebuilding, anticorruption, social accountability, and democracy efforts that are determined, designed, and directed on their behalf by elites or external actors.
- *Respect* the wishes and judgments of civic actors and regular people on the ground. In some contexts, international contact and support can be beneficial. However, in other situations, it can be detrimental by delegitimizing the campaign or movement, harming the credibility of civic leaders, and in some cases, leading to harsh repression and physical harm.

Recommendations

The following overall recommendations are presented for the international community, including the anticorruption, development, peacebuilding, human rights, and democracy/good governance realms.

Protection

It is unfortunately all too common for anticorruption advocates in the civic realm and within governments, as well as investigative journalists, to face harassment, intimidation, and violence from both state and nonstate entities.[30] The CIVICUS 2009–2010 Civil Society Index concluded,

The world is presently witnessing a cascade of laws and regulatory measures to restrict the rights of citizens to freely express their views, associate, and assemble. Peaceful demonstrators, activists, journalists, human rights defenders, and ordinary citizens are increasingly facing motivated prosecution, harassment, physical abuse, and threats to their lives for challenging well-entrenched power structures.[31]

In the course of my research, several civic leaders and activists noted that solidarity and protection were among the most valuable contributions the international community could make. One anticorruption activist said, "First, to defend the lives of the people who are involved in these campaigns and movements. Activists in my country are in constant risk." This view was echoed in a study interviewing 500 local stakeholders in fourteen countries on donor democracy support.[32] It found that "much more valuable than slightly increased amounts of money, or slightly changed funding rules, would be more effective international pressure on regimes to loosen civil society and other laws."[33]

Condemning crackdowns can include exposing violations of international or regional conventions signed by aid-recipient governments, and developing joint statements and actions among like-minded governments. An important caveat is that external actors should act in concert with anticorruption advocates under threat, or their associates and family members. They can best determine whether international solidarity will be beneficial or harmful and which forms of support are needed, and in some cases, point to targets of such efforts, such as powerholders, media, third-party intermediaries, or other governments that have leverage.

Wider strategic benefits also come with international exposure, attention, and condemnation of repression against individuals or civic initiatives. First, international solidarity constitutes the civil resistance principle of unity and can create pressure in the international arena through the dynamic of the power of numbers (of people, actors, institutions, entities). Second, protecting a few can empower many and make crackdowns backfire by thwarting oppressors' goals, which include instilling fear, hopelessness, and apathy among anticorruption advocates and the general public; impeding unity among anticorruption organizations and networks; and preventing alliances with other nonviolent struggles, for example, democracy, labor, women, minorities, and the environment.

Genuine Inclusion and Engagement
Grassroots leaders and community figures have vital input that can be systematically and meaningfully included in top-down reform through

policy and program development deliberations conducted under the auspices of external actors, including donor governments, multilateral institutions, think tanks, and academic centers. On the basis of anecdotal accounts conveyed to me, exclusion seems to be more common than inclusion. Civic anticorruption leaders reported instances in which they did not get responses when contacting the local missions of multilateral institutions, or they were not invited to anticorruption forums that involved NGO elites and decisionmakers from their countries. On the other hand, civic actors want meaningful consultations, not a "façade of a democratic process . . . with no option, whatsoever, of real dialogue," said a young CSO leader.[34]

Self-Organization and Capacity Building

International strategies to foster democracy, accountability, and human rights have focused on the creation of in-country (often elitist) NGOs. Civic activists anecdotally report that external actors often do not see or marginalize social networks on the ground, in part because they do not resemble the Global North's notions of organized civil society. Accordingly, less attention has been given to other forms of citizen groups, such as indigenous cultural organizations, people's associations, and social movements.[35] In the anticorruption and accountability context, while some bottom-up initiatives are spearheaded by CSOs, others may be linked to an organization or emerge from one, but essentially operate as a social movement—or they consist of alliances and networks coordinated by an informal group of nonstate actors from across society.

A conceptual transformation of donor support is needed from clientelism to citizenship. The aforementioned donor democracy study states, "It emerges from our interviews that civil society organizations most appreciate local-level projects that assist self-organisation based around issues of practical relevance to individual citizens."[36] At the macro level, this includes

- "Creating capacities for citizenship through the provision of opportunities for social bargaining and social learning within post-conflict societies."[37]
- Building holistic approaches based on the inherent links among anticorruption, human rights, peacebuilding, and development efforts.
- Considering social networks and preexisting relationships when supporting nonviolent initiatives.
- Supporting INGOs, global civic alliances, and international digital

movements that are close to in-country, grassroots civic initiatives; serve as catalysts for peer-to-peer, bottom-up knowledge and skills transfer; protect activists on the ground; wage transnational campaigns linked to internal civic struggles; and provide modest funding directly to local actors to turn ideas into action.

In contrast, international support for self-organization doesn't necessitate institutionalizing bottom-up anticorruption campaigns and movements by encouraging their transformation into conventional NGOs removed from the grass roots. As people power is extrainstitutional by nature, such attempts to standardize the process of social pressure can interrupt its dynamics; divert time, resources, and attention away from the struggle; and harm the campaign's vibrancy, adaptability, local ties, legitimacy, sense of ownership, and social identity. In tandem, credible civic initiatives have the responsibility to practice what they demand—integrity, fiscal responsibility, and accountability.

Access to Information

While information is not a precondition for successful people power, its availability contributes to an enabling environment. Rather than expend precious resources and efforts to acquire information, nonviolent campaigns and movements can bypass the hurdle of acquiring information and directly use it for the anticorruption challenges at hand. To this end, the international community can advocate for access to information among powerholders in aid-recipient countries. It can also set an example of transparency about its own development activities. Additionally, external actors can make available information needed by grassroots civic actors for anticorruption and accountability initiatives, as the latter often face obstacles from their own national and local governments. Finally, what can also be helpful, on occasion, is informally shared information about integrity champions—state and nonstate powerholders who are favorable to anticorruption and accountability efforts, for example, honest officials, legislators, local administrators, reformers, and representatives of organized labor, professional associations, and the private sector.

Exchange and Knowledge

Although there is no dearth of anticorruption forums, fewer opportunities are available for dialogue and peer-to-peer learning among grassroots civic organizations, their leaders, and local activists. The international community can make possible more frequent exchanges and bring together civic actors who fight graft and abuse but come from realms beyond anticorruption and accountability, such as democracy, peace-building, antipoverty, social and economic justice, human rights, women's rights, labor rights, minority and indigenous rights, the environment, and countering organized crime. A noteworthy development was the Fifteenth International Anti-Corruption Conference, with the overall theme, "Mobilising People: Connecting Agents of Change."

Such exchanges have multiple benefits. Their challenges, strategies, tactics, and practical lessons can be circulated widely within the anticorruption and accountability realms. Others can draw inspiration from the sheer ingenuity, courage, and resilience of those engaging in nonviolent action, who often face intimidation and repression. Such encounters may contribute to a "thickening of alliances and relationships" across borders, thereby fostering transnational peer-to-peer networks and the people power dynamic of power of numbers.[38]

Global South-to-South transfers are particularly important. No longer is it the case that the main flow of learning is from the Global North to the Global South. The most fertile source of skills, innovation, strategies, tactics, and ICT applications for gaining accountability, justice, and rights is now the Global South. A fascinating illustration comes from Asia. Launched in 2010, Ipaidabribe.com is a digital portal developed by the Janaagraha Centre for Citizenship and Democracy in Bangalore, India. Through ICT modalities—email, SMS, Twitter, mobile phone video uploads, and so forth—citizens can safely and, if they wish, anonymously, post instances of bribery and resistance to it in public service delivery, as well as interact with one another and Janaagraha members. In spite of the Chinese regime's Internet censorship, the country's savvy digital surfers learned about Ipaidabribe.com and have taken inspiration from it. Several Chinese websites have been launched, such as "I Made a Bribe," the latter calling on citizens to "Please reveal your experiences of paying bribes so embezzlement and corruption have nowhere to hide."[39] Regular visits to the Indian Ipaidabribe.com reveal an ever-increasing number of countries that are developing their own sites, such as Greece, Kosovo, Kenya, Morocco, and Pakistan, and many more are in the pipeline.

The international community can more fully foster South-to-South transfers in which activists are encouraged to assume various degrees of collective responsibility and ownership in the content and pedagogy, rather than rely on standardized training initiatives managed by external actors. An example from this study are the International Budget Partnership workshops, which are designed and conducted by veterans of successful civic initiatives, and have the dual purpose of knowledge and skills transfer and training of trainers, who can then in turn impart what they have learned to others.

External Corruption Drivers

Corruption as fostered by external actors and policies takes many forms, including lack of transparency in payments by companies to foreign governments; opaque company ownership and transactions; weak money laundering and foreign bribery laws, as well as stolen asset tracking measures; and legal, safe tax havens for corruptors and their assets.[40] A recent study found that from 1990 to 2008, approximately US$197 billion moved from the forty-eight poorest countries, mainly into banks, tax havens, and offshore financial centers in developed countries.[41]

One of the most potent anticorruption strategies the international community can employ is the disruption of external corruption drivers. Such measures can be taken in both national and multilateral settings and involve state and nonstate actors. For instance, donor governments can improve oversight and accountability for major reconstruction and development investments. Integrity Watch Afghanistan asserts that corrupt international contractors are part of the development and problems in the country. "The reality," said Karolina Olofsson, then with IWA, "is that when these private companies are found guilty of corruption, the consequences, if any, are low."[42] According to IWA, home country governments are slow to react or continue the contracting relationship.

At the multilateral level, coordinated government measures can disrupt external corruption drivers. One example concerns revenue transparency legislation in the resource extraction sector. On June 26, 2013, the European Parliament and the Council of the European Union (consisting of EU member states) enacted a landmark transparency law affecting the extractive and forestry industries. European Union logging, mining, gas, and oil companies are now required to report what they pay governments over €100,000, on a country-by-country and project-by-project basis.[43] According to Catherine Olier, EU policy adviser for OXFAM, "This is a critical step forward in the fight against corruption and tax dodging that will help ordinary people in the developing world harness their countries' natural resources wealth and lift themselves out of poverty."[44]

UN Convention Against Corruption (UNCAC)

UNCAC is a comprehensive, legally binding, international anticorruption instrument that is considered a valuable tool for bottom-up grassroots civic initiatives. It includes a mandate for civil society organizations and citizens in national accountability processes, and commits signatory governments to a high standard of preventive measures, criminalization of a wide range of corrupt actions, effective asset-recovery provisions, and review processes.[45] Articles 9, 10, and 13 support the use of social accountability activities, such as social audits, budget tracking, and public procurement monitoring, in order to foster citizen engagement and action.[46] UNCAC is considered a vital top-down measure that can empower and even protect homegrown campaigns.[47] A striking instance of its impact comes from Egypt. In 2007 the Mubarak regime cracked down on the shayfeen.com anticorruption campaign and charged the group with incitement, corresponding with a foreign entity, possessing documents challenging government policy (including the Transparency International Toolkit), and spreading negative information about the country. Shayfeen.com successfully sued the government by demonstrating that its activities were legal under UNCAC, of which Egypt was a signatory. Moreover, the government was then forced to publish UNCAC in Egypt's official legal chronicle, which was essential to render it binding in courts of law.[48]

UNCAC is a work in progress, with ongoing review mechanisms and negotiations to adopt resolutions. There is still much on which governments can agree or disagree. Civil society, both globally and national actors, is united around common demands. For example, ahead of the Fifth Conference of States Parties (November 2013), the UNCAC Coalition, an international network of over 350 CSOs in one hundred countries, released eighteen "Asks" related to ratification, corruption prevention, criminalization and enforcement, asset recovery, and the UNCAC country review process.[49] Adoption of such recommendations would go far toward thwarting external corruption drivers, improving challenging situations on the ground, and providing access to information.

Financial Support

External funding is a double-edged sword. On the one hand, grassroots civic initiatives are often in dire need of material and financial support. They may not have access to domestic sources, such as the private sector, and in-country foundations may not exist or have an interest in people power. As importantly, civic initiatives need to maintain their independence from the state and political parties.[50]

On the other hand, external support can, in some instances, have unintended negative impacts on grassroots mobilization. One such outcome is the "channeling effect," which occurs "when a social movement and its leadership redirect their strategies, goals, and alliances away from the original mission toward those acceptable to funders."[51] In the anticorruption context, this can arise when donors require CSOs to engage in formal relationships with state powerholders, frown upon disruptive nonviolent actions, or tie grants to preselected corruption targets. A second possible consequence is demobilization. A recent literature review on the impact of foreign aid on SMOs and social movements concluded, "While much of the literature has focused on the enabling aspects of transnational links . . . such links, particularly ties of money, also have the unintended effect of weakening domestic movements by limiting their capacity for mass mobilization."[52]

There is no one-size-fits-all solution for this conundrum. This research found a demand for flexible funding and small grants that enable grassroots organizations to pilot innovative civic initiatives or conduct homegrown training sessions. In order to avoid the pitfalls, three guidelines for external financial and material support are as follows: (1) the support should not interfere in the civic initiatives' strategies, priorities, objectives, and nonviolent tactics; (2) the support should empower civic leaders to launch homegrown civic initiatives and mobilize citizens rather than execute projects designed by external actors; and (3) the support should be combined with local resources, such as volunteerism, and financial and material support.

Specific Recommendations

The following recommendations for specific groups are intended to illustrate the breadth of positive measures that various actors in the international community can and do take to support bottom-up civic initiatives targeting corruption. They have been derived and adapted from two outstanding sources: *A Diplomat's Handbook for Democracy Development Support* and *Nonviolent Civic Action in Support of Human Rights and Democracy.*[53] Some proposals appear more than once, illustrating their relevance to multiple realms. As a caveat, given that individual country situations are different, interactions with the civic realm need to be tempered with sound judgment and common sense.

For On-the-Ground External Actors

In this section, I provide recommendations for diplomats, development practitioners, and INGO in-country staff.

Include grassroots campaigns and movements in the "field of vision." This can translate into adding civic leaders in their rounds of calls when taking a new country posting, incorporating bottom-up initiatives on the meeting agenda for visiting delegations or home-country teams, and even conferring with civic groups before and after anticorruption negotiations or development meetings with governments. During the UK presidency of the European Union in 2005, for instance, British diplomats and officials consulted with Russian NGOs before the EU-Russia dialogue meetings and debriefed them afterward.[54]

Ensure access to information that the state or other actors refuse to release to civil society, such as development policies, budgets, expenditures, international loans, procurement figures, foreign aid amounts and dissemination, foreign direct investment data, and so on.

Exhibit solidarity through releasing statements in support of civic leaders, campaigns, and movements targeting corruption; honoring activists who exemplify courage, integrity, and resilience; visiting communities and sites linked to grassroots initiatives; and circulating information and activist stories to the international media.

Highlight legitimacy by linking the rights of civic actors and the goals of campaigns and movements to international conventions on human rights, UNCAC, and others.[55]

Bear witness to the nonviolent actions of civic initiatives, trials of civic actors, and imprisonment of activists.

Protect anticorruption leaders and activists, including temporary refuge in diplomatic space and emergency visas for those whose lives are endangered.

Provide funding. Small-grant seed money, as well as emergency and hardship funds from local embassies, can be invaluable for grassroots initiatives, not only to help sustain essential activities and expenses, but also for urgent appeals such as legal aid for detained campaign members or escapes for those who are at risk of torture or death. As an example, the government of Sweden provides its embassies with funding to support democracy development.

For Development Institutions and Bilateral Donor Agencies

Development institutions include, for example, the World Bank and the UN Development Programme, and bilateral donor agencies include organizations such as the Japan International Cooperation Agency and the US Agency for International Development.

Expand conceptualization of citizen engagement and empowerment to incorporate social mobilization, collective action, grassroots civic initiatives, nonviolent campaigns, and social movements.

Support "actor-oriented approaches" that recognize the agency of citizens to demand their rights.[56] Rather than treating people as subjects of citizen voice and accountability projects and interventions, view them as initiators and drivers of change.

Involve bottom-up civic actors in consultations about top-down policies, measures, and reforms. Not only is their input inherently valuable, research finds that when the grass roots have a voice in policy formulation, they are more likely to engage in monitoring of policy outputs and activities.[57] When aid-recipient governments are hostile to such direct civic interactions, the development realm can incorporate grassroots priorities and input into their own communications with state interlocutors.

Consider preexisting relationships and social support networks when supporting nonviolent initiatives. As mentioned earlier, civic actors anecdotally report that external actors often do not see or sideline social networks on the ground, in part because they do not resemble the Global North's notions of organized civil society.

Provide information to grassroots civic leaders about donor and aid activities, for example, development projects, aid policies, budget support to governments, and anticorruption and accountability champions or sympathizers among local and national powerholders.

For Foreign Governments and Regional Bodies

Recommendations for administrations, parliaments, and regional bodies, such as the European Union, are as follows:

Empower embassies, missions, and diplomats to incorporate engagement with bottom-up initiatives targeting corruption and gaining accountability. In a fresh approach, the Czech Ministry of Foreign Affairs created the Transformation Policy Unit to "enable embassies to support democratization, human rights, and transition-related projects in countries with repressive regimes."[58]

Condemn crackdowns on civic and political space in general, and on bottom-up campaigns and movements targeting corruption in particular. This can entail developing joint statements and actions with like-minded governments.

Magnify breaches of international or regional conventions, when homegrown campaigns and movements invoke international or regional conventions signed by their governments that have been violated.

Target external corruption enablers, such as the laws, practices, and professional services that can drive malfeasance—in home countries, third-party countries, and through regional initiatives.

Engage with the grass roots—bottom-up organizations, campaigns, and movements, for example—by including them in government-sponsored international forums, receiving them in home capitals, and meeting with them during country visits.

Reconceptualize support for bottom-up civic initiatives, such as building holistic approaches based on the inherent links among anticorruption, human rights, peacebuilding, and development efforts; and affording solidarity, small grants, and opportunities for practical, grassroots peer-to-peer exchanges, access to information, and consultation on donor country top-down development, anticorruption, and accountability measures.

Strengthen capacities of international civil society to affirm and empower grassroots campaigns and movements—by supporting INGOs with ties to homegrown civic initiatives, global civic alliances, and emerging online international civic empowerment movements. Such movements serve as catalysts for grassroots knowledge and skills transfer, practical dialogue within countries or across borders, protection of activists, transnational campaigning, and sources of modest funding for grassroots actors to turn ideas into action—for example, the Partnership for Transparency Fund.

For International Civil Society

In this context, international civil society can include transnational advocacy networks, INGOs, foundations, unions, professional organizations, and even diaspora, faith-based, and cultural groups. They have resources, capacities, and leverage that can complement and support in-country, bottom-up initiatives targeting corruption and abuse in order to accomplish the following:

- *Expand the arena* of the struggle beyond the domestic setting.
- *Amplify citizens' voices and bottom-up initiatives* on the international stage to policymakers, multilateral institutions, and the media.
- *Provide information and expertise* that civic initiatives need, such as foreign assets of authoritarian rulers, technical skills, relevant multilateral norms and conventions, sources of funding, legal advice, legal action in third-country courts, and media access.
- *Advocate to external powerholders*, such as governments and multilateral bodies, to act in solidarity with a civic initiative, particularly if it is imperiled by corruptors.
- *Protect* those within the civic initiative who face grave threats through exposure of the situation, advocacy campaigns, legal counsel, emergency assistance, and nonviolent accompaniment.

- *Expedite transnational contacts and learning* to facilitate dialogue and exchange of skills and expertise, as well as to build networks and alliances.

Conclusion

In their efforts to understand and support bottom-up, collective action, external actors in a sense are entering uncharted territory. One overriding lesson from the history and scholarship of nonviolent social movements is that international actors cannot bring them into existence. People power is organic; it springs from the grass roots. Top-down efforts to foster and standardize civic initiatives hold pitfalls. At the very least, externally driven programs will have limited or modest impact. Worse, though, they can potentially undercut bottom-up capacity for people power in societies and even put citizens at risk. However, careful forms of international policies, support, and solidarity can affirm, enable, and empower citizens, rather than inadvertently inhibit or interfere in civic initiatives.

In turn, the international community can benefit from civic initiatives to curb corruption and gain accountability. Beyond their most salient impact on malfeasance, protagonists in such campaigns and movements are a source of insights and information for policymakers, anticorruption advocates, and development practitioners. They often have fresh perspectives about genuine democracy, governance, and power relations in their contexts, as well as inventive approaches to addressing oppression, poverty, and peacebuilding that are not necessarily on the radar screens of elites and powerholders. All in all, their varied approaches demonstrate the vast possibilities available when regular people—young and old, women and men—refuse to be victims and combine ingenuity, strategy, and planning with hope, determination, and valor.

Notes

1. Karen Hussman, "Working Towards Common Donor Responses to Corruption," OECD DAC Network on Governance—Anti-Corruption Task Team, October 18, 2009, www.oecd.org.

2. Karen DeYoung, "U.S. Indirectly Paying Afghan Warlords as Part of Security Contract," *Washington Post*, June 22, 2010, www.washingtonpost.com.

3. Confidential conversations with Afghan civic leaders and state officials.

4. Aunohita Mojumdar, "NGOs Call for Improved Afghan Aid," Aljazeera.net, February 12, 2009, http://english.aljazeera.net.

5. Ibid.

6. "Initial Findings from the Listening Project," Collaborative Learning Projects, August 2010, www.cdainc.com.

7. *The Listening Project Issue Paper: Dealing with Corruption* (Boston: Collaborative Learning Projects, February 2011).

8. Integrity Watch Afghanistan, *July Newsletter* 11, no. 7 (July 24, 2011), www.iwaweb.org.

9. Anuradha Joshi and Adrian Gurza Lavalle, "How Social Accountability Can Improve Service Delivery for Poor People," *Research Programme Summary*, Collective Action Around Service Delivery, Centre for the Future State, n.d., www.sasanet.org.

10. Ibid.

11. *People Power Beyond Elections and Revolutions: New Documentary from TVE Asia Pacific Profiles Social Accountability in Practice,* TVE Asia Pacific, 2004, www.tveap.org.

12. The section on the Guatemalan grassroots movement is based on personal communications during April 2010 with Claudia Samayoa, a leading Guatemalan human rights activist, who at the time was cofounder of the Unit of Protection of Human Rights Defenders (UDEFEGUA) and a member of the Advisors Council for Security to the president of Guatemala; Samayoa, "Fragmented Tyrannies: The Nexus of Corruption and Extreme Violence" (presentation and unpublished materials at the Thirteenth International Anti-Corruption Conference, Athens, October 30–November 2, 2008).

13. "Our Mission," Partnership for Transparency Fund, http://ptfund.org /about/ (accessed October 29, 2013).

14. "Concept Note Guidelines," Partnership for Transparency Fund, http://ptfund.org.

15. Stanley Nelson, *Freedom Riders* (documentary film), Firelight Films, 2011.

16. "Concept Note Guidelines."

17. Voice refers to "the range of measures—such as complaint, organized protest, lobbying, and participation in decision-making and product delivery— used by civil society actors to put pressure on service providers to demand better service outcomes" (Anne Marie Goetz and John Gaventa, "Bringing Citizen Voice and Client Focus into Service Delivery," IDS Working Paper no. 138, Institute of Development Studies, Brighton, 2001).

18. Endy Bayuni, "Discourse: The Knowledge Bank That Listens to People," *Jakarta Post*, April 29, 2011, www.thejakartapost.com.

19. Confidential communication with a former staff member of a multilateral development institution.

20. Mary McNeil and Carmen Malena, eds., *Demanding Good Governance: Lessons from Social Accountability Initiatives in Africa* (Washington, DC: World Bank, 2010), 1.

21. Amy Finnegan and Susan Hackley, "Negotiation and Nonviolent Action: Interacting in the World of Conflict," Program on Negotiation, Harvard Law School, Cambridge, MA, January 25, 2008, www.pon.harvard.edu.

22. Benjamin Olken, "Monitoring Corruption: Evidence from a Field Experiment in Indonesia," *Journal of Political Economy* 115, no. 2 (2007): 200–249, 243.

23. Matthew Andrews, "Voice Mechanisms and Local Government Fiscal Outcomes: How Does Civic Pressure and Participation Influence Public Ac-

countability?" In *Bringing Civility in Governance*, vol. 3, *Handbook on Public Sector Performance Reviews* (Washington, DC: World Bank, 2003), 8.3.

24. Goetz and Gaventa, "Bringing Citizen Voice and Client Focus into Service Delivery," 61.

25. Ibid.

26. Lee Smithey, "Social Movement Strategy, Tactics, and Collective Identity," *Sociology Compass* 3, no. 4 (2009): 658–671.

27. Ibid.

28. Sowmya Kidambi, *Right to Know, Right to Live: Building a Campaign for the Right to Information and Accountability*, New Tactics for Human Rights Project (Minneapolis: Center for Victims of Torture, 2008), www.newtactics.org.

29. Integrity Watch Afghanistan, *July Newsletter*; ibid.

30. Mandeep Tiwana and Netsanet Belay, *Civil Society: The Clampdown Is Real* (Johannesburg: CIVICUS, December 2010), www.civicus.org.

31. Ibid., 15.

32. Richard Youngs, "How to Revitalise Democracy Assistance: Recipients' Views," Working Paper no. 100, Fundación para las Relaciones Internacionales y el Diálogo Exterior (FRIDE), Madrid, June 2010.

33. Ibid., 10.

34. Confidential communication.

35. Richard Holloway, *NGO Corruption Fighters' Resource Book: How NGOs Can Use Monitoring and Advocacy to Fight Corruption* (Impact Alliance Resource Center, 2006), www.impactalliance.org.

36. Youngs, "How to Revitalise Democracy Assistance," 5.

37. Peter Uvin, "Fostering Citizen Collective Action in Post-Conflict Societies," *What Really Works in Preventing and Rebuilding Failed States*, Woodrow Wilson Center for International Scholars, Occasional Paper Series, Washington, DC, no. 1, November 2006, 8.

38. John Gaventa and Gregory Barrett, "So What Difference Does It Make? Mapping the Outcomes of Citizen Engagement," Institute of Development Studies Working Paper 2010, no. 347, October 2010, www.ntd.co.uk.

39. "India's Ipaidabribe.com Inspires the Chinese," CNN-IBN Live, June 13, 2011, http://ibnlive.in.com.

40. "Bond Anti-Corruption Paper," Bond Governance Group, September 2010, www.globalwitness.org.

41. "UNDP-Commissioned Report from Global Financial Integrity Now Available," Global Financial Integrity, press release, May 12, 2011, www.gfip.org.

42. Karolina Olofsson, "Facing Corrupt Contractors in Afghanistan," Global Financial Integrity blog, November 28, 2011, www.financialtaskforce.org.

43. Kayleigh Lewis, "MEPs Agree Tough New Rules for Extractive Companies," *The Parliament*, June 12, 2013.

44. Ibid., 2.

45. "About Us," UNCAC Civil Society Coalition, www.uncaccoalition.org (accessed October 29, 2013).

46. *Fostering Social Accountability: From Principle to Practice,* Guidance Note (Oslo: UN Development Programme, Oslo Governance Center, August 2010), http://content.undp.org.

47. "About Us," UNCAC Civil Society Coalition.

48. Shaazka Beyerle and Arwa Hassan, "Popular Resistance Against Corruption in Turkey and Egypt," in *Civilian Jihad: Nonviolent Struggle in the Middle East*, ed. Maria Stephan, 265–280 (New York: Palgrave Macmillan, 2009).

49. "Making UNCAC Work: Coalition Statement Ahead of the Fifth Conference of States Parties in Panama," UNCAC Coalition, n.d., www.uncac coalition.org.

50. Rita Jalali, "Financing Empowerment? How Foreign Aid to Southern NGOs and Social Movements Undermines Grass-Roots Mobilization," *Sociology Compass* 7, no. 1 (2013): 55–73.

51. Ibid., 60.

52. Ibid., 68.

53. These recommendations have been derived and adapted from the following sources: *A Diplomat's Handbook for Democracy Development Support*, 2nd ed. (Washington, DC: Council for a Community of Democracies, 2010), www.diplomatshandbook.org; Veronique Dudouet and Howard Clark, *Nonviolent Civic Action in Support of Human Rights and Democracy* (Brussels: Directorate-General for External Policies, Policy Department, European Parliament, May 2009), http://www.europarl.europa.eu.

54. *Diplomat's Handbook for Democracy Development Support.*

55. For a summary of anticorruption conventions, see http://www.u4.no /themes/conventions/intro.cfm.

56. Gaventa and Barrett, "So What Difference Does It Make?"

57. Rosemary McGee and John Gaventa, with Gregg Barrett, Richard Calland, Ruth Carlitz, Anuradha Joshi, and Andres Mejia Acosta, "Review of Impact and Effectiveness of Transparency and Accountability Initiatives: Synthesis Report" (prepared for the Transparency and Accountability Initiative Workshop, Institute of Development Studies, October 14–15, 2010), http:// www.ids.ac.uk.

58. *Diplomat's Handbook for Democracy Development Support*, 29.

Acronyms

BiH	Bosnia-Herzegovina
CAGE	Citizens Alliance for the General Election
CBI	Central Bureau of Investigation (India)
CBJP	Brazilian Justice and Peace Commission
CBO	community-based organization
CCEJ	Citizens' Coalition for Economic Justice (Korea)
CDF	constituency development funds (Kenya)
CICAK	Love Indonesia, Love Anti-Corruption Commission
CIN	Center for Investigative Journalism (Bosnia-Herzegovina)
CNBB	National Conference of Bishops of Brazil
CoSP	Conference of States Parties
CSO	civil society organization
CTR	Center for Transatlantic Relations
DHP*	Dejemos de Hacernos Pendejos
FAI	Federazione Nazionale Antiracket
FAKTA	Jakarta Citizens' Forum
FIESP	Federation of Industries of the State of São Paolo
GKU	Green Korea United
IACC	International Anti-Corruption Conference
IBP	International Budget Partnership
ICNC	International Center on Nonviolent Conflict
ICT	information and communication technology
ICW	Indonesia Corruption Watch
ILR	Indonesian Legal Roundtable
INGO	international nongovernmental organization
ISAF	International Security Assistance Force (NATO)

IWA	Integrity Watch Afghanistan
KFEM	Korean Federation for Environmental Movements
KPK	Corruption Eradication Commission (Indonesia)
KPP	Judicial Monitoring Coalition (Indonesia)
KRHN	National Law Reform Consortium
KWAU	Korean Women's Associations United
LBH	Jakarta Legal Aid Institute
LeIP	Indonesia Institute for Independent Judiciary
MACC	Malaysian Anti-Corruption Commission
MCCE	Movement Against Electoral Corruption (Brazil)
MKSS	Mazdoor Kisan Shakti Sangathan (Union for the Empowerment of Peasants and Laborers; India)
MOU	memorandum of understanding
MP	member of Parliament
MTI	Indonesia Transparency Society
MUHURI	Muslims for Human Rights (Kenya)
NAFODU	National Foundation for Democracy and Human Rights in Uganda
NGO	nongovernmental organization
NIR	Network for Integrity in Reconstruction
NORAD	Norwegian Agency for Development Cooperation
NRI	nonresident Indian
OAB	Brazilian Bar Association
OSIEA	Open Society Initiative's East Africa program
PAN	National Action Party (Mexico)
PRD	Party of the Democratic Revolution (Mexico)
PSHK	Indonesian Centre for Policy and Law Studies
PSPD	People's Solidarity for Participatory Democracy (Korea)
PTF	Partnership for Transparency Fund
RACA	Institute for Rapid Agrarian Conflict Appraisal (Indonesia)
RTI	right to information
RUF	Revolutionary United Front (Sierra Leone)
SDA	Party for Democratic Action (Bosnia-Herzegovina)
SMO	social movement organization
TIKA	Turkish International Cooperation and Development Agency
TIRI	Making Integrity Work (now Integrity Action)
UNCAC	United Nations Convention Against Corruption
UNDP	United Nations Development Programme
UNODC	United Nations Office of Drugs and Crime
USAID	United States Agency for International Development
YLBHI	Indonesian Legal Aid Foundation

Glossary

Backfire: when an attack against a nonviolent movement, campaign, or grassroots civic initiative creates more support for the subject of the attack and negative outcomes for the perpetrator(s).

Civic initiatives: organized, sustained civic efforts, based on the following criteria:

- They are "popular" initiatives. They are civilian-based, involve grassroots participation, and are led and implemented by individuals from the civic realm, rather than governments or external actors, such as donors, development institutions, and international NGOs.
- They are nonviolent. They do not threaten or use violence to further their aims.
- They involve some degree of organization and planning, which varies depending on the scope—objectives, geographical range, duration—of the civic initiative.
- Multiple nonviolent actions are employed. Thus, instances of one-off demonstrations or spontaneous protests are not considered a civic initiative.
- Objectives and demands are articulated.
- The civic initiative is sustained over a period of time.

Civic realm: collective nonstate, bottom-up initiatives and relationships in a society. This includes nonviolent civic campaigns and movements; civil society organizations (CSOs); nongovernmental organizations (NGOs); community-based organizations (CBOs); social movement organizations (SMOs); civic coalitions and alliances; unions; professional organizations; grassroots networks, committees, and collectives; local citizen groups; activists; community organizers; and citizens.

Civic space: the arena for public expression and dissent.

Civil resistance: a civilian-based method to fight oppression and injustice through people power. It is nonviolent in that it does not employ the threat or use of violence. It is also called "nonviolent resistance," "nonviolent struggle," "nonviolent conflict," and "nonviolent action."

Defining method: a series of sequenced nonviolent actions that together wield people power. It consists of a principle tactic around which a host of nonviolent tactics revolve.

Digital resistance: civil resistance executed in the digital sphere or online world through the use of information and communication technology (ICT) tools—for example, e-petitions, online/SMS monitoring, SMS balloting, and Facebook group mobilizations.

Dilemma action: a nonviolent tactic that puts the oppressor in a situation whereby the actions it takes will result in some kind of negative outcome for it (lose-lose) and some kind of positive outcome for the nonviolent campaign or movement (win-win).

Discourse: narratives, cognitive frames, meanings, and language used in a civic initiative.

Monitoring: a nonviolent tactic that can involve observing, recording, verifying, comparing, overseeing, checking, and inspecting. In the anticorruption context, the targets of such activities are (1) people (for example, election candidates, parliamentarians, government leaders, public officials, civil servants, social service providers, police); (2) institutions (parliaments, public administrations, government agencies, judiciaries, state security forces, municipalities, corporations, universities, schools, hospitals); (3) policies (such as poverty reduction, education, natural resource exploitation); (4) budgets and expenditures; (5) public programs, social services, public works; procurement practices; procurement outcomes; and (6) social and economic development projects conducted by governments or external actors. Monitoring can either be visible (for example, public audits or site inspections) or anonymous (for instance, mobile phone videos or SMS reports of public officials and police demanding bribes). Effective monitoring creates social pressure and disrupts corrupt practices within systems of graft and abuse.

People power: social, economic, political, and psychological pressure exerted by significant numbers of individuals organized together around shared grievances and goals, engaging in nonviolent strategies and tactics, such as civil disobedience, noncooperation, strikes, boycotts, monitoring, petition drives, low-risk mass actions, and demonstrations.

Reverse boycotts: consumers supporting or patronizing particular businesses or establishments.

Social audits: a form of monitoring, consisting of multiple steps such as information gathering; training citizens to interpret documents and budgets, monitor expenditures, and physically inspect public works; community education and mobilization; public hearings with powerholders; follow-up.

Social movement organization (SMO): a nonstate entity that is part of a social movement. It can provide multiple functions for the movement, such as identity, leadership, strategizing, and planning. However, the movement is not bounded by the SMO; neither are SMOs essential for social movements to flourish.

Appendix:
Nonviolent Tactics Used
in the Twelve Cases

Tactics of Disruption[1]

In the Physical World

- Noncooperation with the system of corruption. *Examples*: India (refusing to pay a bribe by handing over a zero-rupee note), Italy (business owners refusing to pay Mafia extortion money together with consumers patronizing these enterprises).
- Civil disobedience (depending on laws in each context). *Example*: Korea (blacklisting candidates, publishing information about politicians' criminal records).
- Exposure of corrupt activities or impunity. *Examples*: Afghanistan, Bosnia-Herzegovina, Egypt, Kenya, Korea, Mexico, Uganda.
- Hunger strikes, partial hunger strikes, symbolic fasts. *Example*: India (solidarity actions with anticorruption activist Anna Hazare).
- Occupying public and municipal spaces. *Examples*: Brazil, Egypt.
- Low-risk mass actions (context specific: what is low-risk in one situation may not be in another situation).
  - Banging pots and pans. *Example*: Turkey.
  - Synchronized turning on and off of lights. *Example*: Turkey.
  - Letter-writing drive to powerholders and mass "mail-in" to legislators. *Example*: Turkey.
  - Radio call-in programs to report/expose corruption. *Example*: Uganda.
  - Phone ringtones. *Examples*: Indonesia, Korea.
  - Phone hotline. *Examples*: Egypt, India.
- Signature drives, petitions, signed pledges, signing banners. *Examples*: Afghanistan, Brazil, India, Italy, Korea, Mexico, Turkey.

- Displays of symbols.
  - Wearables. T-shirts, bandanas, buttons, hats, ribbons. *Examples*: Bosnia-Herzegovina, Egypt, India, Indonesia, Italy, Turkey.
  - Reusables. *Examples*: Egypt (shopping bags, tea glasses), India (shopping bags, water bottles), Turkey (shake toy called the democracy machine).
  - Graffiti. *Examples*: Bosnia-Herzegovina, Indonesia.
  - Stickers. *Example*: Italy (Mafia-free businesses).
  - Cards. *Example*: Korea (red soccer cards signifying "out").
- Selling movement buttons to citizens. *Example*: Egypt.
- Candidate blacklists. *Example*: Korea.
- Public citizen pledges to not vote for blacklisted candidates. *Example*: Korea.
- Mass boycotting of blacklisted candidates when casting votes. *Example*: Korea.
- Candidate integrity pledges (pressuring politicians to sign pledge to enact political reforms should they be elected). *Example*: Korea.
- Public anticorruption pledges. *Example*: India.
- Powerholder integrity pledges/signatures. *Example*: Kenya—Members of Parliament signing their names on a banner to support passage of a Right to Information act, Constituency Development Fund officials signing "accountability charter" to carry out actions to rectify graft-related problems in antipoverty projects.
- Citizen complaint mechanisms (such as complaints desks staffed by volunteers or CSOs, where people can lodge complaints against corruption and seek assistance or redress). *Example*: India.
- Cultural expressions.
  - Music, songs, SMS ringtones. *Examples*: Kenya, Korea, Indonesia.
  - Poetry, poetry contests. *Example*: India.
  - Humor (for example, cartoons, graffiti, billboards, stunts). *Examples*: Bosnia-Herzegovina, Indonesia, Kenya, Korea, Mexico.
  - Dancing. *Examples*: Kenya, Turkey.
  - Street theatre. *Examples*: India, Indonesia, Kenya.
- Student essay contests. *Example*: India.
- Dilemma actions. *Example*: Bosnia-Herzegovina.
- Public commemorations. *Examples*: Egypt and India (International Anti-Corruption Day), Italy (anti-Mafia martyrs).
- Information gathering.
  - Budgets. *Examples*: Afghanistan, Kenya.
  - Antipoverty programs. *Example*: Kenya.

- Development project plans. *Examples*: Afghanistan, Kenya.
- Citizen surveys. *Examples*: Afghanistan, Korea.
- Monitoring (by citizens on a voluntary basis).
  - Citizen inspections of public works, development projects, public services. *Examples*: Afghanistan, India, Kenya.
  - Public offices and social service providers. *Examples*: India, Kenya.
  - Powerholders (such as officials, legislators, police). *Examples*: Afghanistan, India, Kenya, Mexico, Uganda.
  - Elections. *Example*: Egypt.
- "Meet the public" forums, public hearings. *Examples*: Afghanistan, India, Kenya.
- Protests, vigils, marches, processions, sit-ins, demonstrations. *Examples*: Afghanistan, India, Italy, Kenya, Korea, Turkey.
- Hanging banners. *Examples*: Italy (banners and sheets on public spaces); Korea (banners on buildings).
- Sticking notices in public spaces. *Example*: Italy.
- Leafleting. *Example*: India, Kenya.
- Rallies, bicycle rallies, one-person street rally (to get around laws restricting public assembly). *Examples*: Brazil, Korea, Mexico.
- Human chains. *Example*: India.
- Flash actions (such as ten-minute street corner info "booths" at busy intersections). *Examples*: India, Indonesia.
- "Shadowing" candidates (respected civic leaders chosen to shadow corrupt politicians during political campaigning). *Example*: Korea.
- Anticorruption or democracy classes in schools and universities, informal teach-ins. *Examples*: India, Italy, Korea.
- Festivals, fairs, concerts. *Examples*: India, Indonesia, Italy, Korea.
- Games. *Examples*: India (for example, hug integrity ball, kick corruption ball), Korea (fishing corrupt candidate names out of a barrel of water).
- Street theatre, visual dramatizations. *Examples*: Brazil (cleaning the steps of the Congress), Kenya (street theatre), Italy and Korea (imprinting palms dipped in paint onto large banners).
- Anticorruption awareness booths. *Example*: India (universities, weddings).
- Attention-grabbing or humorous stunts. *Examples*: Brazil (washing the stairs in front of the Congress); Indonesia (parachuting off the Indonesian Corruption Eradication building); Mexico (pedaling the bike of light at the Congress); Turkey (play-acting a car accident associated with a scandal at a press conference).

- Vehicle convoys. *Examples*: Korea (trucks), Mexico (bikes).
- Bus tours. *Example*: Korea.
- Press conferences. *Examples*: Korea, Mexico, Turkey.
- Boycotts. *Example*: Korea (corrupt candidates).
- Reverse boycotts (people supporting businesses). *Example*: Italy.
- Nonviolent intervention (between security forces and citizens at street actions). *Example*: Egypt.
- Solidarity activities. *Examples*: India (supporting whistle-blowers by filing Right to Information petitions), Indonesia (protecting jailed anticorruption commission deputy commissioners, raising money and collecting building supplies for a new anticorruption commission building), Italy (supporting businesses that refuse to pay Mafia extortion money).
- Nonviolent accompaniment. *Example*: Italy (attending court proceedings when business owners testify against the mafia).

In the Digital Sphere
- Reporting/exposing corruption via SMS messages, e-mails, phone videos. *Examples*: Egypt, Uganda.
- Voting for anticorruption heroes via SMS. *Example*: Egypt.
- E-mailing messages to powerholders straight from a website. *Example*: Brazil.
- Online calling tool to directly phone powerholders, such as legislators. *Example*: Brazil.
- Registering calls to legislators through a live chat tool, which allows the campaign or movement to publicly tally numbers. *Example*: Brazil.
- Online interactive sites. *Example*: Mexico.
- Online information feeds. *Example*: Brazil.
- Twitter hashtags. *Example*: Brazil, Indonesia.
- Online Twitter buttons to send out signatures/messages directly to powerholders. *Example*: Brazil.
- E-petitions/signature drives via Twitter, Facebook, e-mail, digital devices. *Examples*: Brazil, Mexico.
- Live chat tools. *Example*: Brazil.
- Joining a movement/campaign Facebook protest group. *Examples*: Bosnia-Herzegovina, Brazil, India, Indonesia, Mexico.
- Changing one's Facebook profile picture/profile to identify with a movement/campaign. *Example*: Bosnia-Herzegovina, Brazil, Indonesia.
- Online banners. *Examples:* Indonesia, Italy.

- Posting statements on blogs. *Examples*: Bosnia-Herzegovina, Brazil, India.
- Tweeting, posting alerts to social media sites (such as Facebook, Orkut, M-citizen, Cyworld). *Examples*: Brazil, Indonesia, Korea, Mexico.

Tactics of Engagement

- "Signing" e-petition. *Example*: Brazil.
- Youth recreation. *Example*: Italy (Addiopizzo basketball team).
- Youth clubs, university clubs.
- Socially oriented get-togethers. *Examples*: Italy (Mafia-free gelateria and cafés), Mexico (Café DHP*).
- Public lectures. *Example*: Korea.
- Community meetings. *Examples*: Afghanistan, India, Kenya, Uganda.
- Information gathering through informal discussions with citizens. *Examples*: Afghanistan, Kenya.
- Negotiation. *Examples*: Afghanistan, Kenya, Korea, Uganda.
- Interaction with security forces (to prevent violence). *Example*: Egypt.
- Memoranda of understanding to access information, cooperate on anticorruption/accountability/integrity activities. *Example*: Uganda.
- Citizen-state committees and boards. *Example*: Afghanistan.
- Media outreach (virtually all cases).
- Press conferences. *Examples*: Indonesia, Korea, Turkey.
- Endorsements from popular music, television, and film personalities. *Examples*: Egypt, Indonesia, Korea.
- Endorsements by respected public figures (for example, clerics, civic leaders, scholars, writers). *Examples*: Brazil, Indonesia, Korea.
- Cooperation with integrity champions (exchanging information, people power solidarity). *Examples*: Egypt, Indonesia.
- Citizen contributions for a movement or campaign. *Examples*: Bosnia-Herzegovina (donations to rent billboards), India (advertisements in movement publication, donations of equipment, memberships), Indonesia (symbolic donations of money and building supplies for the Indonesian Corruption Eradication Commission's new building), Italy (online donations), Korea (money to support the Citizens Alliance for the General Election 2000 campaign).

- Citizen-powerholder meetings/exchanges. *Examples*: Afghanistan (provincial monitoring boards), Uganda (community-police meetings).
- Bottom-up ethics and integrity trainings for powerholders. *Example*: Uganda (police).
- Radio call-in programs. *Example*: Uganda.
- Phone hotlines. *Examples*: Egypt, India.
- Anticorruption awareness booths/tables. *Examples*: India (universities, weddings), Mexico (parks).
- Solidarity activities. *Examples*: India (supporting whistle-blowers by filing Right to Information petitions), Indonesia (protecting jailed anticorruption commission deputy commissioners, raising money and collecting building supplies for a new anticorruption commission building), Italy (supporting businesses that refuse to pay Mafia extortion money).
- Nonviolent accompaniment. *Example*: Italy (attending court proceedings when business owners testify against the Mafia).
- Displays of symbols.
  - Wearables. T-shirts, bandanas, buttons, hats, ribbons. *Examples*: Bosnia-Herzegovina, Egypt, India, Indonesia, Italy, Turkey.
  - Reusables. *Examples*: Egypt (shopping bags, tea glasses), India (water bottles), Turkey (shake toy called the democracy machine).
- Selling movement buttons to citizens. *Example*: Egypt.
- Public citizen pledges to not vote for blacklisted candidates. *Example*: Korea.

Tactics of Empowerment

- Education and training in nonviolent action and nonviolent discipline.
  - Workshops and trainings. *Examples*: Kenya, Korea.
  - Manuals on nonviolent action. *Example*: Korea.
  - Peace Charter. *Example*: Korea.
- Training in monitoring (deciphering documents and budgets, examining expenditures, physically inspecting public works, documenting inspections). *Examples*: Afghanistan, Kenya.
- Civic education.
  - Unofficial democracy classes in schools and universities. *Example*: Korea.
  - Movement-led presentations and workshops in schools and universities. *Examples*: India, Italy.

- Informal teach-ins. *Example*: Korea.
- Public lectures. *Example*: Korea.
- Community meetings. *Examples*: Afghanistan, Egypt, Korea.
- Online youth civic education. *Example*: Egypt.
- Right to information. *Example*: India, Kenya.
- Anticorruption awareness booths. *Examples*: India (weddings), Mexico (parks).
- Providing information to citizens. *Examples*: Afghanistan (development project budgets and plans), Brazil (legislator positions, congressional committee meetings), Egypt (election fraud, powerholder integrity, citizen rights), India (Right to Information act), Kenya (Constituency Development Funds budgets and projects), Mexico (legislative activities), Korea (candidates, policies, projects), Uganda (citizen rights vis-à-vis the police).
- Development and distribution of manuals for activists or regular people (for example, on nonviolent discipline, legal issues, political reform). *Examples*: India, Korea.
- Social and economic empowerment initiatives. *Examples*: India, Italy.
- Phone hotline. *Examples*: Egypt, India.
- Youth recreation. *Example*: Italy.
- Coalition- and alliance-building. *Examples*: Brazil, Egypt, India, Indonesia, Italy, Kenya, Korea, Mexico, Turkey.
- Community surveys, national surveys. *Examples*: Afghanistan, Kenya, Korea, Uganda.
- Right to Information clinics and direct assistance to file Right to Information petitions. *Example*: India.
- Training of trainers workshops (for example, to conduct social audits, train citizens to use Right to Information laws). *Examples*: India, Kenya.
- Citizen contributions for the movement or campaign. *Examples*: Bosnia-Herzegovina (donations to rent billboards), India (advertisements in movement publication, donations of equipment, memberships), Italy (online donations), Indonesia (symbolic donations of money and building supplies for the Indonesian Corruption Eradication Commission's new building), Korea (money to support the Citizens Alliance for the General Election 2000 campaign).
- Solidarity activities. *Examples*: India (supporting whistle-blowers by filing Right to Information petitions), Indonesia (protecting jailed anticorruption commission deputy commissioners, raising money and collecting building supplies for a new anticorruption

commission building), Italy (supporting businesses that refuse to pay Mafia extortion money).
• Cross-country trek. *Example:* Mexico.
• Nonviolent accompaniment. *Example*: Italy (attending court proceedings when business owners testify against the Mafia).

Defining Methods

• Social audits. *Example*: Kenya.
• Community monitoring. *Example*: Afghanistan.
• Parliamentarian monitoring. *Example*: Mexico.
• Zero-rupee note empowerment. *Example*: India.
• Refusing to pay Mafia extortion money and reverse boycotts. *Example*: Italy.
• Not voting for blacklisted candidates. *Example*: Korea.
• Synchronized mass turning on and off of lights. *Example*: Turkey.

Note

1. The categories correspond to the functions of the tactics. Readers will notice that tactics often appear in multiple categories. Depending on the struggle context at hand, a tactic can actually have multiple functions. See Chapter 11.

Bibliography

Ackerman, Peter, and Jack DuVall. *A Force More Powerful: A Century of Nonviolent Conflict*. New York: Palgrave, 2000.

Akay, Ezel, and Liam Mahoney. *A Call to End Corruption*. Minneapolis: Center for Victims of Torture, 2003.

Albloshi, Hamad, and Faisal Alfahad. "The Orange Movement of Kuwait: Civic Pressure Transforms a Political System." In *Civilian Jihad: Nonviolent Struggle, Democratization, and Governance in the Middle East*, ed. Maria Stephan, 219–232. New York: Palgrave Macmillan, 2009.

Amato, Joseph. "Danilo Dolci: A Nonviolent Reformer in Sicily." *Italian Americana* 4, no. 2 (Spring/Summer 1978): 215–235.

Andrews, Matthew. "Voice Mechanisms and Local Government Fiscal Outcomes: How Does Civic Pressure and Participation Influence Public Accountability?" In *Bringing Civility in Governance*, vol. 3, *Handbook on Public Sector Performance Reviews*. Washington, DC: World Bank, 2003.

Anti-Corruption Approaches: A Literature Review. Oslo: Norwegian Agency for Development and Cooperation, 2009.

Baker, Damani. *It's Our Money: Where's It Gone?* International Budget Partnership documentary film, n.d.

Ballentine, Karen, and Heiko Nitzschke. "The Political Economy of Civil War and Conflict Transformation." Berlin: Berghof Research Centre for Constructive Conflict Management, April 2005.

Bartkowski, Maciej, ed. *Recovering Nonviolent History: Civil Resistance in Liberation Struggles*. Boulder, CO: Lynne Rienner, 2013.

Beyerle, Shaazka, and Arwa Hassan. "Popular Resistance Against Corruption in Turkey and Egypt." In *Civilian Jihad: Nonviolent Struggle, Democratization, and Governance in the Middle East*, ed. Maria Stephan, 265–280. New York: Palgrave Macmillan, 2009.

Bhakti, I. N. "The Transition to Democracy in Indonesia: Some Outstanding Problems." In *The Asia-Pacific: A Region in Transition*, ed. Jim Rolfe, 195–206. Honolulu: Asia Pacific Center for Security Studies, 2004.

Bolongaita, Emil. "A New Model for an Anti-Corruption Agency? Indonesia's Corruption Eradication Commission." Presentation at the Symposium on the Fundamentals of an Effective Anti-Corruption Commission. Asian Institute of Management, May 6, 2011.

"Bond Anti-Corruption Paper." Bond Governance Group, September 2010.

Brkan, Darko. Recorded interview: Dosta! Movement, International Center on Non-violent Conflict, June 24, 2010, www.nonviolent-conflict.org.

Carson, Lyn, and Brian Martin. *Random Selection in Politics*. Westport, CT: Praeger, 1999.

Chêne, Marie. "Corruption and Anti-Corruption in Bosnia and Herzegovina (BiH)." U4 Anti-Corruption Resource Centre, November 23, 2009.

———. "U4 Expert Answer: Anti-Corruption and Police Reform." U4 Anti-Corruption Resource Centre, May 31, 2010.

Chenoweth, Erica, and Maria Stephan. *Why Civil Resistance Works: The Strategic Logic of Nonviolent Conflict*. New York: Columbia University Press, 2011.

Cockcroft, Laurence. *Global Corruption: Money, Power, and Ethics in the Modern World*. Philadelphia: University of Pennsylvania Press, 2012.

Corruption in Afghanistan: Recent Patterns and Trends. Vienna: UN Office of Drugs and Crime and the Islamic Republic of Afghanistan High Office of Oversight and Anti-Corruption, December 2012.

Corruption and Human Rights: Making the Connection. Geneva: International Council on Human Rights Policy and Transparency International, 2009.

Dininio, Phyllis. "Warlords and Corruption in Post-Conflict Governments." *New Routes Journal of Peace Research and Action* 14, no. 3–4 (2009): 27–29.

A Diplomat's Handbook for Democracy Development Support. 2nd edition. Washington, DC: Council for a Community of Democracies, 2010.

Dudouet, Veronique, and Howard Clark. *Nonviolent Civic Action in Support of Human Rights and Democracy*. Brussels: Directorate-General for External Policies, Policy Department, European Parliament, May 2009.

Elkatshas, Sherief. *Shayfeen.com: We're Watching You*. Independent Television Service International film, 2007.

Finnegan, Amy, and Susan Hackley. "Negotiation and Nonviolent Action: Interacting in the World of Conflict." Program on Negotiation, Harvard Law School, Cambridge, MA, January 25, 2008.

Fostering Social Accountability: From Principle to Practice. Guidance Note. Oslo: United Nations Development Programme, Oslo Governance Center, August 2010.

Garza, Manuela. "Social Audits as a Budget Monitoring Tool." International Budget Partnership, Learning from Each Other Series, October 2012, http://internationalbudget.org.

Gaventa, John, and Gregory Barrett. "So What Difference Does It Make? Mapping the Outcomes of Citizen Engagement." Brighton, UK: IDS Working Paper 2010, no. 347, Institute of Development Studies, October 2010, 54.

Gladwell, Malcolm. "Small Change: Why the Revolution Will Not Be Tweeted." *New Yorker*, October 4, 2010.

Gladwell, Malcolm, and Clay Shirkey. "From Innovation to Revolution: Do Social Media Make Protests Possible?" *Foreign Affairs*, March/April 2011.

Goetz, Anne Marie, and John Gaventa. "Bringing Citizen Voice and Client Focus into Service Delivery." IDS Working Paper no. 138, Institute of Development Studies, 2001.

Holloway, Richard. *NGO Corruption Fighters' Resource Book: How NGOs Can Use Monitoring and Advocacy to Fight Corruption*. Impact Alliance Resource Center, 2006, www.impactalliance.org.

Hussman, Karen. "Working Towards Common Donor Responses to Corruption." OECD DAC Network on Governance—Anti-Corruption Task Team, October 18, 2009, www.oecd.org.

Jalali, Rita. "Financing Empowerment? How Foreign Aid to Southern NGOs and Social Movements Undermines Grass-Roots Mobilization." *Sociology Compass* 7, no. 1 (2013): 55–73.

Joshi, Anuradha, and Adrian Gurza Lavalle. "How Social Accountability Can Improve Service Delivery for Poor People." *Research Programme Summary*. Collective Action Around Service Delivery, Centre for the Future State, n.d.

Joyce, Mary. "Introduction: How to Think About Digital Activism." In *Digital Activism Decoded: The New Mechanics of Change*, ed. Mary Joyce, 1–14. New York: International Debate Education Association, 2010.

June, Raymond, and Nathaniel Heller. "Corruption and Anti-Corruption in Peacebuilding: Toward a Unified Framework." *New Routes Journal of Peace Research and Action* 14, no. 3–4 (2009): 10–13.

Karatnycky, Adrian, and Peter Ackerman. *How Freedom Is Won: From Civic Resistance to Durable Democracy*. New York: Freedom House, 2005.

Kaufmann, Daniel. "Human Rights, Governance, and Development: An Empirical Perspective." In *Human Rights and Development: Towards Mutual Reinforcement*, ed. Philip Alston and Mary Robinson, 352–402. Oxford: Oxford University Press, 2005.

———. "Ten Myths About Governance and Corruption." *Finance and Development*, September 2005, www.imf.org.

Kidambi, Sowmya. *Right to Know, Right to Live: Building a Campaign for the Right to Information and Accountability*. Minneapolis: Center for Victims of Torture, 2008.

Kikoyo, Wanjiru. *The CDF Social Audit Guide: A Handbook for Communities*. Nairobi: Open Society Initiative for Eastern Africa, February 2008.

Kim, Samuel, *Korea's Democratization*. Cambridge: Cambridge University Press, 2003.

King, Mary. *A Quiet Revolution: The First Palestinian Intifada and Nonviolent Resistance*. New York: Nation Books, 2007.

Kıvanç, Ümit. *Action for Constant Light: Turkey, 1997*. Documentary film, 2002, www.gecetreni.com.

Lafayette, Bernard, Jr., and David Jensen. *The Nonviolence Briefing Booklet*. Galena, OH: Institute for Human Rights and Responsibilities, 2005.

Le Billon, Philippe. "Buying Peace or Fueling War: The Role of Corruption in Armed Conflicts." *Journal of International Development* 15 (2003): 413–426.

The Listening Project Issue Paper: Dealing with Corruption. Boston: Collaborative Learning Projects, February 2011.

"A Lucky Real Estate Deal." Center for Investigative Reporting, September 4, 2007.

Mansour, Sherif. "Enough Is Not Enough: Achievements and Shortcomings of Kefaya, the Egyptian Movement for Change." In *Civilian Jihad: Nonviolent Struggle, Democratization, and Governance in the Middle East*, ed. Maria Stephan, 205–218. New York: Palgrave Macmillan, 2009.

———. "From Facebook to Streetbook." International Center on Nonviolent Conflict webinar, February 17, 2011, www.nonviolent-conflict.org.

Marchant, Eleanor. *Enabling Environments for Civic Movements and the Dynamics of Democratic Transition*. Freedom House, 2008, www.freedomhouse.org.

Martin, Brian. *Justice Ignited: The Dynamics of Backfire*. Lanham, MD: Rowman and Littlefield, 2007.

———. "Whistleblowing and Nonviolence." *Peace and Change* 24, no. 1 (January 1999): 15–28.

Masduki, Teten. "A Conversation with Teten Masduki" (part 2). *Voices*. ANSA-EAP Online Channel, February 6, 2011, http://voices.ansa-eap.net.

―――. "A Conversation with Teten Masduki" (part 3). *Voices*. ANSA-EAP Online Channel, February 13, 2011. http://voices.ansa-eap.net.

McGee, Rosemary, and John Gaventa, with Gregg Barrett, Richard Calland, Ruth Carlitz, Anuradha Joshi, and Andres Mejia Acosta. "Review of Impact and Effectiveness of Transparency and Accountability Initiatives: Synthesis Report." Prepared for the Transparency and Accountability Initiative Workshop, Institute of Development Studies, October 14–15, 2010.

McNeil, Mary, and Carmen Malena, eds. *Demanding Good Governance: Lessons from Social Accountability Initiatives in Africa*. Washington, DC: World Bank, 2010.

Merriman, Hardy. "Forming a Movement." Presentation at the Fletcher Summer Institute for the Advanced Study of Strategic Nonviolent Conflict, Tufts University, Medford, MA, June 20, 2011.

Mulcahy, Suzanne. *Money, Politics, Power: Corruption Risks in Europe*. Berlin: Transparency International, 2012.

NORAD. *Anti-Corruption Approaches: A Literature Review*. Oslo: Norwegian Agency for Development and Cooperation, 2009.

Olken, Benjamin. "Monitoring Corruption: Evidence from a Field Experiment in Indonesia." *Journal of Political Economy* 115, no. 2 (2007): 200–249.

Pettinicchio, David. "Institutional Activism: Reconsidering the Insider-Outsider Dichotomy." *Sociology Compass* 6, no. 6 (2012): 499–510.

Ramkumar, Vivek, and Sowmya Kidambi. "Twataka Pesa Zetu [We want our money]: A Public Budget Hearing in Kenya." International Budget Partnership, n.d.

Roberts, Adam, and Timothy Garton Ash. *Civil Resistance and Power Politics: From Gandhi to the Present*. Oxford: Oxford University Press, 2009.

Rose-Ackerman, Susan. "The Challenge of Poor Governance and Corruption." Copenhagen Consensus 2004 Challenge Paper. Copenhagen 2004 Consensus Project, 2004.

RTI Activists: Sitting Ducks of India. New Delhi: Asian Centre for Human Rights, 2011.

Saich, Anthony, David Dapice, Tarek Masoud, Dwight Perkins, Jonathan Pincus, Jay Rosengard, Thomas Vallely, Ben Wilkinson, and Jeffrey Williams. *From Reformasi to Institutional Transformation: A Strategic Assessment of Indonesia's Prospects for Growth, Equity, and Democratic Governance*. Boston: Harvard Kennedy School Indonesia Program, 2010.

Scharbatke-Church, Cheyanne, and Kirby Reiling. "Lilies That Fester: Seeds of Corruption and Peacebuilding." *New Routes Journal of Peace Research and Action* 14, no. 3–4 (2009): 4–9.

Schock, Kurt. "People Power and Alternative Politics." In *Politics in the Developing World*, 3rd edition, ed. Peter Burnell, Vicky Randall, and Lise Rakner, 202–219. London: Oxford University Press, 2008.

―――. *Unarmed Insurrections: People Power Movements in Non-Democracies*. Minneapolis: University of Minnesota Press, 2005.

Sharp, Gene. *Waging Nonviolent Struggle: 20th-Century Practice and 21st-Century Potential*. Boston: Porter Sargent, 2005.

Shin, Eui Hang. "The Role of NGOs in Political Elections in Korea: The Case of the Citizens' Alliance for the 2000 General Election." *Asian Survey* 43, no. 4 (2003): 697–715.

Shinn, Gi-Wook, and Paul Chang, eds. *South Korean Social Movements: From Democracy to Civil Society*. New York: Routledge, 2011.

Smithey, Lee. "Social Movement Strategy, Tactics, and Collective Identity." *Sociology Compass* 3, no. 4 (2009): 658–671.

Stephan, Maria, ed. *Civilian Jihad: Nonviolent Struggle, Democratization, and Governance in the Middle East.* New York: Palgrave Macmillan, 2009.

Stephan, Maria, and Erica Chenoweth. "Why Civil Resistance Works: The Strategic Logic of Nonviolent Conflict." *International Security* 33, no. 1 (Summer 2008): 7–44.

"Third National Integrity Survey." *Inspectorate of Government Final Report.* Kampala: Republic of Uganda, October 2008.

United Nations Development Programme. *Reflections on Social Accountability: Catalyzing Democratic Governance to Accelerate Progress Towards the Millennium Development Goals.* New York: UNDP, 2013.

United Nations Handbook: Practical Anti-Corruption Measures for Prosecutors and Investigators. Vienna: UN Office of Drugs and Crime, 2004.

Unsworth, Sue. *An Upside-Down View of Governance.* Brighton: Institute of Development Studies, University of Sussex, April 2010.

Uvin, Peter. "Fostering Citizen Collective Action in Post-Conflict Societies." Woodrow Wilson Center for International Scholars, Occasional Paper Series, *What Really Works in Preventing and Rebuilding Failed States*, no. 1, November 2006.

Vogl, Frank. *Waging War on Corruption: Inside the Movement Fighting the Abuse of Power.* Lanham, MD: Rowman and Littlefield, 2012.

von Luebke, Christian. "The Politics of Reform: Political Scandals, Elite Resistance, and Presidential Leadership in Indonesia." *Journal of Current Southeast Asian Affairs* 29, no, 1 (2010): 79–94.

World Bank Development Report 2011: Conflict, Security, and Development. Washington, DC: World Bank, 2011.

Wright, Robin. *Dreams and Shadows: The Future of the Middle East.* New York: Penguin, 2008.

Youngs, Richard. "How to Revitalise Democracy Assistance: Recipients' Views." Working Paper no. 100, Fundación para las Relaciones Internacionales y el Diálogo Exterior (FRIDE), Madrid, June 2010.

Zirker, Daniel. "The Brazilian Church-State Crisis of 1980: Effective Nonviolent Action in a Military Dictatorship." In *Nonviolent Social Movements: A Geographical Perspective*, ed. Stephen Zunes, Lester Kurtz, and Sarah Beth Asher, 260–261. Malden, MA: Blackwell, 1999.

Index

January 25 Revolution (2011), 15, 211, 216, 245; nonviolent struggle, history of, 211; shayfeen.com, 15, 211–217, 248, 280; UN Convention Against Corruption and, 216
Egyptian Movement for Change, 211
Egyptians Against Corruption, 215–216, 245, 248
ElBaradei campaign for reform (Egypt), 211
elections: Bosnia, 227; Brazil, 70–71, 76; Egypt, 213–214, 217; Indonesia, 90; IWA, 173–174; as rebellion, 246; Turkey, 210
electoral reform. *See* Citizens Alliance for the General Elections (CAGE) 2000 (Korea); Ficha Limpa campaign (Brazil)
elites, political, 79, 89, 215, 241n56
e-mail campaigns, 234, 235
empowerment: DHP* campaign (Mexico), 232; expanding conceptualization of, 282; 5th Pillar (India), 157, 163; Integrity Watch Afghanistan (IWA), 183–184; NAFODU (Uganda), 195–196; RTI empowerment tactic (India), 141–143; social accountability and, 267; tactics, 300–302; third-party actors and, 274; top-down approaches and, 166. *See also* people power
enabling environments, 265–267
engagement, tactics of, 299–300
engagement dynamic, 31–32. *See also* citizen engagement
e-petitions, 72–73
Erbakan, Necmettin, 209
essay contests, 145
ethical consumerism, 120–122, 129
ethics training, 193–194, 200
European Commission, 9
European Parliament, 279
European Union, 279, 282
exacting accountability, 56, 226, 269
exchange and knowledge, 277–279
external audits, 269
external corruption drivers and enablers, 279, 283
external third-party actors: CICAK (Indonesia), 108–109; guiding principles for, 274; Integrity Watch Afghanistan (IWA), 184; NAFODU

(Uganda), 199; recommendations, general, 274–281; recommendations for specific groups, 281–285; role of, 258–259. *See also* policy implications; transnational inspiration and connections
extortion, 119, 141. *See also* Addiopizzo movement; bribery; 5th Pillar movement
extrainstitutional pressure: CICAK (Indonesia), 106; MUHURI (Kenya), 224; NAFODU (Uganda), 199–200; people power and, 31. *See also* people power

Facebook: CICAK group, 94, 104; DHP* campaign (Mexico), 232, 235; Dosta! (Bosnia), 229; 5th Pillar (India), 152
Falcone, Giovanni, 116
fasts, 150
Faver, Marcus, 68–69
faxes, mass, 207–208
Federazione Nazionale Antiracket (FAI), 129
Ferrara, Calogero, 128
Ficha Limpa campaign (Brazil): backfire, 73–74; beginnings, 68–70; case analysis, 80–83; citizen engagement, 75; communications and media, 73; context, 67–68; lessons, 83–85; MCCE-Avaaz partnership, 70; minicampaigns, 72–73, 81; number of legislators facing charges, 22n68; online recruitment and signature drive, 71–72; organization and coordination, 74; other tactics, 73; outcomes, 75–79; strategies, 70–71; Supreme Court decision on, 76; tactical planning and sequencing, 74; unity, 75
field of vision, 281–282
5th Pillar movement (India): case analysis, 160–165; challenges and strategies, initial, 140–141; digital technology, 152; discourse, 145–146, 149, 150–151, 162; district branches and local chapters, 148; dual nature, 150; education, 141–142, 145–146; Freedom from Corruption campaign, 141, 142, 145, 146, 162; implementation pressure, 29–30;

About the Book

How do citizens counter corruption and exact accountability from powerholders? What strategic value does people power bring to the anticorruption struggle? Can bottom-up, citizen-based strategies complement and reinforce top-down anticorruption efforts?

Addressing these questions—and demonstrating the critical role of grassroots efforts in the anticorruption/accountability equation—Shaazka Beyerle explores how millions of people around the world have refused to be victims of corruption and become instead the protagonists of successful nonviolent civic movements to gain accountability and promote positive political, social, and economic change.

Shaazka Beyerle is senior adviser at the International Center on Nonviolent Conflict and also visiting scholar at the Center for Transatlantic Relations, School of Advanced International Studies, Johns Hopkins University.